BLACKS OF THE ROSARY

BLACKS OF THE ROSARY

Memory and History in Minas Gerais, Brazil

ELIZABETH W. KIDDY

THE PENNSYLVANIA STATE UNIVERSITY PRESS

UNIVERSITY PARK, PENNSYLVANIA

Library of Congress
Cataloging-in-Publication Data

Kiddy, Elizabeth W., 1957–
    Blacks of the rosary : memory and history in
    Minas Gerais, Brazil / Elizabeth W. Kiddy.
          p.   cm.
Includes bibliographical references and index.
ISBN 0-271-02693-6 (alk. paper)
1. Blacks—Brazil—Minas Gerais—Religion.
2. Brotherhoods—Brazil—Minas Gerais—History.
3. Minas Gerais (Brazil)—Religious life and customs.
4. Rosary, Our Lady of the—Cult—Brazil—Minas Gerais—History.
I. Title.

BX1467.M56K53 2005
267'.1828151'08996—dc22
                            2005005085

The Pennsylvania State University Press
is a member of the Association of American
University Presses.

It is the policy of
The Pennsylvania State University Press
to use acid-free paper. Publications on
uncoated stock satisfy the minimum
requirements of American National Standard
for Information Sciences—Permanence of
Paper for Printed Library Material,
ANSI Z39.48–1992.

TO THE *congadeiros* OF MINAS GERAIS.

CONTENTS

ILLUSTRATIONS AND MAPS

ILLUSTRATIONS

MAPS

ACKNOWLEDGMENTS

I have to begin by thanking the *congadeiros* of Minas Gerais and, in particular, the participants in the *congados* of Jatobá and Oliveira, without whom this book would not be possible. In Jatobá I want to thank Dona Maria Geralda Ferreira, for sharing so many stories, and her son João Lopes, *capitão-mor* of the festival, for giving me permission to film and interview him over the course of three years. Célia Lourdes Ferreira opened her home to me during the fieldwork and always made me feel welcome. Her brother and captain of the Mozambique in Jatobá, José Expedito da Luz Ferreira, helped me immensely with insights into the devotion and faith of the congadeiros, and their sister Lia and brother-in-law José dos Anjos offered wonderful meals and many laughs. In Oliveira the extended family of Ester Borges Rufina took me in as though I were a family member. I will always treasure the time I spent in your *quartel* and with the Mozambique of Our Lady of Mercies. I spent many happy hours following you all over the city of Oliveira during the eight days of the festival. Of the family, my special thanks go to Captains Antonio Eustáquio dos Santos and Pedrina de Lourdes Santos and to Amásia do Rosário, Lena, and especially Efigênia, who tragically passed away when I was in Brazil doing fieldwork. I also want to thank the Associação dos Congadeiros de Oliveira and their president and guiding light, Dona Maria Conceição do Bispo Maurício; her daughter Heloisa Helena Maurício; and the entire extended family. The Federação de Congadeiros de Minas Gerais also always invited and patiently answered my questions and welcomed my presence in their meetings. Finally, warm thanks to Ephigenio Casemiro, Capitão Eustáquio Cristiano, Dona Iracema Pereira Moreira, Seu José Inocêncio, Dona Leonôr Pereira Galdino, Capitão Pedro Aponízio dos Santos, Capitão Sebastião Pinto de Souza, Seu Raimundo Lopes dos Santos, Titane, Dona Zélia Dissimira Soares dos Santos, and all the congadeiros who generously and patiently answered my questions and offered me their warm *mineiro* hospitality.

The generous support of the Comissão Mineiro de Folclore, and especially its president at the time I was doing my research, Sebastião Rocha, helped me immeasurably in the initial stages of my work, as did Frei Chico, whose insights on the Brazilian church in general and Afro-Brazilian culture helped me to understand the complexity of the Afro-Mineiro traditions. Doralice

Mota in Curvelo always opened her generous home to me, helping me to better understand the culture and hospitality of Minas Gerais. The help of Lucy Fontes Hargreaves of Tiradentes was fundamental to my work in São João del Rei, as was the generosity of the Brotherhood of Our Lady of the Rosary in São João del Rei and that of its secretary, Nelson Antunes de Carvalho. In Mariana, I want to thank the Ecclesiastic Archive, for allowing me to study its collections, and the hardworking functionaries there who responded quickly and cheerfully to all my questions and requests. In Belo Horizonte, ethno-musicologist Glaura Lucas and her husband, Anderson, were always there to share ideas with me. My dear friends Lael Keen, Aluísio Gonçalves, and especially Nicole Mir, of Belo Horizonte, always generously opened their homes and their hearts to me during my research trips. The Mandala Restaurant, and its owner Daniel, in Belo Horizonte always offered a healthy meal and a welcoming atmosphere. I extend my most sincere thanks to all these organizations and individuals for their help, both personal and professional.

In the United States there is a long list of colleagues, friends, and family who have made this book possible. At the University of New Mexico my dissertation advisor and friend Judy Bieber helped me through the dissertation process that was the basis for the book. Marta Weigle offered valuable insights and encouragement on the anthropological sections of the book and Ted Sturm and Linda Hall offered advice on many drafts of the dissertation. The Latin American and Iberian Institute and the Office of Graduate Studies at the University of New Mexico supported my work through a series of grants and fellowships that made both the research and the writing of my dissertation, and this book, possible. Johns Hopkins University granted me the Mellon Foundation Post-doctoral Fellowship that allowed me to begin work on this book. I thank A. J. R. Russell-Wood for his always insightful comments and enthusiasm and all his work that paved the way for this study. I also thank Kenneth R. Maxwell for his helpful comments on a paper that became part of this study. The comments and encouragement of Africanists Linda Heywood, John Thornton, and Joseph Miller have been instrumental in helping me to understand the brotherhoods and their festivals as part of the Atlantic World. Thank you also to the two readers from Penn State Press who offered the detailed and well-thought-out advice that encouraged me to finish the book. Finally, I thank Kenyon College and Albright College for grants that allowed me to complete the research and writing of this book. Special thanks go out to Stephen Mech at Albright College, who worked with me for many hours, uncomplaining, as we created the maps. I also want to thank DCC Photo in Reading, Pennsylvania, for their careful work on the reproduction of the photographs.

There are many friends who have helped me along the way. Deepest thanks go to Mestre Acordeon, my teacher and friend, who first opened my eyes to the rich complexity of Brazilian culture, who stepped in as a friend when I most needed one, who taught me when to duck and how to stay in the *jogo* through the long game of graduate school and work, and who always supported my decisions. I want to thank Joseph McPherson for accompanying me to Brazil as my research assistant in 1995 and cheerfully helping me through that entire trip, as well as for looking after my house in New Mexico when I was away doing research.

My parents, Anthony and Harriet Winchell, put up with my independent spirit with a great amount of patience, and with their guidance I found my way back onto the professional path of my grandfather and great-grandfather. My in-laws, Fred and Sandy Kiddy, offered incredible financial and moral support that made graduate school, and this project, possible. Finally, I give my deepest thanks to my husband, Greg, for his hard work on the project, both in the archives and in the field; for his patience through the long years of the research and writing; and for his love throughout the whole process. Without that support this book certainly never would have been written.

ABBREVIATIONS

The following abbreviations are used in the footnotes and bibliography.

PLACE-NAMES, UNIVERSITIES, AND CENTERS

CEDEPLAR	Centro de Desenvolvimento e Planejamento Regional, Faculdade de Ciências Econômicas, UFMG
BH	Belo Horizonte
MG	Minas Gerais
RJ	Rio de Janeiro state
UFMG	Universidade Federal de Minas Gerais

ARCHIVES AND COLLECTIONS

ACC	Arquivo da Casa da Cultura Carlos Chagas, Oliveira, MG
ACO	Arquivo da Catedral de Oliveira, Oliveira, MG
ACBH	Arquivo da Cúria Metropolitana, BH, MG
AEAM	Arquivo Eclesiástico da Arquidiocese de Mariana, MG
AINSR	Arquivo da Irmandade de Nossa Senhora do Rosário, São João del Rei, MG
AN	Arquivo Nacional do Brasil, Rio de Janeiro, RJ
APM	Arquivo Público Mineiro, BH, MG
APM JGP	Arquivo Público Mineiro, Junta do Governo Provisório
APM SC	Arquivo Público Mineiro Seção Colonial
APM SG	Arquivo Público Mineiro, Seção Governmental
APM SP	Arquivo Público Mineiro, Seção Provincial
APM SPPP	Arquivo Público Mineiro, Seção Provincial, Presidente da Província
CBG	Casa Borba Gato, Sabará, MG
CC	Casa dos Contos, Ouro Preto, MG
BN	Fundação Biblioteca Nacional, Rio de Janeiro, RJ
MASSJR	Museu de Arte Sacra, São João del Rei, MG

JOURNALS

AHR	*American Historical Review*
HAHR	*Hispanic American Historical Review*
LARR	*Latin American Research Review*
RAPM	*Revista do Arquivo Público Mineiro*

INTRODUCTION

Esse Congado vem do princípio do mundo. Ninguem
sabe o princípio dele, e ninguem sabe o fim.

[This Congado comes from the beginning of the
world. No one knows the beginning of it, and no one
knows the end.]

—Dona Maria Geralda Ferreira, Jatobá

Dona Maria said this to me on a sunny, dry day in August 1995 as we sat on
her front porch looking out on the yard, where the annual festival for Our
Lady of the Rosary was about to begin.[1] Dona Maria, born 4 July 1906, has
spent most of her life as part of the Festa do Reinado de Nossa Senhora do
Rosário (Feast Day of the Crowning of Our Lady of the Rosary), known in
the vernacular as the Congado (Fig. 1). She plays an important role in the
festival in Jatobá, a region on the industrial periphery of Belo Horizonte, the
capital of the Brazilian state of Minas Gerais. Her brother had been an
important and powerful captain of the congado (ritual group) known as the
Mozambique; she was the widow of the man who had been the leader, or
capitão-mor, of the festival for more than forty years, and she was the
mother of the current leader, João Lopes. In her own right Dona Maria has
long been a *benzedora*, or healer, using prayers and herbs to treat the sick,
who come from miles around to ask for her help, and during the festival, all

1. The preceding quotation from Dona Maria Geralda Ferreira, matriarch of the festival
in Jatobá, is from an interview with the author, Itaipu, BH, MG, 17 August 1995. All translations
mine unless otherwise noted.

the leaders come to ask for her blessing before going out to do the ritual work of the festival. One participant described her as having a "spiritual [force], a knowledge, and she maintains the blood of the brotherhood to not let it fall."[2] On her porch that day in 1995 we waited for the costumed groups of Mozambiques and Congos to arrive with the King and Queen of Congo, whom they had escorted from their homes to the yard, now a ritual space, in front of Dona Maria's house and the chapel of Our Lady of the Rosary. When they arrived, the yard filled with the syncopated rhythms, swirling colors, and large and small rituals that make up the annual feast day celebration.

Dona Maria and all *congadeiros,* as participants in the festivals are called, are heirs of the rosary brotherhood tradition, which dates from the first years of colonization in Minas Gerais. Congadeiros are primarily black, both phenotypically and economically, and live in the working-class and poor neighborhoods of the large cities and small towns of Minas Gerais. During the festivals, congado groups, some using the names of African nations and wearing the colors of the saints, play drums and shakers, sing and dance, and escort their kings and queens. The festivals include the coronations of these kings and queens in the part of the festival known as the Reinado.[3] The festivals open up a ritual space in which the participants can call on Our Lady of the Rosary and the other saints associated with the festival to intercede on their behalf or to thank them for their intercession. In order to ensure the good reunion of the people without any trouble from seen or unseen forces, the participants engage in special rituals at the crossroads and in the privacy of their homes to guarantee the protection of the *pretos velhos,* the spirits of old, black, African slaves.[4] The festivals are the apex of the ritual year for the communities that celebrate them, and they work to reinforce their links to the unseen world, to the past, and to one another.

Dona Maria in many ways embodies some of the paradoxes inherent in the study of the rosary brotherhoods and festivals in Minas Gerais. She identifies herself as an Afro-Brazilian, celebrates the relationship between Our Lady of the Rosary and blacks, and affirms the link between Our Lady

---

2. Célia Lourdes Ferreira, secretary of the Federation of Congadeiros of Minas Gerais, interview with the author, Tirol, BH, MG, 25 December 1996.

3. *Reinado* refers not only to the time in the festival that the coronations occur but also to the kings, the queens, and their retinues. There is some discussion among participants on whether the entire festival should be known as the Reinado, rather than the Congado, because for them the focus is the coronation.

4. João Lopes (pseud. Alcides André), *capitão-mor* (captain-major), Irmandade de Nossa Senhora do Rosário de Jatobá, interview with the author, 5 October 1996, Belo Horizonte, MG.

FIG. 1.   Dona Maria Geralda da Silva overseeing the Feast Day of the Crowning of
Our Lady of the Rosary from her porch, Jatobá, August 1995

of the Rosary and the emancipation of slaves. "The blacks are the sons of Our Lady, and that is why slavery ended. From slavery there was freedom and from freedom came the Congado, the festival of Our Lady. . . . Our Lady helped everyone and here all of the blacks are very happy with Our Lady of the Rosary."[5] However, when asked about the personal history of her family, she recounts that her family was not enslaved, but rather had been slave owners in the nineteenth century. Like Dona Maria's own memory of her family's history and its devotion to Our Lady of the Rosary, the rosary brotherhoods and their festivals in Minas Gerais blur boundaries erected by scholars to understand the history of Africans in the Americas in general, and in Brazil in particular, in three distinct ways.

First, scholars, for the most part, followed the lead of contemporary commentators who considered the brotherhoods and their festivals to be "slave" organizations, even though through much of their history a majority of the membership was free. The communities, built on both kinship and affective ties, were based on a common heritage rather than a shared legal status. Second, the relationship between the brotherhoods and the church and the state authorities made them appear to be accommodating, in the traditional accommodation/resistance dichotomy. Indeed, there can be no argument that the rosary brotherhoods were Catholic lay organizations that Africans and their descendents enthusiastically joined. Nevertheless, participants have long either ignored or resisted attempts to change or abolish rituals that tied them to their African past, such as the coronations of their kings and queens and the drumming and call-and-response singing that continues to define the festivals. Finally, at the time of independence, and then almost a century later after the abolition of slavery, rosary festivals seemed to fade away in many parts of Brazil, but not in Minas Gerais. There, the festivals only grew stronger as the twentieth century progressed.

How, then, can we understand the brotherhoods of the rosary in Minas Gerais? The current day celebrations, the rituals, and the legends developed from the colonial rosary brotherhood traditions in Minas Gerais in which African- and Brazilian-born slaves and free blacks formed communities, celebrated their saints, and helped one another on to the other world through rituals of death.[6] The formation of communities developed concurrently

5. Ibid.

6. For other interpretations of the rosary brotherhoods in the colonial period, see Fritz Teixeira Salles, *Associações religiosas no ciclo do ouro* (Belo Horizonte, Brazil: Universidade Federal de Minas Gerais, 1963); Patricia Mulvey, "Black Brothers and Sisters: Membership in the Black Lay Brotherhoods of Colonial Brazil," *Luso-Brazilian Review* 17 (1980): 253–79; Julita Scarano, *Devoção e escravidão: A irmandade de Nossa Senhora do Rosário dos Pretos no*

with the rituals and celebrations and with all activities within groups of recently arrived slaves in Brazil. Joseph C. Miller points out that slaves would have drawn "on differing aspects of their home backgrounds as they searched for a morally restorative sense of humane community among themselves."[7] The seeming contradictions in the rosary brotherhoods can be understood when they are viewed as a process of the formation and maintenance of transnational and multiethnic communities of the African diaspora. The idea of community that has emerged among these groups is not exclusively one of place, or of neighborhood, but rather of a people who have worked to maintain a group identity through generations—an identity formed by the annual reaffirmation of a shared, remembered history as descendents of Africans and devotees of Our Lady of the Rosary.

The remarkable resilience of the rosary brotherhoods has resulted from centuries of negotiation and compromise with secular and ecclesiastic authorities and within their own populations. Historian Thomas A. Abercrombie in his discussion of the Aymara people of Bolivia argues that "the institutional matrix and cultural meanings of 'ethnic' cultural survival in the Andes have been shaped by native peoples' active and collective engagement with, rather than flight from, the power-infused cultural programs of state elites."[8] Likewise, Africans and their descendents in Minas Gerais actively participated in organizations that simultaneously linked them to the European power structure while allowing them to continue practices that served as a foundation for their existence and endurance as communities. The strategy of these groups exposes the limitations of the resistance/accommodation model, replacing it with the examination of processes of negotiation, change, and continuity. This book, then, is a history of the descendents of a group of

---

distrito diamantino no século XVIII (São Paulo: Nacional, 1976); A. J. R. Russell-Wood, "Black and Mulatto Brotherhoods in Colonial Brazil: A Study in Collective Behavior," HAHR 54 (1974): 567–602; Donald Ramos, "Community, Control, and Acculturation: A Case Study of Slavery in Eighteenth Century Brazil," The Americas 42 (April 1986): 419–51; Caio César Boschi, Os leigos e o poder: Irmandades leigas e política colonizadora em Minas Gerais (São Paulo: Editora Ática, 1986); Célia Borges, "Irmandades do rosário: Participação e dinâmica social em Minas no séc. XVIII," Anais Universitários: Ciências Sociais e Humanas 6 (1995): 239–53.

7. Joseph C. Miller, "Central Africa During the Era of the Slave Trade, c. 1490s–1850s," in Central Africans and Cultural Transformations in the American Diaspora, ed. Linda M. Heywood (New York: Cambridge University Press, 2001), 43. See also Joseph C. Miller, "Retention, Reinvention, and Remembering: Restoring Identities Through Enslavement in Africa and Under Slavery in Brazil," in Enslaving Connections: Changing Cultures of Africa and Brazil During the Era of Slavery, ed. José C. Curto and Paul E. Lovejoy (Amherst, N.Y.: Humanity Books, 2004), 81–121.

8. Thomas A. Abercrombie, Pathways of Memory and Power: Ethnography and History Among an Andean People (Madison: University of Wisconsin Press, 1999), 22–23.

slaves and free blacks who creatively used the cultural materials at hand, who were, in the phrase of historians João José Reis and Eduardo Silva, "between Zumbi and Pai João," in order to ensure their survival as a community, maintain their devotions and the link to their ancestors, and foster a pride in their African roots.[9]

Identity, Memory, and History

This book explores the long history of the congadeiros through the examination of the main themes of community, devotion, and identity, set into the context of the endemic asymmetry of power in Brazilian society. I do not use the word *identity* in the sense of an individual's sense of uniqueness as an autonomous being, but rather to indicate an individual's sense of belonging in a group. Brazilian anthropologist Roberto DaMatta asks whether "the notion of the individual really has absolute validity in social systems where it is conceived as merely residual if not negative social category."[10] In both Brazilian and African societies in the eighteenth century, the family or kin group composed the smallest social unit, and autonomy from such a group often meant marginality. Therefore, the identity of individuals was intimately wrapped up in the identification with a group. This certainly would have been the case for Africans, who, as Miller points out, "thought of themselves primarily in terms of social identities constructed out of family and other local communities."[11] The groups with which many Africans in Minas Gerais chose to align themselves were the brotherhoods of the rosary *of the blacks.*

The rubric *of the blacks* brings up the problematic question of "race" in Brazil, where this is a category that has both been fluid and slippery. Max Weber defines race as something that "creates a 'group' only when it is subjectively perceived as a common trait: this happens only when a neighborhood or the mere proximity of racially different persons is the basis of joint (mostly political) action, or conversely, when some common experiences of members of the same race are linked to some antagonism against members

---

9. João José Reis and Eduardo Silva, *Negociação e conflito: A resistência negra no Brasil escravista* (São Paulo: Companhia das Letras, 1988), 13.

10. Roberto DaMatta, *Carnivals, Rogues, and Heroes: An Interpretation of the Brazilian Dilemma,* trans. John Drury (Notre Dame: University of Notre Dame Press, 1991), 8–9. On the corporate nature of society in the Iberian Peninsula, see the recent work by Howard J. Wiarda, *The Soul of Latin America: The Cultural and Political Tradition* (New Haven: Yale University Press, 2001), 50–75.

11. Miller, "Central Africa," 22.

of an *obviously* different group."[12] This definition, which stresses the relativity of race, serves well for the rosary brotherhoods. The antagonism of the groups in Brazil came from the hierarchical social system in which the members of the rosary brotherhoods, both slave and nonwhite free men and women, had the least power within the society. Once they joined the community of the brotherhood, they joined a group of *blacks*. They sought incorporation with others who shared both "subjectively perceived" common physical traits as well as a common heritage and also shared experiences of slavery, poverty, or both. The brotherhoods provided a forum for the development of identities based on "race," or being black in the colonial period, that rosary brotherhoods in the following centuries could build upon.

The concept of being black in the rosary brotherhoods was erected on two foundations that brought the community together. The first was the devotion to Our Lady of the Rosary, the patron of the blacks. The second was expressed in the annual festival to Our Lady of the Rosary, in which blackness was reinforced by the constant rearticulation of links to Africa through songs, drums, and ritual action and the calling on the *pretos velhos*. The participants have continuously constructed a social memory and thus built and reinforced a group identity, through the action, or work, of the festival. Sociologist Maurice Halbwachs argues that through membership in groups people are able to "localize and recall their memories." Paul Connerton takes this idea a step further by locating the formation of social memory in the action of rituals, both religious and commemorative.[13]

Although sociologists have worked to understand how groups remember their past, the term *memory*, both because of and despite its recent popularity, has come under fire in the field of history. Kerwin Lee Klein recently critiqued the emergence of the term in the discipline, pointing out that memory is most often paired with identity and with a "clustering of quasi-religious terms."[14] He warns that the use of *memory* represents a desire to "re-enchant our relation with the world and pour presence back into the past."[15] Despite Klein's discomfort with the term, the use of the links that remembering provide are not only helpful but necessary when discussing a people who

12. Max Weber, "Ethnic Groups," in *New Tribalisms: The Resurgence of Race and Ethnicity*, ed. Michael W. Hughey (New York: New York University Press, 1998), 17.

13. Paul Connerton, *How Societies Remember* (New York: Cambridge University Press, 1989), quote at 36; and see also Maurice Halbwachs, *The Collective Memory*, trans. Francis. J. Ditter Jr. and Vida Yazdi Ditter (New York: Harper and Row, 1980).

14. Kerwin Lee Klein, "On the Emergence of Memory in Historical Discourse," *Representations* 69 (Winter 2000): 127.

15. Ibid., 144–45.

perceive their past as inseparable from their beliefs. One of the earliest historians to talk about history and memory, Pierre Nora, poetically identified memory as lived history, as "life, borne by living societies founded in its name . . . a perpetually actual phenomena, a bond tying us to the eternal present."[16] More recently, Abercrombie articulates Nora's ideas by juxtaposing memory and history, demonstrating the ways in which social memory is constructed in an Andean village through myth and ritual in relation and opposition to Western historical discourse.[17] History and memory are presented as being on different sides of an unequal equation—an equation that places rational/secular, written history on one side and remembered, ritualized, "sacred" history on the other. Abercrombie exposes the danger in this equation, demonstrating that writing the history of a people "without a history," using a Western model, ends up producing a history that the people themselves would not recognize, in effect recolonizing the peoples' past.[18] Understanding nondominant groups involves using all the resources available for discovering that past, including the ways that the groups themselves construct that history.

Analyzing how memory works, however, involves understanding the mechanisms through which the remembering is achieved. *Memory*, the noun, implies a static concept, a substantive "thing" that may only dwell in the minds of individuals.[19] Yet memory is not a static concept but an active one. People do not simply *have* memories; they actively remember through ritual and storytelling.[20] Remembering, then, is a practice, and it is both similar to and linked to the act of believing. Marilyn Motz points out that "a belief exists only because people believe it: it is not an attribute or property but the evidence of a process."[21] In exactly the same way, a memory exists only because a person, or group, remembers it, and like believing, it is a process better defined by the verb than the noun. The processes of believing and remembering are both articulated in the rituals and narratives of the Congados—in fact, they are inseparable. Through the ongoing and intertwined practices of believing and remembering, the congadeiros maintain a

---

16. Pierre Nora, "Between Memory and History: *Les Lieux de Mémoire*," trans. Marc Roudebush, *Representations* 69 (Winter 2000): 8.

17. Abercrombie, *Pathways*, 10–25.

18. Ibid., xxiii.

19. See Klein's concerns in "On the Emergence," 135.

20. Abercrombie, *Pathways*, 10–21.

21. Marilyn Motz, "The Practice of Belief," *Journal of American Folklore* 111 (1998): 349.

strong and positive sense of community identity and their own "blackness"
through reinforcing a living link to an African past.[22]

The scope of this book is broad both chronologically and geographically. I
divide the book chronologically into three parts. In Part 1, I examine the
antecedents of the *mineiro* (that is, of Minas Gerais) brotherhoods both in
Europe and in Africa. The brotherhoods in Minas Gerais, and the devotion that
evolved within them, began at the intersection of a cluster of sub-Saharan cosmologies, many of which already included elements of European culture and
Catholicism, and eighteenth-century Iberian folk practices in the social milieu
of a slave society in the interior of Brazil. In Chapter I, I investigate the roots of
the devotion and the nature of lay Catholicism in early modern Europe in
order to demonstrate the complexity of Catholicism and the importance of lay
activity at the time of the explorations of Africa and the Americas. The mental-
ities of that period served as a cultural backdrop for the Portuguese and as a foil
for the Africans who came into contact with it. I explore the development of
brotherhoods and specifically the brotherhoods of the rosary and other lay
organizations formed for Africans on the Iberian Peninsula. I also address the
explorations and settlement of the Portuguese in Africa and Brazil and the
beginning of the slave trade. The focus of Chapter 2 is Africa and the primary
locations from which slaves destined for the mines were taken. Specifically, I
examine the dynamic histories of West and Central Africa during the first
centuries of the slave trade, discuss local worldviews and practices from those
areas, and explore the emergence of dynamic creole cultures.

   In the late seventeenth century, gold was discovered in Brazil, in the
highlands region that came to be known as Minas Gerais. In Part 2, I examine
the brotherhoods of the rosary of the blacks in Minas Gerais from the time
of the arrival of the first Europeans and Africans and through to the end of
slavery in Brazil in 1888. Again, the chapters are divided chronologically.
Chapter 3 centers on the development of the brotherhoods in the chaotic
gold-mining boom that occurred in Minas Gerais from 1690 to about 1750.
In that wild, frontier context, brotherhoods, including rosary brotherhoods
of blacks, emerged as fiercely independent organizations. The autonomy of
the organizations during this formative period would shape the ways they
confronted outside pressures in the following centuries. By 1750 the boom
had gone bust, the frontier society of Minas Gerais began to settle down,

---

22. See also Elizabeth W. Kiddy, "Ethnic and Racial Identity in the Brotherhoods of the
Rosary of Minas Gerais, 1700–1830," *The Americas* 56, no. 2 (October 1999): 223–24.

and the first new diocese was created in Minas with the city of Mariana at its hub. Life was changing in the metropolis, too, as the marquis de Pombal came to, then fell from, power and Brazil moved closer to independence. Chapter 4, then, concerns the period from the mid-eighteenth century to 1822 and these external pressures on the rosary brotherhoods, as well as the internal dynamic of the organizations as they confronted increasing oversight by state and church authorities. It was toward the end of this period that travelers began to leave records of the rosary festivals and their coronations and dances. Chapter 5 begins in 1822 and follows the rosary brotherhoods through the transitional period of the Brazilian Empire and to the end of slavery, with another look at both the societal pressures of church and state and the internal reactions of the brotherhood members. Through the colonial period and the empire, although the brotherhoods constantly negotiated with the state and church authorities, little changed in the actual brotherhood structure, and the organizations continued to be based on foundations laid in the early colonial period. By the nineteenth century it was apparent that the Afro-Brazilian festivals to Our Lady of the Rosary had become customary and accepted celebrations among many sectors of society in Minas Gerais.

This relative stability came to an abrupt end in the late nineteenth century, and in Part 3 I examine the rosary brotherhoods and the ongoing methods used by congadeiros to keep their festivals alive from 1889 to 1980. The subject of Chapter 6 is how the reorganization of the church after the abrupt division of church and state at the founding of the First Republic in 1889 affected the brotherhoods. Oral testimony and archival sources recount the evolution of the festivals in the twentieth century and their struggle to survive in a rapidly modernizing Brazil. It turns out, however, that the rosary devotion of the blacks had the power to shape and influence popular sentiment in Minas Gerais, and despite changing attitudes of the church, the rosary organizations and festivals survived. Although I bring in the voices of the congadeiros throughout the book, in the final chapter I step away from the historical narrative and allow participants in the Congado communities today to express their own thoughts about their devotion, their history, and their identity as devotees of Our Lady of the Rosary of the blacks.

The scope of the project required me to use a variety of sources. My interest in studying the history of the rosary brotherhoods in Minas Gerais came out of my personal experience with the festivals dedicated to Our Lady of the Rosary. I traveled to Minas Gerais in 1994, 1995, 1996, and 1997 to research the material in this book, and during those years I attended several festivals. I decided to concentrate on two festivals, one in the town of Oliveira in the agricultural region of Minas Gerais southwest of the capital, Belo Horizonte, and the other in Jatobá, located in the industrial periphery of the capital. The participants in these festivals expressed strong ties to an African past and a pride in their "blackness"—both elements also apparent in the rituals that made up the festivals—which seemed to contradict much of what I had learned about attitudes toward blackness in Brazil. Soon the energy of the festivals, the stamina and devotion of the participants, the rituals with the crowns and the rosaries, the lyrics of the songs, and the words of the tales all drew me into the story of the past as lived by the congadeiros themselves.

While not attending festivals, I haunted large and small archives in Minas Gerais. The books of the brotherhoods are not housed in a central location but instead are spread across an array of various archives. The State Archive in Belo Horizonte (Arquivo Público Mineiro) had some of the brotherhood books, especially for the period of the Empire to the present, and also contained valuable correspondence, laws, and other materials that helped to construct the story of the brotherhoods. The most comprehensive collection of documents for the colonial brotherhoods is housed in the Ecclesiastic Archive in Mariana (Arquivo Eclesiástico da Arquidiocese de Mariana), but I also worked with the documents of some brotherhoods in small archives of particular brotherhoods, such as that in the rosary brotherhood of São João del Rei, the Museum of Sacred Art in that city, and the local archives in Oliveira. There is no telling how many small parishes have their own collections of rosary brotherhood documents. Because of the variation in storage techniques, some of the documents had been lost to the corrosive elements of nature, but fortunately many survived. What remained supplied an abundance and variety of documents that enabled me to piece together a picture of the history of the rosary brotherhoods over several centuries. Finally, documents in the National Archive and the National Library in Rio de Janeiro helped to supplement the brotherhood documents and put them in a larger context. For the chapters on Europe and Africa I relied heavily on published primary sources and the work of scholars of those areas. Those works, and the present-day festivals, legends, and stories, shed light on the documents contained in the archives and enabled me to put together this long story. Although some amount of depth has been sacrificed in order to achieve this breadth, my hope is that authors of future studies will be able to look more closely at particular periods, places, and events in order to continue to build a comprehensive understanding of these important organizations and the people who participate in them.

This study as a whole, then, explores the history of the rich and complex religious and social traditions alive in the Afro-Brazilian communities of

Minas Gerais. Within the infrastructure set by the dominant sector of society, Africans and their descendants creatively and actively organized and used the brotherhoods to create a community in a new place. Far from being a co-optation of their religion and culture, or simply a conscious form of cultural resistance, a study of the brotherhoods of the rosary offers a look into the messier and less-easy-to-categorize strategies of survival that abounded not just in Brazil, but throughout the Americas wherever large numbers of slaves were taken. The centerpiece of these strategies was the ability to form strong and long-lasting communities. The study of the rosary brotherhoods of blacks in Minas Gerais shows the success of groups in one particular region, and the congadeiros today express their achievement through the vibrancy of their faith and the strength of their communities, in which the devotion to Our Lady of the Rosary continues to flourish.

PART ONE

1   EUROPEAN ORIGINS OF THE ROSARY DEVOTION OF THE BLACKS

As contas do meu rosário
São balas de artilharia.

[The beads of my rosary
Are artillery bullets.]

—Popular saying in Minas Gerais

The devotion to Our Lady of the Rosary in the congadeiro communities today emerges from the Africans' appropriation of and adaptations to Christian mystic traditions associated with the Virgin Mary and the rosary prayer beads and the practice of expressing that devotion in, and organizing society through, lay religious brotherhoods.

Rosary brotherhoods in Brazil did not constitute a threat to the social order of Portuguese colonial, and later Brazilian, society, even though they provided places in which black men and women regularly gathered together in large numbers. The Portuguese not only accepted but also encouraged these organizations because they represented a fundamental way that life, and death, was organized in Portuguese society. The Portuguese acceptance of the rosary brotherhoods as existing specifically for blacks grew out of the confluence of several factors, most important of these being the popular nature of Marian devotion, the use of prayer beads, and the development and spread of lay religious brotherhoods. These factors came together in the mid-fifteenth century, just as the unprecedented Portuguese expansion into sub-Saharan Africa got under way.

Marian devotion, the use of prayer beads, and lay religious brotherhoods have three important elements in common. First, they can all be traced to pre- or extra-Christian practices and beliefs. Second, even when initially started by the church, they took on a life of their own when embraced by the lay population. Finally, all grew in popularity because of peoples' desire for intercession between heaven and earth during life and heaven and hell after death.[1] Although the church would not frame them as such, Marian devotion, prayer beads, and lay religious brotherhoods all became active avenues of communication with the spirit world and the world of the dead, which resonated not only with early modern Europeans but also with Africans who were exposed to Christianity. In Europe, rosary prayer beads and the brotherhood tradition came together when Jacob Sprenger, an infamous witch hunter and coauthor of the famous work on demonology, *Malleus maleficarum*, began the first official brotherhood of the rosary in Cologne in 1475. By the sixteenth century, conditions were right for the formation of brotherhoods of Our Lady of the Rosary of the blacks in Portugal and areas of the Portuguese Empire, especially Brazil.

Rosaries and Brotherhoods

The rosary and Our Lady of the Rosary are central to the devotion of blacks throughout the state of Minas Gerais in Brazil; in fact, in the popular saying that opened this chapter, congadeiros maintain that the beads of the rosary are their bullets, giving the rosary not a passive character but the power of a weapon to fight the battles of life.[2] The congadeiros wear the full rosary slung over each shoulder and crossed in front, like the bandoliers of the Mexican revolutionaries. Worldwide, the modern rosary remains one of the most important devotions to Catholics, who use the rosary as a meditative device, as a means of reaching a closer union with God, and for requesting the intercession of Mary. The modern rosary consists of fifteen decades of beads, each decade punctuated by two single beads. The supplicant prays one Hail Mary for each bead in the decade and a Pater Noster (Our Father) and a Glory Be to the Father (Creed) for the single beads dividing the decades. Each decade represents a mystery, an event in the life of Christ, and during

1. Anne Winston-Allen, *Stories of the Rose: The Making of the Rosary in the Middle Ages* (University Park: Pennsylvania State University Press, 1997), 28–30.
2. This popular saying was told to me by Célia Lourdes Ferreira (interview, 25 December 1996); also printed in Leda Maria Martins, *Afrografias da memória: O reinado do rosário no Jatobá* (São Paulo: Editora Perspectiva, 1997), 48.

the repeated prayers of that decade the person meditates on that mystery. The mysteries divide up into three sets of five: joyful, painful, and glorious.[3] The rosary in Brazil includes the entire set of 150 beads. The shorter chain, containing only fifty beads (five sets of ten), is commonly called a *terço* (third) or a *coroa* (crown) in Brazil. The current rosary has developed over many years, but the use of the prayer beads, the repetitive prayers, and the mysteries all developed out of lay practices that were later codified by the church.[4]

The Hail Mary, or Ave Maria, repeated 150 times during a full rosary, is the centerpiece of the rosary devotion. In the seventh century, Pope Gregory XIII (d. 604), also known as Gregory the Great became the first to link "Gabriel's Ave," "Hail, thou that are highly favored, the Lord is with thee, blessed art thou among women" (Luke 1:28), with Elisabeth's greeting to Mary, "Blessed art thou among women, and blessed is the fruit of thy womb" (Luke 1:42).[5] In so doing, he created the earliest example of the Hail Mary. It was not, however, until the sixteenth century that the final supplication of the Ave Maria, "Pray for us sinners now and at the hour of our death," was officially incorporated.[6] In fact, Gregory the Great did not suggest the Hail Mary for use as a prayer of intercession. Instead, he identified it as appropriate for use in the Mass of the fourth Sunday of Advent.[7] Gregory the Great, however, did play a pivotal role in the development of the concept of purgatory, a liminal afterlife, middle place between hell and heaven in which the fate of the dead could be negotiated by the living through prayer. He promoted devotions intended to intercede for the dead, including Masses for the dead.[8] The Ave Maria, which would become the most widespread prayer calling on the Virgin's intercession, was not prayed by the general public until the prolific Benedictine cardinal Peter Damian (d. 1072) recommended its use. A century later, a synod recommended that the clergy say the Hail Mary alongside the Our Father and the Creed. It was also around this time that

---

3. Many of the congadeiros reviewed the fifteen mysteries with me to make sure that I understood the basis of the rosary. João Lopes, interview, 21 May 1997; José Expedito da Luz Ferreira, captain of the Mozambique of Jatobá, interview with the author, Tirol, BH, MG, 21 August 1995.

4. Winston-Allen, *Stories of the Rose*, 28–30.

5. For works on the development of Marian devotion, see Marina Warner, *Alone of All Her Sex, The Myth and the Cult of the Virgin Mary* (New York: Vintage Books, 1976); and Geoffrey Ashe, *The Virgin* (London: Routledge and Kegan Paul, 1976).

6. Warner, *Alone of All Her Sex*, 306.

7. Warner, *Alone of All Her Sex*, 8; and Anne Winston, "Tracing the Origins of the Rosary: German Vernacular Texts," *Speculum: A Journal of Medieval Studies* 68 (July 1993): 620.

8. The actual use of the word *purgatory*, however, did not come into use until many centuries later. Philippe Ariès, *The Hour of Our Death*, trans. Helen Weaver (New York: Oxford University Press, 1991), 153, 158–59.

the Franciscans and Dominicans began to recommend the prayer to the laity as a substitute for more sophisticated and harder-to-remember prayers.

By the twelfth and thirteenth centuries, then, the Hail Mary, the Our Father, and the Creed all became popular repetitive prayers that were prayed together. The supplicants kept track of the prayers by moving from one bead to the next on chains of early Christian prayer beads. Anecdotes of individuals praying chains of Ave Marias were common in Marian legends of that period, yet the practice of using prayer beads developed in earlier centuries.[9] No one knows when prayer beads were introduced into Christianity. Both Hindus and Buddhists used prayer beads, and Muslims may have adopted the practice from those Eastern religions. The early crusaders are thought to have adopted the practice from their Muslim adversaries, but even before the first Crusade (1096–98) Christians used prayer beads. For example, the infamous Lady Godiva of Coventry, on her death in 1075, left a string of gems that she used to keep track of her prayers to a statue of the Virgin, "the circlet of precious stones which she had threaded on a cord in order that by fingering them one after another she might count her prayers exactly."[10]

In the eleventh century, strings of prayer beads were most commonly called paternosters because the recitation of the 150 "paters" (Our Fathers) had replaced the recitation of 150 psalms as the "poor man's breviary."[11] Common people often repeated prayers as acts of penance or devotion. As early as the twelfth century, the Hail Mary had begun to replace the Our Father as a popular repetitive prayer. By the thirteenth century the strings of beads used to keep track of prayers were called chaplets, symbolizing a mystical crown placed on Mary's brow. Because of the connection with the psalms, the prayer beads also came to be called Our Lady's Psalter. The devoted usually recited the prayers following the same division as the psalms, in groups of 50, 100, or 150.[12]

The name *rosary* for the string of prayer beads did not become official until the sixteenth century. The idea of the rosary originated in the medieval imagery and symbolism of roses and rose gardens, which had also been important in Greek and Roman traditions. In medieval times, the rose garden became popular as a place of romance in both imagery and stories, and the

9. Winston-Allen, *Stories of the Rose*, 14–15.

10. Alban Butler, *Butler's Lives of the Saints*, vol. 4, ed. and rev. Herbert Thurston and Donald Attwater (New York: P. J. Kenedy and Sons, 1956), 49. As early as the third century, Christian ascetics Paul of Thebes and Saint Anthony were said to have used knotted strings to keep track of their "incessant" prayers. Winston-Allen, *Stories of the Rose*, 14.

11. Winston-Allen, *Stories of the Rose*, 15.

12. *New Catholic Encyclopedia*, vol. 11 (New York: McGraw Hill, 1967), 688.

image of an enclosed garden came to be the symbol of Mary's virginity. Mary was often pictured sitting in a garden that symbolically represented the opposite of Eve's garden, just as "Eva" and "Ave" had come to represent Eve and Mary's opposition and resolution.[13] The rose symbolized, in medieval mystical semiotics, the Holy Cross and the wounds of Jesus Christ. The red rose symbolized love (the blood that Christ spilled out of love for humankind), and the white mercy (or virginity in the case of the Virgin).[14] The repeated Ave Marias became roses through "the identification of the rose with Christ and Christ with the Word."[15] Late fifteenth- and early sixteenth-century prayer books tell countless stories of the transformations of the words of the Ave Maria into symbolic flowers.[16]

By the thirteenth century the circlet of beads had come to be known as the *rosarium,* a chaplet of roses, and had spread to become "almost an article of dress."[17] Yet the mixture of profane and mystical associations of the rose garden made Alanus de Rupe, the founder of the first, unofficial, rosary brotherhood, uncomfortable. In his brotherhood, founded in Douai, France, in 1470, he vehemently opposed the use of the word *rosary* for the prayer beads. Instead, he supported the use of the term Psalter of Our Lady for the devotion. Other early brotherhoods founded around the emerging prayer bead devotions in France and Italy came to be known as brotherhoods of the chaplet. Nevertheless, papal decrees about the devotion in 1476 and 1478 both used the word *rosario,* and Jacob Sprenger, the most influential promoter of the rosary brotherhoods, never wavered in his preference for the term *rosenkranz* (garland of roses).[18] In 1573, a Portuguese Dominican friar, Nicolau Dias, wrote a treatise on the rosary titled *Livro do Rosayro de Nossa Senhora* (The book of the Rosary of Our Lady) in which he acknowledged the three different names for the devotion, the principal being Rosayro; the second, Coroa (Crown/Chaplet); and the third, Psalteyro (Psalter).[19]

By the sixteenth century, however, the rosary was not just a litany of repeated prayers; nor did it remain associated with the psalms. Instead, it included meditations on the life of Christ, to give shape and meaning to the

---

13. Winston-Allen, *Stories of the Rose,* 89–99; on Mary as the second Eve, see Warner, *Alone of All Her Sex,* 57–62.

14. Winston-Allen, *Stories of the Rose,* 99.

15. Ibid., 100.

16. Ibid., 101.

17. Eithne Wilkins, *The Rose-Garden Game: A Tradition of Beads and Flowers* (New York: Herder and Herder, 1969), 37.

18. Winston-Allen, *Stories of the Rose,* 107–9.

19. Fr. Nicolau Dias, *Livro do Rosário de Nossa Senhora (Edição fac-similada da 1a edição de 1573)* (Lisbon: Biblioteca Nacional, 1982), 37–41.

repeated prayers. For many years, scholars ascribed the combination of the life-of-Christ meditations with repeated prayers to Saint Dominic, who was believed to have repeated the Hail Mary using prayer beads while simultaneously meditating on the life of Jesus. According to the legend, Saint Dominic used this method to convert the Albigensians (better known as the Cathars), a gnostic sect in the south of France whose "radically puritanical" views were spreading in the beginning of the thirteenth century.[20] Nineteenth-century scholars disputed Saint Dominic's authorship, claiming a lack of evidence that Saint Dominic ever used prayer beads. They traced the rosary back to Dominic the Carthusian (1384–1460), a fifteenth-century Dominican monk who, in his 1458 work, *Liber Experientiarum,* claimed to have combined the repetitive prayer with meditations on the life of Christ.[21] Later scholars disputed Dominic the Carthusian's claim when they discovered a vernacular life-of-Christ rosary text written about 1300. Other German vernacular texts have also been discovered that predate the Carthusian Dominic's claim as author.[22] Nevertheless, Dominic's text, even if it was not the first to combine a narrative of Christ's life with the beads, became the most widely disseminated. His version of the narrative was composed of fifty meditations on the life of Jesus, but between 1475 and 1550 rosary prayer books prescribed many different numbers of meditations, ranging anywhere from five to two hundred. The development of the rosary, then, emerged out of a mystical tradition in the medieval church and a popular devotion expressed through the publication in the vernacular of the meditations on the life of Christ. The rosary became a principle avenue of communication between laypeople and the divine and became a private way for people to express their devotion.

Just as the rosary became a way for laypeople to express their individual devotion and make private supplications, lay brotherhoods were developing in a way that would bring whole communities together around a single devotion. Lay brotherhoods were intimately associated with fulfilling charitable acts, which, according to the Gospel of Matthew, were caring for strangers and for the hungry, thirsty, naked, sick, and imprisoned. The charitable act of caring for the dead was added to the list during the Middle Ages.[23] In fact, many scholars have placed the question of death at the center of the discussion of brotherhoods by linking their early medieval manifestations to Roman burial societies. According to historian Albert Meyers, religious brotherhoods developed as echoes of the Greek and Roman sodalities whose

20. Wilkins, *Rose-Garden Game,* 15.

21. Winston-Allen, *Stories of the Rose,* 16–17.

22. Winston, "Tracing the Origins," 622–27; and Winston-Allen, *Stories of the Rose,* 23–26.

members worshipped a certain god in a particular temple. People organized their religious life in these sodalities. Early Christianity adopted a similar corporate structure, and as early as the eighth century Saint Boniface (d. 754) saw the organizations as propagating the Christian faith, practicing mutual aid with charitable works, and extending this aid beyond death by praying for the souls of the deceased.[24] Whether or not medieval and early modern brotherhoods in fact evolved from the Greek and Roman sodalities cannot be known concretely, yet there can be no doubt that lay religious brotherhoods, from their inception, were intimately concerned with the proper care of the body and the soul after death. Even the churches themselves became cemeteries, in which the location of the body of the dead was related to the brotherhood member's position in the organization—the higher the position, the closer to the altar; and the closer to the altar, the closer to the divine.[25] As historian James R. Banker points out, the formation of brotherhoods pointed to the "intense socialization of death" already taking place before the second half of the thirteenth century.[26]

Although they were religious and dedicated to a particular saint, brotherhoods expressed a religion that was not private, but public, a type of devotion in which the active, celebratory functions were as important as private contemplation. In fact, these voluntary associations of lay brothers and sisters were not a private place of a personal relationship with God, but rather public spaces in which communities worked out their relationship to one another and to the divine. In addition, the associations were not "popular" as much as they were "lay," organized not by a monolithic church, but rather by the people themselves.[27] Brotherhoods engaged in vast range of activities, but their primary responsibilities were the physical and spiritual care of the dead and the celebration of the saints' days. They included special ways to communicate across the material boundaries and to an unseen space where ultimate fates and destinies would be determined. As Banker points out in

23. Christopher F. Black, *Italian Confraternities in the Sixteenth Century* (Cambridge: Cambridge University Press, 1989), 3 n. 9.

24. Albert Meyers, "The Religious Brotherhoods in Latin America," in *Manipulating the Saints: Religious Brotherhoods and Social Integration in Postconquest Latin America*, ed. A. Meyers and Diane Hopkins (Hamburg: Wayasbah, 1988), 4.

25. See Ariès, *Hour of Our Death*, 45–90.

26. James R. Banker, *Death in the Community: Memorialization and Confraternities in an Italian Commune in the Late Middle Ages* (Athens: University of Georgia Press, 1988), 11; Maureen Flynn, *Sacred Charity: Confraternities and Social Welfare in Spain, 1400–1700* (Ithaca: Cornell University Press, 1989), 64–69.

27. William A. Christian Jr., *Local Religion in Sixteenth-Century Spain* (Princeton: Princeton University Press, 1981), 147.

his discussion of lay religious brotherhoods in medieval Italy: "Religion need not be conceived as supernatural to recognize that it is not just another social reality. The desire to transcend this world and to articulate the significance of human existence constitutes a dynamic but permanent element in man's consciousness. If a popular or folk culture existed . . . it was not pagan or heretical, but a lay culture concerned with achieving social esteem at death and remembrance thereafter within a general Christian framework."[28]

Religious orders, however, were often concerned with the possible pagan practices of the common people. Sprenger's impetus to found the first official brotherhood of the rosary probably emerged from his inquisitorial efforts to rid the poor and illiterate population of pagan beliefs. In the statutes of his rosary confraternity he wrote that "in our brotherhood no one will be kept out, no matter how poor he may be; but rather the poorer he is, the more disdained, and despised, the more acceptable, beloved, and precious will he be in this brotherhood."[29] Even women, who were often excluded from membership in lay religious brotherhoods, were welcomed into rosary brotherhoods. Further, the brotherhood of the rosary made membership extremely easy—there were no penalties for lapsed members, members did not have to make up missed prayers, they could say any version of the rosary that they wished, and they could pray the rosary anywhere and at any time of the day.[30] The exponential growth of the first brotherhood attested to its popularity. Within the first seven years of its founding, the brotherhood in Cologne had more than one hundred thousand members.[31]

The brotherhood of the rosary became extremely popular not only because of the ease of becoming a member but also because membership assured the person fewer years in purgatory. A broadside from 1510 claimed:

> Whoever wants to be of the family of Mother Mary,
> let him enroll himself in the [brotherhood of the] rosary.
> For I tell you, she will protect him from the pain of hell.
> Indeed, she can free him from it eternally.[32]

A series of papal bulls granted years, and at times tens of thousands of years, of redemption for those who prayed the rosary, and even more if it was

---

28. Banker, *Death in the Community*, 8.
29. Winston, "Tracing the Origins," 634 n. 54. On women in the brotherhoods, see Black, *Italian Confraternities*, 38–39, 103.
30. Winston, "Tracing the Origins," 634.
31. Ibid., 630; and Winston-Allen, *Stories of the Rose*, 111.
32. Cited in Winston-Allen, *Stories of the Rose*, 27–28.

prayed on certain holy days and places. Rosary handbooks that proliferated at that time listed the indulgences granted by the popes.[33] This method of gaining indulgences would have been very appealing to the poor, for the other methods of gaining them, such as lengthy pilgrimages or buying statues, were much too expensive for the many poor people in the population. In some cases, this caused the rosary to become a kind of "'arithmetical' piety," an insurance policy against years in purgatory rather than the inward, meditative devotional practice it represented.[34]

Adding to their allure, rosaries were considered to be powerful charms to keep evil away. Their power was said to increase if the beads were kept for a time near a picture of the Virgin. Manuals of the saying of the rosary, broadsides, and popular songs all stressed these powers in their advertisements.[35] Frei Dias used the last book of his manual to tell forty-five stories of miracles that had been granted by means of the rosary and through the mercy of Our Lady. Many of the stories depict the conversion of a doubting person to the "true faith" through the rosary prayers. Others provide examples of much more practical miracles, such as blind, mute, or paralyzed people becoming well; a sterile woman becoming fertile; or people being raised from the dead. According to the stories, praying the rosary could also give the faithful access to material wealth. All the stories attested to the miraculous power of the rosary and the brotherhoods of the rosary as well as the intercessionary powers of the Virgin, especially in the lives of the poor.[36]

Thus, the rosary became a popular devotion as it simultaneously gained church sanction. The life-of-Christ meditations that eventually became the rosary mysteries originally appeared in the vernacular, demonstrating the popular nature of the devotion.[37] As an extraliturgical, private devotion, it addressed the laity's need for a more personal expression of their own devotion. In the late Middle Ages, the members of the laity would even recite the rosary during the Latin Mass, participating in their own way in a ritual that seemed far removed from them.[38] Dominicans, like Sprenger, founded rosary brotherhoods in Dominican monasteries and were

33. Dias, *Livro do Rosário*, 205–88.

34. Winston-Allen, *Stories of the Rose*, 5 and 122, quote at 5.

35. Ibid., 116.

36. Dias, *Livro do Rosário*, 289–383.

37. Although scholars have long thought that the original German rosaries were translations of Latin ones, recent findings have shown that even Dominic the Carthusian's original life-of-Christ meditation was originally written in German and later translated into Latin. Winston-Allen, *Stories of the Rose*, 17.

38. Ibid., 29.

important in the promulgation of the devotion, yet its exponential spread must be attributed to this extreme popularity among the people.

The devotion's popularity finally moved the church to codify it, and Pope Pius V, a Dominican, made it official in 1569, containing the fifteen mysteries of the rosary that continue to be meditated upon today. The same pope, attributing the victory over the Moors at Lepanto in 1571 to the prayers and processions of the brotherhoods of the rosary in Rome during the battle, dedicated the first Sunday of October to Our Lady of Victory. In 1573, Pope Gregory XIII changed the name of the observance to Our Lady of the Rosary and moved it to the actual day of the battle, 7 October.[39] The final mystery, the crowning of Our Lady in heaven, which would serve as a template for the coronations of kings and queens in the rosary brotherhoods of blacks in Brazil, became established almost universally as the final meditation after 1570.[40]

The conflation of popular and church beliefs with the devotion of the rosary supports William Christian's findings on local religion in sixteenth century New Castile. He found that the local religion was profoundly shaped by the laity, and that many of the clergy participated in the local practices even after the Council of Trent.[41] Posited at the basis of popular beliefs was the possibility of an exchange of communication between humankind and the forces of nature and the seen and unseen worlds.[42] Saints were available to help village communities avoid misfortune. One way to keep that misfortune away, or remedy disasters that were already occurring, was to make a vow (*voto*) to a "specialist" saint associated with that particular problem. Sixteenth-century Castilians would also call on that specialist saint if the problem or crisis had occurred on that saint's holy day. Important to note is that many of these promises were not made on the individual level. Instead, the entire community would participate in the formulation and the fulfillment of vows, most commonly to circumvent plagues and diseases, vine pests, grasshoppers, hail, drought, rabies, and storms.[43] The vows the village people made were

39. *New Catholic Encyclopedia*, vol. 11, 398.

40. For an elaboration of the origin and theological significance of the crowning of Our Lady, see Winston-Allen, *Stories of the Rose*, 145–46.

41. Christian, *Local Religion*, 147. Christian points out that all the Council of Trent changed in New Castile was that the Roman church became the universal church, with new power over local churches, yet, as Manuel M. Marzal points out, Trent did not do away with local practices; it only increased tension between the local and universal churchs. Manuel M. Marzal, "Transplanted Spanish Catholicism," in *South and Meso-American Native Spirituality*, ed. Gary H. Gossen (New York: Crossroads, 1997), 140–69.

42. William A. Christian Jr., *Apparitions in Late Medieval and Renaissance Spain* (Princeton: Princeton University Press, 1981), 19–20.

43. Christian, *Local Religion*, 29.

contractual, mirroring their relationship to their earthly lord.[44] Communities often engaged in legal disputes, and "just as they paid their lawyers, sometimes going into debt to do so, so villages and towns entailed their resources in the form of future masses, penance, and work time to pay saints to be their lawyers before God."[45] Thus, in the sixteenth century, villagers had a worldview in which the earthly world and the spirit realm not only were in communion with one another, but also regularly interacted.

Communities rarely called upon the Virgin to perform specific tasks; nor did they make vows to her shrines. Instead, Marian devotion exemplified the other means of communication between the people and the spirit world. That was when the saints, most often the Virgin, called on communities to serve her. Sometimes, local seers would have visions of Our Lady beseeching the communities to pray to or erect a shrine for her, and shrines in New Castile were overwhelmingly dedicated to her.[46] In other cases, a person would find an image in a cave, or a river, or under the ground, and the image would keep returning to the place in which it was found, signifying that it wanted the community to build a shrine there and nowhere else. These apparitions and findings of images were "charters for the relations between the village and the natural world. The seers, like the legendary discoverers of statues, were privileged intermediaries."[47] The seers themselves could be men, women, or children, and their visions occurred while they were fully awake. Unlike ecstatic nuns and *beatas* (lay holy women) of the time, who served as mediums, these seers were chosen by the saints to receive messages for their communities.[48]

Once the shrines were erected, populations used them for various purposes. Individuals made pilgrimages to certain shrines, often staying there for up to nine days. The shrines sometimes housed brotherhoods and became locations of feast day processions and celebrations. Processions often involved both music and dancing, and the all-night vigils included "feasting and drinking, farces and plays, and secular dirty and lewd songs."[49] By the mid-sixteenth century, local authorities in several towns were so alarmed by the festivities that they passed ordinances prohibiting all-night vigils in their local shrines.

44. Christian, *Apparitions*, 14.
45. Christian, *Local Religion*, 56. In the same manner, the congadeiros still call Our Lady of the Rosary their "lawyer."
46. Ibid., 73–75.
47. Christian, *Apparitions*, 22.
48. Ibid., 186–87, 209.
49. Christian, *Local Religion*, 164.

Despite the numerous shrines dedicated to the Virgin in New Castile and the proliferation and codification of the rosary in sixteenth-century Europe, the rosary devotion and the rosary brotherhoods were not widespread in New Castile in the late sixteenth century. In fact, Pedro Ciruelo, in his early sixteenth-century treatise on witchcraft, which he based on local Castilian practices, did not mention the rosary once. Nevertheless, he praised the prayers that had become intimately associated with the rosary, the Our Father, the Hail Mary, and the Creed. Ciruelo suggested that the prayers be recited or written down and worn as an amulet.[50] Interestingly, after condemning the use of amulets and talismans earlier in the same chapter, Ciruelo defended his suggestion that the prayers be used as a talisman: "Someone may ask me, and with reason, what advantage this talisman has over others, if it has no more natural power than other talismans and if it is illicit to put more trust in it than in another. To this question I answer that its advantage derives from its comprehensive devotional nature."[51] Soon, the rosary, encompassing Ciruelo's suggested prayers, would become the symbol of the complete ritual expression encompassed in those prayers.[52]

Rosary brotherhoods do not seem to be as important in sixteenth-century New Castile as they would become in Portugal and its colonies. Between 1575 and 1580, the number of chapels dedicated to the rosary, a sign that a brotherhood existed, was only 4 percent of the total in New Castile.[53] By that time, however, brotherhoods of the rosary had existed in Portugal for more than one hundred years and had already become intimately associated with the growing black population, both slave and free.[54] The first brotherhood of the rosary in Portugal was founded in the Dominican monastery in Lisbon sometime in the 1480s, just a few years after the founding of the first official rosary brotherhood in Cologne.[55] All during the following century,

50. Pedro Ciruelo, *Pedro Ciruelo's A Treatise Reproving All Superstitions and Forms of Witchcraft, Very Necessary and Useful for All Good Christians Zealous for Their Salvation*, trans. Eugene A. Maio and D'Orsay W. Pearson (Cranbury, N.J.: Associated University Presses, 1977), 228–31.

51. Ibid., 230.

52. Ibid., 230 n. 15.

53. Christian, *Local Religion*, 71.

54. On black life and culture in Portugal, see Padre António Brásio, *Os pretos em Portugal* (Lisbon: Pelo Império, 1944); A. C. de C. M. Saunders, *A Social History of Black Slaves and Freedmen in Portugal, 1441–1555* (Cambridge: Cambridge University Press, 1982); José Ramos Tinorhão, *Os negros em Portugal: Uma presença silenciosa* (Lisbon: Editorial Caminho, 1988).

55. In the prologue of the 1565 *compromisso* (statutes) of the brotherhood of the rosary in Lisbon, it is noted that the brotherhood was originally founded in 1460, which would have been before the founding of the original, unofficial brotherhood founded by Alanus de Rupe. "Compromisso of the Brotherhood of Our Lady of the Rosary of Black Men," printed in Patricia

brotherhoods of the rosary in Portugal thrived. Nine brotherhoods of slaves and free blacks were founded in Portugal in the sixteenth century, all of them dedicated to Our Lady of the Rosary.[56] The combination of the spread of the rosary, a devotion specially designed for illiterate and potentially heathen masses, and the Portuguese expansion into Africa gave the Portuguese a perfect way to teach the Africans the basic precepts of Christianity. Africans would be able to re-form communities and rituals in the rosary brotherhoods because of similarities between their worldviews and the early modern layperson's relationship to the unseen world, as mediated by the rosary and Our Lady of the Rosary within the rosary brotherhoods.

Portuguese Expansion and Rosary Brotherhoods of Blacks

The Portuguese interest in Africa centered on two factors—to further Portuguese economic interests and to evangelize the natives—and both became justifications for the slave trade. Portuguese expansion into Africa began with the capture and retention of the fortified city of Ceuta in Morocco in 1415, an event that Dom João I considered to be a logical expansion of the reconquest.[57] This action signaled the "end of the inward-looking European middle ages and the beginning of the outward-looking age of expansion."[58] It was in Ceuta that the infante Henrique, the well-known Prince Henry the Navigator, got his first battle experience. It was also in Ceuta that the Portuguese first heard of the "gold of Guinea." Prince Henry believed that he could reach the rich gold fields by sea, and to that end he set up his center

Mulvey, "Black Lay Brotherhoods of Colonial Brazil: A History" (Ph.D. diss., City College of New York, 1976), 256. A. C. de C. M. Saunders cites another source, which dates the first brotherhood to 1484, whereas Anne Winston-Allen dates the first brotherhood (citing German sources), in Lisbon, to 1478. Saunders, *A Social History*, 151; Winston-Allen, *Stories of the Rose*, 116.

56. Mulvey, "Black Lay Brotherhoods," 283–85. Moorish slaves had been present on the Iberian Peninsula even before the earliest creation of rosary brotherhoods. At the dawn of the fifteenth century a lay confraternity dedicated to Our Lady of the Angels was formed in Seville to serve the Moorish slave population. During their feast day celebrations the blacks gathered together, appointed their own leaders, and participated in their own songs and dances. Ruth Pike, "Sevillian Society in the Sixteenth Century: Slaves and Freedmen," *HAHR* 47 (August 1967): 345. Historian Patricia Mulvey lists eleven brotherhoods of slaves in Spain formed from the early fifteenth century to the mid-eighteenth century. Only one of these was dedicated to Our Lady of the Rosary. Mulvey, "Black Lay Brotherhoods," 283–85.

57. C. R. Boxer, *The Portuguese Seaborne Empire, 1415–1825* (New York: Alfred A. Knopf, 1969), 18–19.

58. David Birmingham, *A Concise History of Portugal* (Cambridge: Cambridge University Press, 1993), 25.

in the far south region of Portugal, the Algarve, turning Lagos, Portugal, into a thriving ship-building center and port.[59] Prince Henry's first expansion was to the uninhabited islands of Madeira and the Azores in the Atlantic. He kept urging his seamen southward, until finally by the 1460s they had reached the Gold Coast, by the 1480s they had found the kingdom of Kongo, and by the end of the century Vasco da Gama was rounding the Cape of Good Hope on his way to India.[60]

The church fully supported the Portuguese expansion, as well as the capture and evangelization of Africans. Popes issued three successive bulls, in 1452, 1455, and 1456, which gave the Portuguese, and specifically Prince Henry, the right to conquer and subdue any pagan peoples, to seize their goods and lands, and to transfer the people to perpetual slavery in order to save their souls from eternal damnation. The bulls decreed that other nations could not interfere with the Portuguese monopoly of discovery, and the king of Portugal signed the bull in a ceremony attended by French, English, Castilian, Galician and Basque officials. Finally, the papal decrees gave the Portuguese Crown the right to build churches and monasteries and to send priests to any lands they conquered. The head of the Order of Christ, a position held by Prince Henry the Navigator and then successive kings of Portugal, had the right to nominate priests and bishops; to impose censures and other penalties; to collect the *dízimo* (10 percent tithe); to censor letters from Rome, and to have the power of an "ordinary"; a prelate with a jurisdiction over specified territories.[61] Through these bulls the church not only fully supported the Portuguese in their imperial endeavor, but also established the *padroado real,* or royal patronage of the church, which would intimately link the Portuguese church and state for the following four hundred years, until the end of the nineteenth century.

In the early decades of the Portuguese expansion, however, slavery was not always associated with blacks, or blacks with slavery. Black slaves had already become a common sight in Lisbon and other Portuguese cities by the late fifteenth and early sixteenth centuries, but Africans also traveled to Lisbon for other reasons. In one instance, in 1486, a chief from the port of Benin went to Lisbon to learn "the Christian way of life," and his visit

---

59. Hugh Thomas, *The Slave Trade: The Story of the Atlantic Slave Trade, 1440–1870* (New York: Simon and Schuster, 1997), 53.

60. Birmingham, *Concise History,* 25–26; Thomas, *Slave Trade,* 55.

61. Boxer, *Portuguese Seaborne Empire,* 21–23; Thomas Bruneau, *The Political Transformation of the Brazilian Catholic Church* (London: Cambridge University Press, 1974), 14.

resulted in the development of a trading center in Benin.[62] The most common motivation to bring African freemen to Lisbon, however, was to train a native clergy. From the earliest contacts along the Senegal River, Portuguese ships took black youths to Lisbon to study for the ministry. This practice became even more common after Kongo became a "Christian" state in 1491, after the king of Kongo accepted Christianity and became Dom João I of Kongo. Dom Henrique, son of King Afonso I of Kongo and grandson of the first Christian Kongo king, became the most famous success in this regard. After studying in Lisbon, Dom Henrique was consecrated by Pope Leo X as a bishop in 1518, after which Dom Henrique returned to São Salvador, Kongo, to serve in that capacity. The same pope promulgated a brief in which he authorized the royal chaplain in Lisbon to ordain "Ethiopians, Indians and Africans" who had reached the moral and educational standards of the priesthood.[63] Throughout the sixteenth century the Kongolese royal family sent sons to Portugal to study in the Lisbon monastery of Saint John the Evangelist, known popularly as Saint Eloi. After the mid-sixteenth century, when the slave trade heated up, the practice of noble Kongolese youth studying in Lisbon became much less frequent, but a trickle of these African students continued.[64]

This apparent "color-blindness" of the Portuguese, however, should not be overly exaggerated. Even in the late fifteenth century, the Portuguese judged blacks by a different standard from that of whites. For example, King Bemoin of Senegal traveled to Lisbon in 1488 and converted to Christianity, in a ceremony at which the king and queen of Portugal acted as his godparents. Despite this, when Bemoin returned on a Portuguese ship to Senegal, the captain, Pero Vaz, simply murdered him and turned his ships around to go home. Pero Vaz was not punished by the king—although by European standards he had committed regicide—because the Portuguese "would not tolerate the execution of a white Portuguese of noble rank for killing a black African, king or not."[65] Historian Anthony Pagden argues that the murder could only have happened away from Portuguese soil, in a locale where the ties that bound Portuguese society together no longer applied.

62. Thomas, *Slave Trade*, 79.

63. C. R. Boxer, *The Church Militant and Iberian Expansion, 1440–1770* (Baltimore: Johns Hopkins University Press, 1978), 3–4.

64. Boxer, *Church Militant*, 3–7.

65. Peter Russell quoted in Anthony Pagden, *European Encounters with the New World* (New Haven: Yale University Press, 1993), 4–5.

Brotherhoods were an important part of the social fabric on Portuguese soil and in the far-flung colonies. They could serve both the social and the religious needs of the growing black population and tie that population to the larger social and cultural milieu, protecting them from the type of violence that befell King Bemoin. The confluence of the repetitive prayers of the rosary, considered ideal for illiterate populations, with the open-membership policies of the brotherhoods of the rosary made those brotherhoods the perfect vehicle for bringing that population into the church and, by extension, into Portuguese society. Frei Dias's sixteenth-century Portuguese rosary manual stated that part of the "excellence" of the rosary brotherhood lay in its acceptance of all types of people: "men, women, large, small, poor, rich, old, young, free, slave, religious, seculars and also the dead."[66] As in Jacob Sprenger's original rosary brotherhood, brothers and sisters of the brotherhood in Lisbon were not obliged to pay any entrance fee; their sole obligation was to pray the rosary every day.[67] Even people who had already died could become members of the rosary brotherhood if living members prayed rosaries in their names. Frei Dias did not mention race anywhere in his treatise, yet he included among his miracle stories the tale of a woman who had been taken captive by the Moors in Granada and managed to gain her freedom through her devotion.[68] The Portuguese and the Africans could easily have applied this tale to the enslavement of sub-Saharan Africans— both their physical enslavement and their metaphorical and diabolical enslavement to pagan gods.

Although the earliest rosary brotherhood in Lisbon had originally been for blacks and whites, by 1496 the blacks had separated from the whites to form their own organization. They were given special permission to collect alms in the ships that by then were regularly sailing for Africa.[69] The 1575 *compromisso* (incorporating statutes) of the Brotherhood of Our Lady of the Rosary of the Blacks in Lisbon showed that by the late sixteenth century the brotherhoods had, in fact, become brotherhoods of blacks and slaves. It explained that the rosary brotherhood was for the blacks "because black men, coming from lands far away from Our Lady of the Rosary and its great miracles, and moved by a Catholic devotion, had been the first to build

66. Dias, *Livro do Rosário*, 45.
67. The brotherhoods in Brazil, and those in eighteenth-century Portugal, did require entrance and annual fees of their members.
68. Dias, *Livro do Rosário*, 349–52.
69. Linda M. Heywood, "The Angolan-Afro-Brazilian Cultural Connections," *Slavery and Abolition* 20, no. 1 (1999): 10–11.

and sustain the very holy Chapel and brotherhood."[70] In addition, the compromisso included certain chapters that related specifically to the slave members. For example, despite the fact that the brotherhood admitted slaves, slaves could not be officers, nor could white Moriscos, mulattos or Indians. The brotherhood had no obligation to free slaves who were already "partly free" (meio forros), but the brotherhood would not stop members from collecting alms for the purpose of freeing their fellow members. Finally, in addition to the administrative officers in the brotherhoods, the compromisso allowed that "any brother who wishes, by their devotion, to be majordomo, Prince, King, Duke, Count, Marquis, Cardinal, or any other dignitary" could do so, setting the groundwork for the establishment of this type of hierarchy in Brazilian rosary brotherhoods.[71] In the mid-eighteenth century the brotherhood in Lisbon became even more important to African and Portuguese-born black slaves, because membership in the organization prevented them from being sold out of Portugal to Brazil, where slavery was rumored to be, and probably was, much harsher.[72]

At the same time that black slavery grew in importance in the Atlantic sugar economy, the rosary became a metaphor for slavery to an unswerving devotion to Mary and Jesus in seventeenth-century Europe. In a prayer published in Antwerp in 1671, the author asked to "be freed from the chains of the infernal enemy in the hour of death so Mary's hands would pull us to heaven by means of the rosary to adore Jesus in the company of the saints."[73] In eighteenth-century Portugal the slavery metaphor remained current. In 1755 a priest published a work in Lisbon that contained a "letter of slavery" to Jesus, Mary, and Joseph in which he presented the rosary worn around his neck as a sign of his slavery. The Jesuit preacher, Antonio Vieira, used a similar idea in his sermon to the slaves of a brotherhood of the rosary on a plantation in that state of Bahia, Brazil, in 1633. He preached, "[T]hat Our Lady of the Rosary is able to free people from the slavery of the body has been seen in the countless examples of those who, finding themselves captives in an infidel land, were freed through devotion to the rosary, and after offering to the altars of the same Lady the broken chains and fetters of

70. "Compromisso of the Brotherhood of Our Lady of the Rosary of Black Men," in Mulvey, "Black Lay Brotherhoods," 256.

71. Ibid., 258–62.

72. C. R. Boxer, *Race Relations in the Portuguese Colonial Empire, 1415–1825* (Oxford: Clarendon Press, 1963), 108–9.

73. Frei Francisco Van Der Poel, *O rosário dos homens pretos* (Belo Horizonte, Brazil: Imprensa Oficial, 1981), 78.

their captivity, as trophies to her power and charity, they hung them in the temples."[74] Thus, the rosary came to be seen metaphorically both as a chain of slavery and as having the ability to break those chains.

As brotherhoods of the rosary became associated with the black population and slavery in Portugal, they similarly became connected with that population throughout the Portuguese seaborne empire. The Dominicans, who were the main propagators of the devotion of the rosary, had special canonical privileges allowing them to create brotherhoods for slaves. By the sixteenth century, brotherhoods of slaves and free blacks dedicated to Our Lady of the Rosary, which had been founded throughout Portugal, were housed mostly within Dominican monasteries.[75] Some Dominicans became missionaries in Kongo and organized brotherhoods there, yet theirs was not the only order to promote the rosary devotion and brotherhoods among Africans. The brotherhoods of the rosary in Africa and Brazil were also started by Jesuits, who created missions in those territories shortly after the formation of their order in 1540, as well as by laypeople and by the secular clergy.

The first lay religious brotherhood dedicated to Our Lady of the Rosary in Africa was formed as a result of a petition made by two black freemen on the island of São Tomé. The Portuguese began to settle this uninhabited island in 1486, and it soon became an important sugar producer and entrepôt in the Atlantic slave trade. The king granted the petition for the brotherhood in 1526, giving it more privileges than those enjoyed by the same brotherhood in Lisbon.[76] By 1610, Dominicans in Kongo mentioned a rosary brotherhood in São Salvador, the capital of Kongo, in which the Kongo royal family held the most important posts.[77]

By the late seventeenth century, several brotherhoods of the rosary had been founded in Angola. By 1690, just before slaves began to be exported to the mines of Minas Gerais, a church had been dedicated to Our Lady of the Rosary of the Blacks in Luanda, the capital of Portuguese Angola. Contemporary accounts described the chaplain of the church as a "cleric, who was not ordained; who is obligated to confess them [the blacks] and accompany

---

74. Padre Antônio Vieira, "'Children of God's Fire': A Seventeenth Century Jesuit Finds Benefits in Slavery but Chastises Masters for their Brutality in a Sermon to the Black Brotherhood of Our Lady of the Rosary," in *Children of God's Fire: A Documentary History of Black Slavery in Brazil*, 2d ed., ed. Robert Edgar Conrad (University Park: Pennsylvania State University Press, 1994), 169.

75. Brásio, *Pretos*, 73–104; Boxer, *Church Militant*, 26.

76. Boxer, *Race Relations*, 14.

77. Padre António Brásio, ed., *Monumenta missionaria Africana, Africa Ocidental (1600–1610)* vol. 5 (Lisbon: Academia Portuguesa da História, 1985), 612; Heywood, "Angolan-Afro-Brazilian Connections," 13–15.

them when they die, at their funerals."[78] A communiqué in 1693 described the church of the rosary in Luanda as housing a brotherhood of "freed blacks and slaves and other officials, [one that] is well served by its chaplain paid by them and celebrating their feasts, with a Mass on Saturdays, Sundays and Saints' Days, and devoted clerics often go there to hear Mass."[79] At least two other churches were dedicated to Our Lady of the Rosary in the territory of Angola: one in the Prezidio de Cambambe, forty-seven leagues from Luanda, and the other in the Prezidio das Pedras, fifty-seven leagues from Luanda.[80] Eventually, brotherhoods of the rosary were also established in Cape Verde, Mozambique, and even Goa.[81] It would be in the slave-driven society of Brazil, however, that the rosary brotherhoods would flourish.

The Discovery of Brazil

The Portuguese first encountered the Brazilian coast in 1500, when Pedro Alvares Cabral, a nobleman from the king's household, was accidentally blown off course on his way to India. Only a few tradable commodities were discovered, so the Portuguese did not rush to exploit the new land. As in Africa, merchants established trading factories along the coasts that dealt mostly in brazilwood, which was valued for the red dye it produced. By the 1530s, growing French competition in the region prompted Dom João III to establish fourteen hereditary, donatary captaincies, which he granted to twelve individuals. Despite fiscal and juridical privileges that the Crown allowed the recipients of those lands, the captaincies never prospered. Only two enjoyed relative success, those of Pernambuco in the north and São Vicente in the south. Generally, however, the new owners of the vast tracts of land did not have the resources to overcome the harsh climate, the constant disputes with the indigenous populations, and the incursions of European challengers.

Finally, acknowledging the failure of most of the donatary captaincies, the king sent a governor-general to establish a Crown captaincy in Salvador, Bahia, in 1549. There, sugar cultivation was beginning to overshadow the earlier brazilwood trade. As sugar cultivation and manufacture boomed, in both Bahia and its northern neighbor Pernambuco, the Indian population

78. Brásio, *Monumenta,* vol. 14, 186.
79. Ibid., 343.
80. Ibid., 188–89.
81. Mulvey, "Black Lay Brotherhoods," 16.

became less and less willing to work on the plantations and in the mills, even when taken as slaves. Exacerbating the Portuguese labor shortage, by the end of the sixteenth century epidemics had decimated many of the indigenous populations of the coastal areas.[82] In order to fill the need for labor in the sugar mills and on the plantations, the Portuguese colonists began to import slaves from Africa in ever increasing numbers. By the end of the sixteenth century, the slave trade from Africa to Brazil had begun in earnest.[83]

Along with the Portuguese administrative system, the first religious orders (regular clergy) and diocesan (secular) clergy arrived in Brazil in the mid-sixteenth century. In 1549 six Jesuits, led by Manuel de Nóbrega, arrived in Bahia and soon set to work converting the Indians to Christianity. The spread of the Jesuits was comprehensive, but they concerned themselves mostly with converting the natives and eventually to working with the enslaved African population. For the Europeans, a diocese was established in Salvador in 1551, and the first bishop arrived there in 1552. This remained the only diocese in Brazil until 1676, when it became an archdiocese with oversight over the newly formed dioceses of Olinda and Rio de Janeiro. A permanent inquisitorial tribunal was never set up in Brazil. Instead, bishops and other agents employed by the Holy Office in Portugal investigated suspected heretics. Because of an ongoing shortage of both secular and religious clergy, the main religious institutions among the Portuguese were the brotherhoods in the cities and the plantation chapels on the rural estates. In both these settings, laypeople organized their own devotions and hired their own chaplains. In this way they largely maintained control over their own devotions.[84]

As the slave trade to Brazil increased at the end of the sixteenth century, brotherhoods of the rosary developed in the cities and on the sugar plantations of the northeast of Brazil. The king of Portugal felt this missionary effort so worthwhile that in 1572 he ordered that for six years, tithes collected from newly converted Africans should be used to build their churches and help their brotherhoods, rather than be returned to the crown.[85] In 1584, the ecclesiastical visitor of the Jesuits in Rome requested the statutes

82. See John Hemming, *Red Gold: The Conquest of the Brazilian Indians* (Cambridge: Harvard University Press, 1978).

83. On the early days of the settlement of Brazil, see C. R. Boxer, *The Golden Age of Brazil, 1695–1750: Growing Pains of a Colonial Society* (Berkeley and Los Angeles: University of California Press, 1962); and Leslie Bethell, ed., *Colonial Brazil* (Cambridge: Cambridge University Press, 1991).

84. Thomas C. Bruneau, *The Church in Brazil: The Politics of Religion* (Austin: University of Texas Press, 1982), 14.

85. Mulvey, "Black Lay Brotherhoods," 78–79.

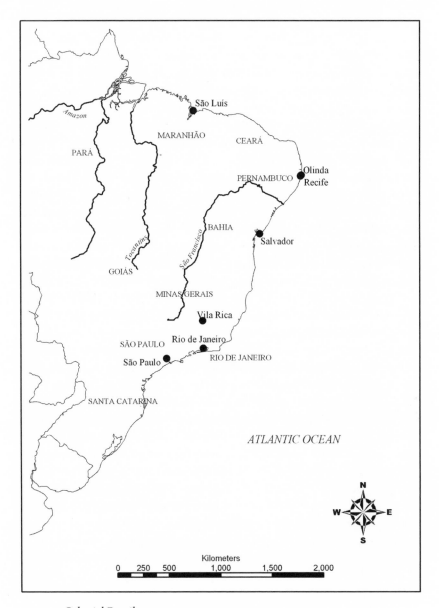

MAP 1.   Colonial Brazil

of the brotherhood of Our Lady of the Rosary for his students to study. The visitor, just two years later, ordered that brotherhoods of the rosary be created for the Indians and the blacks on mills and farms throughout Brazil.[86] Thus, the Jesuits took over the responsibility for the brotherhoods of the rosary in Brazil.

The Jesuits took up their mission to create brotherhoods for the slaves enthusiastically. Two Jesuits in Pernambuco in 1589, for instance, traveled from *engenho* (sugar mill) to *engenho* forming brotherhoods of slaves and boasted of confessing more than eight thousand slaves.[87] By the end of the seventeenth century, there were brotherhoods of the rosary in the cities of Recife and Salvador in the north and of São Vicente in the south and on sugar mills and farms throughout rural Brazil.[88] By the end of the seventeenth century the association of the rosary brotherhoods with blacks had been well established. In 1633 Padre Antonio Vieira urged the members of a rosary brotherhood on a rural estate to accept the bonds of slavery in order to gain freedom in the next life.[89] In 1694 a Jesuit, Padre Pedro Dias, wrote a grammar for the Jesuit fathers to use in converting the blacks in Brazil. The book was titled *Arte da lingua de Angola. Oeferecida [sic] a Virgem Senhora N. do Rosario Mãy, y Senhora dos mesmos Pretos* (The art of the Angolan Language. Offered to Our Virgin Lady of the Rosary, Mother and Lady of those same blacks).[90] By the time that wandering *bandeirantes* (frontiersmen) from São Paulo found gold in the mountains of Minas Gerais in the late seventeenth century, the brotherhoods of the rosary of the blacks were already well established throughout Brazil.

Despite the relative success of economic endeavors such as sugar and tobacco cultivation in Brazil, the Portuguese Crown had always hoped to find gold in its American colony just as the Spanish had found silver in theirs. Finally, in the late seventeenth century the Portuguese realized their dream. Gold was discovered in the mountainous region north of São Paulo and northwest of Rio de Janeiro between 1693 and 1695 by groups of *bandeirantes* who penetrated the area that would come to be called Minas Gerais, or the General Mines. This long-anticipated discovery sparked a gold rush of enormous proportions and opened an entirely new economic and historical period in the history of Brazil. It would be in the mining region that the brotherhoods

86. Serafim Leite, S. J., *História da companhia de Jesus no Brasil*, vol. 2 (Rio de Janeiro: Civilização Brasileira, 1938), 340–41.

87. Ibid., 324.

88. Mulvey, "Black Lay Brotherhoods," 289–90, and Leite, *História*, vol. 2, 324 n. 3.

89. Vieira, "'Children of God's Fire,'" 169.

90. Leite, *História*, vol. 2, 354 n. 4.

of Our Lady of the Rosary of the Blacks would be fully realized, as many of the tens of thousands of Africans forcibly transported there struggled to rebuild their worlds.

Conclusion

It would not be an exaggeration to argue that lay religious brotherhoods were the most significant organizations in the daily life of most Portuguese, in both the metropolis and the colonies. Within the brotherhoods people organized their religious lives, engaged in charitable acts, participated in lavish public festivals, provided social services, and took care of the bodies and souls of their members after death. Lay religious brotherhoods fulfilled these functions because they constituted social and physical spaces that served as domains in which different levels of relationships could be worked out. In the European consciousness, lay religious brotherhoods were domains that mediated between different elements of society in four main ways. On the societal level, they served to mediate between the formal church and the laity and became a place where battles over control of the church would be fought. They served as a liminal space between family and society, creating an extrafamilial corporate society of people with shared interests. They served as a domain in which the people could receive the favors of the divine through the work of the saint who served as an intercessor, or advocate, in the lives of the devoted. Elaborate feast day celebrations expressed this relationship by creating a site in which promises to the saints could be paid. Finally, perhaps the most important function of the lay religious brotherhoods was their position between the living and the dead, as they served the important function of burying and praying for the dead. In these last two functions, brotherhoods articulated a concept of space that extended from the purely physical/material into one that included the realm of the unseen spirits.

In the mid-fifteenth century, just as the Portuguese were expanding into Africa, the devotional tool of the rosary, the emergence of Our Lady of the Rosary, and the rosary brotherhoods were all emerging in Europe. The Portuguese came to consider the rosary, with its repetitive prayers and personal, lay devotion, an effective means with which to catechize Africans. Concurrently, rosary brotherhoods came to be understood as an ideal way to incorporate blacks into Portuguese society. Slaves and free blacks, from many different regions of Africa and the colonies, would establish and support these organizations in an attempt to construct community within a world that considered them to be on the bottom of the social hierarchy. How

Africans and their descendents understood these organizations, however, would have differed from how the Portuguese interpreted them. Africans from many regions formed communities that negotiated their own set of relationships from inside the rosary brotherhoods.

2 AFRICANS IN THE BROTHERHOODS

Eu vem do mar, eu vem do mar
Oi, lê lê, ia
Trazendo Nossa Senhora
O que beleza!

[I come from the sea, I come from the sea
Oi, lê lê, ia
Bringing Our Lady,
Oh, how beautiful!]

—Mozambique of Our Lady of Mercies, Oliveira, MG,
at the raising of the flagpoles

Brazil, in the three hundred years of the slave trade, received more Africans to its shores than any other single colony or nation. The influx of slaves followed the economic needs of the colony and empire. Beginning in the sixteenth century, slaves entered Brazil to work primarily in the sugar industry in the northeast, but by the end of the seventeenth century that industry was in decline because of the growing competition from the West Indies. When gold was discovered in the mountainous region just north of Rio de Janeiro in the late seventeenth century, the slave trade shifted to that area, which came to be called Minas Gerais. The following hundred years saw a huge influx of African labor, as well as slave labor from the economically declining northeast. The Africans came from several different regions and as a population represented a complex array of loyalties, language groups, customs, and worldviews. Many individuals from these groups chose to join the communities of other nonwhites in lay religious Catholic brotherhoods dedicated to Our Lady of the Rosary.

Because the brotherhoods were ostensibly Catholic organizations, it might be tempting to talk about the mixing of religions, yet to their members the rosary brotherhoods represented a much broader reality. Modern Western discourse traditionally posits discreet categories of the way societies divide, and as anthropologist Wyatt MacGaffey points out,

> [o]ur social sciences presuppose categories such as "religion," "government," and "economy," despite the difficulty we have in giving satisfactory definition to them and explaining the relationships among them. It can be argued that these terms of art seem compelling to us, despite their logical obscurity, because they correspond to the functional differentiation of our lives, in which "religion," "government," and "economy" are carried on in different buildings by different groups of specialized personnel.[1]

Non-Western societies and those of the premodern period did not divide or understand their world in the same way, and neither group did so as the West divides and understands its societies today. As discussed in the previous chapter, brotherhoods served as examples of the mixing of society and religion in the European setting. Likewise, African understandings of the world included something that today could be defined as religion, yet that something did not exist separate from the rest of society, and many African languages never had a word for *religion* in the Western sense. Instead, "religion" permeated all of existence, including before birth and after death.[2] A connection to gods, unseen spirits, and ancestors simply wove constantly through the fabric of life. It existed as part of the kinship system and as part of the geography of power in African societies. MacGaffey calls this totality a "cosmology," defining a cosmology as "a body of collective representations of the world as a whole, ordered in space and time, and of man's place in it."[3] Therefore, the more interesting questions reside not in examining the syncretism between African "religions" and Christianity but rather in how the organization of society, the power structure that included the living as

---

1. Wyatt MacGaffey, "Dialogues of the Deaf: Europeans on the Atlantic Coast of Africa," in *Implicit Understandings: Observing, Reporting, and Reflecting on the Encounters Between Europeans and Other Peoples in the Early Modern Era*, ed. Stuart B. Schwartz (Cambridge: Cambridge University Press, 1994), 250.
2. John S. Mbiti, *African Religions and Philosophy* (New York: Anchor Books, 1970), 2–3. Newell S. Booth Jr. also discusses the pervasive aspect of African religions in "An Approach to African Religions," in *African Religions: A Symposium*, ed. Newell S. Booth Jr. (New York: NOK, 1977), 1–5. For a discussion of Central African cosmology, see James H. Sweet, *Recreating Africa: Culture, Kinship, and Religion in the African-Portuguese World, 1441–1770* (Chapel Hill: University of North Carolina Press, 2003), 104–15.
3. Wyatt MacGaffey, *Religion and Society in Central Africa: The BaKongo of Lower Zaire* (Chicago: University of Chicago Press, 1986), 5.

well as unseen forces, spirits, and ancestors, was reoriented as it came into contact with Christianity as expressed both in the lay brotherhood organizations and in colonial *mineiro* society.

Two major African regions were represented in the slave trade to Minas Gerais. In the first half of the eighteenth century, slaves were brought from West Africa—from several different ports in the Bight of Benin—and, to a lesser extent, from Central Africa. In the second half of the century, slaves came primarily from Central Africa, primarily through the ports of Luanda and Benguela. These large culture areas, each of which actually represents a multiplicity of particular peoples, fed the labor pool of the mining district, and all of them contributed to the social and cultural milieu that made up the brotherhoods of the rosary. Once captured, often in the far interior of the continent, the slaves began a long overland journey, a period of waiting on the coast, the long journey in the darkness of a slave ship, then another overland journey to reach the mining region of Brazil. Torn from their local communities, captives would have searched for ways to make sense of their world, aligning with one group or another along the way. This process would have begun a realignment of group identities, which would have continued even after captives arrived in Minas Gerais. These alignments often emerged in the colonial documentation under the rubric of *nação* (nation), which in colonial Brazil was a word often used to identify people from a similar culture rather than from a shared "national" origin in the modern sense.[4] The *nações* in the case of Africans, however, were constructed identities, and can be understood to reflect alliances, particular to certain contexts, which captives forged during their long and dehumanizing journey and after their eventual arrival in the mining district. The Europeans recognized that these alliances represented distinct groups such as "Mina" or "Congo," which then became the "ethnicities" or "nations" recorded in any number of contexts, including brotherhood registries.[5]

As African captives got to know one another, and drew on cultural commonalities to form new groups, the Portuguese attempted to find means to

---

4. Mary C. Karasch, "Minha Nação: Identidades escravas no fim do Brasil colonial," trans. Angela Domingues, in *Brasil: Colonização e escravidão*, ed. Maria Beatriz Nizza da Silva (Rio de Janeiro: Editora Nova Fronteira, 2000), 128.

5. See the Appendix, Table 1, for the different "ethnicities" listed in the books of three rosary brotherhoods in Minas Gerais. The question of how to talk about, or even what to call, African "ethnicities" in the Americas has been the subject of much discussion in recent years. See especially Miller, "Retention, Reinvention," 86–87; as well as Miller, "Central Africa," 42; João José Reis, "Identidade e diversidade étnicas nas irmandades negras no tempo da escravidão," *Tempo* 2, no. 3 (1997): 13; Karasch, "Minha nação," 128–39.

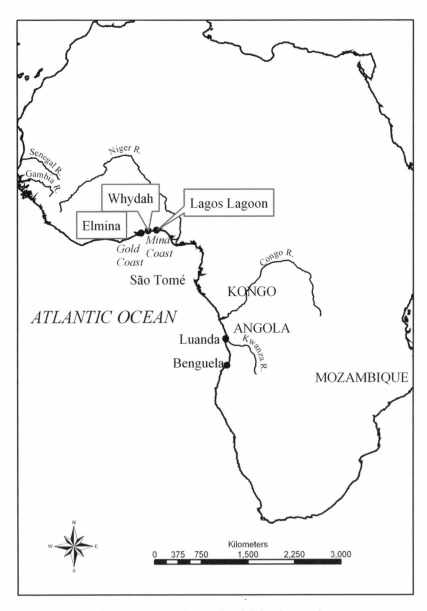

MAP 2.   Major African regions and ports that fed the slave trade to Minas Gerais

incorporate these new groups in a way that made sense according to a Portuguese outlook on the world, the basis of which was the organization of corporate groups. The Portuguese welcomed and encouraged lay brotherhoods of Africans, yet the early years of contact were marked by misunderstandings on both sides. James Lockhart articulates this process of mutual misunderstanding:

> Each side was able to operate for centuries after first contact on an ultimately false but in practice workable assumption that analogous concepts of the other side were essentially identical with its own, thus avoiding close examination of the unfamiliar and maintaining its own principles. The truce obtaining under this partial misconception allowed for a long period of preservation of indigenous structures of all kinds while intercultural ferment went on gradually, hardly attaining the level of consciousness.[6]

Although Lockhart refers specifically to the Nahua-Spanish contact, he describes the African-Portuguese contact as well. Different African cosmologies came together in the rosary brotherhoods, incorporated elements of Christianity that supported their worldviews, interpreted and adapted the hierarchy of colonial Brazilian society and popular religion, and created a new expression—a cosmology that drew on many cultural elements, and on a remembered shared past in Africa. Although the outward expressions might have changed from year to year in the brotherhoods, the worldview changed very slowly over the centuries in Brazil.

The Mina Coast

In the first half of the eighteenth century, the slaves brought into the mining region were primarily from the Costa de Mina, or the Mina Coast, and probably were the majority both in the general population and in the brotherhoods through the 1740s.[7] The term *Mina* implied a varied background that

---

6. James Lockhart, "Sightings: Initial Nahua Reactions to Spanish Culture," in Schwartz, *Implicit Understandings,* 219.

7. Laird W. Bergad, *Slavery and the Demographic and Economic History of Minas Gerais, Brazil, 1720–1888* (New York: Cambridge University Press, 1999), 151–52; Maurício Goulart, *A escravidão africana no Brasil: Das origens à extinção do tráfico* (São Paulo: Editora Alfa-Ômega, 1975), 203–17; Mariza de Carvalho Soares, *Devotos da cor: Identidade étnica, religiosidade e escravidão no Rio de Janeiro, século XVIII* (Rio de Janeiro: Civilização Brasileira, 2000), 73–85.

did not include slaves shipped from the port of São Jorge da Mina (now Elmina, Ghana). Dom João II built São Jorge da Mina in 1481 as a fortress designed primarily to keep other European merchants away from the lucrative gold trade.[8] The Portuguese obtained gold from Akan merchants, in trade for slaves from Kongo and Benin as well as for European manufactured goods. This net import of slaves and export of gold continued until the seventeenth century.[9] In 1637, however, the Dutch captured São Jorge da Mina, and in 1641 the Portuguese signed a treaty that restricted their trade to four ports east of São Jorge da Mina and the Volta River: Grand Popo, Whydah (Ajuda), Jaquin, and Apa. The term *Mina* in Brazil, then, came to imply peoples shipped out from these ports, all of which lay between the Volta River and Lagos in the western half of the Bight of Benin.[10]

The Mina Coast included many different groups through the entire period of the slave trade, although power shifted and kingdoms rose and fell through those centuries. Terms for "ethnicities," which identified individuals as being from that region, appeared on the membership lists of the rosary brotherhoods in Minas Gerais. The most frequent terms to appear on those lists were *Mina* and *Courano*. The Mina, as stated above, probably included slaves originally from several different regions and was a word whose meaning shifted throughout the eighteenth and nineteenth centuries. Although scholars have long maintained that these slaves were all probably from the Bight of Benin and its hinterlands, some evidence supports the idea that some of the Mina slaves may indeed have been from the Gold

8. Philip Curtin, et al., *African History from Earliest Times to Independence*, 2d ed. (London: Longman, 1995), 201–2.

9. This relationship would switch, and by the seventeenth century the port was exporting slaves and importing gold, but by that time it was under Dutch control and did not affect the Portuguese Empire. John K. Thornton, *Africa and Africans in the Making of the Atlantic World, 1400–1680* (Cambridge: Cambridge University Press, 1992), 119.

10. Mary Karasch argues that the slaves identified as Mina may have come from the Asante, Dahomey, Yoruba, and Ibo. The designation may have also included the groups from northern Nigeria: the Hausa, Fulani, Bornu, and Nupe, who would have had more contact with Islam. Mary C. Karasch, *Slave Life in Rio de Janeiro, 1808–1850* (Princeton: Princeton University Press, 1987), 16. For a more detailed breakdown of these areas, see also maps in Thornton, *Africa and Africans*, xii, xiii, xiv, xvi. Karasch points out that in the 1830s in Rio, the name Mina came to be associated with Muslim slaves. By the 1830s Minas were barely present in the brotherhoods of the rosary in Minas Gerais, but it is interesting to speculate on whether they played a part in the eighteenth-century brotherhoods in Minas Gerais, especially with the long tradition of lay religious brotherhoods in Islam. On the origin of the Mina slaves, see also Pierre Verger, *Fluxo e refluxo do tráfico de escravos entre o golfo do Benin e a Bahia de Todos os Santos dos séculos XVII a XII*, 2d ed., trans. Tasso Gadzanis (São Paulo: Editora Corrupio, 1987), 12, and Philip Curtin, *The Atlantic Slave Trade: A Census* (Madison: University of Wisconsin Press, 1969), 208; Boxer, *Golden Age*, 176.

Coast to the west of the bight. In the 1720s, des Marchais, the French slaver, identified twenty nationalities of slaves being sold at the port at Whydah. The group des Marchais identified included one called "Minois." Robin Law asserts that these were peoples who had migrated east from the Gold Coast to the region known as Little Popo (just west of Grand Popo). They probably would have been Fante/Asante and would have had knowledge of mining gold.[11] This may have given credence to the beliefs of Brazilian miners, who claimed that Mina slaves were not only skilled miners but also had a magical ability to find gold.[12] Nevertheless, the Portuguese called this entire region the Mina Coast, so it is unlikely that all of the many slaves identified as Mina in the Brazilian slave lists referred to the "Minois," but certainly some of them may have been.

The dominant ethnic groups, and those most likely to have entered the slave trade from the Mina Coast, would have been the Fon, centered mostly in the kingdom of Dahomey, and the Yoruba, who populated a region of city-states east of Dahomey, the most powerful of which was Oyo. During the period of the slave trade to the mines in Brazil, the traffic was beginning to be controlled by the large kingdoms that had pushed their way, in the late seventeenth century, from the interior to the coast. Their kings became interested in the slave trade at the same time that the Europeans were intensifying their trading along the entire coast of Africa.[13] The other large group brought from West Africa that appeared in the membership lists of the brotherhoods in the mid-eighteenth century was the Courano, or Courá. They were from a village called Curamo on the south shore of the lake that was also called Curamo (now known as the Lagos lagoon), near the present-day city of Lagos, Nigeria.[14] Jean Barbot described the area of the lake as a dependency of the kingdom of Benin, which lay to the east of Oyo. Although little has been written about these people, they represented the largest identifiable group of West Africans after the Mina in the brotherhoods of the rosary in Minas Gerais. From the scanty documentation it appears that they were at war with the king of Dahomey, for in 1744 the king demanded that the Portuguese at the fort of Whydah hand over the "Couranas" who were there. The king further announced that if the Portuguese did not hand over

11. Robin Law, *The Slave Coast of West Africa, 1550–1750: The Impact of the Atlantic Slave Trade on an African Society* (Oxford: Clarendon Press, 1991), 189.

12. Boxer, *Golden Age*, 175.

13. Soares, *Devotos da cor*, 71–72.

14. Jean Barbot, *Barbot on Guinea: The Writings of Jean Barbot on West Africa, 1678–1712*, vol. 2, ed. P. E. H. Hair, Adam Jones, and Robin Law (London: Hakluyt Society, 1992), 665, 667 n. 2.

those people, he would storm the fort and take them out himself.[15] Although little is known about the Couranas, if they were from Benin they probably shared a similar cosmology to that of their neighbors to the west (Dahomey) and to the northwest (Oyo).

The conglomerate of peoples that made up the identified groups from West Africa shared a general body of beliefs and understandings of the world. They considered themselves to be descended from a common ancestor and held a similar worldview.[16] In fact, in Oyo, Dahomey, and Benin, the kings (*oba*) were linked to the unseen world of the gods through kinship, because the father of the kings, Oduduwa, had come down from the sky to begin the dynasty.[17] Although kings probably were not "worshipped" as such, they did have an important ritual function in the society.[18] Kings connected what Westerners define as religious and political into a single, multifaceted power complex on which the health of the community rested. The kings in West Africa linked the people to deities, which included a creative power, or god, that controlled the universe, but who was not necessarily the creator of the universe. Along with the supreme god, there was an extensive pantheon of local deities that had supernatural powers and that were often linked to the environment. These lesser gods could be more important than the supreme god because they were more active in the everyday lives of the people, and the people sought to keep in their favor by erecting altars and engaging in rituals in their honor.[19]

Ancestors, an important part of the kinship complex, were also revered and honored through ritual, and the people engaged in rituals of death to make sure that the dead would continue to help the living. In the early eighteenth century, The Dutch slave trader William Bosman talked about the "fear" of death of the king of Dahomey and about the sanctions against speaking about death in the presence of the king.[20] These practices should be interpreted as

15. Pierre Verger, *Trade Relations Between the Bight of Benin and Bahia from the Seventeenth to the Nineteenth Century*, trans. Evelyn Crawford (Ibadan, Nigeria: Ibadan University Press, 1976), 176 n. 29. See also Luiz Mott, *Rosa Egipcíaca, uma santa africana no Brasil* (Rio de Janeiro: Editora Bertrand Brasil, 1993), 14.

16. George Brandon, *Santeria from Africa to the New World: the Dead Sell Memories* (Bloomington: Indiana University Press, 1997), 9–10.

17. D. A. Strickland, "Kingship and Slavery in African Thought: A Conceptual Analysis," *Comparative Studies in Society and History* 18 (July 1976): 378.

18. Law, *Slave Coast*, 76–78.

19. Sylvia R. Frey and Betty Wood, *Come Shouting to Zion: African American Protestantism in the American South and British Caribbean to 1830* (Chapel Hill: University of North Carolina Press, 1998), 11–13.

20. William Bosman, *A New and Accurate Description of the Coast of Guinea*, originally published 1705 (London: Frank Cass, 1967), 351–52.

special treatment toward the king, a person considered to have exceptional ritual and temporal power, and toward the king's death. Bosman talks less about the burial practices of the common people, but Barbot mentions that the people of Whydah were buried in their huts "where they died, because they have no cemeteries or special [burial] places."[21] Both authors remain relatively silent on the issue of ancestors, interpreting "religion" as the worship of gods and not recognizing the role of ancestors in the lives of the people of West Africa. Bosman, however, records a conversation between a European priest and an important person in the king's court:

> This Priest in my Company being once in Discourse with one of the King's Grandees, who was a witty Man, said in a menacing manner, *That if the* Fidasians *continu'd their old Course of Life, without Repentance, they would unavoidably go to Hell, in order to burn with the Devil;* to which the sharp Fidasian reply'd, *Our Fathers, Grandfathers, to an endless Number, Liv'd as we do, and Worship'd the same Gods as we do; and if they must burn therefore, Patience, we are not better than our Ancestors and shall comfort our selves with them.*[22]

The trade on the Slave Coast, as elsewhere in Africa, was conducted through a factory system. The Europeans built forts along the coasts and engaged in trade with the African monarchs or local leaders. In general, the Portuguese and the other European nations who conducted trade in slaves and other goods were not interested in establishing colonies of Europeans. Instead, they built trading forts (factories) along the coasts and sought to monopolize trade, both between Africa and Europe and between different African areas.[23] Although there was considerable European contact along the coasts, this contact did not extend far into the interior of the region. Some missionaries did try to work in the interior of West Africa, but they did not meet with much success. Europeans found Christian symbols, such as the cross, from their earliest explorations of the region, but those symbols reflected a local worldview, not a Christian one. For example, in the sixteenth century an ambassador of the king of Benin told them that there was a great

21. Barbot, *Barbot on Guinea*, 640.

22. Bosman, *New and Accurate Description*, 385–86. Bosman uses the Dutch *Fida* for *Whydah*. Italics are in the original.

23. The exception to this was the previously uninhabited islands of the Azores, Madeira, and São Tomé. Brazil also became an exception after it was threatened by other European powers, most specifically the French.

monarch to whom all the local kings paid homage, a ruler who "was held in as great veneration as is the Supreme Pontiff."[24] When a king of Benin ascended to the throne, news of it would be sent to this monarch, who in return would send a cross of brass that the king of Benin would wear as his sign of authority. Upon leaving the court of the king, the ambassador also received a small cross, signifying his freedom to travel and his privilege in his native land.[25] Further, contemporary accounts attested that the kings in West Africa were especially fond of the rosaries made from bright blue stones that the Portuguese brought to trade from Central Africa.[26] Lay traders and merchants often engaged in informal missionary work along the coast, and the growing popularity of the rosary in fifteenth- and sixteenth-century Europe would have made it a perfect way for the lay traders to begin to show the Africans the Christian faith.[27]

In addition to sending the lay traders, the Portuguese had sent missions into the interior from the beginning of their explorations, and the Spanish and French expeditions in the second half of the seventeenth century noted the presence of Portuguese-speaking Christians in the region. The missionaries met with some interest, but nothing that would match the spectacular conversion of the king of Kongo in Central Africa. For example, the king of Benin said that he was interested in adopting Christianity, but the sixteenth-century historian João de Barros pointed out that he "was very much under the influence of his idolatries, and sought the priests rather to make himself powerful against his neighbours with our favour than from a desire for baptism."[28] The king of Allada in 1658 had requested missionaries from the king of Spain and expressed a desire to be baptized but balked when he found out he could no longer practice polygamy.[29] On the whole, missions were small and ineffective, both because of the rapid death of many of the missionaries and because of the strength of the local beliefs.

24. From the *Décadas da India* by João de Barros (1496–1570), in *The Voyages of Cadamosto and Other Documents on Western Africa in the Second Half of the Fifteenth Century*, ed. and trans. C. R. Crone (London: Hakluyt Society, 1937), 126.

25. João de Barros, *Décadas da India*, 126–27.

26. This information was included in a report written by Leo the African for Pope Leo X. Thomas, *Slave Trade*, 83.

27. John K. Thornton, "On the Trail of Voodoo: African Christianity in Africa and the Americas," *The Americas* 44 (January 1988): 264. For another argument against the superficiality of the conversion, see Richard Gray, "'Como vero Prencipe Catolico': The Capuchins and the Rulers of Soyo in the Late Seventeenth Century," *Africa* 53 (1983): 39–54.

28. João de Barros, in Crone, *The Voyages*, 125.

29. Law, *Slave Coast*, 153.

Perhaps as a result of the request of the king of Allada for missionaries in 1658, Italian Capuchins wrote a catechism in the local language. This catechism from Allada demonstrates the lengths to which missionaries were willing to "syncretize" certain elements of Christianity with African concepts of the world. For example, at the time in Allada, the supreme god was a dual figure called by the names Vodu and Lisa. The catechism substituted these names for those of God and Jesus Christ.[30] This syncretism created, as it did elsewhere in Africa, a situation in which both the Africans and the Christians used the language to further their own ends, without these groups really communicating with each other, an example of the mutual misunderstandings that were ubiquitous during the first decades of cultural contact.[31] The presence of the Capuchins and their attempts at evangelization, however, did not lead to the conversion of many Africans in this region. Despite the exposure of the West Africans to Christianity, it did not make significant inroads into that region until the introduction of Protestantism in the nineteenth century.[32]

The documentation demonstrates that Brazilians had started importing Mina slaves into the port of Rio de Janeiro at the beginning of the eighteenth century, and many of those slaves were destined for the mines. These slaves became the earliest members of the rosary brotherhoods in Minas Gerais and participated in shaping the heterogeneous communities that the brotherhoods would become. Within the brotherhoods, West African slaves could begin to reconstruct their worlds around common cultural elements such as kinship, kingship, expressions of hierarchy, and a link with the ancestors. In many fundamental ways, the Mina slaves interpreted the brotherhoods and Christianity through their own understandings of the world and would have found, in the lay religious brotherhoods, a place in which they could reconstruct those worlds.

---

30. Thornton, *Africa and Africans,* 253. These are the same gods that are worshiped in that region today, except that Vodu has been replaced by Mawu. See Thornton, *Africa and Africans,* 253 n. 67.

31. Wyatt MacGaffey insightfully calls this mutual misunderstanding a "dialogue of the deaf." MacGaffey, *Religion and Society,* 200. He points out that the phrase "dialogue of the deaf" was coined by A. Doutreloux in *L'ombre des fétiches* (Louvain: Editions Nauwelaerts, 1967), 261.

32. The exception to this is the kingdom of Warri, to the east of the kingdom of Benin, which, despite the lack of priests, did have a history as a "Christian" state from the late sixteenth century into the nineteenth century. See A. F. C. Ryder, "Missionary Activity in the Kingdom of Warri to the Early Nineteenth Century," *Journal of the Historical Society of Nigeria* 2 (1960): 1–26.

Central Africa

After the middle of the eighteenth century, and especially in the 1760s, 1770s, and 1780s, the population of West Africans in the brotherhood registers, and indeed in the general population of Minas Gerais, declined and that of the Central Africans grew considerably. Central Africa stretches from present-day Gabon in the north to the port of Benguela in southern Angola. This large and geographically diverse region was home to several different large groups that had their origin in the Bantu migration centuries earlier. To the north, around the Zaire River Basin and just to the south of that, was Kongo, the regions that would later divide up into the larger kingdoms of Kongo, Loango, and Tio. The area just south of that region was inhabited by Mbundu peoples in what came to be called Ndongo. Finally, the most southern region was inhabited by people collectively called Ovimbundu. In the valley east of the coast of the Portuguese port of São Paulo de Loanda (Luanda) lived people who called themselves Pende, but by the seventeenth century that region was taken over by the two kingdoms of Matamba and Kasanje. People who lived farther east than this were collectively called the Ngangela.[33] These regions would be represented by "nations" in the rosary brotherhoods of Minas Gerais by groups called Congo; Angola; Benguela; and, of lesser importance, Ganguela.[34]

Kongo became the first kingdom in the region with which the Portuguese set up a close trading relationship. Kongo civilization stretched from present-day Gabon in the north to Angola. In 1485 the Portuguese set up friendly relations with the king of Kongo, Nzinga Nkuwu.[35] The Portuguese Crown recognized the Kongolese royal family as a potential ally, and set out to create a Christian state in Africa.[36] Finally in 1491, Nzinga accepted baptism and became the Christian King João I.[37] Nzinga returned to his native faith after only three years, but his son Afonso, and some other members of the aristocracy,

---

33. Joseph C. Miller, "The Paradoxes of Impoverishment in the Atlantic Zone," in *History of Central Africa*, vol. 1, ed. David Birmingham and Phyllis M. Martin (London: Longman, 1983), 124.

34. Congo, with a *C*, refers to the Brazilian ethnicity, which was made up of people who may or may not have been from the African kingdom of Kongo.

35. The kingdom of Kongo in the late fifteenth century extended roughly 250 miles east from the coast and 250 miles from north to south. It emerged with two neighboring kingdoms, Tio and Loango, both to the north. The three made up part of the same regional political processes. Curtin, et al., *African History*, 227–28.

36. The Portuguese, along with catechizing in Kongo, tried to Europeanize the population. They sent craftspeople, agricultural laborers, masons, and even housewives to teach the Kongolese European ways. Thomas, *Slave Trade*, 82.

37. Thomas, *Slave Trade*, 77–82.

remained Christian.[38] With the help of the Portuguese, Afonso won the battle of succession that followed the death of Nzinga Nkuwu. He worked to improve relations with the Portuguese and to centralize and consolidate his power. Christianity became a Kongo royal cult, but the king remained frustrated in gaining control over his church.[39] The pope would not allow Afonso I patronage over his church; instead the former granted this right to the King of Portugal. Nevertheless, Afonso developed Christianity as the important state religion. He had the great trees that surrounded the royal cemetery cut down and built a church on that site, making Christianity the "new cult of the royal predecessors." The site became the center of Christian life in the capital, Mbanza Kongo (São Salvador) and was dedicated to Our Lady of Victory.[40]

Like Afonso, Diogo I, Afonso's grandson, tried to maintain and legitimize his governance over his kingdom through Christianity and control of the slave trade. Despite difficulties, he proved highly successful at this and became relatively autonomous of Portuguese influence. His heirs continued to remain independent of outside control. In 1568, however, the Jaga (a Kongo label for foreign invaders) attacked Kongo, and the king of Kongo was forced to appeal to Portugal for help.[41] With Portuguese assistance, Kongo drove out the Jaga and restored royal power, but the centralized authority of the king among the people decreased as the kingdom became more dependent on the Portuguese and their monopoly over the export slave trade.[42] In the seventeenth century, Kongo entered a period of civil war and unrest that would not be resolved until the beginning of the eighteenth century.[43] Even in the eighteenth century, when slaves identified as "Congo" appeared in the lists of brotherhoods, the authority of what had been called Kongo remained decentralized, spread among several chiefs in different districts.[44] Nevertheless, by the middle of the nineteenth century, the King of Congo would become an important presence, a "unifying symbol" in the hierarchy of the rosary brotherhoods in Minas Gerais, and in Afro-Brazilian communities and rituals throughout Brazil.[45]

38. MacGaffey, "Dialogues of the Deaf," 254.

39. Paul E. Lovejoy, *Transformations in Slavery: A History of Slavery in Africa.* (Cambridge: Cambridge University Press, 1983), 38.

40. Anne Hilton, *The Kingdom of Kongo* (Oxford: Clarendon Press, 1985), 63–64.

41. Ibid., 65–68.

42. Curtin, et al., *African History,* 230.

43. See John K. Thornton, *The Kingdom of Kongo: Civil War and Transition, 1641–1718* (Madision: University of Wisconsin Press, 1983), 69–113.

44. Hilton, *Kingdom of Kongo,* 210–21.

45. See Miller, "Retention, Reinvention," 99; Elizabeth W. Kiddy, "Who Is the King of Congo? A New Look at African and Afro-Brazilian Kings in Brazil," in Heywood, *Central Africans,* 169–81.

Just as the Portuguese relationship with the kingdom of Kongo was unique in the Portuguese Crown's attempt to establish friendly relations with another recognized monarch, Portugal's relationship with Angola was unique in that it was the single instance, until the nineteenth century, in which a European power attempted to establish a colony through military force in Africa.[46] In 1575, Paulo Dias de Novaes received the lands south of Kongo as a donatary captaincy. In a process unlike the initial peaceful, mercantile penetration of the kingdom of Kongo, Novaes sought to profit directly through military conquest. His program proved untenable, however, and he only succeeded in building a fortified city he called São Paulo de Loanda on an island just off the coast. Luanda served as a base of operation for the military campaigns and became home to European and Afro-European traders and Jesuits. Even after the Portuguese-Spanish combined Crown took over the captaincy after Novaes's death in 1592, these powers were unable to penetrate the interior militarily, but they did set up a profitable trade in slaves from the interior.

In the beginning of the seventeenth century the Imbangala (known to the Portuguese as Jaga, but a different Jaga from the people who invaded Kongo) became important players in the political scene of Angola. Imbangala became a collective name for roving bands of warriors who had fled from the drought-wracked highlands and invaded what is now northern Angola. The Portuguese, in an attempt to overthrow the main Mbundu king, allied themselves with the Imbangala in the early seventeenth century. In later decades the Portuguese switched alliances and allied themselves with the local Mbundu king against the Imbangala. After the death of the Mbundu king, the famous Queen Nzinga, the slave-born half sister of that king, formed an alliance with the Imbangala against the Portuguese. Queen Nzinga, however, was not strong enough to take over her brother's kingdom, and the Portuguese succeeded in creating a military zone just east of Luanda between the Dande and Kwanza Rivers, which they called Angola, after the title of the kings of the region, *ngola*.[47]

Between 1620 and 1640, the political map of the region took shape. The Portuguese held the land east of Luanda, Queen Nzinga conquered Matamba to the northeast, and the Imbangala set up a kingdom to the south of Matamba, a region that came to be called Kassanje. Kassanje (Cassange) would become

---

46. David Birmingham, "The African Response to Early Portuguese Activities in Angola," in *Protest and Resistance in Angola and Brazil,* ed. Ronald H. Chilcote (Berkeley and Los Angeles: University of California Press, 1972), 19.

47. Miller, "Paradoxes," 140–41; Curtin, et al., *African History,* 230.

a major inland slave-trading entrepôt for slave caravans coming from the east. These three kingdoms became the most important players in the slave trade in the late seventeenth century, and their dominance lasted well into the nineteenth century.[48] All these African kingdoms rallied around the Dutch when they invaded Luanda in 1640, but the Portuguese were able to gain control over it in 1648 and to retain that control until the twentieth century.

By the end of the eighteenth century, slaves identified as Benguela had become demographically dominant in the African population of Minas Gerais, as well as in many of the brotherhoods in that area. In 1617, São Filipe de Benguela (known as Benguela) became the third most important coastal trading port of slaves and commodities. It was founded by Euro-Africans who sought to establish trade out of the influence of the increasingly metropolitan-oriented Luanda.[49] After the Dutch attacked and occupied Luanda from 1641 to 1648, Brazilian ships came to drive the Dutch out. The Brazilians attempted to enter the Luanda trade, but Europeans had more appealing trade goods, and Euro-Africans had better connections. The Brazilians found that they could not obtain slaves by peaceful means. For this reason, the Brazilians went south to the port of Benguela, where the Euro-Africans were open to trading with anyone.[50] Nevertheless, Benguela would not become an important slave port until the eighteenth and early nineteenth centuries, when drought in the nearby Ovimbundu highlands, along with an aggressive policy on the part of the local governor to profit from the slave trade, drove thousands of villagers into slavery.[51]

The Benguela highlands consisted of kingdoms collectively known as the Ovimbundu, the origin of many of the slaves exported from Benguela. The Ovimbundu were grouped around what has commonly been called "warlords," leaders who had important ritual powers.[52] A large military expedition, launched by the Portuguese in the 1770s, displaced the warlords on

48. Curtin, et al., *African History*, 230–31. In African works, Queen Nzinga's name is often given as Njinga or Anna Njinga, and she herself spells her name Ginga in her extant letters. See John K. Thornton, "Legitimacy and Political Power: Queen Njinga, 1624–1663," *Journal of African History* 32, no. 1 (1991): 25–40. Queen Nzinga would appear in Afro-Brazilian festivals, often with the King of Congo, with her name spelled spelled Xinga, Zinga, Ginga, and Jinga.

49. James Duffy, *Portugal in Africa*, (Baltimore: Penguin Books, 1962), 52.

50. Miller, "Paradoxes," 134–35.

51. Rosa Cruz e Silva, "The Saga of Kakonda and Kilengues: Relations Between Benguela and Its Interior, 1791–1796," in *Enslaving Connections: Changing Cultures of Africa and Brazil During the Era of Slavery*, ed. José C. Curto and Paul E. Lovejoy (Amherst, N.Y.: Humanity Books, 2004), 245–59.

52. Douglas L. Wheeler and René Pélissier, *Angola* (Westport, Conn.: Greenwood Press, 1978), 25.

the highland plateau and established a string of merchant princes along the slave-trading routes. These princes funneled slaves to the port of Benguela.[53] The trade was driven in large part by the uncertainty of rain. On the drought-ridden plateau, rain became a determining factor in the slave trade from Benguela. In fact, the trade swelled in the late seventeenth century because of a devastating ten-year drought between 1785 and 1794. Coupled .with the drought, from the 1780s the governors and merchants from Benguela engaged in an aggressive campaign to capture slaves for the Brazilian market. The increase in "Benguela" slaves in the brotherhoods of the rosary in the late eighteenth century strongly suggests that many of them eventually ended up in the highlands of Minas Gerais.

Throughout Central Africa, local society and religion were based primarily on extended kinship groups that ranged from large kingdoms, as in the case of Kongo and later Matamba and Kasanje, to small, parochial villages. The languages of the people all came from Bantu roots, and the general cosmology of the people was shared. Of all the regions, Kongo religion has been the best documented and has undergone the most nuanced analyses.[54] Primary sources document to some similarities between Kongo metaphysical beliefs and those of the group's southern and eastern neighbors. Unfortunately, the seventeenth-century European accounts do not allow for a subtle view of the underlying cosmology found in the different religious beliefs of the people, but the similarity of the outward form with the practices of Kongo demonstrates that there may have been an underlying continuum (as with the language) throughout the region.[55]

Kongo cosmology posits a hierarchy of spirits (nzambi), of which the highest was often called Nzambi a Mpungu, often translated as God. Nzambi, however, can include many different types of spirits, importantly, but not exclusively, spirits of the dead. Using contemporary sources, John K. Thornton identifies many layers of "spirits," a host of supernatural beings that were territorial, ancestral, and others, that often resided in charms or in "wicked

53. Miller, "Paradoxes," 149–50. Miller argues in a later article that Benguela slaves, who shared a common language and culture, may have been one of the most important early "ethnic" arrivals to Minas Gerais, but they do not appear in the brotherhood documentation until later in the eighteenth century. Miller, "Central Africa," 53–54. In a more recent work, Rosa Cruz e Silva points out that many of the African kings in the region tried to stem the aggression of the Benguela traders and keep their people from being captured in the slave trade. Silva, "Saga of Kakonda," 250.

54. See, for instance, Hilton, Kingdom of Kongo, 1–31; and MacGaffey, Religion and Society.

55. Wyatt MacGaffey, Kongo Political Culture: The Conceptual Challenge of the Particular (Bloomington: University of Indiana Press, 2000), 1.

people."[56] Numbered among these occupants of the other world, the ancestors played an extremely important role in the hierarchy of spirits and in the lives of the living. The seventeenth-century accounts of both João António Cavazzi de Montecúccolo and António de Oliveira de Cadornega attest to the importance of ancestors among the Jaga (a term they used to designate all non-Christians). Cadornega, for instance, recounts that Queen Nzinga, while she was discussing religion with a priest, insisted that after she died she wanted to join her ancestors. When the priest told her that her ancestors were burning in the fires of hell, she continued to insist that she wanted to join them. The priest left in frustration.[57] Some years later, Queen Nzinga did accept baptism, but only after a spirit medium communicated her dead brother's "willingness to forego offerings due to him."[58]

Cavazzi also noted the concern over ancestors, from that of ancestors wanting to contact the living after their deaths, to those about the dead wandering around homes uninvited after death, in which case they would have to be exorcised.[59] Graves, and graveyards, were the "principle medium through which the living communicated with the dead."[60] The graveyards became crossroads, intersections between the land of the living and the land of the dead. The relationship to the dead and to ancestors, then, was not only about what Westerners call the sacred but also about power.

Power, or politics, in Central Africa could not be separated from this relationship to ancestors. Joseph Miller makes the important point that Central Africans would have not been as familiar with the idea of states—no matter how much the Portuguese dealt with representatives of what they considered to be kingdoms—but rather with local and powerful patron-client relationships. Thus power was understood "in metaphors of protective powers exercised by strong, personal patrons on behalf of loyal clients through continual *ad hoc* demonstrations of efficacy, often through metaphorical reliance

56. John K. Thornton, "Religious and Ceremonial Life in the Kongo and Mbundo Areas 1500–1700," in *Central Africans and Cultural Transformations in the American Diaspora*, ed. Linda M. Heywood (New York: Cambridge University Press, 2001), 80.

57. António de Oliveira de Cadornega, *História geral das guerras angolanas, 1680*, ed. José Matias Delgado, vol. 3 (Lisbon: Agência-geral do Ultramar, 1972), 268.

58. John K. Thornton, "Religious and Ceremonial Life in the Kongo and Mbundo Areas 1500–1700," in Heywood, *Central Africans,* 87.

59. See Pe. João António Cavazzi de Montecúccolo, *Descrição histórica dos três reinos do Congo, Matmba e Angola*, trans. Pe. Graciano Maria de Leguzzano, O. M. Cap. (Lisbon: Junta de Investigações do Ultramar, 1965), 207–20. See also Thornton's excellent analysis and description of the care of the dead and ancestors in Central Africa in Thornton, "Religious and Ceremonial," 73–83.

60. Hilton, *Kingdom of Kongo,* 11.

on ancestors and other spiritual figures."[61] It was through this understanding of power, Miller posits, that Central Africans would invoke especially powerful figures, such as the king of Kongo and Queen Nzinga, in their organizations in the Americas.[62]

It was into this understanding of power that Christianity inserted itself, and by the eighteenth century Christianity was widespread in Kongo, even among the common people. It is clear, however, that this cult was understood through the lens of traditional Kongo cosmology. The king of Kongo's conversion, along with those of leaders of neighboring kingdoms, gave the Europeans great hopes for a Christian state in Africa. The conversions, however, must be understood within the framework of the African cosmology. First, the Central Africans' conversion was facilitated by their belief that the people delivering the message of Christianity were, as seen in their white color, visitors from the land of the dead and thus potentially dangerous spirits. As MacGaffey so eloquently points out, "when the first Portuguese arrived in Kongo in 1485 they exhibited the principal characteristics of the dead: they were white in color, spoke an unintelligible language, and possessed a technology superior even to that of the local priestly guild of smiths . . . [and thus they] were considered visitors from the land of the dead."[63] Christianity appealed to the leaders of these kingdoms as a new way through which to increase their power and influence by giving them access to a new, and seemingly more powerful, realm of spirits and charms.

Certain physical objects relevant in the Christian doctrine were interpreted through the lens of local customs. For example, the cross was already significant to the people of Kongo; in fact, it symbolized "all that exists" in Kongo cosmology. In addition, Kongo beliefs included the important use of *minkisi*, which were magic complexes that were often materialized in charms, which were used to protect the wearer from evil influences, including magic spells. Like such sacred Kongo items, objects of veneration among Christians also received the name of *nkisi*, such as a church (*nzo a nkisi*), and the Bible (*nkanda nkisi*).[64] Although there is a paucity of information on the use of the rosary in much of Africa, it would not be a stretch to assume that Central Africans would have understood the rosary as a sort of charm, not unlike lay Iberians, who interpreted its power in a similar way.

---

61. Miller, "Central Africa," 42.
62. Miller, "Retention, Reinvention," 99.
63. MacGaffey, *Religion and Society*, 198–99.
64. John K. Thornton, *The Kongolese Saint Anthony: Dona Beatriz Kimpa Vita and the Antonian Movement, 1684–1706* (Cambridge: Cambridge University Press, 1998), 108. Also see Sweet, *Recreating Africa*, 104–17.

The Jesuits arrived in Central Africa with Paulo de Novaes in 1575, and although they zealously carried out their missionary work, there were never more than a handful in the region at any given time. They became intimately involved in the slaving missions as well as setting up agricultural estates in Luanda.[65] Like the Capuchins in Allada, the Jesuits published a KiKongo translation of the Christian catechism in 1624. The catechism shows how little the missionaries understood the KiKongo cosmology and language.[66] The missionaries, in their zeal to communicate Christianity, translated it in such a way that the Africans could only understand it according to the paradigm of the latter's own cosmology. The Capuchins also played an important role in spreading Christianity through the rural areas of Central Africa and contributed to the syncretization of Christianity along African lines. In the mid-seventeenth century, they became extremely important in Kongo, where they began to fill the role of the royal priest. In addition, they created congregations that emphasized the cult of the dead, something with which all Central Africans could have identified.[67] The willingness of the missionaries to syncretize elements of Christianity, compounded by an uneven understanding of the local languages, undoubtedly led to reinterpretations of the Christian doctrine along African lines even among the general populace.[68]

The doctrines and apparatus of Christianity spread less evenly to other regions of Central Africa and became more and more Africanized as they spread to the periphery of Afro-Portuguese contact.[69] According to Cavazzi, in the seventeenth century Christianity had not reached the Ovimbundu highland plateau, and the people there "professed the rituals of the Jagas."[70] Cavazzi described religion among Jagas in which ancestors were often called upon for help, both with harvests and with day-to-day problems. The *xinguila* (ritual specialists) could receive the spirits of the dead who wanted to communicate with the living. In addition, if the death was not correct, the souls of the dead would wander around the earth bothering the people of the village, and the *xinguila*, who acted as exorcists, would have to rid the village of these interfering spirits.[71] Nevertheless, by the mid-eighteenth century, a century after Cavazzi's mission, when the flow of slaves from this region to

65. Miller, "Paradoxes," 132–33.
66. MacGaffey, *Religion and Society*, 200.
67. Hilton, *Kingdom of Kongo*, 160–61.
68. See Thornton, "Religious and Ceremonial," 83–90.
69. Linda M. Heywood, "Portuguese into African: The Eighteenth-Century Central African Background to Atlantic Creole Cultures," in Heywood, *Central Africans*, 105–11.
70. Cavazzi de Montecúccolo, *Descrição histórica*, 24.
71. Ibid., 207–12. See also Sweet, *Recreating Africa*, 140–42.

Brazil increased, the highland plateau had been invaded by Portuguese, and the new ruling families were intermarrying with the Afro-European and Afro-Brazilian slave traders and introducing Christianity.[72]

The impact and influence of Christianity in different regions of Central Africa, including the Benguela highlands, varied greatly, and in fact Christianity became one aspect of a bundle of cultural elements that evolved into varying forms of Afro-Portuguese creole culture. Except for the regions dominated by Portuguese culture, such as the ports of Luanda and Benguela, European culture, including Christianity, was interpreted, and indeed transformed, through local traditions, practices, and beliefs.[73] This uneven spread of symbols and meanings created a situation in which the difference between African and European became much more shaded and gradual, and much more varied, than has traditionally been articulated in the literature about slavery and the slave trade.[74] It became a process, abrupt for some and more gradual and familiar for others—but for all of them it was a journey, both physical and metaphysical, of forced reorientation. In the transfer of captives from Central Africa to Brazil, then, the process of interpreting meanings and finding correlations in meanings between what Africans had known and what they came to know in Brazil intensified as captives strove to make sense of their world and reestablish their humanity.

Our Lady of the Rosary

By the second half of the eighteenth century, the rosary brotherhoods of Minas Gerais, like the general population, had become significantly more Central African. Nonetheless, the brotherhoods never became ethnically exclusive and always retained a membership that included several different ethnicities. The Fon, Yoruba, Bini, Mbundu, Ndongo, Ngangela, and Kongo and all the other groups came together with many shared understandings of the world. Jan Vansina confirms that "it has become clear that in Africa social structures and religion are aspects of a single thing: a human community living the drama of its own existence."[75] The newly formed groups within the brotherhoods, then, would not have been able to establish community without also rebuilding a coherent cosmology. The community also needed a

---

72. Miller, "Paradoxes," 149.
73. Heywood, "Portuguese into African," 109–12.
74. Miller, "Central Africa," 53.
75. Jan Vansina quoted in MacGaffey, *Religion and Society,* 1.

type of charm, a figure, around which to shape its new community/religious complex—both to give the community cohesion as a group and to give it ritual efficacy in the outward expression of its cosmology.[76] The central symbol that was both offered by the Portuguese and chosen by the Africans was Our Lady of the Rosary.

A story that Dona Maria of Jatobá told me sheds light on the way that the present-day community remembers the formation of that community. The adherence of blacks in Minas Gerais to the devotion to Our Lady of the Rosary began when two runaway slaves saw Our Lady bobbing out in the waves. The slaves ran back to their master and told him. The master went down to the shore and tried to convince her to come out of the water, but with no success; nor were the priest or the bishop able to persuade her to come to the shore. Finally, the white authorities decided to let the blacks have a try at coaxing her out of the water. Various nations of blacks—first the Congo, then the Mozambique—went to the shore with their instruments to dance and sing, trying to lure her from the waves. Only when the "three oldest blacks" of the Candombe (according to legend the mythical ancestor of the congado), with their three sacred drums went to the shore and played did Our Lady begin to stir. Not until the Congo and the Mozambique joined the Candombe and all the African nations played, sang, and danced together, did Our Lady finally come out of the waves and sit on the largest drum.[77]

Although versions of this story vary from place to place, the main elements of it remain constant, and the theme of the coming together of disparate groups is central in all versions. At first glance, the legend appears to be an adaptation of traditional medieval exempla, and in fact its significantly Christian nature cannot be denied. Mary had long been associated with the sea even before the medieval period. Saint Jerome, the fourth-century father of the church, called the Hebrew Miriam in the Gospels *stilla maris*, a drop of the sea. This became (perhaps through a copyist's mistake) *stella maris*, the star of the sea, giving birth to the antiphon Ave Maris Stella.[78] In addition, the apparition tradition was common in Europe in the medieval period, and the refusal of

---

76. In her discussion of the adaptation of Central African religious traditions in Rio de Janeiro, Mary Karasch points out that Our Lady of the Rosary and other saints adopted by the blacks served as a charm, in the sense of a *nkisi*. Karasch also discusses the importance of the reformulation of community in the establishment of those religious complexes. Mary C. Karasch, "Central African Religious Tradition in Rio de Janeiro," *Journal of Latin American Lore* 5 (1979): 233–53.

77. Dona Maria Geralda Ferreira, interview, 28 August 1996. The story was repeated by Leonôr Pereira Galdino, Queen of Congo of Jatobá, interview with the author, Lindéia, BH, MG, 2 October 1996. For the complete narrative of Dona Maria's story, see Chapter 7.

images to move from the site where they had been discovered or revealed was a common motif in the apparition genre.[79]

The question then becomes, What did Africans see when they looked at Our Lady of the Rosary through African eyes? Looking at discreet cultural elements offers some insight into this question, such as the use of drums to call Our Lady of the Rosary to shore, which comes from a strong pan-African tradition of using drums to mediate between the two worlds. Many African traditions see the sea as the passage between the worlds. The presence of the different Afro-Brazilian "ethnicities" identifies the legend as unique to that tradition. The most significant aspect of the legend, however, and the one that remains constant in many variations of the story, is necessity of the different groups to join together in one community to ensure the efficacy of all their efforts. In fact, the establishment of community around the devotion to Our Lady of the Rosary is the central theme of the legend. That community, in the broadest cultural sense, was first made up of West and Central African slaves and freed blacks.

Despite the lack of depth of exposure to Christianity and European culture, Mina slaves and other groups from the Mina Coast participated enthusiastically in the lay religious brotherhoods in the first half of the eighteenth century. During this period, Our Lady of the Rosary may have been associated with Yemanjá, the goddess of the sea in the Yoruban tradition. In the iconography of present-day Candomblé (an Afro-Brazilian religion of Yoruban origin mostly found in Bahia), Yemanjá is pictured emerging from the sea, as is Our Lady of the Rosary in Minas Gerais today. Our Lady of the Rosary was found to be associated with Yemanjá in the Xangôs (also an Afro-Brazilian religion of Yoruban origin) of the northern Brazilian state of Pernambuco.[80] The rosary itself, to the early adherents of the brotherhood, may have been linked with Ifá, a divinatory tool in which a *babalawo* (diviner) threw sacred palm nuts, or a chain of eight half nuts, to make predictions about the future.[81] Unfortunately, these associations must remain in the realm of speculation. I

78. Warner, *Alone of All Her Sex*, 262.

79. Stafford Poole, *Our Lady of Guadalupe: The Origins and Sources of a Mexican National Symbol, 1531–1797* (Tucson: University of Arizona Press, 1995), 24.

80. Mulvey, "Black Brothers and Sisters," 256. See also a brief reference to this for Minas Gerais in Roger Bastide, *The African Religions of Brazil: Toward a Sociology of the Interpenetration of Civilizations*, trans. Helen Sebba (Baltimore: Johns Hopkins University Press, 1978), 54.

81. José Ramos Tinhorão, *As festas no Brasil colonial* (São Paulo: Editora 34, 2000), 96; for the Ifá divination in Africa, see J. D. Y. Peel, "The Pastor and the *Babalawo:* The Interaction of Religions in Nineteenth-Century Yorubaland," *Africa* 60 (1990): 340.

have not found evidence of specific connections of discreet cultural associations, at least not in the state of Minas Gerais.

Central Africans also understood Our Lady of the Rosary as a centralizing figure who had the ability to intercede on behalf of humans. As discussed earlier in this chapter, Central African cosmology posited that people in the land of the dead were white. Our Lady of the Rosary's white color would have identified her as a spirit from the land of the dead, who, according to Christian belief, had the ability to mediate between the two worlds. Linguistic misunderstandings also led to an African interpretation of Our Lady of the Rosary. Along the coast, African terms came to be used for Christian concepts, yet their meaning in the local African languages remained quite different from that in the Christian. For example, *Holy Mother* had been translated into KiKongo as *ngudi a nkisi*, but in the original language it meant something closer to "source of magic."[82] A tie to a "source of magic" enabled newly arrived Africans, and their offspring, to combat the witchcraft that, in their view, had caused them to fall into the horrible reality of slavery in the Americas.[83]

The inclusion of Mozambiques in this version of the legend, and as part of many present-day festivals, and the presence of a group called Candombe both reflect influences from the nineteenth and twentieth centuries. Mozambiques, or slaves from East Africa, despite their presence in Rio de Janeiro at the beginning of the nineteenth century, rarely appeared in the brotherhood lists.[84] Nevertheless, they were one of the first "nations" to appear in brotherhood accounts of their own festivals in the early nineteenth century.[85] Without membership lists to substantiate the presence of participants who identified themselves as Mozambiques, it is difficult to confirm whether the group called Mozambique was completely or partially composed of participants from East Africa. The dance and ritual known as Candombe was also recorded in Rio de Janeiro in the early nineteenth century, but it is better known as an Afro-Argentine and Afro-Uruguayan tradition.[86] It never appeared in the books of the brotherhoods or in any documentation I examined in Minas Gerais, despite its importance in the current festival. The point of the origin story of the Congado, as told by Dona Maria, is that it was only when all the groups joined together that Our Lady of the Rosary came out of the water. The symbolic importance of the act of coming together, and the remembrance of Africa that the storytelling reveals, identifies the legend as evidence of a process of identity, and community, formation.

82. MacGaffey, "Dialogues of the Deaf," 263.
83. Miller, "Retention, Reinvention" 90–92; and Sweet, *Recreating Africa*, 104–6.
84. Karasch, *Slave Life*, 8–13, 21–25.

Our Lady of the Rosary served as a cross-cultural symbol that reflected the European discourse while simultaneously embodying an ethos and worldview that incorporated cultural elements and understandings from a diverse array of African backgrounds. Looking at Our Lady of the Rosary through African eyes suggests that her white color, which has long been interpreted as a symbol of passive acceptance of a European worldview, actually represented a more complex interplay of ideological influences. Our Lady of the Rosary served as the centralizing symbol of the cosmology that emerged in the rosary brotherhoods. She became a cultural bridge between what the Africans had known in their native lands and what they came to know in their captivity, a symbol that created meaning in the lives of the people devoted to her.

Conclusion

The journey of the Middle Passage, across the land, the sea, and then the land once again, began a journey of reidentification for the slaves. Throughout history and certainly during the three hundred years of the slave trade, Africans did not identify themselves as a homogeneous group of "blacks," or even as Africans, but rather as members of distinct groups. Whatever these distinct groups were in Africa, they came to be translated into what were called "nations" in Brazil. Although the African nations of Brazil were entities created by the dynamic of the slave trade itself, sufficient evidence exists in the documentary record that blacks did self-identify with one or another particular nation, or ethnicity as these groupings are most commonly called today.[87] These ethnicities were tied to one another through shared cultures, societies, economies, politics, religions, and histories. The reformulation of the captive Africans' identity began when, through capture or sale, they left their communities in Africa and embarked on a forced and often lengthy overland march to the coast, followed by a dark, terrifying sea voyage. The

85. "Compromisso da Irmandade de Nossa Senhora do Rosário do Arraial de Nossa Senhora do Monte do Carmo, Freguesia de Nossa Senhora da Conceição de Pouso Alto, Bispado de Mariana," 1820, APM SP 959, chapter 20.

86. Karasch, *Slave Life,* 289 n. 98; Néstor Ortiz Oderigo, *Calunga: Croquis del Candombe* (Buenos Aires: Editorial Universitaria de Buenos Aires, 1969); Tomás Oliveira Chirimini, "Candombe, African Nations, and the Africanity of Uruguay," in *African Roots/American Cultures: Africa in the Creation of the Americas,* ed. Sheila S. Walker (Lanham, Md.: Rowman and Littlefield, 2001).

87. See Reis, "Identidade e diversidade," 13.

effect of the Middle Passage on Africans, including the overland journeys that bracketed the sea voyage for the slaves taken to the mines in Brazil, has been debated by scholars for many years.[88] Yet whatever the specific nature of transformation during the journey, there can be no doubt that it must have left an indelible scar on the slaves and that it constituted a dark rite of passage.[89] However, the torturous rite did not erase the captives' pasts; rather, it initiated a process of reorientation toward a new identity and hence identification with new groups. Those who shared similar journeys began to redefine the boundaries of their own identities and to interact, as best as they could, with one another and with the new worlds in which they found themselves.[90]

The lay religious brotherhoods in Brazil, originally organized by Europeans, would come to serve as a social space in which Africans and their descendents could rebuild their communities and, as a result, in which the mixing of African cosmologies and European religious forms could occur. It was in this space that fundamental social structures such as kinship, hierarchy, and the relationships to ancestors could be reformulated around a powerful image, Our Lady of the Rosary, who could intercede on behalf of the community. Africans from diverse backgrounds participated in the reformulation of community in the brotherhoods, and each would add its distinctiveness to the new community of "blacks" in the mining region of Minas Gerais.

88. For a discussion of the historiography of cultural connections and the slave trade, see Linda M. Heywood's introduction to Heywood, *Central Africans*, 2–8.

89. See Joseph C. Miller, *Way of Death: Merchant Capitalism and the Angolan Slave Trade, 1730–1830* (Madison: University of Wisconsin Press, 1988); and for Brazil, see Robert Edgar Conrad, *World of Sorrow: The African Slave Trade to Brazil* (Baton Rouge: Louisiana State University Press, 1986).

90. Miller, "Retention, Reinvention," 81–84; see also Michael A. Gomez, *Exchanging Our Country Marks: The Transformation of African Identities in the Colonial and Antebellum South* (Chapel Hill: University of North Carolina Press, 1998), 158.

PART TWO

3 EARLY FORMATION OF THE BROTHERHOODS, 1690–1750

Eu vim de Angola, eh
Vim aqui curimar [trabalhar]!

[I came from Angola, *eh*
I came here to work!]

—Mozambique of Our Lady of Mercies,
Oliveira, MG

The first half of the eighteenth century in Minas Gerais was a time in which the formation and shaping of the patterns of society took place. The social frameworks established during this period would be negotiated for the following centuries, yet they would remain in some ways remarkably stable. The early period stretched from the first discovery of gold in the region and the subsequent gold rush to the rapid decline of gold production in the middle of the eighteenth century. The gold rush would establish Minas Gerais as the largest slaveholding region in Brazil, not only during the rush, but also well into the nineteenth century. The nature of the mining economy itself, along with the decline of mining and the rise of a more diversified economy, would lead to a remarkably diverse population containing a large number of free nonwhites. In fact, by the end of the colonial period, free nonwhites were in the majority. By the middle of the century the Crown had established the borders of the captaincy, the major urban centers, a system of roads going to and from the coast, and systems of tax collection and justice. The Crown had also attempted to regulate the clergy, and to this end it established a diocese in 1745, with its seat in the newly incorporated city of Mariana. The Crown had forbidden religious orders to establish themselves in the mining district because of its fear, probably well founded, that members of religious orders engaged in contraband of precious metals and gems. This ban created a gap in the religious field of the mining district that the brotherhoods rapidly filled.[1]

Because of the frontier nature of the settlement and the lack of religious clergy, brotherhoods became more than an incidental part of the religious life; they became the center of religious expression. The region's urban nature, which emerged from the very earliest settlement patterns, facilitated the development of the brotherhoods in colonial Minas Gerais.[2] In addition, the *padroado* gave the Portuguese kings and queens control over every aspect of the diocesan church in Brazil.[3] The church, in effect, had become a branch of the government, and it squabbled endlessly with the secular authorities over jurisdiction, weakening the control of both over the religious life of the colony.

The disputes between the state and the church left both practice of religion and its infrastructure in the hands of the laity in the form of religious brotherhoods. In the beginning of the captaincy, the state was content to allow the brotherhoods to organize and administer the religious life of the colony, because the brotherhoods assumed much of the financial burden of the physical structure and ornamentation, the personnel, and the rituals of the church. Even the poorest of the brotherhoods took over the expense of maintaining their own altars, of building churches when they could, and of hiring their own chaplains. The independence of the brotherhoods over their affairs created a lay religious infrastructure that was related to, but not necessarily under the authority of, the official diocesan organization. Not surprisingly, this autonomy would be challenged by the church, after the middle of the eighteenth century until well into the twentieth.

In this formative period, then, the people themselves established their social organizations by coalescing into corporate groups within brotherhoods, and as the society became more complex and hierarchical, more brotherhoods were established.[4] On the top of the hierarchy were the white brotherhoods of old Christians dedicated to the Santíssimo Sacramento (Most Holy Sacrament), and on the bottom were the rosary brotherhoods of the blacks. Despite their position at the bottom of the social ladder, brotherhoods of the rosary of the blacks in the colonial period were the most numerous of all brotherhoods, and by midcentury, any town or village of any significance

---

1. Despite the ban, there were always some orders present in colonial Minas Gerais. See Boschi, *Os leigos,* 84 n. 33, 34.

2. A. J. R. Russell-Wood, *The Black Man in Slavery and Freedom in Colonial Brazil* (New York: St. Martin's Press, 1982), 128.

3. Bruneau, *Political Transformation,* 14.

4. See Salles, *Associações religiosas.*

had a rosary brotherhood. They became the most significant way in which Africans from different regions of Africa, and from Brazil, both free and slave, gathered together to re-form communities. Despite their differences, the brotherhood members used the organizations to build an identity on what they had in common: a link to Africa, which played a part in their identification as being "black," and their devotion to Our Lady of the Rosary. These factors allowed the brotherhoods in colonial Minas Gerais to develop as grassroots organizations that flourished because of the lack of church/state control, rather than the imposition of that control.[5]

Finding Gold in Minas Gerais

The earliest years of settlement in the mountainous region that would come to be known as Minas Gerais were marked by disorder and confusion, compounded by the promise of incredible wealth. A Jesuit named Antonil, a traveler to the mining district in the early eighteenth century, wrote, "Every year fleets bring crowds of Portuguese and foreigners to the mines. From the cities, towns, *recôncavos*, and backlands of Brazil come whites, mulattos, and blacks, together with many Indians employed by the Paulistas. The mixture is of every condition of people: men and women, young and old, poor and rich, nobles and commoners, laymen and clergy, and religious of different orders, many of whom have neither house nor convent in Brazil."[6] The gold rush in Brazil, in fact, was probably the largest in the world to that date, and Portuguese officials took some time to catch up to what was occurring in that region. In fact, the church was the first institution to attempt to establish administrative infrastructures in the captaincy. The official church arrived in Minas Gerais in 1703, when the bishop of Rio de Janeiro sent Cônego Gaspar Ribeiro Pereira to establish churches and set administrative boundaries.[7] Antonil, however, noted that despite the presence of pastors and *visitadores* (ecclesiastical visitors), little could be done to subdue the chaos of those early years, for priests "were little feared or respected in those towns that moved from one place to another like the sons of Israel in the desert."[8] Yet

---

5. See also Donald Ramos, "A influência africana e a cultura popular em Minas Gerais: Um comentário sobre a interpretação da escravidão," in *Brasil: Colonização e escravidão*, ed. Maria Beatriz Nizza da Silva (Rio de Janeiro: Editora Nova Fronteira, 2000), 142–62.

6. Andre João Antonil (pseud.), *Cultura e opulência do Brasil por suas drogas e minas* (São Paulo: Melhoramentos, 1976), 167.

7. Boxer, *Golden Age*, 57.

8. Antonil, *Cultura*, 168.

Antonil's negative commentary belies the fact that the people themselves often started lay religious brotherhoods in this early period, a time during which the first churches were built and the first brotherhood of the rosary, the first confraternity recorded in the mining districts, was established in the town of São João del Rei in 1708.[9]

By the end of the first decade of the eighteenth century, Dom João V had realized that he had to bring an end to the disorder in Minas Gerais in order to take full advantage of the wealth the land was already producing. His excuse to impose order came in 1709, when the War of the Emboabas erupted between Paulistas, who had discovered the gold in Minas Gerais, and immigrants from elsewhere in Brazil and from Portugal.[10] The war was a bloody battle of factions that threatened the Crown's ability to generate revenue from the mines. The Crown responded by separating the mining area (Minas Gerais) and São Paulo from the captaincy of Rio de Janeiro and by establishing a Portuguese administration. The king named Antônio de Albuquerque Coelho de Carvalho the first governor of the new captaincy in a royal letter (carta régia) of 9 November 1709 and ordered him to establish towns.[11] In 1711 the new governor elevated three of the most prominent mining villages, Ribeirão do Carmo (Mariana), Vila Rica d'Albuquerque (Vila Rica), and Nossa Senhora da Conceição do Sabará (Sabará), to the status of towns, each with its own municipal council. In 1714, he established the first three districts (comarcas) in the captaincy, Vila Rica, Rio das Velhas, and Rio das Mortes.

Despite the attempt at Crown control, the mining centers remained anarchic. However, this early period came to a close in 1720, when a rebellion erupted in the town of Vila Rica, the capital, in opposition to the Crown order to establish smelting houses to facilitate the collection of the royal tax. The governor of the combined captaincies of Minas Gerais and São Paulo between 1717 and 1721, Dom Pedro de Almeida, the conde de Assumar, responded quickly and without mercy, drawing and quartering the ringleader and burning all of the insurgents' houses to the ground. On his urging, the Portuguese Crown separated the mining region from the captaincy of São Paulo and created the captaincy of Minas Gerais.[12] A royal letter established the collative

9. Certificados de Missas 1790–1918, MASSJ book 4.03, 3. The first church was erected in Minas Gerais in 1690, even before gold was discovered. Cônego Raymundo Trindade, *Arquidiocese de Mariana: Subsídios para a sua história*, vol. 1, 2d ed. (Belo Horizonte, Brazil: Imprensa Oficial, 1953), 68.

10. Boxer, *Golden Age*, 61–83.

11. "Nomeação de Antônio de Albuquerque," RAPM 11 (1906): 685.

12. Donald Ramos, "A Social History of Ouro Preto: Stresses of Dynamic Urbanization in Colonial Brazil, 1695–1726" (Ph.D. diss., University of Florida, 1972), 405–27.

parishes in 1724.[13] The new governor of Minas Gerais, Dom Lourenço de Almeida, ushered in what became literally the "golden age" of Minas Gerais.

Once towns were established and the royal and Church administration began to take root, the Crown turned its attention to normalizing life in the mines. It considered the teachings of the church to be important for bringing morality and probity to the population, yet it mistrusted most of the clergy that represented that church. Not only did the king deny licenses to religious orders, he ordered that any secular clergy who dared to remain in Minas without licenses be jailed.[14] In addition, many of the secular clergy themselves led licentious lives, and Crown officials frequently complained that most of the clergy were corrupt and a bad influence on the morals of the miners and the slaves. The priests were accused of charging exorbitant prices for their services and many were charged with ignoring royal orders to leave the captaincy, even under threat of excommunication.[15] One worried correspondent wrote the king about

> the deplorable state that almost all of the ecclesiastics in this region, without wanting to offend your royal ears I will only say the most minor vice is to live publicly with their concubines . . . you can distinguish their concubines because they are the most ostentatious and well dressed and for whom the ecclesiastics fight duels and have public quarrels with the most profane . . . and do not believe, Your Majesty, that I am exaggerating, because it is a common practice among the majority of the ecclesiastics that in these Mines they cannot live without a concubine.[16]

Despite persistent attempts to expel secular clergy who did not serve as good examples to the population and to replace them with clergy who would behave like "men of God," copious correspondence about licentious and corrupt priests continued throughout the eighteenth century.[17]

---

13. José Ferreira Carrato, *As Minas Gerais e o primórdios do Caraça* (São Paulo: Companhia Editora Nacional, 1963), 106.

14. Ordem de 21 de Fevereiro de 1738, in "Religioens, clerigos e mater.ᵃˢ Eclesiasticas," *RAPM* 16 (1911): 398.

15. Letter from Dom Bráz Baltazar da Silveira to the king, Dom João V, 2 June 1716, APM SC 04, 447–49. See also the letter from Dom Bráz Baltazar da Silveira to the king, Dom João V, 4 May 1715, APM SC 04, 402.

16. Letter from town of São João del Rei to the king, Dom João V (no name), 22 August 1719, APM SC 04, 693–97.

17. "Religioens, clerigos e mater.ᵃˢ Eclesiasticas," *RAPM* 16 (1911): 393–403.

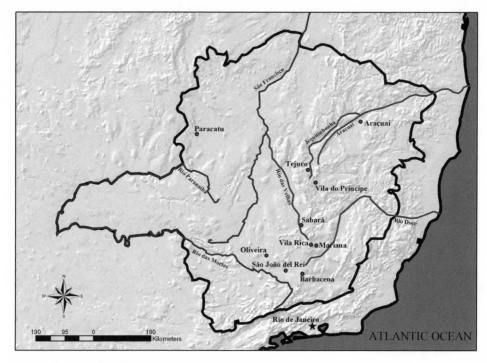

MAP 3.   Colonial Minas Gerais

One of the main concerns of the Crown officials in regards to the clergy centered on their belief that the church would help to subdue the population—not only the miners but also the slaves who were pouring into the region. Within the first years of the settlement, Minas Gerais became the most significant destination for slaves in Brazil. The Portuguese government authorities based the size of the claims, known as *datas*, on how many working slaves the claimant possessed, providing a powerful incentive to miners to arrive in the region with slaves, or acquire slaves once they had arrived.[18] In the first years after the discovery of gold the majority of slaves were marched south from the captaincy of Bahia to Minas Gerais, via a long overland journey.[19] Antonil estimated the journey at between 186 and 237 leagues, depending on the route. He described the road as wide and easy to move along as well as rich with provisions for the travelers as they passed through the wide open *sertão* (arid and remote interior) of southern Bahia

18. Antonil, *Cultura*, 215–16.
19. Goulart, *A escravidão*, 149–50.

and northern Minas Gerais.[20] Because the demand was so high, slaves transported along these routes came not only from Africa but also often from
farms and sugar mills already established in Bahia. The need for slaves in
the mines became so great, in fact, that coastal plantations began to become
depopulated, prompting the Portuguese Crown to make several unsuccessful
attempts to limit the number of slaves allowed into the mining region.[21]

By 1706, the Overseas Council in Lisbon suggested that Rio de Janeiro,
which would become the Brazilian capital in 1763, be given a contract to
import slaves from Angola and the Mina Coast in order to halt the flow of
slaves from the northern sugar and tobacco plantations.[22] Soon Rio de
Janeiro began to supplant Bahia as the primary slave-importing city in
Brazil, both because of the proximity to the mines and because colonial
authorities wanted the slaves who were brought to the northern ports to
remain on the plantations of the north. Despite its closer proximity, the
caminho novo (new road) that ran north from Rio de Janeiro was much
more difficult to travel in the early decades of the eighteenth century. Three
major rivers had to be crossed by boat or raft, and travelers often had to
camp in the woods. Antonil wrote that although the trip was only approximately eighty leagues, much shorter than the trip from Bahia, it would take
ten to twelve days to go from Rio de Janeiro to Vila Rica, because of the difficulty of the terrain.[23] Nevertheless, by the third decade of the eighteenth
century, traffic along the northern routes had dwindled significantly and the
route from Rio de Janeiro had become the main route from which gold and,
later, foodstuffs were exported from the colony and by which manufactured
goods, migrants, and slaves entered Minas Gerais.[24]

Despite the long journey, slaves in huge numbers were brought into the
mining district along these routes. Historian of Brazilian slave demography
Maurício Goulart estimates that between the opening of the mines and
1715, approximately 2,600 slaves entered the region annually. During the
height of the mining period, between 1717 and 1723, between 4,400 and
5,000 slaves entered Minas Gerais each year, and between 1723 and 1735
that number increased to between 5,700 and 6,000. The importation of slaves
into Minas Gerais reached its highest point at the end of the 1730s, when
between the years 1739 and 1741, 7,360 slaves were imported annually, after
which the numbers tapered off to about 4,000 a year between 1760 and

20. Antonil, *Cultura*, 246–47.
21. Boxer, *Golden Age*, 45.
22. Goulart, *A escravidão*, 151.
23. Antonil, *Cultura*, 242–47.
24. Bergad, *Slavery*, 10.

1780, diminishing to 2,000 annually for the duration of the colonial period.[25] Slaves in the mining district throughout the first half of the eighteenth century became a significant part of the population, on average probably constituting between 40 and 50 percent of the overall population.[26] Recent captives from the Mina Coast and from Angola mixed with the many slaves brought from the plantations of Bahia, a population that included *crioulos* (Brazilian-born blacks) and Africans who had already attained some level of familiarity with Brazil. Even from the beginning of the captaincy, then, the slave population of Minas Gerais was heterogeneous.

The labor regime for slaves in the mining district could be a cruel reality. One contemporary doctor, Luis Gomes Ferreira, commented that slaves worked relentlessly, with "their feet always in the cold earth, on stones, or in water, when they rest or eat their pores close and they become so chilled that they are susceptible to many dangerous illnesses, such as very severe pleurisies, apoplectic and paralytic fits, convulsions, pneumonia, and many other diseases."[27] This type of treatment contributed to the ever increasing number and size of *quilombos*, or runaway slave communities, in Minas Gerais.

Yet the mining district, and the mining regime, also offered opportunities to slaves that were not available in other regions of Brazil. Many of the mining claims were scattered and distant, so often it would have been impossible to supervise slaves closely. Many slaves working in the mines were able to accumulate capital, especially those who paid their masters a certain sum and were able to keep the rest. Eventually, if these slaves survived, they could accumulate enough to buy their freedom. In the towns of Minas Gerais, slaves led similarly autonomous lives, sometimes even living separately from their masters.[28] Female slaves often worked as street vendors, which enabled them to amass savings, and in fact, female slaves manumitted themselves, or were manumitted, much more frequently than men. The overall high manumission rate may also have been a result of the fact that because of the extremely high ratios of men to women, slave women often became the

---

25. Goulart, *A escravidão*, 164–70, and Russell-Wood, *Black Man*, 109.

26. Bergad, *Slavery*, 87.

27. Luis Gomes Ferreira quoted in Eduardo Galeano, *Open Veins of Latin America*, trans. Celdric Belfrage (New York: Monthly Review Press, 1997), 53–54. See also Kathleen J. Higgins, *"Licentious Liberty" in a Brazilian Gold-Mining Region: Slavery, Gender, and Social Control in Eighteenth-Century Sabará, Minas Gerais* (University Park: Pennsylvania State University Press, 1999), 70–73. The French naturalist Auguste de Saint-Hilaire similarly described the harshness of slave labor that he observed in the diamond-mining district in the early nineteenth century. Auguste de Saint-Hilaire, "Slave Workers at the Diamond Washings of Tejuco, Minas Gerais, in the Early Nineteenth Century," in Conrad, *Children*, 140–42.

28. Higgins, *"Licentious Liberty,"* 68–69.

concubines of white men, who would often recognize their mulatto offspring and free them. As historian Kathleen J. Higgins so cogently points out, this undermined the link, so common in the Americas, between slaveholding and whiteness. It created a large population of nonwhites who were free; in fact, by 1805 nonwhites outnumbered whites in the free population by two to one.[29] Many of these nonwhites participated in brotherhoods of the rosary of the blacks.

The autonomy of much of the slave population caused the conde de Assumar to comment that "the freedom which the blacks of this captaincy have [is] unlike that in other parts of America, certainly it is not true slavery the manner in which they live today as it more appropriately can be called licentious liberty."[30] Some of the attempt to bring these slaves under control was to be through the teachings of the church, even though the clergy did not always conform to the church's moral precepts. How slaves were to be taught the catechism had been laid out in the Constituições primeiras, or Primary Constitutions, written by the archbishop of Bahia in the early years of the eighteenth century. The Primary Constitutions standardized the catechism of the slaves into a series of questions and answers about God, Jesus, Mary, and the Holy Spirit as well as about heaven and hell.[31] The clergy often abbreviated even this simple catechism, however; for example, one ecclesiastic visitor to the mining region in the mid-eighteenth century only required the slaves to understand "the Trinity, Incarnation, and one God as rewarder of good and punisher of evil."[32] Crown officials accused the clergy of failing to offer slaves even this basic instruction in the faith and complained that slaves were not baptized before attaining adulthood; nor were they even taught the fundamental principles of the religion.[33] Masters also came under the fire of state officials, for not giving the slaves Sundays and saint's days off and for abusing their power.[34]

Some slaves, such as those from northeastern Brazil, and from Angola, Kongo, may have had some exposure to the symbols of Christianity and to Afro-Portuguese creole culture, others may have had little or no contact. The reaction to catechism and Christianity, however, can be understood to

29. Ibid., 38–40.

30. Quoted in Kathleen J. Higgins, "Master and Slaves in a Mining Society: A Study of Eighteenth-Century Sabará, Minas Gerais," Slavery and Abolition 11, no. 1 (1990), 59; also quoted in Russell-Wood, Black Man, 104.

31. Primary Constitutions, excerpted in Conrad, Children, 154–57.

32. D. Ramos, "Community, Control, and Acculturation," 441.

33. Ibid.

34. Letter from the conde de Assumar to the king, Dom João V, 4 October 1719, APM SC 04, 713.

be a continuation of the process of mutual misunderstanding followed by creolization. Key rituals may have been understood through African interpretations. Baptism, for example, could have been interpreted as an initiatory rite of incorporation in a new community, as baptism itself had been understood by many cultures in Africa.[35] In fact, the conde de Assumar, once again criticizing apparent slave freedoms, complained that even baptized slaves "choose as their godparents others who in their lands are of [ ] a higher authority [ ] and relatives of native kings who govern those who recognize them, with some kind of superiority, and they are so subjected that they don't only obey the leaders when possible, many times they give the daily earning of their masters without fear of the punishment that they will receive."[36]

Already in the early days of the captaincy, slaves quickly began to establish affective ties along hierarchical lines through the initiatory ritual of baptism, which undermined the authority of the slave system. Nevertheless, even the conde de Assumar would not have suggested that slaves not be baptized. Instead, he suggested that the slaves be forced to take white godparents, a practice that had been banned elsewhere in Brazil.[37]

Despite the conde de Assumar's warnings, most officials viewed the doctrines of the church as one of the most viable preventative measures to slave uprisings and the formation of runaway-slave communities (quilombos). Authorities were all too aware of the havoc wreaked by the Quilombo dos Palmares just decades earlier in the northern captaincy of Pernambuco.[38] Although none of the quilombos of Minas Gerais grew to be as large as Palmares, there were many famous and long-lasting quilombos throughout the colonial period.[39] The slaves who ran away to these settlements survived by mining; through agriculture; and probably to a great extent by looting

35. Frey and Wood, Come Shouting, 18–19.
36. Letter from the conde de Assumar to the king, Dom João V, 28 November 1719, APM SC 04, 740–48.
37. See Stuart B. Schwartz, Sugar Plantations in the Formation of Brazilian Society, Bahia, 1550–1835 (London: Cambridge University Press, 1985), 406–12.
38. Letter from the conde de Assumar to the king, Dom João V, 20 April 1719. RAPM 3 (1898): 265. The Quilombo dos Palmares grew to be a legendary runaway slave community in the backlands of colonial Pernambuco, today the state of Alagoas. It probably began in about 1605 and was finally defeated by the Brazilian militias in 1695. See R. K. Kent, "Palmares: An African State in Brazil," in Maroon Societies: Rebel Slave Communities in the Americas, ed. Richard Price (Garden City, N.Y.: Anchor Press, 1973), 170–91; and Stuart B. Schwartz, Slaves, Peasants, and Rebels: Reconsidering Brazilian Slavery (Urbana: University of Illinois Press, 1996), 122–28.
39. See Roger Bastide, "The Other Quilombos," in Price, Maroon Societies, 191–201; and Carlos Magno Guimarães, A negação da ordem escravista: Quilombos em Minas Gerais no século XVIII (São Paulo: Icone Editora, 1988).

in the captaincy, where lawlessness was still prevalent.[40] They created hierarchies that were headed by what the Portuguese officials called kings and queens.[41] Officials greatly feared the *quilombos*, and they were much written about and actively tracked down and destroyed.[42] Other slaves, however, chose to join lay religious brotherhoods as a way to combat the alienation of the slave system, probably much to the relief of the Crown officials. The choice between running away to a *quilombo* and joining a brotherhood has long been understood to be one representing a model of opposites: resistance (*quilombos*) or accommodation (brotherhoods). Despite the different motivations slaves might have had to enter a brotherhood or run away to a *quilombo*, both represented the same impulse—to re-create communities within this new, alienating environment in which Africans found themselves. In both types of communities, slaves and free blacks re-created hierarchies and established affective ties. In both systems, the naming of kings and queens became an important way to articulate that hierarchy.

The authorities greatly feared the practice of having black kings and queens when it occurred in the *quilombos*, and although the authorities never spoke out against the existence of black brotherhoods, they never completely accepted the election of black leaders within those organizations. One of the conde de Assumar's greatest fears, in fact, was the penchant of the blacks to name their own leaders, their "kings" and "princes." In his correspondence about a rumored slave uprising, the conde de Assumar pointed out that the slaves had already "named among themselves a King, Prince, and military officials" and that although at first he thought this was some "ridiculousness" of the blacks, he had heard a similar rumor from a nearby town.[43] He suggested that they capture and throw out of the town all the blacks from Mina and Angola who called themselves kings.[44]

The conde de Assumar, because of his fear of slave self-determination, especially in the application of monikers of royalty, provided the earliest

40. Waldemar de Almeida Barbosa, *Negros e quilombos em Minas Gerais* (Belo Horizonte, Brazil: n.p., 1972); Guimarães, *A negação;* and Carlos Magno Guimarães, "Mineração, quilombos e Palmares, Minas Gerais no Século XVIII," in *Liberdade por um fio: História dos quilombos no Brasil*, ed. João José Reis and Flávio dos Santos Gomes (São Paulo: Companhia das Letras, 1996), 147–49.

41. Kiddy, "Who Is the King of Congo,"162.

42. Alda Maria Palhares Campolina, C. Melo, and M. Andrade, *Escravidão em Minas Gerais: Cadernos do arquivo 1* (Belo Horizonte, Brazil: Secretaria de Estado da Cultura, 1988), 45–51.

43. Letter from the conde de Assumar to the king, Dom João V, 20 April 1719, *RAPM* 3 (1898): 263–64.

44. Ibid., 264.

documentation showing the existence of the *reinado* (the ritual coronation of kings and queens) inside the brotherhoods of the rosary in Minas Gerais in the first decades of the eighteenth century. In 1720 he posted a proclamation condemning the crowning of kings and queens in religious festivals, a problem that, he wrote, had been eliminated in most of Minas Gerais except in the district of Serro do Frio, the diamond-mining district. It is interesting to note that the practice of crowning black kings and queens had already been practiced and, according to the official report, eliminated in Minas Gerais before 1720, when the conde de Assumar wrote the letter. He complained that in Serro do Frio the blacks "at their feast days acclaim and crown black Kings and Queens in a solemn act," which, to the count was "a repugnant act considering the humble condition of the slaves that must be preserved."[45] The letter suggested punishments for all who participated in the ritual—including priests, who should lose their ecclesiastical allowance (*côngrua*) if they dared to crown the African kings and queens. Yet less than nine years later, when Minas Gerais was under a new administration, the statutes of the brotherhood of the rosary in Vila do Príncipe (present-day Serro) in the diamond-mining district included a clause that established the annual election of a king and queen.[46]

The Count's concerns about the recognition of slave leaders supports a legend popular among the participants in the rosary feast day celebrations today, the story of Chico Rei. The story tells of the origin of the reinados and congados (the ambassadors to the kings and queens) in the colonial period. Oral tradition and nineteenth-century histories tell the story of Francisco (Chico), who had been a king in Africa but was captured and brought as a slave to Brazil. On the journey he lost his wife and family except one son, and together they were taken to the mines. Chico resigned himself to his fate, worked hard, and finally was able to free his son, then himself, and eventually all the members of his nation. Together, the Africans created a state within a state with Chico as king, his second wife as queen, and the rest of his family as princes. They constructed the church of Saint Iphigenia on the Alto da Cruz, the highest hill in Antonio Dias (a neighborhood in Vila Rica). The church continues to be home to the brotherhood of the rosary. The royal African family participated in the sung mass in the chapel and afterward danced and sang and played their African instruments in the

---

45. Letter from the conde de Assumar to the king, Dom João V, 20 May 1720, APM SC 11, 288v.

46. *Compromisso da Irmandade de Nossa Senhora do Rozário na freguezia da Conceyção da Villa do Príncipe do Sêrro do Frio no Anno de 1.728* (Serro, MG: Irmandade de Nossa Senhora do Rosário, 1979), 1.

streets. According to this legend, Chico Rei's coronation was the first Reinado of Our Lady of the Rosary of the blacks, a practice that was then imitated in all the villages of Minas Gerais.[47]

This legend has become part of the collective memory of Minas Gerais and is an important origin story that the congadeiros tell about themselves and celebrate on an annual basis. Although not confirmed by manuscript sources, it contains elements that accord with documentary evidence from the early colonial period. Leaders or relatives of African leaders did play a role in the colonial black society; blacks entered lay religious brotherhoods and built their own churches; and they did find ways to become free from slavery. The legend posits that Chico Rei came from a single region of Africa and his followers were from a single nation, yet he started the first Reinado of the blacks. Chico Rei, as the King of Congo would later do, represented the emergence of a new identity, one made up of shared histories of Africa, the memory of the Middle Passage, and the solidarity formed from being nonwhite in colonial *mineiro* society. Slaves and free blacks, both African and Brazilian born, sought out a situation in which they could name their own leaders without fear of reprisal, nurture a link with the unseen world and with ancestors, and care for the recent dead. Slaves who did not run away, like the legendary Chico Rei, chose to negotiate their way through the system and create a place for themselves within society through their participation in the brotherhoods of Our Lady of the Rosary.[48]

The Rosary Brotherhoods of the Blacks in *Mineiro* Society

The administrative system of Minas Gerais in which slaves such as Chico Rei would have to maneuver was largely in place by the late 1720s. By 1720, brotherhoods of the rosary had already been established in all the official towns in Minas Gerais, including São João del Rei (1708); Mariana (before 1715); Vila Rica, which included both Ouro Preto (1715) and Antonio Dias (1718); Sabará (1713); and Vila do Príncipe (1716).[49] The brotherhoods of the rosary were not restricted to the largest towns. One of the earliest documented brotherhoods was established in the small village of Cachoeira do Campo, in the outlying district of Ouro Preto, with a compromisso dated

47. Diogo Vasconcellos, *História antiga das Minas Gerais,* vol. 2 (Rio de Janeiro: Imprensa Nacional, 1948), 243–44 n. 1; and Pedrina de Lourdes Santos, interview, 24 August 1995.

48. See also Chapter 7.

49. Boschi, *Os leigos,* 214–24.

1713.[50] Overall, during the colonial period, brotherhoods of the rosary were the most numerous of all the brotherhoods in the captaincy. Historian Caio César Boschi found that rosary brotherhoods of the blacks were just one of fifty-two different types of brotherhoods, yet they accounted for 19.3 percent of the total brotherhoods in colonial Minas Gerais, outnumbering all other types.[51] As the frontiers of Minas Gerais expanded, the presence of rosary brotherhoods expanded with them, until almost every town and hamlet had its own chapter.

The first official act of a brotherhood was to write its statutes, a compromisso that lay out all the rules and regulations by which the brotherhood would be governed. Often a brotherhood would be created and function for many years before the membership wrote a compromisso and sent it to the authorities for approval, so in most cases, it only legitimized organizations that had already existed for many years. Although these documents were modeled after their counterparts in Lisbon, they differed widely in their styles of presentation and focus. In addition, the marginalia and the provisos, often added years after the writing of the original statutes, offer invaluable insight into the processes and negotiations between the brotherhoods and the authorities and the organization of difference within the brotherhood membership.

The compromissos of the *mineiro* rosary brotherhoods, however, shared many similarities. Like their counterparts in Europe and Africa, *mineiro* rosary brotherhoods allowed people of any race and nation and of either gender to join. Positions of power, as articulated in the statutes, were of two main types: administrative and celebratory. The administrative positions were those of secretary, treasurer, and procurator (of which there were often two). Those officials were responsible for negotiating with the church and state authorities, because they took care of the books of the brotherhoods, including the accounts, minutes of the meetings, election lists, and records of masses.

The celebratory positions were just as important as the administrative offices in the internal running of the brotherhoods. The black rosary brotherhoods were unique because they included a king and queen, positions that were often identified in the colonial compromissos as the most important in

50. "Compromisso da Irmandade de Nossa Senhora do Rosário novamente Erecta na Igreja Matris de Nossa Senhora da Nazareth do lugar da Caxueira no distrito das Minas . . . o anno de 1713." AEAM A22, 8.

51. These numbers are taken from Caio César Boschi's comprehensive list of brotherhoods in colonial Minas Gerais. The figures can be considered to be low, however, for many books have not survived to the present, or remain in individual parishes. Boschi, *Os leigos*, 189–90.

the brotherhood. In addition, there were to be male and female judges for each of the saints venerated by the members. All these positions were filled through election, and each required a hefty contribution from the office-holder. The document laid out how elections would be run and how much each officer should pay. In addition, the brotherhoods might have several officers installed *por devoção* (through the strength of their devotion). These were people who volunteered for certain celebratory positions because they wanted to pay a promise, or simply participate more fully in the activities of the brotherhoods.

Many of the early rosary brotherhoods were not brotherhoods exclusively "of the blacks." For instance, the compromisso of the brotherhood in Cachoeira do Campo (1713) overtly restricted membership to whites.[52] Just a decade later, however, the brotherhood had opened its membership to blacks, perhaps because of pressure from the ecclesiastical visitor. Often these visitors, and especially Padre Antonio de Lima, who visited Minas Gerais in the early 1720s, blatantly sided with the blacks within the brotherhoods. For instance, Padre Antonio wrote a proviso into the back of the statutes of Cachoeira do Campo in 1723 that directly addressed the *pretinhos* (little blacks) in the brotherhood (despite the fact that the original compromisso had banned the membership of blacks). He warned the blacks not to let the whites have a vote on the ruling board (*mesa*), because the whites wanted to dominate the blacks *in their own brotherhood*.[53] Between 1713 and 1723, then, the brotherhood had gone from being an entity exclusively for whites, according to the statutes, to one for blacks, according to practice, as articulated in a note within that same document by the ecclesiastic visitor.

Sometimes brotherhoods that started with both black and white members eventually divided into two brotherhoods. The brotherhood of the rosary in Antonio Dias of Vila Rica (the brotherhood, according to legend, started by Chico Rei) cleaved along racial lines in 1733, when the whites left to form their own brotherhood in the next valley, Padre Faria.[54] In Campo dos Carijós (1743) blacks wrote to the king of Portugal expressing their desire to create a brotherhood only for blacks, because they had been expelled from the brotherhood of the whites and never wished to be subject to the whites again. The black rosary membership of Campo dos Carijós further requested

52. "Compromisso da Irmandade . . . da Caxueira," AEAM AA22, chapter 1.
53. Ibid., 7. Italics mine.
54. "Compromisso da Irmandade de NS do Rozario dos Pretos denominada do Alto da Cruz . . . , Antônio Dias, 1733," CC Paróquia de Nossa Senhora da Conceição de Antônio Dias, rol 58.

that they be allowed to worship at their own altar in the chapel of Our Lady of the Rosary, which they had helped to construct: "[W]e also ask, Your Royal Highness, to concede the authorization, if we are not able to worship at the altar of the Brotherhood of the Rosary of the Whites[,] that you help us to erect [our own altar] in order to have our festivals and worship Our Lady of the Rosary without having to encounter the whites on the days of their obligation."[55] The bishop of Rio de Janeiro agreed to these statutes, making no changes in the text.[56] By 1750, rosary brotherhoods had become intimately associated with the slave, free, and freed black population and often added the qualifier to the name of the brotherhood: the Brotherhood of Our Lady of the Rosary of the Blacks.

When brotherhoods separated along racial lines, whites maintained their devotion to Our Lady of the Rosary often in their own brotherhoods, as had occurred in the case of the brotherhood in Padre Faria. Whites did not shun the devotion, or participation in brotherhoods dedicated to Our Lady of the Rosary, simply because blacks had so enthusiastically embraced the devotion and membership in the brotherhoods. The use of the devotional tool of the rosary was widespread among the entire population, and motivations for joining one brotherhood or another, or many brotherhoods, would have been complex and personal. This participation can be understood to emerge from a desire of a person to fulfill his or her Catholic responsibilities of charity and community participation while at the same time ensuring that as many masses as possible would be celebrated for his or her soul after death.[57] Europeans or Euro-Brazilians might be motivated to join a rosary brotherhood in particular because incredibly good fortune occurred on the feast day of Our Lady of the Rosary, or to fulfill a promise made to her. These and any number of other reasons might compel a white to join a rosary brotherhood of the whites, or even of the blacks.

Men and women in Minas Gerais, and throughout the Iberian world, with enough resources would join more than one brotherhood, and some people belonged to several. For example, Kathleen Higgins talks about the case of Mathias de Castro Porto, an early white settler in the mining town of Sabará, Minas Gerais, who upon his death chose to be shrouded in the habit of the Third Order of Saint Francis, a prestigious brotherhood that only admitted whites and of which he was a member. In addition, he left substantial

55. "Compromisso dos Pretos devotos de N. Senhora do Rosário da freguesia do Campo dos Carijós para se governarem por eles, 1743," APM SP 959-1743, chapter 1.

56. Ibid.

57. A. J. R. Russell-Wood, "Prestige, Power, and Piety in Colonial Brazil: The Third Orders of Salvador, HAHR 69, no. 1 (1989): 61–89.

sums of gold to seven other brotherhoods in which he claimed membership, including that of Our Lady of the Rosary.[58]

This example should not lead to easy conclusions, for it does not imply that a recognition of racial difference and prejudice did not exist in Minas Gerais or that the brotherhood structure did not reflect a hierarchical social structure. Mathias de Castro Porto chose to be buried in the shroud of the most prestigious brotherhood that he belonged to, and his membership in multiple brotherhoods was an outward expression of his wealth. In these ways he expressed the class structure of his time and fulfilled the charitable acts expected of a person of his social and economic standing. At the same time, de Castro Porto had no legal heirs upon his death, so he recognized his seven illegitimate children, all of whom were of mixed descent, and bequeathed to them one of the largest fortunes in the region. De Castro, in his will, also freed a slave, who went on to become a slave owner.[59] In the frontier atmosphere of the mining region, all these different forces—blood relations, patron-client relations, social hierarchy, class, and piety—worked together to shape the decisions of the population.

By the middle of the eighteenth century, brotherhoods had been established not only for blacks and whites but also for other groups, those who chose to identify themselves as mulattos and *pardos* (people of mixed descent), and as *crioulos* (Brazilian-born blacks). Vila Rica, the administrative capital of the captaincy of Minas Gerais, serves as a good example of how the society divided itself into the different corporations. In the eighteenth century, twenty-nine brotherhoods were founded in Vila Rica: fifteen for whites, five for mulattos, two for *crioulos*, two for blacks (both rosary brotherhoods), one for Portuguese, and one integrated. Three of the brotherhoods did not have a designation. The first ten brotherhoods, all founded before 1720, were either black or white, and only when the population became more complex did people start to define themselves through more discrete groupings.[60] Membership in a brotherhood gave an individual a chance to join a community. Part of any community's identity is based on the perceived differences with another group; thus the emergence of mulatto and *crioulo* brotherhoods after 1721 demonstrates that some nonwhites began to align with groups other than "blacks."[61]

58. Higgins, "*Licentious Liberty*," 94.
59. Ibid., 87.
60. Marcos Magalhães de Aguiar, "Vila Rica dos confrades: A sociabilidade confrarial entre negros e mulatos no século XVIII" (master's thesis, Universidade de São Paulo, 1993), 23.
61. See Weber, "Ethnic Groups," 17.

In the colonial period, the term *black* represented a wide range of elements having to do with phenotype, legal status, economic standing, and cultural ties, as it does today. Many people, including nineteenth-century travelers and present-day scholars, have argued that the term *black* was synonymous with *slave*, and that ex-slaves would self-identify as *pardos* to escape the stigma of the "black" label.[62] Nevertheless, the rosary brotherhoods were brotherhoods of blacks (*dos pretos*), yet they were not exclusively slave. On the contrary, many members of the brotherhoods of blacks were free, yet they willingly participated and often took leadership positions in brotherhoods of blacks. Why, then, did people willingly and enthusiastically become members of an organization already stigmatized in its title "of the blacks?" On a social level, "of the blacks" referred to the larger brotherhood structure in the society against which the rosary brotherhoods created an identity. The nonwhite status of the brotherhood pertained not only to the skin color of the members but also to economic status, which bundles the term *black* with an issue of class. Finally, *black* referred to the cultural practices within the brotherhoods, which often included the coronation of kings and queens, dances to the drums of the nations, and other surface manifestations that echoed and remembered an African past.

The social space of the brotherhood, which helped to define difference with the larger community, needed to be contained within a physical space, and the soaring physical space of the baroque brotherhood churches became a tangible and powerful symbol of the rosary brotherhood members' existence as a community. Often, and especially when they were first founded, the black brotherhoods would reside within the *matriz*, or main church of the parish, as was the case in Cachoeira do Campo. When they could afford to, brotherhoods built their own chapels or churches. To build a church, they needed to apply for and receive a license from the Crown and church authorities.[63] Whether the license was granted depended in large part on the brotherhood's having enough funds to be able to afford the large, expensive undertaking, something that was not often possible for brotherhoods of blacks. For example, the 1782 compromisso of the brotherhood of Calambao included a chapter about the graves they would have inside their new church when they built it. The proviso, written by the queen, pointed out that the brotherhood "could not construct a chapel without a license from the Queen, granted through the tribunal of the Mesa de Consciência e Ordens [Board of Conscience and

---

62. See, for instance, Henry Koster, *Travels in Brazil* (London: Longman, Hurst, Rees, Orme, and Brown, 1816), 396.

63. Boschi, *Os leigos*, 127–29.

Orders] without having established a patrimony."[64] The Mesa de Consciência e Ordens in Lisbon regulated the religious branch of the government and was directly under the control of the Portuguese Crown.

Despite the expense, brotherhoods worked hard to construct their own churches, which gave the brotherhoods autonomy from the control of the *matriz* and the parish priest, at least for the period of the eighteenth century. The churches provided a physical place that the members of the rosary brotherhoods could call their own and in which they could celebrate their masses and festivals, worship, and care for their dead. The churches housed the important belongings of the brotherhoods, including the lamps, robes, host, and saints and all the necessary items that served to express their devotion. Today, brotherhood members who still practice their devotion in colonial churches comment that although all colonial churches were built with slave labor, only the rosary churches were built voluntarily by, and for, slaves and free blacks.

The space within the churches consisted of a sanctuary with a main altar and usually at least two lateral altars. The main altar held the images of the primary saint of the organization. The space of the main altar, the choir, was divided from the main body of the church by a low balustrade, called a *grade*. The *grade* separated the altar from the body of the church. Lateral altars, which might also serve as altars of other brotherhoods, held images of additional saints who were important to the congregation of the church.[65] In Minas Gerais, the main altar of the church of the rosary brotherhood contained an image of Our Lady of the Rosary, and the lateral altars held the images of other saints who were revered by the membership, usually Saint Benedict and Saint Iphigenia. The main body of the church did not have rows of pews, as churches do today. People attended mass and other activities in the church standing, kneeling, or sitting on woven mats.[66] Behind the altar was the *con-sistório* (meeting room), where meetings of the brotherhood administration took place and which also held huge chests of drawers that contained the

64. "Compromisso de Calambao (filial de Guarapiranga), 1782," AEAM Livros das Irmandades 25, chapter 5 and proviso.

65. The rosary brotherhood in Mariana is an example of this, the lateral altars of the church holding images of the brotherhoods of St. Iphigenia and St. Benedict. Nevertheless, the brotherhoods were closely associated: the elections of the three brotherhoods were kept in the same book, they shared in the expenses of the church, and they often celebrated their festivals together. "Termos de Meza," Irmandade de Nossa Senhora do Rosário, Mariana, AEAM P27.

66. João José Reis, *A morte é uma festa, ritos fúnebres e revolta popular no Brasil do século XIX* (São Paulo: Companhia das Letras, 1991), 174–75. Interestingly, the present day chapels dedicated to Our Lady of the Rosary in Minas Gerais also do not have pews, but long benches that can be moved to the center when they are needed.

valuables of the brotherhoods. The brotherhoods that had enough funds to build and maintain their own churches spent a large portion of their funds on the maintenance of the physical structure of the church such as repairing the roof, fixing the windows so the rain would not come in, and building new towers.[67]

The physical space of the rosary churches allowed the brotherhoods to have a tangible presence in the society of Minas Gerais. Legally, rosary brotherhoods had all the rights and responsibilities of any brotherhoods in the society. One of those responsibilities was to have their compromissos approved by church or state authorities or both. Another was having their accounting books reviewed by a local authority on an annual basis.[68] Although the oversight of the books seems to be another attempt at control, in reality, in the first half of the eighteenth century, that control was considerably weakened because of heated jurisdictional battles between civil and religious authorities. Such disputes occurred because of the ambiguity in the nature of the organizations and disagreement about whether they should be seen as primarily secular or sacred. The practical side of the debate centered both on a question of control over the organizations and on the more pragmatic matter of who would collect the revenue generated by the oversight of the books of the rosary brotherhoods.

The compromissos were the first books of the brotherhoods to be reviewed by the authorities, and for the most part, in the first half of the eighteenth century, their oversight remained under the jurisdiction of the religious authorities. The *Primary Constitutions* stated that compromissos, and any subsequent changes to those documents, had to be approved by a bishop.[69] In the first half of the century, that requirement either meant sending the book to Rio de Janeiro to be approved or waiting for the ecclesiastic visits of the bishop or his representatives to the mining districts. The religious authorities considered the statutes to be within their jurisdiction because in addition to mundane considerations they included clauses on masses, care of the dead, the responsibilities of the chaplains, and the annual festival. In most cases, the formation of the brotherhood itself predated by years, and sometimes decades, the formalization of that brotherhood as signaled by the approval of the compromisso.

67. See, for instance, "Termos de Meza," Irmandade de Nossa Senhora do Rosário, Mariana, AEAM P27; "Termos de Meza," Irmandade de Nossa Senhora do Rosário da Arrial de Bacalhau, filial de Guarapiranga, AEAM Y12.

68. Boschi, *Os leigos*, 112–39.

69. *Constituições primeiras do Arcebispado da Bahia, feitas, e ordenadas . . . 12 de junho de 1707* (São Paulo: Antônio Louzada Antunes, 1853), book 4, title 60.

The annual review of the accounting books of the brotherhoods became the most hotly contested jurisdictional battle between the local secular and ecclesiastic authorities regarding the brotherhoods. Just as the *Primary Constitutions* ruled the religious life of the colony, the *Código filipino* (Philippine Code), was the main canon of secular law in the Portuguese Empire. These laws granted the Provedores das Capelas e Resíduos (Supervisors of Chapels and Testaments) the right to regulate the chantries and testaments of the people of the empire, including the books of the brotherhoods.[70] A Crown authority in the local government usually held the position of *provedor* (supervisor). For example, in the late eighteenth century in Mariana the *juiz de fora* (Crown judge) served as the *provedor,* while in Vila Rica and Sabará it was the *ouvidor* (justice of the peace).[71] The *provedor's* job as it pertained to brotherhoods was to examine their accounting books annually to make sure that the books of the brotherhoods remained in line with the rules as articulated in the compromissos and to make sure that there were no accounting irregularities.[72] Despite the secular laws, ecclesiastic authorities had assumed the responsibility of overseeing the brotherhood accounting books from the beginning of the captaincy.[73] Crown authorities tenaciously fought to wrest control of the job from them, and for the first half of the eighteenth century, the jurisdictional lines were so unclear that it is impossible to trace any kind of chronology of who oversaw the accounting books.[74]

Equally as important to the rosary brotherhoods' participation in bureaucratic matters of the society was their participation in the festive life of their towns. Often, the church authorities in the first half of the eighteenth century expressed a sympathetic view toward the slaves' plight, defending the right of the blacks to participate fully in the religious life of the colony. For example,

70. CBG, *Código filipino,* book 1, title L, 93–95.

71. "Memória Histórica da Capitania de Minas-Geraes," *RAPM* 2 (1897): 425–518. Marcos Magalhães de Aguiar points out in his master's thesis that the authorship of this account, which officially has no date or author, has been attributed (by means of paleographic evidence) to Xavier da Veiga and to have been written in 1787. Aguiar, "Vila Rica,"27 n. 25.

72. Aguiar, "Vila Rica," 166.

73. The ecclesiastic authorities did this despite successive provisos written at the end of the seventeenth and into the eighteenth century that clearly banned the right of those authorities to oversee the accounting books. Boschi, *Os leigos,* 123 n. 121.

74. As early as 1729, the *ouvidor* from the district of Rio das Mortes wrote a furious letter to the king, accusing the ecclesiastic visitors from Rio de Janeiro of charging exorbitant prices for checking the accounting books of the brotherhoods. The *ouvidor* also charged the ecclesiastic visitors with insubordination and flagrant disobedience of his, and thus the king's, orders. Boschi, *Os leigos,* 123–24. Yet just a few years later, in 1733, the *visitador* Dom Frei João da Cruz examined the accounting books of the brotherhood in Antonio Dias of Vila Rica, apparently without interference. CC Antônio Dias, rol 60, "Receitas e Despezas," 24.

the same ecclesiastic visitor who urged the black members of the rosary brotherhood in Cachoeira do Campo not to allow the whites a vote on the board (an internal matter) upheld the rights of the rosary brotherhood in Mariana to participate in the local Easter celebration in 1727.[75] That year, the Brotherhood of Senhor dos Passos in Mariana (the brotherhood responsible for the procession before Easter to several "stations" depicting the passage of Jesus to the cross) sent a petition to the same ecclesiastic visitor about not wanting to leave the statue of Jesus at the Church of the Rosary of the Blacks on the Thursday before Good Friday. The members of the brotherhood of Senhor dos Passos complained that it was out of their way to get it there, but the visitor decided in favor of the blacks.[76] Clearly, some members of the church explicitly showed sympathy for blacks who were attempting to participate in the celebratory life of the towns.

Perhaps the best known example of the rosary brotherhood participation in public celebrations from the first half of the eighteenth century was the *Triunfo Eucharístico,* the account of a sumptuous procession of 1733 in which the sacrament was carried from the rosary church of the blacks to the newly completed *matriz*. The eyewitness account described Minas Gerais at the apex of the gold boom and depicted an ostentatious procession that included allegorical floats; personages representing the sun, moon, and all the planets; and horses decked out in diamonds. The brotherhood of the rosary played a major role in the festival, its church having been chosen for the safekeeping of the sacrament. During the procession, numerous brothers of the rosary proceeded in long robes (*opas*) of white silk, with three officials in the middle carrying the statues of Saint Anthony of Catagerona, Saint Benedict, and Our Lady of the Rosary, images that were beautifully adorned "with gold and silver silks, and expensive works of gold and diamonds."[77] The choice of the rosary church to house the sacrament while the *matriz* was built demonstrates the ways in which the church attempted to include the corporations of blacks in the larger society. The participation of blacks shows that they were more than willing to enter this door into the European power structure. Through participation in the festivals, and in the economic life of the captaincy, rosary brotherhoods were able to interact with the society in which they were embedded, while the members could shape their own identity as a "black" community in Brazil.

75. "Compromisso da Irmandade . . . da Caxueira," AEAM, AA22, 7.

76. "Livro da Irmandade de Nosso Senhor dos Passos," AEAM, P23, 2.

77. Affonso Avila, *Resíduos seiscentistas em Minas: Textos do século do ouro e as projeções do mundo barroco,* vol. 1, *Triunfo Eucarístico* (Belo Horizonte, Brazil: Centro de Estudos Mineiros, 1967), 97–98.

Emergence of a New Identity in the Brotherhoods

Against the backdrop of the larger society, and certainly through the lens of history, the term *black* implies a level of homogeneity that did not exist within the rosary brotherhoods. An examination of the organization of difference in the black organizations serves as a window through which to examine how the black population defined difference within its own community. It also sheds light on a strategy of the blacks that combated the flattening effect of the European hierarchy, which placed them on the bottom, through the creation of their own hierarchies. The creation of these hierarchies also served as a transnational strategy through which a distinctly African community could be built in Brazil.

The documents left by the black members of the black brotherhoods demonstrate that one of their motivations for joining the rosary brotherhoods was to achieve a level of self-determination in their own organizations, a goal supported by some of the clergy as well. Despite their desire to create an identity distinct from that of the whites, black brotherhoods had to include rules in their compromissos that called for some number of the officers to be white. Scholars have considered the presence of white officers in the brotherhoods to have been a mechanism of control over the brotherhoods.[78] The tradition of having at least one white officer began in the black brotherhoods in Portugal, and it has been generally accepted that white officers were necessary for brotherhoods in which the vast majority of members could not read or write. In Brazil, it was often masters of some of the slave members who became officers of the brotherhoods. Although scholars have suggested that the masters wanted to serve as officers in the brotherhoods of the blacks to maintain power over their slaves, it also cannot be assumed that their motivations stemmed only from this desire.[79] The impulse to participate in the brotherhood may have emerged from a feeling of noblesse oblige, or from a paternalistic understanding that slaves were part of an extended household, albeit households structured in line with the harsh power relationships of the time. However, because many Africans came from systems in which power was understood through local patron-client relationships,

78. Both Julita Scarano and Caio César Boschi view the presence of white officers as a form of social control. Scarano questions the motives of the white members and ends up concluding that these white officers took away much of the independence of the blacks. Boschi agrees with Scarano and goes on to state even more strongly that the presence of the white officers demonstrates an ideological domination to which the blacks were subject. Scarano, *Devoção e escravidão*, 130–31; Boschi, *Os leigos*, 138–39.

79. Scarano, *Devoção e escravidão*, 131.

blacks in the rosary brotherhoods may have sought the protection of whites who they knew to be sympathetic to and friends with blacks.[80] These whites would have helped the blacks with the legal requirements that tied the brotherhood structure to the larger political and economic structure of the captaincy.

Although the impetus for allowing whites to participate in the administrative functions of the brotherhoods cannot be known with certainty, when whites did participate in the brotherhoods, blacks found ways to curb their power, through mechanisms that were delineated in the statutes and subsequently approved by the church and state authorities. The compromisso from the brotherhood in Serro, for example, did not specify color in the positions of treasurer, secretary, and procurator, but it did insist that the judges who voted for these positions be black.[81] In Campos dos Carijós, where the black members had been expelled from the white brotherhood, the compromisso simply stated that the brotherhood would have a secretary and a treasurer who had to be white, while later stating that they would never be subject to a white brotherhood.[82] The brotherhood in Antonio Dias, which had also split from the whites, declared in its statutes that "the Treasurer, Secretary, and Reverend Chaplain who are elected by the board . . . can vote, agreeing with the black members in everything that is just and reasonable."[83] The compromisso of the brotherhood in Ouro Preto stated that the white brothers would be members of the brotherhoods during their term and could enjoy all of the benefits but that they would only have a vote on the board when they served in those offices. The brotherhood was not obliged to accompany the burial of the wives or children of these officers unless their relatives were members. If the children of the white officers married one of the black brothers or sisters, however, they would be buried by the brotherhood, but the brotherhood would not be obliged to say masses for their souls.[84] These examples suggest that the whites' role in the brotherhoods was

80. Miller, "Central Africa," 42.

81. *Compromisso da Irmandade . . . da Villa do Príncipe*, 2.

82. "Compromisso dos Pretos devotos de N. Senhora do Rosário da freguesia do Campo dos Carijós pará se governarem por eles, 1743," APM SP 959-1743.

83. "Compromisso da Irmandade de NS do Rozario dos Pretos denominada do Alto da Cruz da Freg.ª de Nossa Senhora da Conceição de Antonio Dias de V.ª Rica do Ouro Preto, CC Paróquia de Nossa Senhora da Conceição," rol 058, doc. 123–24, chapter 22. Donald Ramos discusses several more examples of the blacks curbing the power of the whites in rosary brotherhoods in "A influência africana," 156–57.

84. Augusto de Lima Júnior, *História de Nossa Senhora em Minas Gerais* (Belo Horizonte, Brazil: Imprensa Oficial, 1956), 60.

more complex than that of simply "having power" over the brotherhoods, and that blacks had a say in shaping the terms of that relationship.

The relationship between whites and blacks in the brotherhoods should not be allowed to overshadow the vast differences compressed into the term *black*. That blacks and whites participated in the same organization is worthy of discussion, but even more remarkable is that such a varied population of "blacks" were able to come together to make a new community. Not only were there divergences in backgrounds, with all the variations in worldviews, language, and custom, but the population was diverse in terms of legal status and gender as well. The scope of the differences in the brotherhood membership can be gleaned from the registration books for new members. When new members joined the brotherhoods, the secretary entered their names into a registration book (*livro de entradas*) with whatever data he considered pertinent. The secretary then signed the book and the new members would either sign (less common in the eighteenth century) or they would make their mark, the sign of the cross. The intricate designs on many of the crosses attest to an expression of individuality and pride among this population. Some slaves, however, even in the eighteenth century, learned to write, and on rare occasions slaves would sign their names in the entrance books—one of the only sources historians have that demonstrate at least some level of slave literacy. For example, in Mariana, one slave member of the rosary brotherhood, João Mina, in 1762 "corrected" his earlier entrance by signing his name where before he had only made the sign of the cross. The corrected entry read "Clearly this brother corrects his entrance, signing his name today because he knows how to write."[85]

All secretaries of the rosary brotherhoods entered the names of the members, whether they were slave, freed (*forro*), or free, and if slave, the name of the master. Racially, the categories "slave" and "freed" implied black or *pardo* or mulatto in same cases, but never white. The members who were listed as free could be black, *pardo*, or white, and unfortunately the documents offer few clues on the color of the free members. In the case of the free members, they often appeared in positions restricted to blacks, such as the position of king. For this reason, and because of the significant population of free people of color in colonial Minas Gerais, it can be assumed that many free members listed in the entrance books without a racial signifier were nonwhite. In the second half of the eighteenth century, secretaries also entered the African ethnicity or whether new members were *crioulo*, where they lived, and to whom in the brotherhood they were related.

85. "Entradas de Irmãos," Mariana, 26 December 1762, AEAM P28.

The registration book from the rosary brotherhood in Ouro Preto, which listed membership entrances from 1724 to 1760, was designed in such a way as to suggest that "households" of slaves joined the brotherhoods together, often all on the same day. There, the secretary listed the slave members under their masters' names. This was the only book I encountered in which the secretary entered the new members in this way. Over the period the book covered, more than 80 percent of the membership was slave, with more than a third of the free population identified as freed.[86] After the slaves from a given household were entered, the secretary left a space in which the names of slaves purchased later by the same master could be entered. The masters themselves were predominantly white and male, but all the brotherhoods also included masters who were women and who were *forros* or *pardos*. Some of the masters served as one of the white officers in the brotherhoods. Other masters, especially those who themselves were *forros*, also became members. For example, Catarina de Senna, a *forra*, became a member in 1732, along with her two slaves, Luiza and Mariana. That same year Antonio dos Santos (no race given) joined the brotherhood with his spouse (*mulher*), Micaela de Matos, a *preta forra*, and her slave, Antonio Barbosa.[87]

Most rosary brotherhoods had a smaller slave membership than that of Ouro Preto. The registration list for Cachoeira do Campo, which also began in 1724, showed the slave membership to be the majority for the first six years. After 1730, however, the slaves were never again the majority membership, and in the following decades their population in the brotherhood never went above 50 percent.[88] Unfortunately, the secretary did not indicate the race of the free population, yet if the population of Cachoeira do Campo followed the pattern of Minas Gerais in general, then a large part of the free population was nonwhite. The brotherhood never grew enough in importance in the community to be able to build its own chapel. Instead, it remained at a lateral altar in the *matriz*, Our Lady of Nazareth. In contrast, the brotherhood in Ouro Preto grew to be very important in its community, building its own church in the early eighteenth century and participating in important capacities in public festivals such as the ostentatious Triunfo Eucarístico.[89]

86. See the Appendix, Table 7.
87. "Entradas de Irmãos," Irmandade de Nossa Senhora do Rosário, Ouro Preto 1724–1760, CC Paróquia de Pilar, rol 81.
88. "Entradas de Irmãos," Cachoeira do Campo, AEAM AA25 and AA26. See the Appendix, Table 6.
89. Brotherhoods of the rosary, considered slave brotherhoods, were often more well off than the brotherhoods exclusively for free blacks and *pardos*. See Aguiar, "Vila Rica."

In many of the brotherhoods during this early period, *forro* members constituted a significant segment of the membership. The members of most of the rosary brotherhoods in Minas Gerais did not include clauses in their statutes that discussed the collection of alms to help to free slave members as the early Lisbon rosary brotherhood had done.[90] One exception was the 1728 compromisso from Vila do Príncipe, however, which specifically indicated that the members who had freed themselves through their own hard work could receive aid in food and clothing from the brotherhood. The document stated immediately after this, in an obtusely worded phrase, that any members who managed to escape and thus free themselves from a cruel master would receive the same sort of aid.[91] Other compromissos did not include this clause; nor is there evidence that brotherhoods used their funds to actively free members, although there were many members who were freed, some during the years of their membership.[92] The extant colonial registration book from São João del Rei, for example, had been copied from an earlier book and indicated that some members had been slaves at the time of their entrance but had subsequently been manumitted. The 1747 entry for Josefa Teixeira identified her as the slave of Maria Teixeira, but the margin note claimed that "today [she] is free." Similarly, Felipe Tavares de Silva had been originally listed as the slave of Josefa Nunes de Carvalho, but by the time of the entry in the new book, in 1757, she was free.[93]

Rosary brotherhoods were open to men and women, and both "brothers" and "sisters," as the members were called, could serve on the ruling boards as judges and as kings or queens, the highest celebratory positions in the brotherhood. The women participated equally in paying their dues in the brotherhoods and received equal benefits from the brotherhoods upon their deaths. This, however, did not mean that the brotherhoods were egalitarian in gender terms. Demographically, men usually joined the brotherhoods in larger numbers than did the women, even after the ratio of men to women

90. See "Compromisso of the Brotherhood of Our Lady of the Rosary of Black Men," chapter 7, in Mulvey, "Black Lay Brotherhoods," 261.

91. *Compromisso da Irmandade . . . da Villa do Príncipe*, 4.

92. The conde de Assumar, in a letter to the king, Dom João V, suggested that the practice of freeing slaves in the captaincy should be stopped because it caused such great disorder. Nevertheless, the practice continued to be quite common in Minas Gerais, especially after the decline of the gold production. Letter from the conde de Assumar to the king, Dom João V, 28 November 1719, APM SC 04, 742.

93. This occurred in twelve entries in São João del Rei between 1747 and 1770. "Entradas de Irmãos," Irmandade de Nossa Senhora do Rosário dos Pretos, São João del Rei, 1747–1806, AINSR.

evened out in the second half of the eighteenth century.[94] Also, the women, after they had made their marks in the entrance books, never signed any of the other documents of the brotherhoods, not even with their marks, though some of the minutes of the meetings record having female judges and occasionally the queen present. The offices of the brotherhoods—the secretary, treasurer, and procurators—were never open to women. Whatever the gender roles had been in the African traditional societies, the men in the brotherhoods took the leadership roles within the administration, following the Portuguese patriarchal model.[95]

For the first half of the eighteenth century, there are few clues to the origins of the slaves and free blacks in the rosary brotherhood membership. One sign that the membership might have been diverse can be seen in the compromissos themselves, which did not restrict brotherhood membership to one or another ethnicity, as did many rosary brotherhoods in cities on the coast, such as those in Recife, Salvador, and Rio de Janeiro. The registration book from the rosary brotherhood in Mariana offers some information about the ethnicity of the slaves in the brotherhoods. That book began in 1754 and listed not only the members who joined that year but all the current members who had joined in previous years. In that year the secretary listed the ethnicity of 85 percent of the membership, and that divided between the Atlantic Islands, Brazil, Central Africa, and West Africa. By far, the largest percentage of those listed were West African, 62 percent of the total. The next largest groups were the Central Africans, Brazilians, and Atlantic Islanders. Even within this group many different discrete ethnicities were listed. The high percentage of West Africans, the majority of whom were identified as "Mina," agrees with the numbers within the general population in the first half of the eighteenth century. The high percentage also differs from the rosary brotherhoods on the coast, which often had memberships restricted

94. In the entrance books that I used men always outnumbered women; see, for example, the Appendix, Tables 4 and 5. Marcos Magalhães de Aguiar found that an exception was the rosary brotherhood in Ouro Preto, in which women outnumbered men in the second half of the eighteenth century. Aguiar, "Vila Rica," 319–25. For gender ratios in general, Donald Ramos gives the example of the slave male and female ratios through the eighteenth century in Vila Rica, showing that they evened out dramatically in those years. D. Ramos, "Community, Control, and Acculturation," 23. More recently, in an essay on the demographics of slavery in Mariana, Laird W. Bergad also confirms the decline in the gender ratio between 1750 and 1808. Laird W. Bergad, "After the Mining Boom: Demographic and Economic Aspects of Slavery in Mariana, Minas Gerais, 1750–1808," *LARR* 31, no. 1 (1996): 75–85.

95. That is not to say that the women may not have played extremely important roles in the spiritual health of the brotherhoods, as they do today, but unfortunately, this is impossible to trace in the documentary record.

to Angolas and *crioulos*. Although in the following decades the populations in the rosary brotherhoods would become increasingly Central African and Brazilian, there can be no doubt that West Africans played a role in the formation of these brotherhoods and joined together with blacks from other regions to form the communities.

The brotherhood population represented a diverse group that gathered together to worship, celebrate, and mourn and to take care of the rituals of death. In these communities they established new affective ties with one another using kinship metaphors. In the broadest sense the brotherhood provided a fictive kin system, in which the members became brothers and sisters. In addition, family membership was not uncommon for slave, free, and freed members. Often the name of a woman was followed by "mulher de" (woman of) and then the name of one of the brothers, or a new member was listed as the daughter or son of someone in the brotherhood.[96] The books also listed many of the free and freed members as living in the house of someone, or as *agregado* (a non-related household member) in someone's household, and even occasionally as *exposto* (foundling).

Once a person became a member of a brotherhood, he or she was responsible for paying an entrance fee and subsequent annual dues. The member elected to be a judge or a king or queen would have the added responsibility of making a very high payment; in the early eighteenth century that charge was often as high as twenty *oitavas* (drams) of gold. The registration books listed whether the new members paid their entrance fees, and occasionally, if they did not, a marginal note declared the entrance void because the member could not pay. Scholars examining the brotherhoods have often wondered where the members got the money to pay for the entrance fee, the annual dues, and the extremely high payment due if that person was elected to be a judge, or the king or queen. The secretaries of the brotherhoods rarely recorded the masters' paying any of the fees for their slaves. The slaves may have got their fees through their own work. In Minas Gerais in the eighteenth century, many slaves worked for a daily wage, only part of which they turned over to their master. The slave members of the brotherhoods would then have had this money at their disposal to donate to the brotherhood. The free and freed blacks would have had an even harder time in a world in which they had to feed and shelter themselves, and studies comparing rosary

---

96. The phrase *mulher de* often indicates "wife of" someone, but not necessarily in the sense of being legally married. For the slave and free black population, it might often have meant simply a "living together" arrangement, constituting relationships that were extremely common in colonial Minas Gerais.

brotherhoods to brotherhoods with exclusively nonslave membership have demonstrated that rosary brotherhoods usually did better financially.[97]

The accounting books of the brotherhoods give some clues to the money's origins. The books from 1726 and 1727 in Cachoeira do Campo show that some of the members paid their dues through a barter system. Two members, for instance, paid by donating several pounds of beans; another offered the money that he earned in the raffle of a slave; and others paid by donating eggs and chickens.[98] In other brotherhoods later in the eighteenth century, some members would pay for a sermon, others would donate wax for the festivals, or would work off their entrance fee by doing repairs on the church. A popular legend in Minas Gerais today tells how the blacks mining for gold would surreptitiously hide gold dust, and even nuggets of gold, in their hair. When they got to the church of the rosary, they rinsed their hair in the baptismal font and the gold fell out into the water.[99] However the blacks got their money, there can be no doubt that they were often successful in raising funds, for the churches of those rosary brotherhoods that had churches were decorated in the golden splendor of the Brazilian baroque.

The conscious separation of blacks into their own brotherhoods and the limitation of power of the white officers attest to the beginning of new communities with their own identities within rosary brotherhoods. The question arises of why Africans from many different ethnicities; Brazilian-born blacks, free and slave; and men and women joined together in this organization "of the blacks." In fact, the nonwhite status of the members, and the devotion to Our Lady of the Rosary became the significant commonalties in the communities forming within the rosary brotherhoods. Our Lady of the Rosary herself acted as a cross-cultural symbol in the brotherhoods, as discussed in the previous chapter. Our Lady of the Rosary became an appealing intercessor for the Africans and recent descendants of Africans in Brazil.[100] The rosary brotherhoods, however, were not passive receptacles in which identity formed simply as a result of contact between different peoples and cultures. On the contrary, they were a site, social and physical, in which the rosary membership *worked*, by means of rituals and narrative, to create community.

97. Aguiar, "Vila Rica."

98. After 1730 these types of payments, or at least the recording of them in this manner, did not continue. "Livro de receitas e despezas," Irmandade de Nossa Senhora do Rosário de Cachoeira do Campo, 1724, AEAM AA23, 6v-7.

99. This legend also serves to demonstrate the positive images of blacks that are expressed through the legends associated with Our Lady of the Rosary, this one countering the often negative feelings about certain types of hair.

100. See Elizabeth W. Kiddy, "*Congados, Calunga, Candombe:* Our Lady of the Rosary in Minas Gerais, Brazil," *Luso-Brazilian Review* 37, no. 1 (2000): 47–61.

The Work of the Brotherhoods

The work of the brotherhoods was expressed most vividly in the two rituals that most commonly brought the community together; the annual feast day celebrations and the rituals of death. These occasions, one joyous and the other sad, presented opportunities for the community to gather together and tend to their links with the unseen world. The expression inherent in both rituals provided opportunities for multiple interpretations and understandings of the way the world functioned, creating a space in which an African-based community could draw on cultural elements in ways that made them able to nurture their links to their common past, ancestors, and spirits.

Each lay religious brotherhood put on an annual feast day celebration, and the communities competed to see which would have the most extravagant festival.[101] The festivals included religious observances as well as lavish processions in which all the brotherhoods of the town would participate. The event of the election and coronation of the black kings and queens, the reinados of the brotherhoods, was a cornerstone of the annual feast day celebration of Our Lady of the Rosary throughout Brazil. The annually elected kings and queens played an important financial role within the rosary brotherhoods. As in the first half of the century, they paid the highest contribution in the brotherhoods, funds that went toward financing the annual festival.[102] In compromissos from the first half of the eighteenth century, the ecclesiastical visitors instructed the brotherhood not to use the money from the annual dues for the festival; instead, they should use the contributions of the king and queen. The ecclesiastical visitor to Cachoeira do Campo suggested that to raise money for the annual feast day celebration the members would not have to spend from the alms they had collected or spend from the annual dues paid by the brothers. Instead, because it was the custom to "also have judges, and stewards, king and queen, it is possible to have the festival without spending from the brotherhood, attending more to the service of God than to your merriment."[103] The same visitor wrote a proviso in the accounting book from Antonio Dias in Vila Rica (Alto da Cruz) prohibiting the use of the annual dues for the celebration of the festival.[104] The provisos

101. Bruneau, *Political Transformation,* 18.

102. The kings and queens of most festivals today are responsible for paying for the lunches served to all the participants and visiting guests, which can mean feeding up to five hundred people. In other festivals the people in those positions are responsible for making a large donation to the association that runs the festival.

103. "Compromisso da Irmandade . . . da Caxueira," AEAM AA22, 8.

104. "Receitas e Despesas," Irmandade de Nossa Senhora do Rosário de Alto da Cruz, CC Paróquia de Antônio Dias, rol 60, 24.

written later in the eighteenth century did not include this prohibition, but the tradition that the annual king and queen sponsor the yearly festival has continued until today.

Although the evidence demonstrates that the brotherhoods elected and crowned kings and queens, for the first half of the eighteenth century no descriptive accounts exist of these festivals in Minas Gerais. In Salvador, Bahia, blacks also crowned kings and queens during the rosary feast day celebrations. In 1729 a proclamation was published in Bahia "about the Reinado of the Blacks and their pastimes" stating that "in this city there have been introduced many abuses, not only scandalous and pernicious in respect to the service of God, but harmful to the public peace and being the principal of these the Reinados of the blacks, who in order to do the act with grandeur rob even their own altars."[105] The proclamation stated that from that day forward the Reinado would have no function and that the festival of the rosary would go on only inside the church of the rosary. This description links the reinados to the annual feast day celebration and is interesting for the history of Minas Gerais because of the large number of black slaves who were transported to the mines from Bahia and its hinterlands. Blacks already familiar with the celebrations may have carried the Bahian traditions to Minas Gerais. In Minas Gerais, the compromissos and accounting books in the first half of the century usually only referred to the religious requirements of the festival, a Te Deum, a sung mass, music, and a sermon if the brotherhood had enough funds. It would not be until the second half of the eighteenth century and the end of the colonial period that descriptions of these festivals would emerge in the documentary record.

Another important ritual obligation, and an important part of the reconstruction of communities, was the necessity to take care of the dead and the souls of the dead. The proper care of the dead, and the rituals for their souls after death, were one of the main preoccupations of the brotherhood members, and in the compromissos often several chapters were taken up by explanations of how and where burials were to take place and how many masses would be celebrated for the dead. In addition to conducting these masses at the time of death, the brotherhoods engaged in masses for the dead throughout the year, on an either weekly or monthly basis, depending on the financial status of the brotherhood. The money paid for these masses was one of the major expenses of the brotherhoods, yet providing it was also one of its most important functions. The high fees paid by officeholders—the judges and kings and queens—not only helped to support the brotherhood

105. Quoted in Mulvey, "Black Lay Brotherhoods," 115 n. 27.

but also assured the officeholders that they would receive more masses for their souls after their deaths, thus speeding their entrance into heaven.[106] The brotherhoods' conceptions of death and of the care of the soul after death played a huge role in the lives of the eighteenth-century *mineiros*. Through the celebration of masses the dead were not only helped in the other world but were also remembered through rituals, and thus remained part of the community of the living.

Visitors to Minas Gerais rarely commented on the funerals of the blacks. However, one, the visiting bishop Antonio de Guadalupe, wrote in 1726 that slaves "got together at night singing and playing instruments for their dead, getting together in stores where they bought various food and drinks, which after they ate they threw into the grave."[107] This reference did not mention the brotherhoods of the rosary, yet it shows the perception of Europeans toward certain practices of Africans having to do with death. Members of the brotherhoods did attempt to control the burials of their members. For instance, traditionally throughout Brazil, the brotherhoods of the Santas Casas de Misericórdia (Holy Houses of Mercy) were the keepers of the funeral biers.[108] In Minas Gerais, however, most brotherhoods possessed their own bier and used it without any interference from the elite Santas Casas.[109] Even the very early brotherhood of the rosary in Vila do Príncipe, with a compromisso from 1728, stated that they had their own funeral bier.[110]

Rosary brotherhoods were also concerned with having their own graves within the churches. The rosary brotherhood in Cachoeira, for example, occupied a lateral altar in the *matriz* dedicated to Our Lady of Nazareth. In their early compromisso, the brotherhood wrote that they had six *sepulturas* (graves), in the Church of Nazareth, for the members.[111] Nevertheless, in 1738, these graves were still in dispute, but by a proviso written that year the brotherhood was given six graves within the church, provided that the brotherhood honored their responsibility to participate in the upkeep of the church. The local priest assigned specific grave numbers to the members (1, 3, 14, 15, 24, and 25), for the burial of the brothers and sisters of the rosary. In 1758 the question of graves came up again—they asked for and received

106. See "Livro do Compromisso da Irmandade de Nossa Senhora do Rosário dos pretos da freguesia de São Caetano (Monsenhor Horta)," 1762, AEAM Livros das Irmandades 22, Chapter 13.

107. Dom Antônio de Guadalupe quoted in Reis, *A morte é uma festa*, 160.

108. A. J. R. Russell-Wood, *Fidalgos and Philanthropists: The Santa Casa da Misericórdia of Bahia, 1550–1755* (Berkeley and Los Angeles: University of California Press, 1968), 201.

109. Aguiar, "Vila Rica," 228–29.

110. *Compromisso da Irmandade . . . da Villa do Príncipe*, chapter 3.

111. "Compromisso da Irmandade . . . da Caxueira," AEAM AA22, 8.

eight graves within the *matriz*, for which they agreed to pay two *oitavas* of gold annually for the upkeep of the *matriz*.[112]

The placement of the corpses in the church floor may have represented several different things to the African members of the rosary brotherhood. On the one hand, it recalled the custom of burying members of the family within the family compound, as practiced in parts of West Africa.[113] For the Central Africans, who buried their dead far from the family homes, it may have represented the conflation of the church (the main ritual area of the brotherhoods) with the cemetery, the place where the veil between the two worlds was thinnest and most permeable.[114] Both these understandings of the placement of the dead would have had multiple meanings in the brotherhoods' membership. Both understandings would have also led to the comforting conclusion that the bodies and souls of the dead were being properly cared for so that they could become, in later years, the ancestors—the *pretos velhos*—who would help to tie the brotherhood membership to their remembered African past.

In the first half of the eighteenth century, the chaotic years of the gold rush in Minas Gerais, brotherhoods of the rosary of the blacks began to be formed to serve the needs of the "black" population of Minas Gerais. Within the organizations, the diverse membership worked together to create a new community within the structure that they inherited from the Portuguese. They reconstructed that world by creating hierarchies within their own populations as well as establishing affective ties with one another. They built patron-client relationships with whites while also attempting to carefully maintain a certain level of autonomy. Finally, the members of the rosary brotherhoods engaged in rituals that drew them together as a community and linked them with the larger society of Minas Gerais.

Conclusion

During the first half of the eighteenth century, rosary brotherhoods, like all brotherhoods, helped to shape the religious life of Minas Gerais while remaining fairly autonomous from the official, Portuguese, church. This period coincided with the time that the majority of the membership would have been closer to their African past. This meant that they brought with

---

112. "Inventários e Posse," Cachoeira do Campo, AEAM AA25, 1–7.
113. Barbot, *Barbot on Guinea*, 640; Falen, "Benin's Vodun."
114. Cavazzi de Montecúccolo, *Descrição histórica*, 124–33; Hilton, *Kingdom of Kongo*, 10–11; MacGaffey quoted in Karasch, *Slave Life*, 247–48 n. 101.

them into the brotherhoods their conceptions of death and the community and of the relationship between the living and the dead and the unseen world. The second half of the eighteenth century and the end of the colonial period would bring increased church/state control over the brotherhoods, at the same time that rosary brotherhood membership became increasingly Brazilian born. Yet patterns of ritual and tradition had already been uniquely crafted inside the rosary brotherhoods in the formative period of the mining districts of Minas Gerais. In addition, the general population became accustomed to the practices of the rosary brotherhoods and incorporated the rosary groups into their own festivities. Officials were content to have the nonwhites in their own brotherhoods while they could work out the bigger questions of running the mines and getting rich. Records of festivals throughout the nineteenth and twentieth centuries have documented the existence of an ongoing mixture of "folk" Catholicism with African traditional worldviews within rosary brotherhoods. The groundwork of the mixture lay on the foundation that was established in the first half of the eighteenth century, during the wild and formative frontier days of Minas Gerais.

4   THE LATE COLONIAL PERIOD, 1750–1822

O marinheiro é hora,
É hora de curimar [trabalhar]
Eiá, eiá, eiá,
Menino de Angola, eiá

[Oh sailor it's time,
It's time to work,
Eiá, eiá, eiá,
Child of Angola, eiá.]

—Mozambique of Our Lady of Mercies as they
proceed through Oliveira

In 1745 the Portuguese king established a new diocese in Minas Gerais that had its seat in Mariana, which was raised to the status of the first city in the captaincy.[1] The new bishop, Dom Frei Manoel da Cruz, arrived in Minas Gerais in 1748 in a joyous celebration described by an anonymous author in the *Aureo trono episcopal* (The golden episcopal throne). The celebration, opulent in the same manner as was described in the 1733 *Triunfo Eucharistico*, shows a society heady with wealth on the eve of its decline. The arrival of the new bishop heralded a new period for the brotherhoods, not so much because of the actions of the bishop himself but because of changes in Minas Gerais and the Portuguese Empire in general. The middle part of the eighteenth century represented many things—a downturn in the mining economy and the concurrent changes in the demographic makeup of Minas Gerais, the rise in power of the marquis de Pombal in Portugal and his efforts at centralizing

1. The diocese in Mariana, however, served only the central mining region of Minas Gerais. The northern portions of the state remained under the control of the dioceses of Bahia and Olinda (in the state of Pernambuco) established in the sixteenth and seventeenth centuries, respectively. The southern areas of Minas Gerais came under the jurisdiction of the diocese of São Paulo, established in 1746. Monsenhor Paulo Florêncio da Silveira Camargo, *História eclesiástica do Brasil* (Petrópolis: Editora Vozes Limitada, 1955), 397–410.

power and authority in Lisbon; and the increased desire in the captaincy of Minas Gerais to bring the brotherhoods in general, and the rosary brotherhoods in particular, under tighter control. After 1808, when the Portuguese court fled Lisbon for Rio de Janeiro, this more rigid oversight would be orchestrated by the government there. By the end of the colonial period, the church would try to assert more control by regulating more closely the collection of alms and insisting on the payment of the tax on graves within the churches. More important, by the end of the colonial period the parish priests would demand and receive more control over the brotherhoods.

After having developed their organizations in the relatively chaotic atmosphere of the gold rush in Minas Gerais, the members of the rosary brotherhoods reacted in many different ways to the desire of the authorities to have more control. Their primary strategy was to carry on as best they could in the independent manner that had been established in the first half of the eighteenth century. The brotherhood members were able to engage in strategies that James C. Scott so aptly calls "weapons of the weak" in order to keep alive the practices that defined and created their community.[2] They often simply ignored the requests of the authorities to see their books, they used the courts when possible to address problems, and they carried on with their festivals and coronations despite prohibitions against them. In many cases, local townspeople supported these efforts by the rosary brotherhoods to maintain their traditions, demonstrating that the local population had begun to, at least in part, identify the culture within the rosary brotherhoods as an integral part of the culture of Minas Gerais. Although practices within the brotherhoods changed as the internal demographic and the relationship to authorities developed through time, in this period the practices within the rosary festivals emerged as recognizable predecessors to the rosary festivals today. At the same time, members of the rosary brotherhoods continued to assert their reformulated identity as "blacks," even as increasing numbers were free and freed. That black identity continued to be linked to the active maintenance of what was becoming a shared memory of an African past.

Brotherhoods and the Authorities

At the same time that the new bishop was appointed to and arriving in Minas Gerais, changes were occurring in Portugal that would affect the church in

---

2. James C. Scott, *Weapons of the Weak: Everyday Forms of Peasant Resistance* (New Haven: Yale University Press, 1985), xv–xvii.

Minas Gerais even more greatly. Dom José I (1750–77) rose to the throne in 1750, bringing into power his autocratic minister the marquis de Pombal (Sebastião José de Carvalho e Melo). Through a series of reforms, known as the Pombaline reforms, Portugal centralized the power of its far-flung empire in Lisbon.[3] The Pombaline reforms had their largest impact on the economic structure in Brazil, but Pombal's zeal to centralize power also affected the relationship between church and state. After expelling the Jesuits from Portugal and Brazil in 1759, Pombal evicted the Núncio (the papal ambassador) from Portugal and severed relations with the Vatican. For ten years the church in both Portugal and its colonies was completely national. Relations with the Vatican were reestablished in 1770, but Pombal's attack on the church in Portugal weakened the church in Brazil.[4]

Pombal also introduced reforms to the brotherhoods that reflected his desire to centralize the power of the state over the brotherhoods. For instance, in 1765 Pombal ordered all the compromissos (even those that had previously been approved) to be sent to Lisbon to be reviewed by the Mesa de Consciência e Ordens. Other measures included the abolition of the requirements of some brotherhoods to prove the "purity" of their bloodline, the reduction of the dues of the judges and other board members, and, most important for the brotherhoods of the rosary, a prohibition on the annual coronation of kings and queens in the black brotherhoods.[5] These reforms brought the brotherhoods under increased scrutiny by the Crown and continued even after the death of Dom José I and Pombal's ouster in 1777.

The Mesa de Consciência e Ordens, as best it could, strictly upheld the requirement that the brotherhoods send their compromissos to Lisbon. The compromisso from Cachoeira do Campo, for example, included a proviso from 1780 in which the *Mesa* scolded the members of the brotherhood for having had their compromisso approved only by a high official of the church in Minas Gerais. The *Mesa*, however, placed the blame on the "incompetent" church official for not knowing his jurisdiction.[6] Nevertheless, sending the books to Portugal could prove to be a lengthy, and sometimes futile, process. The documents could easily be lost during the long journey, as was the case for the rosary brotherhood in Mariana; noted in its minutes in 1769 was the

3. For an overview of the Pombaline reforms, especially their economic aspects, see Kenneth R. Maxwell, "Pombal and the Nationalization of the Luso-Brazilian Economy" HAHR 48 (November 1968): 608–31.

4. Bruneau, *Political Transformation*, 20.

5. Boschi, *Os leigos*, 121–22.

6. "Compromisso da Irmandade . . . da Caxueira," AEAM, AA22, 10.

brotherhood's intent to write a new compromisso to send to Portugal because the one that had already been sent had never been returned.[7]

On the local level, the oversight of the brotherhood books increasingly became a concern of officials, who continued to squabble over jurisdiction. As soon as the new bishop, Dom Frei Manuel da Cruz, arrived in Mariana he became embroiled in these jurisdictional fights. The ouvidor of Vila Rica, Caetano da Costa Matoso, accused the bishop of charging excessively for the oversight of the accounting books of the brotherhoods, of keeping the fees for his personal use, and not giving alms to the poor.[8] As a result of this dispute, by the 1760s accounting books were being examined almost exclusively by secular authorities, and in 1802 the bishops' jurisdiction legally came to an end.[9]

The actual control over the brotherhoods by state officials who were overseeing the brotherhood books, however, should not be overstated. Many of the rosary brotherhoods did not bring their accounting books in to be checked every year, and sometimes five or more years would go by without their being examined by the authorities.[10] In other cases brotherhoods of the rosary would ignore what the authorities told them when they did take their books to be checked. Tomás Antonio Gonzaga, the ouvidor geral and himself a member of a rosary brotherhood of blacks (and famous mineiro poet and participant in the 1789 rebellion against the Crown) found that in one brotherhood of the rosary in Santo Antonio de Itatiaia there was no proper book of receipts in 1782.[11] Despite his irritated entries in their accounting books in which he accused the brotherhood of ignoring his provisos, they continued to disregard his orders for another two years. Apparently, the brotherhood never did start a book of receipts, because in 1788, the next ouvidor also scolded the brotherhood for ignoring the order, calling their lack of obedience "rebelliousness" and "obstinacy." He threatened to suspend the secretary of the brotherhood from his office if he did not fulfill the

7. "Termos de Meza," Mariana, 16 April 1769, AEAM P27, 43v.

8. "Minuta de parecer do ouvidor da comarca de Vila Rica Caetano da Costa Matoso sobre rendimentos do bispado de Mariana," Códice Costa Matoso (Belo Horizonte, Brazil: Fundação João Pinheiro, 1999), 737–42.

9. Aguiar, "Vila Rica," 157–64 and Trindade, Arquidiocese, 120–22, 173. See also Boschi, Os leigos, 115–25.

10. "Livro de Receitas e Despezas," Irmandade de Nossa Senhora do Rosário, São João del Rei 1803–1825, AINSR.

11. Tomás Antonio Gonzaga, along with fellow inconfidente (participant in the 1789 uprising against the Portuguese Crown) Cláudio Manuel da Costa were both members of the rosary brotherhood of blacks in Antonio Dias (Alto da Cruz). D. Ramos, "A influência africana," 158.

proviso.[12] Punitive measures were often threatened, as witnessed in the brotherhood of the rosary in the Arraial de Bacalhau, in the outlying districts of Mariana. There, the *provedor* wrote a proviso ordering the treasurers who had served up until then (1798) to bring the books within three days under threat of prison sentences.[13] In Cachoeira do Campo, the *provedor* told the ruling board in 1788 that they had ten days to turn in the accounting books covering the period from 1777 to 1788 for him to review.[14] Clearly, the authorities, when not arguing among themselves, tried to get the brotherhoods to comply with their orders, but continuing complaints suggest that they were often unsuccessful.

In the late eighteenth century, however, the most pressing concern of the ecclesiastic authorities was not the jurisdiction over the oversight of the brotherhood books but the deepening struggle between the parish priests and the chaplains hired by the individual brotherhoods. Foundational historian of the Brazilian Catholic church Eduardo Hoornaert posited that the increasing romanization of the church in Brazil, which would reach its apex in the late nineteenth century, could be traced by following the increasing power of the parish priests within the brotherhoods.[15] Yet in the late eighteenth century, when the Brazilian church remained firmly under the control of the monarch of Portugal, the struggle between the parish priests and the brotherhoods focused more on financial concerns of the parishes.

Diminishing revenues coming from the mining region as it entered into its long, steady economic decline reduced the amount of money a parish priest could earn. Parish priests wrote the king, blaming the difficult financial situation of the colony on the independent and pernicious nature of the brotherhoods, and recommended that the *matrizes* of the towns be financially reinforced to combat them. The parish priests primarily complained that the brotherhoods did not submit to their orders but rather to the orders of the chaplain whom each brotherhood hired. Even representative of the Crown Martinho Mello de Castro wrote to the Overseas Council in Lisbon in 1794 criticizing the brotherhoods for the "arrogant spirit, of sovereignty and independence that dominate those Corporations, especially those of Pardos and Blacks."[16] Although the Crown asked for the advice of two former officials of the colony, who firmly stated that the priests' claims were unfounded and should be ignored, the Crown sided with the priests. The king passed an

12. Boschi, *Os leigos*, 126–27.
13. "Livro de Receita e Despeza," Arraial de Bacalhau, 1795–1865, AEAM Y27, 7.
14. "Livro de Receita e Despeza," Cachoeira do Campo, 1779–1840, AEAM AA24, 36.
15. Eduardo Hoornaert, *História da igreja no Brasil* (Petrópolis: Editora Vozes, 1977), 386.
16. Quoted in Scarano, *Devoção e escravidão*, 148.

Episcopal law on the eve of the nineteenth century stating that the parish priests should be given more say in the internal affairs of the brotherhoods.[17] Putting brotherhoods more under the watchful eyes of the parish priests, who were essentially under the control of the Crown, would also serve its purpose of keeping the brotherhoods under better control.

The rosary brotherhoods, however, resisted as best they could the attempt to increase the control of the parish priests and the official church in the running of their corporations. The 1787 compromisso of the rosary brotherhood in São João del Rei offers insights into both the brotherhoods' desire to stay independent and the Crown's attempts to make sure the parish priest had a say in the running of the organizations. The members of the brotherhood asserted in their statutes that the brotherhood would "remain entirely exempt from the parish jurisdiction in their festivals because they are held in a private chapel" and that the ruling board would always meet under the chairmanship of the chaplain.[18] Further, in the compromisso it was declared that all the rituals and celebrations in the annual festival would be officiated by the reverend chaplain of the brotherhood and that the members would exhibit the Holy Sacrament "without dependence on the Church official."[19] The official in Lisbon who read the statutes underlined those passages and wrote margin notes referring the reader to the proviso at the end of the document, in which it was declared that the "parish priest will preside over all of the acts of the brotherhood; without damage to [the brotherhood's] rights."[20] Despite resistance, the presence of parish priests presiding over brotherhood activities continued to increase through the nineteenth century.

After the Portuguese court moved to Brazil in 1808, the most prominent figure in trying to get the brotherhoods of the rosary to follow the laws of the church was Monsenhor José de Sousa Pizarro e Araújo, who was the *procurador geral das ordens* (general procurator of the orders) and an important member of the Mesa de Consciência e Ordens.[21] Monsenhor Pizarro wrote notes to the king within the margins of the beautifully illuminated compromisso of the Brotherhood of the Rosary of Barbacena, in the district of Rio das Mortes, in 1809. Pizarro launched a vitriolic attack on the use of

17. Boschi, *Os leigos*, 75–77.

18. "Compromisso da Irmandade de Nossa Senhora do Rosário dos Pretos," São João del Rei, 1787, MASSJ, book 04.04, chapter 9.

19. Ibid., MASSJ, book 04.04, chapter 12.

20. Ibid., MASSJ, book 04.04, proviso.

21. Monsenhor Pizarro was also a prolific historian who wrote the ten-volume history of Rio de Janeiro, *Memórias históricas do Rio de Janeiro* (Rio de Janeiro: Imprensa Nacional, 1943–51).

chaplains by the brotherhoods, accusing the chaplains of taking away the power of the parish priests who had been placed in the parishes by the Grand Master (the king himself). Pizarro then accused the brotherhood chaplains of making themselves "leaders of hateful upheavals, destroyers of the public peace, and [of being] rebellious against the suggestions of the pastor of the parochial diocese."[22]

Despite the eloquent attacks, the brotherhoods continued to try to maintain control. In 1810, the members of the brotherhood in Santa Luzia, in the district of Sabará, wrote to the Mesa de Consciencia e Ordens to complain that the parish priest had taken advantage of their rural ways and had expelled their chaplain, who had served them well for forty-one years. They commented that the priest had done this, and had not given them the right to choose the successor, even though they had founded the brotherhood more than seventy years earlier and that they were the ones who paid for the activities of the brotherhood. Clearly the rosary brothers and sisters had a sense of their own autonomy in the system and struggled in this period to maintain it.[23]

The church and state, however, were actively attempting to regain control over the brotherhoods on many different fronts. How alms were collected became another area of concern for officials, and restrictions on asking for alms in the streets of the cities became the other major correction most often made in the provisos of the compromissos. Brotherhoods had always been required to receive permission to ask for alms on the street, and most brotherhoods received that permission in the early part of the eighteenth century. By the end of the century, however, secular and religious officials were attempting to clamp down on the practice of brotherhoods asking for alms. For example, the compromisso of the rosary brotherhoods in São João del Rei stated that the brotherhood would have a *ermitão* (hermit) who would beg for alms not only in São João but also in the outlying districts. In addition, members of the brotherhood would ask for alms with the *bacia* (collection plate) every Sunday.[24] The king wrote a proviso within the statutes that forbade the hermit to ask for alms outside of São João.[25] In a compromisso written five years earlier, however, from the northern city of Paracatu, the

22. "Capítulos do Compromisso que fas a Irmandade de Nossa Senhora do Rosário da Freguesia de Nossa Senhora da Piedade da Villa de Barbacena, 1809," AEAM Livros das Irmandades 35.

23. "Requerimento da Irmandade de Nossa Senhora do Rosário dos Pretos, Arrayal de Santa Luzia, 2 Abril 1810," AN, caixa 293, Mesa de Consciência e Ordens, SDA 4J, pacote 1, doc. 49.

24. "Compromisso da Irmandade," São João del Rei, MASSJ, book 04.04, chapter 7.

25. Ibid., MASSJ, book 04.04, proviso.

royal proviso clearly stated that the brothers and sisters should not ask for alms, because they should support their brotherhood only with the dues and offerings given by the members themselves.[26] In his proviso to the brotherhood of Barbacena in 1809, Monsenhor Pizarro also stated that the brotherhood's request to ask for alms either with the *bacia* or with the *caixinha* (a small collection box) should not be permitted, because the public should not have to support the brotherhoods. Clearly knowledgeable of the provisos written in other compromissos, Pizarro, to support his case, quoted the proviso of the brotherhood of Paracatu prohibiting the collection of alms in that town.

Despite these attacks, the collection of alms with the *bacias* continued in Barbacena and throughout Minas Gerais.[27] The rosary brotherhood in Cachoeira do Campo, for example, consistently recorded in their accounting books the collection of alms with the *caixinha* between 1789 and 1839.[28] The accounting books from the rosary brotherhood in São João del Rei similarly demonstrate that between 1804 and 1831 the members of the brotherhood continued to ask for alms with both the *bacia* and the *caixinha* in the streets of that city.[29] Such contributions were then recorded in the accounting books, which were overseen and approved by the local *provedor* without opposition. Thus, despite the rigorous oversight of the statutes by the board in Lisbon and then in Rio de Janeiro, and the rulings of the Portuguese monarchs themselves, the distant authority had little to do with the daily running of the brotherhoods, or with the local authority that oversaw them on a regular basis.

The official church had monetary reasons for getting the brotherhoods back under official church, and by extension state, control. One way to collect more revenue was to force the brotherhoods to fulfill the requirement to pay a tax to the *matriz* for graves within *any* church in the parish, not just in the *matriz* itself. Even after rosary brotherhoods built their own churches, they were required by the *Constituições primeiras* to pay a tax to the *matriz*

26. "Compromisso da Irmandade de Nossa Senhora do Rosário, que fazem os pretos livres do Arraial de São Luiz e Santa Ana Minas do Paracatu, 1782," APM SP 959, royal letter.

27. In Barbacena, money is listed as collected with the *caixinha* after 1823, which might show a change of local administration of the town. The accounting books show that between 1804 and 1831, the members of the brotherhoods consistently asked for alms in the streets of the city with both the *bacia* and the *caixinha*. "Livro de Receitas e Despezas," Irmandade de Nossa Senhora do Rosário, Barbacena, 1812–1827, AEAM C32.

28. "Livro de Receitas e Despezas," Cachoeira do Campo, 1779–1840, AEAM AA 24, 36.

29. "Livro de Receitas e Despezas," Irmandade de Nossa Senhora do Rosário, 1805–1831, São João del Rei, AINSR.

for the use of graves inside their own churches.[30] Nonetheless, in the second half of the eighteenth century many rosary brotherhoods wrote clauses into their statutes stating outright that they were not required to pay that tax. In the 1782 compromisso of Calambao, for example, the membership indicated that they did not want to pay the *matriz* the tax for the burial of the member, even though they did not have their own church.[31] In her proviso, the queen referred this problem to the local prelate. The members of the rosary brotherhood in São João del Rei stated in their 1787 statutes that they did not have to pay the tax to the *matriz*, because they had their own church. The marginalia of the *compromisso*, written by the official who approved the document, stated that this could not be allowed, as it would hurt the finances of the *matriz*.[32] Not surprisingly, the most virulent objections came from Monsenhor Pizarro in Rio de Janeiro, in the comments he wrote in the 1809 compromisso from the brotherhood in Barbacena. The membership of that brotherhood also claimed that they did not have to pay the *matriz* for burying their dead in their own church. Citing the clause from the *Constituições primeiras*, Pizarro firmly declared that that brotherhood must pay the tax because the income of the parish depended in part on those funds.[33]

In the early nineteenth century, questions of the tax paid for members buried in the church floor became moot, as prohibitions against burying the dead within the floors of the churches began to be promulgated. In the marginalia of the statutes of the rosary brotherhood in São João del Rei, notes, which must have been inserted in the early nineteenth century, stated that the "use of graves inside of churches is explicitly prohibited by the Royal Decree of 11 January 1801."[34] Monsenhor Pizarro, in the 1809 Barbacena compromisso, commented on the clause about burying the dead in the church, stating that it would cause public harm. Dom João, the regent, following only this section of Pizarro's advice, passed all the clauses of the Barbacena document except the one that tried to place graves in the church.[35] Acquiescing to

30. This law, found in Livro 4, 56 n. 856 of the *Constituições primeiras*, was cited by Pizarro in the proviso of the "Capítulos do Compromisso . . . da Villa de Barbacena," 1809. AEAM Livros das Irmandades 35.

31. "Compromisso of Calambao (filial de Guarapiranga)," 1782, AEAM Livros das Irmandades 25, chapter 5.

32. "Compromisso da Irmandade," São João del Rei, MASSJR, chapter 11 and marginalia.

33. "Capítulos do Compromisso . . . da Villa de Barbacena," AEAM Livros das Irmandades 35, chapter 13 and proviso.

34. "Compromisso da Irmandade," São João del Rei, MASSSJR, chapter 11 and marginalia.

35. "Capítulos do Compromisso . . . da Villa de Barbacena," AEAM Livros das Irmandades 35, proviso.

the regent's demand, the brotherhood of Barbacena agreed in their meeting of 19 September 1825 that they would build a cemetery with an *oratório* (oratory), at which they could perform the ritual of the commendation of the souls (*encomendações das almas*).[36]

In the tight economic climate of the late colonial period, even other brotherhoods were trying to reclaim what they considered to be their rights in the ritual of death. In 1806, the Santa Casa de Misericórdia of Ouro Preto wrote to the brotherhood of the rosary citing its privilege, held since 1593, of a monopoly on the carrying of the dead on its funeral biers. Although this assertion may have come as a result of a practical need for funds in the declining economy of the mining district, the timing coincided with a larger movement by the church to reclaim old privileges that had been explicitly ignored. In a lengthy reply, however, the rosary brotherhood argued that it should be able to have its own bier because the Santa Casa's rules had been written during the Spanish occupation of Portugal. In the end, the rosary brotherhood was able to maintain control over the burials of its members.[37]

In the first half of the eighteenth century, the brotherhoods of the rosary of the blacks, like other brotherhoods in Minas Gerais, had developed outside the control of the church and state. The middle of the century, from the earliest days of Pombal's influence to the end of the colonial period, was a period of increased attempts of the church and state, in Lisbon then in Rio de Janeiro, to regain control over the brotherhoods. Nevertheless, the brotherhoods resisted that control and continued to try to run their affairs in the independent manner that had been established earlier in the century. Yet this was not just an argument between the authorities and the blacks of the brotherhoods. The documents also demonstrate what appears to be a lack of agreement between local authorities and the state, a disconnection between the local authorities' tacit acceptance of certain practices such as the collection of alms through the town, and the official prohibitions coming out of the centers of power in the metropolis.

Inside the Brotherhoods in the Late Colonial Period

In Calambao, an outlying district of Mariana, the secretary of the rosary brotherhood recorded a meeting of the board in 1782 at which the members expressed their reasons for forming a new brotherhood of the blacks. They

---

36. "Termos de Meza," Irmandade de Nossa Senhora do Rosário, Barbacena, 1824–1932, AEAM C21—19 September 1825. The ritual of the *encomendação das almas* is a "folk" Catholic

wrote that there were more than two thousand blacks living in their district, located more than three leagues from the closest brotherhood of the rosary.[38] They did not mention slave or free status in their reason for forming the brotherhood, they simply used the racial designator "of the blacks." The phrase *of the blacks*, however, continued to conflate a population diverse in legal status, ethnicity, and gender. The demographic trends within the rosary brotherhoods in the second part of the colonial period mirrored those of the larger society, with an increasingly *crioulo* slave population, an increase in diversity in the African population, and a growing number of free people of color. Since the 1720s, brotherhoods had been established to serve a growing mulatto and *crioulo* population of Minas Gerais, yet many freed slaves and free blacks continued to participate in already established rosary brotherhoods of the blacks and to form new rosary brotherhoods.[39] As in the first half of the century, the population within the brotherhoods had to continue to find ways to organize difference within their populations in order to successfully form communities and engage in the work of the brotherhoods.

During the second half of the eighteenth century, the overall population in Minas Gerais continued to change significantly. Following the decline in gold production after the 1730s, the importation of African slaves into Minas Gerais began to diminish.[40] Despite that decline, the captaincy of Minas Gerais managed to diversify its economy significantly, in some regions even as early as 1730, and after 1780 the region remained economically active in agriculture, ranching, and even some textile production. Nevertheless, changes in the overall population reflected changes in the mining economy. After 1786 the slave population began to decline and would continue to decrease in numbers until the 1820s and 1830s. As a percentage of the overall population, that segment dropped from its peak in the late eighteenth century as 48 percent of the overall population, to only 26 percent at the end of the colonial period. It would

---

tradition (not part of the official church) that has continued throughout the rural regions of Minas Gerais, and not only among "blacks." It takes place during Lent, which is the time when "the souls of the dead wander freely through the world of the living." The ritual serves to "maintain equilibrium between this world, and the other." See Núbia Pereira de Magalhães Gomes and Edimilson de Almeida Pereira, *Do presépio à balança: Representações sociais da vida religiosa* (Belo Horizonte, Brazil: Mazza Edições, 1994), 368–69.

37. "Termos de Meza," Irmandade de Nossa Senhora do Rosário dos Pretos, Ouro Preto, 1791–1897, CC, Freguesia de Nossa Senhora do Pilar, rol 82, 29 January 1806, 42.

38. Termo de Meza, 2 January 1782, in the "Compromisso . . . Calambao, 1782," AEAM Livros das Irmandades 25.

39. Aguiar, "Vila Rica," 23.

40. Goulart, *A escravidão*, 170.

41. Bergad, *Slavery*, 90–93.

continue to drop as a percentage of the overall population through the period of the empire, even when it began to increase again in real numbers. Conversely, the nonwhite, free population increased significantly during the late colonial period. That population increased from 31 percent of the overall population to 41 percent, where it would remain relatively consistently through the end of the empire.[41]

The brotherhood membership reflected these demographic changes. As in the first half of the century, the "black" designator of the majority of rosary brotherhoods linked them to the slave population, but in fact the membership was far from exclusively slave and became even less so as the century went on. For example, the new seat of the diocese, Mariana, had a rosary brotherhood that started its book of entrances in 1750. In the first eighty years of recording new memberships, 959 new members joined the brotherhood, and of them, slaves joined more frequently than either *forros* or free men and women.[42] The first decade listed in the book, 1750–60, included more than a third (396) of the entrances for the entire period because it included members who had already been participating in the brotherhood. In that first decade, slaves represented the largest group and *forros* made up the majority of the nonslave group. In subsequent decades, although the slave entrances remained relatively constant and even grew as a percentage of the total, the number of *forro* members decreased as the number of free members increased, again, a demographic trend that mirrored the larger population changes in Minas Gerais.[43]

The rosary brotherhood in São João del Rei experienced similar changes. Despite the fact that this brotherhood had existed since 1708, the earliest extant registration book covered the years between 1754 and 1805, during which the secretary entered 1,506 new members.[44] As in Mariana, slaves entered at a higher rate than either *forros* or free people; unlike in Mariana, the percentage of entering *forros* remained fairly constant. Despite the differences in the trajectories of the *forro*/free/slave populations in these two brotherhoods, the main point to be made here is that the populations entering the brotherhoods remained diverse in terms of their legal status. Although brotherhoods of the rosary were characterized as brotherhoods of slaves, their populations always had a large percentage of nonslave members, and this population increased as the colonial era drew to a close.

42. See the Appendix, Table 8. "Assentos de Irmãos, Irmandade de Nossa Senhora do Rosário," 1750–1886, Mariana, AEAM P28.
43. See Bergad, "After the Mining Boom," 67–97.
44. "Entradas dos Irmãos," Irmandade de Nossa Senhora do Rosário dos Pretos, São João del Rei 1747–1806, AINSR.

The ethnic diversity within the rosary brotherhoods complemented the diversity in legal status. The brotherhood in Calambao, the same one that indicated that they needed a brotherhood of the blacks because of the large black population in their region, demonstrated this type of diversity. The meeting from which the request was issued was attended by four white officers; four black officers (including the black king); and twenty-seven board members, twenty-six of whom were African of various ethnicities. The black king was Angolan, and the other officers were listed as Mina. Of the board members, eleven were listed as Angola, nine as Mina, and six as Benguela, with one *crioulo* and one listed with no place of origin.[45] The mixture of ethnicities of the board members in the brotherhood in Calambao reflected the complexity of the overall populations in the rosary brotherhoods in the second half of the eighteenth century.

The snapshot of diversity that the Calambao example provides, however, differs from the general trends that can be traced in the lists of new members in the rosary brotherhoods. By the mid-eighteenth century the secretaries of the brotherhoods began to regularly identify the ethnicity of the Africans who joined. The entrance books from Mariana and São João del Rei offer examples of how ethnicity appeared in the entrances of the rosary brotherhoods.[46] In Mariana, the secretaries listed some description, either naming the member's African-based ethnicity or noting that the member was Brazilian born, for 645 of the members. Of the thirty-five different designations used, thirty were African identifications, one was *crioulo*, and the rest were color designations: *cabra, pardo, preto,* and *branco.* Around half the members in São João del Rei (749 members) of the entering population had their ethnicity identified or were described in color terms. The secretaries used thirty-two different descriptors, of which most, as in Mariana, were African ethnicities. Overall, the members of the rosary brotherhoods in São João del Rei and Mariana represented well more than thirty different African groups. The overall trend in both brotherhoods, however, was a secular rise in Brazilian-born members in the last decades of the eighteenth century. In São João del Rei, *crioulos* represented the largest single entering group, and their presence continued to increase vis-à-vis the other groups. *Crioulos* entered the rosary brotherhood despite the fact that a Brotherhood of Our Lady of Mercies, most often associated with the *crioulo* population in Minas

45. Termo de Meza, 2 January 1782, in the "Compromisso . . . Calambao, 1782," AEAM Livros das Irmandades 25.

46. "Assentos de Irmãos," Irmandade de Nossa Senhora do Rosário, 1750–1886, Mariana, AEAM P28.

Gerais, had been established in São João del Rei in 1751. Why *crioulos* continued to align with a group designated as "of the blacks" cannot be answered with any certainty through the documentation. If the definition of blackness, however, is based in part on a shared history linked to Africa, the choices that the *crioulos* made suggest that they wanted to nurture and remember those ties, rather than sever them.[47]

These individuals of different ethnicities, slave and freed, and members of the Brazilian population all participated in the administration of the brotherhoods of the rosary. The lists of the elections that were recorded annually in the books of the board meetings demonstrate that the diversity within the general population in the brotherhoods was reflected in the leadership positions. No one group dominated the rosary brotherhoods in Minas Gerais. The book of the elections for the brotherhood in Cachoeira do Campo began in 1748, when the brotherhood had already been "integrated" for more than twenty-five years. Although the secretary did not list the African ethnicities of the participants, the lists show that the leadership positions switched between slave and nonslave members. In the first five years of the listing of elections, between 1748 and 1753, the nonslave population held more than 90 percent of the leadership positions. Then, suddenly, the number of positions held by the slave and *forro* population radically increased.[48] Unfortunately, no reasons are given in the books of the minutes of the meetings to indicate why this radical change took place, yet it does suggest a shift of power within the brotherhood.

An election list from a brotherhood in the hamlet of Bacalhau, located near Mariana, offers a detailed view of the distribution of the positions of authority over a sixty-nine year period (1761–1830).[49] With 4,467 names, it includes white officers and those who are black (secretary, treasurer, procurators), kings and queens, judges, brothers and sisters of the board, and other positions listed as *por devoção*. Demographics of the elected members of the brotherhood in Bacalhau share some similarities with those of the entering membership represented in the registration lists in the larger urban areas, the city of Mariana and the town of São João del Rei. For example, slaves

---

47. See the Appendix, Table 2.

48. "Eleições," Irmandade de Nossa Senhora do Rosário, Cachoeira do Campo, 1748–1776, AEAM AA27.

49. There was an eleven-year period from 1778 to 1789 during which the elections were not listed due to a conflict within the brotherhood. A cross-check with the 1831 census demonstrates that some of the officeholders of the brotherhood, and their masters, lived in the nearby town of Guarapiranga, at least at the end of the colonial period. CEDEPLAR, 1831 census in Minas Gerais, database, compiled and organized by CEDEPLAR, Faculdade de Ciências Econômicas, UFMG.

held just over 50 percent of all the positions, whereas one-third of the free elected officials were *forros*.[50] Toward the end of the colonial period, the brotherhood in Bacalhau experienced a gradual decrease in the presence of slave leaders and an increase in free leaders. Yet even by the beginning of the Brazilian Empire in 1822, slave leadership still remained in the majority.

For more than half the population in the Bacalhau election lists, an ethnicity was listed. Of these, *crioulos* were by far the largest group holding positions in the brotherhood, its numbers almost twice those of the next most numerous group, the Benguela. Overall, *crioulos* held just less than half the total positions in the brotherhood. The high presence of Brazilian-born blacks in leadership positions very likely points to their better grasp of the Portuguese language and their greater familiarity with the society at large. The distribution of leadership positions among African ethnicities in the election lists from Bacalhau show that Benguela, Angola, and Congo were the three most significant. Members from West Africa held less than 5 percent of the total leadership positions over the entire period. The people in the highest positions in the brotherhoods (kings, queens, and judges) reflected the same general distribution across group lines, with *crioulos* most often holding those positions.[51]

In the rosary brotherhood of Bacalhau, it was not uncommon for members to hold several different positions over the course of several years. White officers tended to hold their positions for many years. Alferes João Dias Braga, for example, was the white procurator from 1816 to 1827. Blacks did not tend to stay in their positions as long as the whites; instead, they rotated in and out of different positions in the brotherhood. The exception to this, and the only position dominated by a group other than the *crioulos*, was that of the black treasurer, which was held throughout the period in question by Benguela members, many of whom held the positions for several years.[52] Most blacks, however, moved from one position to another. For example, the free black man Caetano Gomes de Oliveira held the position of black treasurer in 1810, 1811, and 1819, was the black secretary in 1814, and a board member in 1816 and 1826. Even slaves occasionally returned several times to participate in the running of the brotherhood. Antonio Angola, slave of Antonio Correia, served as a brother of the board in 1763, 1766, and 1769 and as a

---

50. Of elected officials, 2,243 were slave, 839 were *forro*, and 1,385 were free. "Livro de Termos de Meza," Irmandade de Nossa Senhora do Rosário, Arraial de Bacalhau, Freguesia de Nossa Senhora da Conceição de Guarapiranga, 1758–1893, AEAM Y12.

51. See the Appendix, Table 3.

52. "Livro de Termos de Meza," Arraial de Bacalhau, AEAM Y12.

judge in 1768. Women slaves also returned to serve several times; for example, Felipa, the *crioula* slave of João Ferreira de Souza, volunteered to be a queen *por devoção* in 1810 and was elected as a board member in 1815 and 1821. Most often, however, members served for only one year. Interestingly, the return to positions does not show a movement up through a hierarchy, as occurred in brotherhoods elsewhere in Brazil.[53]

The heterogeneity displayed in the overall membership and in the leadership positions in all the rosary brotherhoods demonstrates that the participants were able to create a corporate group out of many disparate peoples. Indeed, the brotherhoods of the rosary in Minas Gerais never split along ethnic lines, as they did in Bahia, where the Angolan slaves formed a brotherhood dedicated to Our Lady of the Rosary exclusively for themselves, or in Rio, where slaves also formed into different brotherhoods according to their nations.[54] No similar examples exist in Minas Gerais of slaves or freed slaves of one or another African nation splintering off from the rosary brotherhood to form their own brotherhood.[55]

Instead, divisions within the rosary brotherhoods in Minas Gerais usually occurred along color lines, as in the cases from the first half of the eighteenth century when white and black rosary brotherhoods split. In the second half of the century, divisions tended to occur between blacks and *pardos* or *crioulos*, with the last two groups often choosing to found their own brotherhoods. In one case, in the diamond-mining region of Tejuco (present-day Diamantina), *crioulos* and *pardos* originally joined the brotherhood of the rosary but in 1771 decided to leave, citing as their reason the fact that the organization was "black." They started a brotherhood of Our Lady of Mercies and obtained an altar of their own in a white church; they then grew dissatisfied and asked to join the brotherhood of the rosary again, but were refused because of the constant discord between the groups.[56] There is little evidence beyond this

53. In Recife, Pernambuco, for example, the rosary brotherhood of the blacks was linked to a labor hierarchy that had clear rankings through which members would pass—until they became King of Congo in the rosary brotherhood. See José Antonio Gonçalves de Mello, "Aditamentos e correções," in *Anais Pernambucanos*, ed. F. A. Pereira da Costa, vol. 10 (Recife, Brazil: n.p., 1983).

54. E. Valerie Smith, "The Sisterhood of Nossa Senhora da Boa Morte and the Brotherhood of Nossa Senhora do Rosário: African Brazilian Cultural Adaptations to Antebellum Restrictions" *Afro-Hispanic Review* 11 (1992): 63; and Bastide, *African Religions*, 119; on Rio, see Karasch, *Slave Life*, 272; and on Bahia, Reis, "Identidade e diversidade," 14.

55. Donald Ramos did find evidence of a brotherhood of Our Lady of Mercy in Antonio Dias that split into two; one of the resulting groups specifically excluded "gente dos Reinos da Guiné e Luanda." D. Ramos, "A influência africana," 157.

56. Russell-Wood, "Black and Mulatto Brotherhoods," 581; Bastide, *African Religions*, 431 n. 31.

one case, however, that this type of strife existed between the Africans and the Brazilian-born members in the brotherhoods of the rosary in Minas Gerais. In another singular case, the brotherhood in the northern mining city of Paracatu was founded exclusively for nonslaves. The Paracatu brotherhood was the exception and may have been different from those in the south because it was in the diocese of Olinda, far to the north and not as affected by other brotherhoods in the same captaincy.

In addition to the occasional strife between members of the rosary brotherhoods and *crioulos* and mulattos, the black members of the brotherhoods had to continue to deal with the presence of white officers in their organizations. Until the 1780s, brotherhoods continued to temper the requirements for white officers, as they had in the first half of the century. For instance, the statutes of the brotherhood in São Caetano (1765) only indicated that the secretary and the *zelador*, who in this brotherhood served as the protector, should be white. Later, the chapter that described the jobs indicated that the secretary should know how to read and write, but if he did not, he should be "substituted by *any* brother or by the white *zelador*" (italics mine).[57] The compromisso also specified, however, that the procurator should be black.[58]

By the 1780s, however, compromissos less frequently limited the power of the whites. For instance, the brotherhood in Calambao (1782) specifically called for the protector, secretary, procurator, and treasurer to be white, and stated that nothing in the brotherhood could be determined without the white officers being present.[59] The 1784 statutes from the village of Santa Rita in the district of Sabará explained that blacks "lacked the intelligence" to fill the positions of secretary and treasurer, and so they should be filled by whites.[60] Some brotherhoods found creative solutions to the question of having whites in positions of power, such as the brotherhoods of Bacalhau and Calambao, which both had a full set of white officers and a full set of black officers. These changes toward the turn of the nineteenth century may represent an awareness of the attempts to bring about increased oversight at that time. The members may even have ignored these requirements in their

---

57. "Compromisso da Irmandade . . . de São Caetano," 1762, AEAM Livro das Irmandades 22, chapter 4. Russell-Wood points out that in Salvador in 1789 many of the black brotherhoods already had black treasurers and scribes and that this also occurred in Rio de Janeiro in the early twentieth century. Russell-Wood, "Black and Mulatto Brotherhoods," 597.

58. "Compromisso da Irmandade . . . de São Caetano," 1762, AEAM Livro das Irmandades 22, chapter 1.

59. "Compromisso . . . Calambao, 1782," AEAM Livro das Irmandades 25, chapter 2.

60. "Compromisso da Irmandade do Rozario dos Pretos, Arraial de Santa Rita da Freguezia de Santo Antonio do Rio Asima na Comarca de Sabará," 1782, ABG.

own compromissos in practice, as they did with the presentation of their books to the authorities and the collection of alms, but included them in order to avoid unnecessary friction from the outside.[61]

Around the time of independence, many brotherhoods began again to place more limitations on the white officers. The 1820 compromisso of the brotherhood in the village of Nossa Senhora do Monte do Carmo in the town of Pouso Alto in southern Minas Gerais declared that if at all possible, all the positions should be filled by blacks or free *crioulos* because they would have keys to the safe and so access to all the possessions of the brotherhood.[62] This requirement demonstrated a blatant distrust of the whites. If Pouso Alto followed the same general trend in Minas Gerais to have more Brazilian-born members, perhaps by 1820 there were enough nonwhite members who could read and write to not require white officers. The proviso written by the king did not mention these clauses. This same tendency can be seen by the brotherhood in Curvelo, which, in statutes written the year after those of Pouso Alto, stated that they would have a white treasurer and secretary, or a *pardo* if the person had the qualities to hold the job.[63] As in the first half of the eighteenth century, the relationship of the diverse population of "blacks" to the whites who participated in their brotherhoods was a complex one and probably reflected an array of responses and motivations to particular local conditions.

The compromissos were not the only recourse that blacks in the brotherhoods had to regulate the power of whites in their brotherhoods. As seen in the early eighteenth century, blacks could split from white rosary brotherhoods to form their own organizations. In at least one case, blacks in the rosary brotherhoods used the courts to act against perceived injustices of the whites within the brotherhood. The leadership in Bacalhau suffered a rupture in 1776 when some "scheming whites, enemies of the peace," took over the administration of the brotherhood and expelled the former white officers. This disruption completely halted the record keeping of the brotherhood, and from 1778 to 1789, no elections were listed and no minutes of meetings

61. In a case from Salvador, Bahia, the black brotherhood of St. Benedict asked the Crown to "revoke the statutory clause that incumbents of these posts should be white" because now enough members could read and write. "In 1789 the governor reported that the concession of this privilege would not constitute a precedent, for six black brotherhoods of Salvador already had blacks as scribes and treasurers." Russell-Wood, "Black and Mulatto Brotherhoods," 597.

62. "Compromisso de Nossa Senhora do Rosário dos Pretos da Arraial de Nossa Senhora do Monte do Carmo da Freguesia de Nossa Senhora da Conceição de Pouso Alto, Bispado de Mariana," 1820, APM SP 959.

63. "Compromisso da Irmandade dos pretinhos de Nossa Senhora do Rosário da Freguesia de Santo Antônio do Curvelo, Arcibispado da Bahia, 1821," APM 959, chapter 1.

recorded.[64] In 1789, after the case had gone to the courts in Rio de Janeiro, the expelled officers were returned to their positions and the books of the brotherhood began again. In addition to being reinstated, the officers were to be paid all the money the brotherhood owed to them.

Although this conflict appeared to be a power play between whites, blacks did begin to appear in the documentation when, in 1789, they insisted on electing new white officers because they did not, and never would, accept those reinstated by the court in Rio de Janeiro. In fact, the reinstated officers served only one year, and in 1790 they were replaced by new officers. In 1791, the blacks boycotted the brotherhood by refusing to turn in the alms they had collected until the new white officers took their seats, and until they were relieved of a debt from the chaplain who had been expelled in 1776, a debt they had been ordered to pay by the courts. The new white officers were instated, but the brotherhood did not receive a discharge from the debt until 1795, when the ex-chaplain finally released them from it.[65] The dispute within the brotherhood of Bacalhau, and other examples, demonstrate that the "blacks" had forged an identity within the brotherhood of the rosary and would act as a group in defense of their interests. The blacks from Bacalhau did not object to having white officers, and again, this might be related to the recognition of the advantages that powerful patrons could bring. Instead, they objected to a certain group of white officers, and they had means of making their objections known, and acted upon.

The identity of being part of a community "of the blacks" had been forming since the earliest days of the colony, when black rosary brotherhoods began to separate from white brotherhoods. Yet skin color was not the only factor that brought these communities together, and perhaps it was not even the most important. The color identification was based on a shared history, of having ancestors who came from Africa, and the desire to maintain practices that linked the community to that history. Those shared practices expressed devotion to Our Lady of the Rosary. In the second half of the eighteenth century, and throughout the nineteenth century, the rituals and symbols that actively created that memory begin to emerge in the documentary record. Sometimes the expression of the tie to Africa was overt. For instance, the 1809 compromisso from Barbacena included a cover page with an image of Lady of the Rosary with a rosary made of African cowry shells, known as *búzios* in Brazil, which came to have a ritual importance in the divination practices of Candomblé. The presence of a rosary of *búzios* on the

64. "Livro de Termos de Meza," Arraial de Bacalhau, 1758–1893, AEAM Y12, 30v–48.
65. Ibid.

cover of a rosary brotherhood compromisso is certainly thought provoking, yet it is the only example of this type of expression that I have encountered.[66] The most prevalent external expression of a conscious link to an African past was through the work of the brotherhoods in which the membership maintained its relationship to their ancestors and to the unseen world. The presence of kings and queens, and the ritual coronations that accompanied them, along with the dances and songs of the "nations" that accompanied the collection of alms and played a role in the coronations, all served as ritual spaces in which the memory of the African heritage could be kept alive and the hierarchy within the brotherhood could be expressed, along with the power that obtained from the maintenance of those connections to Africa, to the ancestors, and to the unseen worlds.

Death in the Brotherhoods

As in the first half of the eighteenth century, in the second, rosary brotherhoods continually expressed a concern with the proper burial of the dead and with masses celebrated for souls of the dead. Funerals must have been common in the harsh labor structure of Minas Gerais, yet their very frequency provided occasions, albeit sad ones, for the community to gather. After 1750, the hierarchy of death emerges in the documentary record, demonstrating a community that organized itself hierarchically not only in life. One example of this was the attention paid to the location of the graves within the churches. In the popular conception of the time, the closer one was buried to the altar, the "closer" one would be to heaven.[67] In the small town of Guarapiranga, near Mariana, in 1750, there was a single church, the matriz, that had four "official" brotherhoods (those with compromissos), including a brotherhood of the rosary of the blacks.[68] As revealed in the 1745 statutes of that black brotherhood, its members had negotiated with the authorities for graves within the matriz. They asked for two graves inside the balustrade, nearer to the altar, for the king, queen, and male and female judges, and for four in the main body of the church. By 1782, the hierarchy of death was becoming even more pronounced in the captaincy of Minas Gerais. In the compromisso of Calambao, the brotherhood of the rosary designated that the dead would

66. "Capítulos do Compromisso . . . da Villa de Barbacena," 1809, AEAM Livros das Irmandades 35, front cover.
67. Ariès, Hour of Our Death, 78–82.
68. "Informação das antiguidades da freguesia de Guarapiranga," Códice Costa Matoso, vol. 1, 258.

be buried in the Chapel of Santo Antonio. The chaplain of the brotherhood and the black and white officials would be buried in the *capela-mor* (main chapel), the black and white ex-officials inside the balustrade, and the other members outside it.[69]

The compromissos after the mid-eighteenth century also give further insights into the ritual of the funerals in the black brotherhoods. Once a member died, he or she had to be buried with pomp, in the style of the religious baroque of eighteenth-century Minas Gerais. The brothers and sisters would be informed of the death and called to the funeral by the ringing of the bells of the church or by the procurator or *andador*, both elected positions in the brotherhoods. The statutes required that all members and the chaplain attend the funerals of fellow brotherhood members; members who missed funerals might be subject to expulsion from the brotherhood. In the funeral processions the brothers wore their *opas*, carrying their cross and their banners in front of the funeral bier from the location of the wake, often the home of the member, to the church where the brotherhood had its graves.[70] The leaders of the brotherhoods carried their symbols of power—the judges their staffs and the kings and queens their crowns.[71] All the compromissos stipulated that the members who were buried had to be in good standing, yet they always included clauses stating that if a brother or sister had fallen on hard times, the brotherhood would raise funds to pay for the burial and masses as part of the charity of the organization. In addition, children and wives of members would be buried by the brotherhoods.

Sometimes the brother or sister may have been too far from the church to permit all the members to go to the site of the death to accompany the body back to the brotherhood church or altar. Some brotherhoods made provisions for those cases. In São Caetano, a member who died would be brought to the border of the town and met there by two of the brotherhood members.[72] The brotherhood of Guarapiranga requested of the authorities that, if members died far from the *matriz*, but near other chapels in the town, burial of the members be allowed in those churches, because of the difficulty of getting the dead to the *matriz*, "as is notorious."[73] In the landscape of death,

69. "Compromisso . . . Calambao, 1782," AEAM Livros das Irmandades 25, chapter 5.

70. For only a few examples of the explanations of the rituals of death, see *Compromisso da Irmandade . . . da Villa do Príncipe*, chapters 3 and 15; "Compromisso da Irmandade . . . do Alto da Cruz" 1733, CC Antonio Dias, rol 58, doc. 123–24, chapter 18; "Compromisso da Irmandade do Rosário de Acurui (Rio das Pedras)," 1756, Prateleira A doc 21, chapter 3; "Compromisso da Irmandade . . . de São Caetano," 1762, AEAM Livros das Irmandades 22, chapter 14.

71. "Compromisso . . . Calambao, 1782," AEAM Livros das Irmandades 25, chapter 4.

72. "Compromisso da Irmandade . . . de São Caetano," 1762, AEAM Livros das Irmandades 22, chapter 14.

then, brotherhoods tried to take all possibilities into account in order to ensure that their members would receive a proper burial.

Clearly one of the most important functions of the lay religious brotherhoods was the care of the body and the soul of the members after death, and rosary brotherhoods made this one of their priorities. The corpse made not only a physical journey from home to a resting place in an important ritual space but also a symbolic journey from the things of this world to the other world, symbolized by the church itself. Africans and their descendants may have interpreted the ritual of the funeral through their own understandings of death and the afterlife. The street, where the funeral processions occurred, may have symbolized the journey, and the pomp and discipline that accompanied the corpse was necessary to protect the liminal condition of the dead. All the members had to be present in their regalia and symbols of power not simply for show but in order to protect the soul in the space between the land of the living and that of the dead. They also had to help transport the corpse from the private home to the "home" of the community, the chapel or church where the brotherhood met—to be buried in a space that then became, like cemeteries in Africa, a route of communication between the living and the dead.[74] No matter how the brothers and sisters of the rosary brotherhoods interpreted the symbols of death, they were important rituals that brought people together to do the "work" that allowed them to continue as a community.

Kings, Queens, and Festivals

As in the first half of the eighteenth century, the other important work of the brotherhoods was the celebration of the feast day of Our Lady of the Rosary, which included the reinados, the coronations of kings and queens. Documentation from the later part of the colonial period began to include descriptions of congados, the costumed groups that accompanied the royalty, dancing and singing, through the towns during the annual festivals. These congados, as they continue to be called today, are the same groups that have become the cornerstone of the apparition narrative of Our Lady of the Rosary and that continue to play a fundamental role in the annual festivals.

73. "Compromisso, Irmandade de Nossa Senhora do Rosário dos Pretos, Freguesia de Nossa Senhora da Conceição de Guarapiranga," 1745, AEAM, Livros das Irmandades 49, 14.

74. Linda Heywood discusses the clergy's criticisms of the syncretic practices in "Christian" funerals in Luanda in "Portuguese into African," 99–100.

The election of kings and queens was exclusive to the brotherhoods of the rosary of the blacks, and stemmed from its consideration as a slave brotherhood, even though the demographics show that in many cases the free and freed population was as numerous or outnumbered the slave population in some brotherhoods.[75] Other brotherhoods of *crioulos* and *pardos*, such as the brotherhoods of Our Lady of Mercies or those dedicated to Saint Benedict, did not have kings and queens. Despite bans on the practice of black coronations throughout the colonial period, they continued. By the second half of the eighteenth century, the brotherhood statutes demonstrate that the presence of kings and queens in the rosary brotherhood had come to be considered custom. The members of the rosary brotherhood of São Caetano, for example, wrote in their 1762 compromisso that "in order not to break the inveterate custom of this town, and this America, there will be in this Brotherhood also a king and queen."[76] The brotherhood in the village of Santa Rita, near Sabará, wrote in its statutes that it was the custom of the brotherhoods of the blacks to nominate a king and queen, a practice that increased the devotion of the members.[77] In other brotherhoods, such as that in São João del Rei, kings and queens were not mentioned in the statutes, but the accounting books and the elections from the same brotherhood always had a king and queen listed as having paid their annual contribution.[78] The compromisso from Barbacena did not list a king and queen, yet later in the nineteenth century the accounting books always included an entry of funds collected at the annual Reinado.[79]

Although the main kings and queens in the festivals today are called Kings and Queens of Congo, and they hold their positions for life, this title did not emerge in the brotherhood documentation until very late in the colonial period and did not appear in the compromissos in Minas Gerais

75. During the Feast Day of the Holy Spirit, members of the brotherhood associated with that devotion elected an emperor, a practice that, like the coronations of black kings and queens, continues to today. For an excellent analysis of this practice in Rio de Janeiro in the nineteenth century, and earlier practices in France, see Martha Abreu, *O império do divino: Festas religiosas e cultura popular no Rio de Janeiro, 1830–1900* (Rio de Janeiro: Nova Fronteira, 1999), 39–41.

76. "Compromisso da Irmandade ... de São Caetano," 1762, AEAM Livros das Irmandades 22.

77. "Compromisso pelo qual se deve regular a Irmandade de N. Senhora do Rozário dos Pretos erecta no arraial de Santa Rita da Freguezia de Santo Antonio do Rio Assima," 1784, ABGS, chapter 3.

78. "Compromisso da Irmandade," São João del Rei, 1787, MASSJR 4.01; "Livro de Receitas e Despezas," Irmandade de Nossa Senhora do Rosário dos Pretos, São João del Rei, 1803–1825, AINSR.

79. "Capítulos do Compromisso ... da Villa de Barbacena," 1809, AEAM Livros das Irmandades 28; "Livro de Receita e Despeza," Irmandade de Nossa Senhora do Rosário de Barbacena, 1868–1899, AEAM C22. In some cases, as in Ouro Preto, the practice of having kings and queens disappeared from the election books in 1799 and then reappeared in 1823.

until the late twentieth century. Yet early nineteenth-century travelers to Brazil were often enchanted with the exotic festivals put on by the blacks and wrote about the black kings whom they called Kings of Congo, although they often denied the significance of black kings and queens. The German scientist Karl Friedrich Philipp von Martius wrote an account of a dynastic festival, the ascension of Dom João VI to the throne (6 February 1818), which he witnessed in Tejuco (Diamantina). Martius wrote that it was traditional throughout Brazil for the blacks to annually elect a king and his court, observing that this king had no power whatsoever and citing the lack of power as the reason why the Portuguese did not oppose the elections. Martius described the visit of the newly crowned King of Congo, a freed black shoemaker, to the house of the superintendent of the diamond-mining district. According to Martius, the superintendent greeted the black court in his nightgown and cap and invited them into his house. When the superintendent invited the king to sit on the sofa, the king was so shocked that he let his scepter fall on the ground. The superintendent picked it up, saying, "Your Majesty dropped your scepter!"[80] This account suggests that the white population participated in the coronations of the blacks, but the appearance of the superintendent in his pajamas, despite his politeness to his visitors, demonstrated the condescending attitude of the whites toward the ruler of the blacks.

Martius recorded the election, coronation, and visits not only of a King of Congo, but also of a Queen Xinga—a figure that emerged from the memory of the infamous Queen Nzinga of Angola and Matamba. In the minds of Europeans, Queen Nzinga may have served as a mythic heroine—an African queen who accepted Christianity. Her presence in the festivals of the blacks, especially standing side by side with the King of Congo, to Europeans represented the triumph of Christianity over heathenism.[81] For the Africans and their descendents, Queen Xinga very likely represented the triumph of African traditions in the face of almost overwhelming attempts at European cultural domination, very much what the politically astute Queen Nzinga had accomplished during her reign in Matamba. No accounts of Queen Xinga in the festivals of the rosary appear again until the twentieth century, when

---

80. Karl von Martius quoted in Luís da Câmara Cascudo, *Antologia do folclore brasileiro* (São Paulo: Livraria Martins Editora, 1965), 93.
81. Queen Nzinga's story probably was known by intellectuals in Europe in the eighteenth century through several published seventeenth-century accounts, most notably that of Pe. António Cavazzi de Montecúccolo. Thornton, *Africa and Africans*, 258–59.

she participated with the King of Congo in some festivals known as Congos in northern Brazil and Congadas in the southern regions.[82]

Although Queen Xinga did not appear frequently in Afro-Brazilian festivals, the figure of the King of Congo would become extremely important in the rosary brotherhoods. In the colonial period, however, it is difficult to find references to Kings of *Congo*, despite the fact that kings and queens had long been important within the brotherhoods. It might be tempting to suggest that these were labels assigned by foreign visitors who would have been familiar with the conversion of the king of Kongo and Queen Nzinga and so placed these titles on the black kings and queens in their writings. Occasionally, however, the title King of Congo appeared from where it was hidden in colonial rosary brotherhood records, leaving the question open of who first used these titles and when. The entrance books for São João del Rei, for example, identified the slave Brizida as the "Queen of the Congos" in 1773.[83] Twenty years later the same book listed Thereza de Sobral e Souza, a freed black, as the "wife of the King of Congo."[84] The name King of Congo did not appear again in the extant books of that brotherhood. In the brotherhood in the hamlet of Bacalhau in 1830, a list of elected officers identified the slave José Congo as the King of Congo in the same year that they listed a black king and queen who were both *crioulos*.[85] In 1830, the last year of the extant list of elections, the title King of Congo appeared on the list. The records point to a position called the King of Congo in the brotherhoods that may have differed from the position of the black king and queen, who were elected every year. The documentation does not give enough information from which to draw any firm conclusions, but it does suggest that a King of Congo existed slightly beneath the surface of the official documentation of

82. Mário de Andrade and other folklorists write at great length about Queen Xinga in festivals where she or her ambassador is represented. For example, in the northeast in celebrations at which Xinga or her ambassador appears, it is not at the side of the King of Congo, but rather as his adversary. The version Mário de Andrade collected was from a script for the drama of the Congos given to him by a participant of that festival of the rosary in Natal in the state of Rio Grande do Norte. Mario de Andrade, *Danças dramáticas do Brasil* (São Paulo: Livraria Martins Editora, 1962), 40–105. Similarly, Alceu Maynard Araújo described a festival of congadas that he witnessed in Xiririca (now Eldorado) São Paulo during which Queen Xinga is mentioned but never appears. Alceu Maynard Araújo, *Folclore nacional: Festas, bailados, mitos e lendas*, vol. 1 (São Paulo: Edições Melhoramentos, 1964), 263–65. Linda M. Heywood also points out some places where Queen Nzinga appears or is referred to in present-day festivals. Heywood, "Angolan-Afro-Brazilian Connections," 20–21.

83. "Entradas dos Irmãos," São João del Rei 1747–1806, AINSR, 6 January 1773.

84. Ibid., 6 January 1793.

85. "Livro de Termos de Meza," Arraial de Bacalhau, 1758–1893, AEAM Y12.

the brotherhoods in Minas Gerais, mostly hidden from the eyes of the authorities.

One of the characteristics of the present-day Kings and Queens of Congo in the rosary festivals is that they hold their positions for life and pass them on upon their death to another family member. In the colonial period, the practice of having black kings and queens for life was known in some regions of Brazil. Henry Koster, describing the customs of the blacks in Pernambuco around 1815, pointed out that the King and Queen of Congo were elected only if one had died or been dismissed for some reason during the previous year.[86] The first concrete evidence in Minas Gerais of the practice of having kings and queens for life appeared in the brotherhood of Pouso Alto. Their statutes stated that the positions of king and queen were so important that without them the festival would lack brilliance. To avoid this possibility, the brotherhood named a black king and queen for life to pick up the crown in case one of the elected royalty died.[87] Either the lifelong kings and queens, Kings and Queens of Congo, formed part of the tradition that needed to remain hidden from the view of the authorities (and thus out of the documentation), or the practice of having these hereditary positions did not come into widespread practice until the nineteenth century.

Even if the tradition of kings and queens for life did not start until the nineteenth century, Martius's opinion that the kings and queens within the brotherhoods had no meaning reflects the views of a visitor who only witnessed the celebration from the outside. This veneer of insignificance allowed the blacks to continue with their coronations even after they had been outlawed by the authorities. The position of kings and queens, however, was far from insignificant; in fact it had great meaning for the members of the rosary brotherhood. In the eighteenth century the black kings of Minas Gerais held enough power to prompt the vicar, Padre Leonardo de Azevedo Castro, of a small town near the city of Mariana to write a petition in 1771 to the governor of Minas Gerais complaining about the abuses of kings in the rosary brotherhoods. Like the conde de Assumar fifty years earlier, Padre Leonardo complained that the titles of king and queen were "indecent, abominable, and incompatible" with slavery. He attached a series of documents to the complaint that, in his view, proved the bad character of the blacks. In one example Padre Leonardo complained that the black king went to the jail to order the freedom of some prisoners. When the jailer asked for the order of the judge, the king responded that he did not care what the

---

86. Koster, *Travels in Brazil*, 273–74.
87. "Compromisso . . . de Pouso Alto," 1820, APM SP 959, chapter 17.

judge ordered, that he was the king and that it was he who gave the orders. In another case, the king and his retinue passed two shoemakers who did not remove their hats or stand up when the group walked by. In response, the blacks started a brawl that the chief of police had to break up. These accounts demonstrate that the kings of the brotherhoods had an understanding of their temporal, local power as leaders of the black population. Whites also respected the black kings, according to Padre Leonardo. He cited a case from Tejuco, the same town in which Martius later witnessed the festival he described, in which the black kings, year after year, gave audiences and dispensed favors to both blacks and whites who came to them.[88]

Kings also played a part in the religious/magical complex present in the brotherhoods. Padre Leonardo complained that in his city the blacks knew that the reelected king was their true king because an oracle had foretold of it. Members of the brotherhood respected the king as a fortune-teller, and people came from all over seeking his advice.[89] Although this type of reference to the supernatural power of black kings and queens was rare in the colonial documentation, the importance of having a king who oversaw a diverse hierarchy echoes the African past, when societies themselves organized along strictly understood hierarchies.[90]

The kings and queens participated in the joyous occasion of the feast day celebration, which was also part of the obligation of the living community of the rosary brotherhoods. The majority of festivals dedicated to Our Lady of the Rosary in colonial Minas Gerais were held at Christmastime despite the fact the feast day fell on 7 October.[91] This timing for the festival occurred for two reasons. First, the association of the rosary brotherhood with slavery made Christmas a good time to give the slaves some time off. The association with slavery is borne out by the fact that that white rosary brotherhoods, or rosary brotherhoods associated with nonslaves, such as the Paracatu rosary

88. Several recent scholars have talked about the extent to which whites also used African diviners and ritual specialists in colonial Brazil. See D. Ramos, "A influência africana," 142–55; Sweet, *Recreating Africa.*

89. Padre Leonardo's letter and accompanying documents were published in the notes of Gilberto Freyre, *Sobrados e mucambos: Decadência do patriarcado rural e desenvolvimento do urbano,* vol. 2, 5th ed. (Rio de Janeiro: Livraria José Olympio Editora, 1977), 412–15.

90. The practice of consulting oracles, the existence of curing ceremonies, and the use of magic were common in colonial Minas Gerais and throughout Brazil, not only among blacks but within many segments of the population. See Laura de Mello e Souza, *O diabo e a terra de Santa Cruz* (São Paulo: Companhia das Letras, 1989), 151–273; D. Ramos, "A influência africana," 144–55; Sweet, *Recreating Africa,* 119–37.

91. This date was usually written in the *compromissos* as the first, second, and third *oitava* of Christmas.

brotherhood, held their festivals on the feast day of Our Lady of the Rosary. That date for the festival would become more common in the second half of the nineteenth century for many rosary brotherhoods. Second, the celebration of the rosary festival in the Christmas period stemmed from the association of the King of Congo with one of the three kings, or wise men, of the Christmas story, Balthasar, who is portrayed as black and whose feast day is 6 January.[92] For example, in Rio de Janeiro Congo slaves "celebrated the old Kingdom of Kongo in their songs, honored the Wise Man Balthasar as King of Congo, and crowned their own kings and queens."[93] In Minas Gerais, although festivals were often held during the Christmas season, the connection to the wise men in the biblical story would not be overtly made in the documents of the rosary brotherhoods until the nineteenth century.

The compromissos offer few clues about the nature of the festivals themselves. Most of them, as in the first half of the century, called for a sermon, a sung mass, and a litany. The accounting books duly recorded the cost of these activities. Yet the statutes, as documents that were overseen, at least to some extent, by the authorities, may have contained information that the members deemed "safe" for the authorities' eyes. Yet in many of the compromissos was also the warning that the festivals should proceed with as much solemnity as possible, implying that this might not have always been the case. One 1756 statute, from Rio Acima, tried to ward off some of the disorder that must have been part of the festivals, stating that "it is well known the disorder with which our black brothers participate in their festivals."[94] It was described in the document how the brothers and sisters were to conduct themselves in chapel on the day of the festival, special strictures being placed upon the female judges; they were allowed to bring only one *fâmula* (lady-in-waiting) to help them arrange their clothes, and if the female judges needed to bring more servants to help them, they could not sit inside the *grades*, the seats of honor.

Parts of the rituals that are considered "traditional" in the festivals today, beyond the crowning of kings and queens, had their origins in the colonial period. In the current festivals, the kings and queens are always picked up

92. Many of the brotherhoods of the rosary today still celebrate the Folia de Reis, sometimes called the *reisado*, from Christmas to 6 January. The Folia de Reis is a popular festival that includes dances and songs celebrating the visit of the three kings to the infant Jesus.

93. Karasch, *Slave Life*, 19. Not all brotherhoods held their festivals on Christmas, for instance the festivals associated with the white brotherhoods of the rosary, like that in Cachoeira do Campo, were held on the first Sunday of October, near the time of the official feast day of Our Lady of the Rosary (7 October). Serro has always held their celebration on the last weekend of July.

94. "Compromisso da Irmandade de Nossa Senhora do Rosário, Rio das Pedras," 1756, AEAM A21, chapter 9.

(*buscados*) in their houses by the congados and accompanied to the chapels or areas where the festival will take place. The 1750 compromisso from Ouro Preto gives hints of the origin of this practice in the colonial period. It is suggested therein that in order to avoid disturbances the kings and queens did not have to be picked up at their homes, or even met at the door of the church. However, if there was good order in the brotherhood, the members could go to get the kings and queens in their homes if they wished and accompany them to the church.[95] This account serves to link the kings and queens to the feast day celebration and to demonstrate the way in which the brotherhood asserted its physical presence out into the streets.

Today, the congados, the groups of costumed dancers and musicians who serve as "ambassadors" to the court of the king and queen, continue to have the responsibility of picking up the kings and queens in their homes, but the colonial documentation did not use the term *congado* until the nineteenth century. Nevertheless, some groups that resemble present-day congados were noted in the eighteenth century. One of the earliest extant documents that describe these groups comes from the *Aureo trono episcopal*, written in 1748 about the celebration of the arrival of the first bishop to Minas Gerais. The account described a group of eleven young *mulatinhos* with skirts and headdresses made of long plumes, holding bows and dancing energetically through the streets.[96] Although the festival was not connected specifically with the feast day celebrations of Our Lady of the Rosary, the groups described in this account, now called *caboclos* and *caboclinhos*, still participate in the festivals of the rosary throughout the Serro do Frio region. The same plumed figures appeared in the late eighteenth-century stylized watercolors depicting the festival of the rosary and the Day of Kings celebration that were painted by Carlos Julião, a captain of the royal army (Fig. 2). Julião wrote that his images came from Rio de Janeiro and Serro do Frio in Minas Gerais, and his watercolors could have portrayed rosary festivals in either region.[97] The figures in the images do bear a close resemblance to the dancers described in the *Aureo trono episcopal* and to those of congado groups in that region today (Fig. 3).

The term *congada* first appears in the documentation in the description of the festival by Karl von Martius. He used the word to describe a group of

95. "Compromisso da Irmandade de Nossa Senhora do Rosário, Ouro Preto, 1750," APM SPPP 1/35 caixa 02, doc. 44.
96. Laura de Mello e Souza, *Desclassificados do ouro: A pobreza mineira no século XVIII* (Rio de Janeiro: Editora Graal, 1986), 22 n. 10.
97. Carlos Julião, *Riscos illuminados de figurinhos de Brancos e Negros dos usos do Rio de Janeiro e Serro do Frio*, introduction by Lygia da Fonseca Fernandes da Cunha (Rio de Janeiro, 1960), plates xxxv, xxxvi, xxxvii.

FIG. 2.   Coronation of a King on the Day of Kings, watercolor, from Carlos Julião, Riscos illuminados de figurinhos de Brancos e Negros dos usos do Rio de Janeiro e Serro do Frio. Courtesy of the collection of the Fundação Biblioteca Nacional, RJ.

FIG. 3. *Caboclinhos* from the rosary festival in Serro, one of the only festivals that has continued without serious interruptions from the colonial period.

participants in the festival of blacks in Tejuco in 1818, commenting that the king and the queen of the brotherhood "received the official visit of a foreign ambassador to the court of the Congo (which is called the *congada*)."[98] The participants in the Congada jumped, leaped, made faces, and bowed deeply and were accompanied by the riotous sound of drums and shakers, "creating such a bizarre spectacle that you would imagine that you were in a band of monkeys."[99] Almost two centuries earlier, Gaspar Barlaeus, a visitor to Dutch Recife, described a similar performance that occurred during the visit of the ambassador of the king of Kongo to Recife in 1642. According to Barlaeus's description, the Kongelese ambassador and his retinue gave a performance that included "original dances, leaps, formidable swordplay, [and] the dazzle of eyes simulating anger against an enemy."[100] In that ritual drama, the Kongolese

98. Karl von Martius quoted in Cascudo, *Antologia*, 94.
99. Ibid., 95.
100. Gaspar Barlaeus, *Historia dos feitos recentementes praticados durante Oito Anos no Brasil*, trans. Cláudio Brandão (Rio de Janeiro: Ministério de Educação, 1940), 272.

FIG. 4. *Feast Day of Our Lady of the Rosary, Patroness of the Blacks*, by João Maurício Rugendas. Rugendas traveled through the interior of Brazil as part of a Russian-sponsored expedition in the second quarter of the nineteenth century. Courtesy of the collection of the Fundação Biblioteca Nacional, RJ.

ambassador represented the king of Kongo and received representatives from different embassies from various nations, who paid homage to him, "according to the ceremonies used among their nations, in their deportment, courtesies, and reverential behavior."[101] The description of this ritual, enacted by the emissaries of the king of Kongo, closely resembled the rituals that would be enacted by the members of the rosary brotherhoods in colonial Minas Gerais. The similarities suggest that the performance of these embassy representatives in the brotherhoods echoed African practices that had occurred centuries earlier.

The colonial documentation of the brotherhoods offers few clues about what Karl von Martius had called the *congada*, although descriptions would become more prevalent later in the nineteenth century. In colonial documentation, the groups Martius described appeared in receipt books, which listed them singing and dancing through the streets in order to collect alms for the festival.[102] In the early nineteenth century, the accounting books from São João del Rei often included entries noting alms collected by the "dances on the riverfront," or the "dances of the blacks on Sundays," or "at the door of the church [by] the revelry of the drums of the nations."[103] The "nations" referred to members of the African ethnicities who collected alms for the brotherhoods. The 1820 compromisso from Pouso Alto in southern Minas Gerais specifically named one of those nations, Mozambique, whose members had the custom of going out into the town to collect alms.[104]

Like the Mozambiques who appear in the apparition story of Our Lady of the Rosary, the presence of congado groups called Mozambiques in the colonial documents raises the question of whether the participants in those groups were actually from the discrete locations that the name implied. Unfortunately, there was no accompanying documentation from Pouso Alto that might have shown a presence of members from East Africa, and Mozambiques were rarely listed on the admissions records of the rosary brotherhoods and other documentation such as election lists. In his comprehensive study of slavery in Minas Gerais, Laird Bergad found that between 1715 and 1888 slaves identified as Mozambique never constituted more than 2.7 percent of the population.[105] Nevertheless, by the late nineteenth century these titles certainly were not directly linked to African ethnicities. By then, *Congos, Mozambiques,* and

101. Ibid.
102. The collection of alms by dancing groups was not unique to the congados, or to the brotherhoods of blacks. See Abreu, *Império do divino*, 39–40.
103. "Livro de Receitas e Despezas," São João del Rei, 1803–1825, AINSR.
104. "Compromisso da Irmandade . . . de Pouso Alto," 1820, APM SP 959, chapter 20.
105. Bergad, *Slavery*, 151.

other names had become ritual designations of nations within the festivals of the rosary in Minas Gerais, remnants of both an African past and, in the case of the group known as *caboclinhos*, the heterogeneous past of a united community.

Conclusion

Despite their many differences in origin and legal status, members of the rosary brotherhoods came together to form a community in which the significant commonalities were "race" and devotion to Our Lady of the Rosary. Their consciousness of being black allowed them to assert themselves collectively in the dominant society. Equally important, however, the practice of the devotion to Our Lady of the Rosary in the feast day celebrations made space for the continuation of ethnic identities in the members' rituals, simultaneously asserting their unity as blacks and making room for a collective memory that linked the heirs to the tradition with an African homeland. This demonstrates that for the members of the rosary brotherhoods in Minas Gerais, the move from ethnicity to race was not an unbroken chain but rather a complex process of reidentification that signaled an acceptance of the new society while simultaneously fostering ties to the old. Fundamental to the process was the ability of blacks to form communities, create hierarchies within those communities, and maintain links to the ancestors and to unseen beings through rituals of death, thanks, and devotion.

Yet the end of the colonial period saw a general decadence in the institutions of the brotherhoods of the rosary. All the books of the brotherhoods show a decline in membership and funds in the last decades of the eighteenth and the beginning of the nineteenth century. This decline can be attributed both to the creation of brotherhoods for more specific groups within the population that once participated in the brotherhoods of the rosary and to the general economic decline in the captaincy.[106] The accounting books reveal that by the end of the eighteenth century many of the brotherhoods were struggling to keep up certain practices that they had previously enjoyed. The church of the rosary in Mariana, for instance, had always housed three brotherhoods, dedicated to Our Lady of the Rosary, Saint Benedict, and Saint Iphigenia. Each of the three brotherhoods through the eighteenth century had hired its own chaplain. In the early nineteenth century, the brotherhoods decided together that they could afford only one chaplain, to share

---

106. Salles, *Associações religiosas*, 47.

between the three, "following the example of the brotherhoods of Alto da Cruz, that have only one chaplain, and in the same way that of Ouro Preto."[107] As repairs became necessary on their churches, many brotherhoods canceled their annual festivals or radically simplified them.[108]

Nevertheless, the general decadence of Minas Gerais in the late colonial period did not destroy the brotherhoods; it simply caused them to adapt and evolve, as they had always done and continue to do. In fact, in the nineteenth century the brotherhoods experienced a great resurgence. Far from disappearing at the end of the colonial period, they continued, and became even stronger, under the new provincial government of Minas Gerais in imperial Brazil.

107. "Termos de Meza," Irmandade de Nossa Senhora do Rosário dos Pretos, Mariana, 1747–1844, AEAM P27, 1807.

108. The brotherhood in Ouro Preto wrote in their minutes that they would not have the *festa* in 1808 and 1814 "vista a grande decadência em que se acha o país e grande falta de esmolas que dão os Juizes." The brotherhood in Mariana canceled their *festa* three times in the second decade of the nineteenth century and radically simplified the others. "Termos de Meza," Irmandade de Nossa Senhora do Rosário dos Pretos, Ouro Preto, 1788–1897, CC rol 82–83; and "Termos de Meza," Mariana, 1747–1844, AEAM P27.

5 THE BROTHERHOODS IN THE BRAZILIAN EMPIRE

Minhas perna me dói, aê,
o meu corpo me dói, aê,
os meus braço já me dói, aê,
o meu ombro me dói, aê,
minha cabeça me dói, aê.

[My legs hurt,
my body hurts,
my arms hurt,
my shoulders hurt,
my head hurts.]

—*Vissungo* (work song) from the time of slavery

The political and social changes that occurred in Brazil in the sixty-seven year empire that followed the declaration of independence in 1822 impacted the rosary brotherhoods in Minas Gerais in various ways. Yet the continuities in the system, especially in the slave system; in the slave trade, which lasted through 1850; and in the extension of the *padroado real,* also created the conditions in which the rosary brotherhoods would not experience any large ruptures within their basic organizational and celebratory framework. Instead, the relationships and strategies set in the colonial period continued, and rosary brotherhoods and their festivals thrived, because of both the internal coherence of the organizations and the support of the organizations and their festivals by the general population of Minas Gerais. By the end of the empire in 1889, the African slave trade had been closed down for thirty-eight years, yet the records of "African" practices in the brotherhoods continued. In fact, the documents of the brotherhoods in the nineteenth century provide links both to the twentieth-century festivals and to the African and colonial past of the participants. The brotherhoods continued to serve as sites where blacks, both slave and free, could create a shared identity built on the foundation of their

common link to an African past—and symbols of that past—and their active
memory of that past through their devotion to Our Lady of the Rosary.

Independence and the Beginning of the Empire

Independence in Brazil came about after a series of events largely set into
motion by the Napoleonic invasion of the Iberian Peninsula and the Portuguese Crown's subsequent flight to Brazil in 1808. Upon his arrival in Brazil,
Dom João VI opened the Brazilian ports to free trade, reversing Pombal's
mercantilist and monopolistic reforms. In 1810, Dom João VI set up prefer-
ential tariffs to England in thanks for that country's transporting the court
safely from Portugal to Brazil. All these measures helped the Brazilian
economy but abolished the monopoly that Portugal had had on Brazilian
goods, the latter a move that the Portuguese came to view as the cause of
an economic depression in Portugal. The Portuguese became desperate to
bring back the traditional system, and they believed that the return of the
king to the mother country would convince him to revert to the old system.
Instead of returning, however, in 1815 Dom João VI raised the status of the
Portuguese colony in America and created the "United Kingdom of Portugal,
Brazil, and Algarves."[1]

The tension between the people wanting to return to a monopolistic
system and those favoring free trade became increasingly heated. The issue
came to a head when the liberal revolution of 1820 in Spain swept into Portugal. Despite Dom João VI's superficial attempts to placate Portuguese
merchants after the Spanish revolution, a liberal uprising erupted in the
Portuguese city of Oporto in 1820. The leaders of the revolution convened
the parliament (Côrtes) and ordered a constitution to be written, but the real
intent of the revolutionaries was to reverse the liberal concessions made to
Brazil.[2] The revolutionaries in Portugal demanded the immediate return of
the king. Against his will, Dom João VI returned to Portugal to face a hostile
parliament. He left his son Pedro as regent, telling him, "Pedro, if Brazil
breaks away, let it rather do so for you who will respect me than for one of
those adventurers."[3] Under mounting pressure from the Brazilian elites,

---

1. Roderick J. Barman, *Brazil: The Forging of a Nation, 1798–1852* (Stanford: Stanford
University Press, 1988), 45–53; Emília Viotti da Costa, *The Brazilian Empire: Myths and Histories* (Chicago: University of Chicago Press, 1985), 12–15.

2. E. V. d. Costa, *Brazilian Empire*, 15.

3. Barman, *Brazil*, 72.

coupled with the intransigence of the Portuguese Côrtes, Dom Pedro declared independence from Portugal on 7 September 1822, naming himself the first emperor of Brazil.[4]

Once independence was achieved, the Brazilian elite, many of them large land and slave owners, sought to gain control of the young nation, and they imported liberalism as the political ideology with which to do this. As Emília Viotti da Costa so cogently points out, the Brazilian elites shaped liberalism to fit their specific needs. Before independence, they had used liberalism as a rallying cry to free Brazil from Portuguese control. Once independence was achieved, they sought to use the ideology to attain economic and political control of the country.[5]

The rhetoric of liberalism, however, affected not only the elite. Its ideas reached into the consciousness of even the blacks, who interpreted liberal discourse in their own way. In 1822, shortly before independence, Antônio Paulino Limpo de Abreu, a local judge in Minas Gerais, wrote a letter to the president of the provisional government of Minas Gerias, justifying his decisions about a black "who is, or who calls himself, the King of the Congos."[6] Limpo de Abreu explained that the blacks interpreted the discussions about liberty in the constitutional congress to signify that on Christmas, or shortly afterward on the Day of Kings, they would receive their letters of freedom. Although Limpo de Abreu concluded that the notice of the uprising was only the whisperings of the wishes of the blacks rather than a plan, he ordered the authorities to prohibit "all gatherings of blacks, to take away their weapons, and to severely punish those who deserved to be punished."[7] The date on which the blacks understood that they would receive their freedom coincided, not by chance, with the feast day celebrations of Our Lady of the Rosary of the blacks, and the King of Congo noted by Limpo de Abreu may well have been the head of the local rosary brotherhood.

Neither the elites nor the emperor, however, had any intention of freeing the slaves or granting rights to the disenfranchised masses. On the contrary,

4. Although independence was relatively "bloodless" and did result in a unified Brazilian state (as opposed to the mayhem of the Spanish American independence movements) it sparked a rash of revolts from regional factions that did not want to submit to a strong central authorities. In the 1830s and 1840s there were significant regional revolts in Rio Grande do Sul, Maranhão, Pernambuco, Alagoas, and Pará, and minor revolts throughout the new country. Judy Bieber Freitas, "Marginal Elites: Politics, Power, and Patronage in the Backlands of Northern Minas Gerais, Brazil, 1830–1889" (Ph.D. diss., Johns Hopkins University, 1994), 16.

5. E. V. d. Costa, *Brazilian Empire*, 53–57.

6. Letter from Antonio Paulino Limpo de Abreu to the president and deputies of the provisional government, 14 February 1822, APM SP JGP 1/6, caixa 01, doc. 28.

7. Ibid.

the ruling groups had an interest in maintaining the status quo. This stance was made clear both in the proceedings of the National Convention, assembled in 1822 to write a constitution, and in the emperor's constitution of 1824. The desire of the elites to gain political hegemony put them in direct conflict with the emperor, a problem that came to a head during the National Convention. At the convention, the elites relentlessly attacked the emperor. They moved to put the provincial governments, the ministers, and even the army under legislative control and even to abolish the right of the emperor to veto legislation. The emperor responded by closing down the convention, ordering the arrest of some representatives, and sending others into exile. In 1824, the emperor's council of state wrote a constitutional charter, which, in an attempt to placate the elites, followed the project drafted by the convention. However, beyond creating the conditions for a strong oligarchy and assuring the continuation of slavery, it gave significant powers to the emperor. The constitution also defined the new nation's policy about the relationship between church and state, continuing the preeminent position of the Catholic Church in Brazilian society.[8]

Most significantly, the new constitution continued the *padroado* by ceding Dom Pedro I the right to censor acts and decrees from Rome, to collect the *dízimo*, and to name bishops. The mood had changed in Rome, however, and, in large part because of the challenges of liberalism throughout Europe and the Americas, throughout the nineteenth century the Vatican became increasingly intent on centralizing power in Rome and unifying doctrine and practice, in a movement known as the Ultramontane reforms. The conflict between the state and the church that had occurred on the local level in the colonial period had manifested in the latter part of the eighteenth century primarily in the increased presence of parish priests in the running of the brotherhoods. In the nineteenth century the conflict became an international struggle of wills between successive popes and the emperors of Brazil.[9]

One example of the conflict was in the pope's refusal to recognize the emperor's right to name bishops, and the pope's insistence that the nominations be sent to Rome for review. This conflict manifested in several different contentious cases in the province of Minas Gerais. When the diocese of Diamantina was formed in 1854, the pope compromised by letting the emperor choose the new bishop. The emperor, Dom Pedro II, did not recognize the right of the pope to interfere in the church affairs of Brazil and angrily wrote

8. E. V. d. Costa, *Brazilian Empire*, 55–59.
9. Pedro A. Ribeiro de Oliveira, "Catolicismo popular e romanização do Catolicismo brasileiro," *Revista eclesiástica brasileira* 36, no. 141 (1976): 131–41.

that it was his right to name the bishops, without any permission from the pope. The dispute over the right of the emperor to the *padroado* continued throughout the century as more ecclesiastical authorities openly expressed their resentment over the intrusion of the Crown into the affairs of the church. In the diocese of Mariana, the conflict came to a head over the promotion of José de Souza e Silva Roussim, a man of "notoriously scandalous customs."[10] Roussim tried four times for the post of *cônego da Sé* (a high administrative post in the church) in Mariana, and four times was rejected by the bishop, Dom Antônio Ferreira Viçoso (1844–75). Dom Viçoso objected to Roussim's appointment because of Roussim's questionable personal reputation. Finally, in 1855, Roussim was posted to the position by imperial decree. When the bishop objected in a long letter to the government, the ministers of state voted to keep Roussim in the position. Finally, when Dom Viçoso refused to follow the order, because he considered it against the laws of the church, one of Dom Pedro's ministers threatened, "I can make bishops and much more so, priests."[11]

Although Dom Pedro II tenaciously held on to his power over the church, he allowed his bishops to attend the First Vatican Council, called by the ultramontanist Pope Pius IX (1846–78). Seven of the eleven Brazilian bishops attended the conference and, in 1870, brought back to Brazil an ultramontanist agenda that proposed to free the church from state control and settle it under the wing of the pope in Rome.[12] The growing conflict finally came to a head in an incident known as the Religious Question of 1874. The young bishop of Olinda, Dom Vital Maria Gonçalves de Oliveira, refused to allow the clergy to attend or participate in a mass given by a brotherhood that included Masons among its members. Freemasonry had been flourishing in Brazil since before independence and had played a major role in Brazil's break from Portugal.[13] Many clerics and even some bishops were Masons, as was Dom Pedro II, and the Roman church considered the white brotherhoods to be hotbeds of Masonic activity. Dom Vital's attack, therefore, purposefully aimed at the very fabric of the Brazilian church. The brotherhood retaliated by publishing a list of laymen and clergy who were members of brotherhoods and also Masons. Dom Vital ordered that the Masons be expelled from the brotherhoods and the clergy give up their

10. Dom Pedro II quoted in Waldemar de Almeida Barbosa, *História de Minas*, vol. 2 (Belo Horizonte, Brazil: Editora Comunicação, 1979), 401.

11. Quoted in Barbosa, *História de Minas*, vol. 2, 402–3.

12. Bruneau, *Political Transformation*, 22–28.

13. For discussions of the Freemason's involvement in the independence movement, see Barman, *Brazil*, 79, 82, 94, and 98–99. It is important to point out that unlike in Europe, in Brazil Masonry was not anticlerical; in fact, many clerics were Masons.

affiliation with the Masons. Dom Macedo Costa, the bishop from Pará, joined Dom Vital in the struggle. The brotherhoods complained to the government, upon which the emperor ordered the imprisonment of the two bishops and imposed sentences of five years of hard labor. Although the bishops' sentences were eventually reduced and they were finally pardoned, this conflict symbolized the increasing tension between the Brazilian government, the lay religious brotherhoods, and the Vatican.[14]

Despite the bishops' loyalty to Rome, the whole institution of the church did not turn with one great movement toward Rome. Much of the clergy continued to lead lifestyles that were less than "ideal," according to the most basic precepts of the Roman Catholic doctrine. Thomas Ewbank, an American who visited Rio de Janeiro in the mid-nineteenth century, noted that although priests vowed to live a celibate life, "you will find nearly the whole with families; and it is a substantial fact, which admits of no argument, that in their amours they are ever partial to women of color—blacks or mulattos."[15] The controversial minister of justice in 1831 and 1832, Diogo Feijó, himself a priest and most likely the son of a priest, had a mistress and five children and, not surprisingly, openly criticized clerical celibacy. He also spoke out against the "pretensions of the Pope."[16] Feijó, despite his family, was nominated to be bishop of Mariana in 1835 (he refused the position). In Minas Gerais, the situation of the clergy was no better. Dom Viçoso made it part of his mission to reform the clergy, who "for the most part lived as if they were married."[17] The Catholic Church in Brazil, then, was far from a unified ideal that the ultramontane church would have liked it to be. It remained a complex organism, which by the nineteenth century had developed its own personality in Brazil, as the Brazilian Catholic Church, in which brotherhoods continued to play a fundamental role.

The Rosary Brotherhoods and the State

The imperial government continued the tradition of Portuguese colonial rule by retaining a supervisory role in the brotherhoods. Although Dom Pedro I closed the Board of Conscience and Orders in 1828, he ruled that the brotherhoods would be regulated by secretaries of the state after the religious

14. Bruneau, *Political Transformation*, 22–29.
15. Thomas Ewbank, *Life in Brazil* (New York: Harper and Brothers, 1856), 141–43.
16. Barman, *Brazil*, 171. Trindade, *Arquidiocese*, vol. 1, 208–14.
17. Trindade, *Arquidiocese*, vol. 1, 208–14, quote at 221.

sections of the compromissos had been approved by the church.[18] The provinces followed the lead of the federal government, and in 1837 the legislative assembly of Minas Gerais passed a law that gave the bishop authority to approve compromissos.[19] The compromissos from Minas Gerais during this period also included provisos with the approval of the provincial government, but there is no record that they were sent off to the federal capital. In 1859 the imperial government and the General Assembly sent out a "circular" advising the presidents of the provinces that they wanted copies of the brotherhood statutes, including the provisos written by the provincial government with the alterations they had suggested.[20] It was probably this circular that prompted the provincial assembly in Minas Gerais to pass a decree ordering that compromissos be registered in the *livros de provedoria* (purveyor's books).[21] In the early 1860s, the president of the province also sent out a call to the various municipalities to send him copies of the statutes, probably also in compliance with the imperial decree.[22]

Beyond the oversight of the compromissos, the increasing presence of the parish priests in the decision making of the brotherhoods gave both state and church authorities an increased presence within the brotherhoods of the rosary. In the nineteenth-century statutes, the parish priest was often given the right to officiate, that is, hold the *presidência* (presidency), over the meetings. In the early nineteenth century, some brotherhoods attempted to undercut the power of the parish priest, such as had occurred in Barbacena in 1809, but the proviso always effected changes in those clauses to include the parish priest in the running of the brotherhoods.[23] By the mid-nineteenth century, the brotherhoods no longer tried to replace the priest with a hired chaplain. The 1849 compromisso from São Sebastião de Capituba included a requirement for the president to be the parish priest and the vice president another priest.[24] The

18. *Código Filipino*, Primeiro Livro das Ordenações, ABG, 270–72.

19. The law itself was the Lei Provincial R.[mo] 66 Art. 2 de 18/3/1837. "Compromisso da Irmandade de Nossa Senhora do Rosário, Arraial de Corregos," 1851, APM SP 959, proviso.

20. *Colleção das leis do Império do Brasil, 1860*, vol. 23, part 2 (Rio de Janeiro: Typografia Nacional, 1860), 246.

21. The decree was the second part of "artigo 33 do decreto 9 no. 2:711 de 19 de dezembro de 1860." "Compromisso da Irmandade de Nossa Senhora do Rosário de Paroquia de S. Gonçalvo de Contagem," 1867, ACBH, proviso.

22. Letter from Antonio Carlos Monteiro de Moura to the president of the province, 21 April 1862, APM SP 959.

23. "Capítulos do Compromisso . . . da Villa de Barbacena," 1809, AEAM Livros das Irmandades 35, proviso.

24. "Compromisso, Irmandade de Nossa Senhora do Rosário de São Sebastião de Capituba," 1860, AEAM 0253 Dom Antonio Ferreira Viçoso 1868, 03 02 014, chapter 15.

statutes from Betim (1855), Oliveira (1860), and Contagem (1867) included similar clauses.[25] The rosary brotherhood in Bacalhau started recording its elections again in 1860, after a thirty-year pause, and these new elections were supervised by the parish priest (*sob a presidência*).[26] This increased presence of the parish priest did give the diocesan church more oversight over the brotherhoods, but there is little evidence that the brotherhoods altered the basic administrative or ritual structure as a result.[27]

The provincial assembly further regulated the brotherhoods through the passage of municipal laws that affected the festivals and other rituals of the rosary brotherhoods. The Postura das Câmaras Municipais da Província de Minas Gerais (Rules of the Municipal Councils of the Province of Minas Gerais) confirmed by the Conselho Geral (State Assembly) in 1830 set forth many regulations concerning the running of brotherhoods on the municipal level, especially where they overlapped with questions of public order and health.[28] For example, they officially banned the burial of the dead within churches, which had come to be viewed as a public health issue. Burying people inside of the churches throughout the Portuguese Empire had been outlawed in a royal letter of 1801, but this had been largely ignored. An imperial law of 1828 renewed the prohibition, which was fought by towns, parishes, and brotherhoods. In 1829 the vicar general (*vigário-geral*) reinterpreted this law to say that the towns had to build cemeteries but that some burials could still occur inside the churches. The argument went back and forth until finally the State Assembly banned the practice altogether in the Postura.[29]

The section about public security in the Postura included many clauses about other activities of the brotherhoods. Article 99 prohibited the asking of alms "under whatever invocation" and listed a fine of four *mil reis* and four days' imprisonment for any infractions. This rule, however, excepted

---

25. "Estatutos, Irmandade de Nossa Senhora do Rosário da Freguesia de Nossa Senhora do Carmo do Betim," 1855, APM SP 959, chapter 3; "Compromisso da Irmandade . . . de Contagem," ACBH, article 11.

26. "Livro de Termos de Meza," Arraial de Bacalhau, AEAM Y12, 97–172v.

27. "Termos de Meza," Irmandade de Nossa Senhora do Rosário dos Pretos, Mariana, 1747–1844, AEAM P27; "Termos de Meza," Irmandade de Nossa Senhora do Rosário dos Pretos, Barbacena, 1812–1932, AEAM C30 and C21; "Livro de Termos de Meza," Arraial de Bacalhau, AEAM Y12.

28. After 1834 the Conselho Geral (literally General Council) came to be called the Assembléia. For a discussion of the relationship between the *município* (town), the province, and the central government, see Freitas, "Marginal Elites," 22–28.

29. "Postura das Câmaras Municipais da Província de Minas Gerais confirmado pelo Conselho Geral da mesma Província," AEAM, 0158 Dom Frei José da Santíssima Trindade, 1823 02-2-034, chapter 1, article 66. Also see Trindade, *Arquidiocese*, vol. 1, 197–98.

certain brotherhoods, such as the Misericórdia and the Santíssimo das Almas (the two brotherhoods of the white elite) and others that had already been granted licenses to collect alms.[30] Although this was not targeted specifically at the black brotherhoods, it might have affected the ability of the different groups of "African nations" of going about their traditional practice of asking for alms in the streets. Despite the ban, by the 1860s these groups, the congados, from the black brotherhoods of the rosary continued to collect alms in the streets.

The Postura included a chapter about public safety that was directed primarily at the activities of the slaves and blacks. For instance, a slave could not be given a license to open a business, and if the license was given because the slave "maliciously hid" the fact of his or her "condition," he or she would be fined and the business closed down.[31] The *batuque* (a dance of African origin that had long been regarded as dangerous) was expressly forbidden, even in private homes, during the day or night. The following article, however, allowed the slaves to "play, sing, and dance in the streets and plazas of the villages," but, it was added, the local justice of the peace could reverse that ruling.[32] Finally, and most important for the discussion of the brotherhoods of the blacks, the next article permitted "the *quinbites*, or reinados, that the slaves are accustomed to have on certain days of the year, as long as they are not held at night."[33] This municipal law officially ended the prohibition against the coronation of black kings and queens that had been enacted under the Pombaline reforms. The lifting of the ban was immediately reflected in the election books of the brotherhood of the rosary in Ouro Preto (the provincial capital). Although elsewhere in Minas Gerais the coronations had continued despite the ban, it must have been more difficult to continue the practice in the seat of power. There, the crowning of kings and queens was not recorded between 1800 and 1823 but began again the year that the first draft of the Postura was written.[34] The reappearance of the king and queen in the documentation in Ouro Preto so shortly after the passage of the local law demonstrates that just as blacks were aware of the discourse on liberalism, the members of the brotherhoods of the rosary were aware of the legislation of the time that affected their practices. Nevertheless, the placement of the Reinados in the laws dealing with the behavior of slaves demonstrates that

30. "Postura das Câmaras Municipais," chapter 1, article 99.
31. Ibid., chapter 3, article 5.
32. Ibid., chapter 2, articles 135 and 136.
33. Ibid., chapter 2, article 137. I have not found a translation of the word *quinbite*; nor have I seen it used in other settings.
34. "Eleições da Irmandade de Nossa Senhora do Rosário, Paróquia do Pilar, Ouro Preto," 1761–1891, CC Paróquia do Pilar, rol 80.

in the minds of the elite there was a continuing association of the rosary brotherhood and their coronations with slaves.

The acceptance of the Reinados of the blacks by the lawmakers, and thus the elites, of Minas Gerais also demonstrates that the celebration had become part of the society and culture of local Minas Gerais. This acceptance of the reinado in Minas Gerais diverged from the tendency of provincial lawmakers elsewhere in Brazil during the same period. For example, the 1845 laws from the city of Desterro in the southern province of Santa Catarina specifically outlawed *batuques,* "as well as those which have as their purpose the supposed African royal ceremonies [*reinados africanos*], which they are accustomed to performing during their celebrations."[35] In Rio de Janeiro, just before independence, the dances of the rosary blacks were banned, and in compensation the king personally ordered that fifty *mil reis* be given to the rosary brotherhood annually for five years to make up for the losses in their income.[36] After 1830, the dances during the rosary feast day celebrations disappeared from the streets of Rio de Janeiro, and even the French traveler Jean Baptiste Debret commented that the "loud costumed festivals" of the black brotherhoods were no longer allowed in Rio de Janeiro and that in order to see them you had to travel to other parts of Brazil.[37] The rosary brotherhood in Rio de Janeiro even suspended the practice of crowning kings and queens.[38]

In Minas Gerais, however, sanctioned by the new provincial laws, the feast day celebrations continued in the nineteenth century and on into the twentieth, accepted by the provincial authorities and local populations as nonthreatening events, as Martius had seen them in his description of the festival in Tejuco in the decade before independence. The passage of the provincial/municipal laws accepting the Reinados demonstrates the continuation of a pattern from the eighteenth century of white interest, and even participation, in Afro-*mineiro* activities. As historian Judy Bieber points out, these tendencies "contributed to construction of a distinctive regional identity at odds with imported European norms."[39] Rosary brotherhoods, therefore, were able to continue public celebrations—increasingly using the

35. Conrad, *Children,* 260–65, quote at 260.

36. BN, Rio de Janeiro, Seção de Manuscritos, II—34, 28, 25.

37. Jean Baptiste Debret, *Viagem pitoresca e histórica ao Brasil,* vol. 2, trans. and ed. Sérgio Milliet (São Paulo: Livraria Martins Editora, 1954), 225; see also Abreu, *Império do divino,* 35–36.

38. Joaquim José Costa, *Breve notícia da irmandade de Nossa Senhora do Rosário e São Benedito dos homens pretos do Rio* (Rio de Janeiro: Tipografia Politécnica, 1886).

39. Judy Bieber, "Postmodern Ethnographer in the Backlands: An Imperial Bureaucrat's Perceptions of Post-independence Brazil," *LARR* 33, no. 2 (1998): 59.

financial backing of white patrons—that linked them, as Africans of many ethnicities, to their own past and reinforced their unity as a community of blacks in Brazil.

The Brotherhoods of the Rosary During the Brazilian Empire

Despite continuities from the colonial period, the rosary brotherhoods were not static institutions during the empire. They remained flexible as their members tried to adapt to demographic changes within their population and to changing pressures and attitudes of the local, provincial, and national authorities. Many of the colonial brotherhoods had records that stretched through the nineteenth century, and some into the early twentieth century. Some of the colonial brotherhoods of the rosary revised their compromissos in the nineteenth century in response to changes in the larger social and political world, and many new rosary brotherhoods were founded during the empire. The other books of the brotherhoods, such as accounting books, from before 1830 represent a continuation of the late colonial period. After 1830, the records of brotherhood activity drop off significantly—no new brotherhoods were started, new membership dropped drastically or remained fairly low, and in some cases the books of the brotherhoods stopped altogether.[40] In the 1850s, activities started up again, with many new brotherhoods forming and others experiencing a renaissance both in membership and, following increases in membership, in finances.

There may have been several reasons for the drop-off of the documentary record for the period between 1830 and 1850. The 1831 law freeing all slaves who arrived from outside Brazil may have had an effect on the rosary brotherhood activity. The possible fines for buying slaves may have disinclined masters to allow their slaves to join corporate organizations, from which they might learn more about their rights. Moreover, this twenty-year period coincided with the unrest that erupted throughout Brazil after the abdication of Dom Pedro I. Despite the early coronation of the new emperor, Dom Pedro II, on his fifteenth birthday in 1840, Brazil continued to be buffeted by internal struggle for the following decade. The years 1830–50 were marked

---

40. The rosary brotherhoods in both Sabará and São João del Rei did revise their compromissos in that period—1840 and 1841 respectively. See "Estatutos da Irmandade de Nossa Senhora do Rosário dos Pretos da Cidade de Sabará," 1840, APM SP 959; and "Estatutos da Imrandade de Nossa Senhora do Rosário dos Pretos, São João del Rei," 1841, MASSJ 4.01. In addition, the number of new entrants in the rosary brotherhood in Mariana started to increase significantly after 1840, but jumped to new levels after 1850. See the Appendix, Table 8.

not only by elites battling among themselves but also by "class and racial conflicts [and] tensions between the poor and the rich, between foreigners and natives or between blacks and whites."[41] This confusion may have caused a general feeling of unrest that made participation in the brotherhoods less significant than it had been in the past. Alternatively, because the records of the brotherhoods come largely from official documentation, it may have been that the chaotic decades following independence simply made record keeping within the brotherhoods both impossible and unnecessary.

By the middle of the century Brazil began to settle, however uneasily, into its own nationhood. In 1850 the central government passed a law that finally effectively ended the African slave trade. In 1852, a new cooperation, known as the *conciliação* (compromise), emerged at the national level between the liberals and conservatives, who constituted the two parties that emerged from the chaos. Coinciding with this new stability, new brotherhoods of the rosary were officially formed, membership in the older brotherhoods soared, and the records in accounting books and books of the minutes of the meetings that had stopped around 1830 resumed. By the 1860s, the brotherhoods were expanding again in Minas Gerais.[42] It was in this later period that the books and written accounts of the festivals began to describe events that echo the festivals of today while demonstrating a continuation of colonial traditions.

Within Minas Gerais, the brotherhoods experienced demographic changes during the empire that were linked to changes in the economy. The mining economy had already turned downward at the end of the eighteenth century, and the population of Minas Gerais had to rely less on mining and export commodities in general for their revenue. The economy began to be based more on agriculture and stock raising and some small manufacture, all for both local consumption and export to national markets.[43] Although this trend

41. E. V. d. Costa, *Brazilian Empire*, 68–69.

42. Four of the brotherhoods founded during that period still have ongoing, vibrant festivals dedicated to Our Lady of the Rosary, including that of Oliveira (founded in 1860) and of Contagem, which is the home of the Festival of the Rosary of the Arturos (a brotherhood founded in 1868). The Festa do Rosário of the Arturos, which occurs in the Comunidade Negra dos Arturos (Afro-Brazilian Community of the Arturos) in Contagem, has been one of the most studied festivals of Minas Gerais, perhaps because of the unique Afro-Brazilian family-based community in which it occurs. See Núbia Pereira de Magalhães Gomes and Edimilson de Almeida Pereira, *Negras raízes mineiras: Os Arturos* (Juiz de Fora: Editora da Universidade Federal de Juiz de Fora, 1988); and the recent excellent ethnomusicological study by Glaura Lucas, "Os sons do rosário: Um estudo etnomusicológico do congado mineiro—Arturos e Jatobá" Vols. 1–2 (master's thesis, University of São Paulo, 1999).

43. Amilcar Martins Filho and Roberto B. Martins, "Slavery in a Nonexport Economy: Nineteenth-Century Minas Gerais Revisited," *HAHR* 63 (1983): 556.

had already started in some regions in the eighteenth century, the nineteenth century saw a significant expansion in nonmining activities, even though some diamond and gold mining continued in the metallurgic regions of the province. By the end of the empire, the southern region of Minas Gerais had begun to participate in the coffee boom.[44]

Despite the increasing lack of direct ties to an export economy, slaves continued to be imported into Minas Gerais. Amilcar Martins Filho and Roberto B. Martins, in their influential article on slavery in nineteenth century Minas Gerais, estimate that Minas may have been the largest importer of Africans in that century, with a share of perhaps 30 percent of the total Brazilian imports.[45] There is also evidence to show that conditions began to favor natural reproduction in the slave population. In 1823 the population of native-born slaves was 60 percent of the total *mineiro* slave population.[46] Laird Bergad's detailed research into the demography of Minas Gerais in the eighteenth and nineteenth centuries also demonstrates a steady increase in Brazilian-born slaves and a decrease in African-born slaves in the three main regions that he studied. In fact, in all of the these regions, Brazilian born slaves outnumbered African born slaves by the end of the eighteenth century, a trend that steadily increased until the abolition of slavery in 1888.[47] The overall number of slaves increased in the nineteenth century, although they declined significantly as a percentage of the overall population, from 27.2 percent of the population in the 1831 census, to only 18.2 percent in the 1872 census.[48]

Scholars have long posited that there was a redistribution of slaves in the nineteenth century to the southern coffee-growing regions. Martins and Martins Filho postulate that there was, in fact, no significant redistribution of slaves prior to 1873, and Bergad agrees that the coffee economy, which would have been the factor pulling slaves south, was not significant in Minas Gerais until after 1870, when they did move south.[49] By 1886, in the coffee-growing areas of the Zona da Mata and the south, the slave population had increased to 57.8 percent of the total in the state, the mining region had 17.3 percent, and the rest of the slave population was distributed throughout the state.[50]

44. Bergad, *Slavery*, xx.

45. Martins Filho and Martins, "Slavery in a Nonexport Economy," 549.

46. Douglas Cole Libby, "Proto-industrialisation in a Slave Society: The Case of Minas Gerais," *Journal of Latin American Studies* 23 (1991): 11.

47. Bergad, *Slavery*, 123–26. See also Maria do Carmo Salazar Martins, "Revisitando a província: Comarcas, termos, distritos e população de Minas Gerais em 1833–35" in *Quinto seminario sobre a economia mineira* (Belo Horizonte, Brazil: UFMG/CEDEPLAR, 1990), 13–29.

48. Libby, "Proto-industrialisation," 11.

49. Martins Filho and Martins, "Slavery in a Nonexport Economy," 551–53; Bergad, *Slavery*, 216.

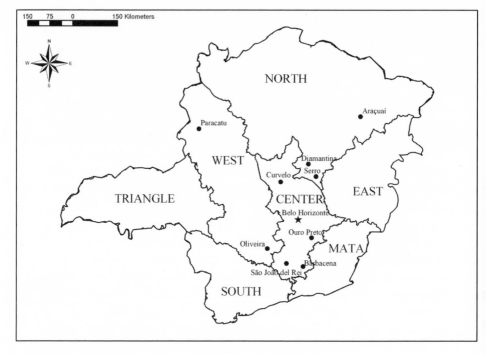

MAP 4.   Regional divisions in nineteenth-century Minas Gerais

As in the colonial period, the membership within the rosary brother-hoods reflected these demographic trends. The admissions of two of these brotherhoods, one in the colonial center of power, Mariana, and the other in the south in Barbacena, just north of the new coffee-growing regions, illustrate the demographic changes in the brotherhoods. The brotherhoods of the rosary in Barbacena and Mariana both had populations on the upswing in the second half of the nineteenth century, and both associations existed well into the twentieth century. Despite the increase in the Mariana brotherhood, after about 1840, the slave population began to decline vis-à-vis the free population, and by the 1870s the brotherhood was almost 90 percent free. The freed (*forro*) population remained miniscule in the overall entrances to the Mariana brotherhood.[51] By contrast, the rosary brotherhood in Barbacena had a slave

50. Martins Filho and Martins, "Slavery in a Nonexport Economy," 551–53.
51. "Assentos de Irmãos," Irmandade de Nossa Senhora do Rosário, 1750–1886, Mariana, AEAM P28.

population that remained significant, in the 1850s and 1860s constituting almost half of the new incoming members.[52]

Many of the members in these brotherhoods continued to be free and freed blacks, who made up a dynamic sector of the *mineiro* population. The population of free nonwhites in Minas Gerais remained significant, both numerically and as a percentage of the overall population. In 1833 there were 321,938 free nonwhites in Minas Gerais, constituting 41.9 percent of the population. In 1872, the number had more than doubled to 829,544, while diminishing only slightly as a percentage of the population, to 39.5 percent.[53] Although the *forro* population also dropped off in general in the brotherhood in Barbacena over the period of the empire, in the 1830s it increased significantly, in that decade accounting for almost one-quarter of the new membership.[54] Barbacena's proximity to the Zona da Mata and its location along the major route from Rio de Janeiro to the metallurgic regions probably played a role in making its slave population more significant. The rosary brotherhoods, varying in their numbers of slaves, remained organizations for a heterogeneous population that was not exclusively, and often not majority, slave, once again contradicting their traditional presentation as "slave" brotherhoods.

One of the most difficult parts of information to glean from the extant books of the rosary brotherhoods in the nineteenth century is the ethnicity, or place of origin, of the members of the brotherhoods. In general, the lists of the members include fewer and fewer identifications of the ethnicity of the entering membership. In Mariana, the percentage of the origins of members registered in the brotherhood dropped from more than 40 percent in the 1820s to less than 5 percent in the 1870s (relevant here is that by the 1870s only 11.4 percent of the entering population in the brotherhood was slave). The registration books from Barbacena listed the origins of only 30 percent of entering members. Of these, the largest group was Brazilian, at 44.1 percent, followed by the Central African at 33.5 percent. The population of West Africans still remained significant, though, composing 18.4 percent of the total.[55]

52. See the Appendix, Tables 8 and 9. The Zona da Mata, by the 1872 census, had a slave population larger than that of Mariana, but still only a quarter of the total population of that region. Douglas Cole Libby, *Transformação e trabalho em uma economia escravista: Minas Gerais no século XIX* (São Paulo: Editora Brasiliense, 1988), 47.

53. Bergad, *Slavery*, 91. Bergad is careful to demonstrate that these percentages varied from region to region within the province of Minas Gerais. See 112–20.

54. "Entradas de Irmãos, Irmandade de Nossa Senhora do Rosário, Barbacena," 1812–1840 and 1841–1863, AEAM C31 and C26.

55. Ibid.

Just as the diversity of the populations within the brotherhoods was expressed through legal status and ethnicity, the brotherhoods continued to include both men and women in their membership. In the brotherhoods of Mariana and Barbacena, women comprised around a third of the entering members consistently throughout the period of the nineteenth century. These numbers are slightly lower than the percentage of women in the population as a whole as represented in the 1833–35 census, but nevertheless demonstrate that at least demographically, women remained a significant presence in the rosary brotherhoods throughout the nineteenth century, adding to the diversity that had to be organized within the associations.[56]

The books of entrances provide insight into the numbers of members, but the rhetoric of the compromissos regarding race, ethnicity, and gender can help to tease out both the extent of diversity in the brotherhoods and how the membership of the brotherhoods organized the diversity within their populations. Through the compromissos the brotherhoods organized diversity among their membership in the same way they had done for more than a century, welcoming people of both genders and of diverse legal and racial status. At the same time as they promoted diversity within their organizations, in the nineteenth century the brotherhoods increasingly tried to regulate that diversity in order to maintain the balance necessary for unity among the members.

The majority of new rosary compromissos to appear in the documentary record emerged after 1850. These statutes demonstrated changing attitudes toward the race of the administrative officers vis-à-vis the preindependence compromissos discussed in the previous chapter. None required the administrative offices to be filled exclusively by whites, and most included the possibility of pardos filling those posts. The members of the brotherhood of Araçuaí in their 1879 statutes wrote that the secretary and the treasurer had to be white or pardo, but, as did many of the colonial brotherhoods, stated that there would also be two black procurators.[57] Some brotherhoods eliminated color stipulations, making instead the status of the person the determining factor in whether that individual could fill administrative posts. In the 1855 statutes from Betim, the three main officers did not have to be white, but rather "free people of reputation."[58] Likewise, in the nearby brotherhood of Contagem, the three offices had to be filled "always by free men of recognized probity and

56. M. d. C. S. Martins, "Revisitando a província," 18–19.
57. "Compromisso da Irmandade de Nossa Senhora do Rosário da Cidade do Arassuahy," in Poel, Rosário, 199.
58. "Estatutos . . . Betim," 1855, APM SP 959, chapter 3.

devotion."[59] The new brotherhood in Santa Anna de Bambuhy called for its administrators to be "Brazilian or naturalized citizens," with enough funds to fulfill their responsibilities.[60] In all these cases the lack of indication that whites were required probably points to the fact that more nonwhites were able to read and write in the mid-nineteenth century. Nonetheless, some of the compromissos continued to use pejorative language to describe the abilities of blacks. For example, according to the statutes from Formiga of 1862, the positions of secretary and treasurer had to be filled by men who were white or "of color" (*de cor*), but flatly stated that blacks did not have the qualities or circumstances to fill those positions.[61] Finally, some brotherhoods maintained that they would not consider race; for example, the brotherhood in São Bento de Tamandua wrote that "this brotherhood does not recognize distinctions by color or condition . . . it accepts all the children of Adam and Eve." Nonetheless, that same brotherhood did not allow its slave members to fill administrative posts.[62]

Contrary to the specific requirements for the administrative positions, the race and ethnic stipulations for positions of power in the celebratory hierarchy tended to qualify the blacks above all for those positions. The requirements demonstrate that the members were concerned that ritual positions of power would be evenly distributed among their diverse populations. The brotherhood in Itabé wrote that the king and queen were to be chosen "without hatred or affection" (*ódio nem afeição*) from among the *crioulos*, Angolas, or Minas.[63] Also, the members of the board were to be nominated from among the "*crioulos* and *pretos*, without exception of Nations."[64] Other brotherhoods insisted that the kings and queens be black. For example, the 1862 compromisso from the town of Formiga called for the election of a king and queen, who had to be black and to have around them their "Estado" (retinue).[65] Kings did not always have to be black, however, and in the brotherhood of Araçuaí, the statutes ruled that if the main judge, a position that was

59. "Compromisso da Irmandade . . . de Contagem,"1867, ACBH, article 19.

60. "Compromisso de Devotos da SS Virgem do Rosário . . . N. Senh. Santa Anna de Bambuhy, Comarca do Rio Grande, Bispado de Mariana," 13 julho 1862, APM SG 847, 34 (chapter 1).

61. "Compromisso da Irmandade do Rosário da Cidade da Formiga," 1862, APM SP 959, chapter 2.

62. "Compromisso da Irmandade de Nossa Senhora do Rosário da Freguezia de São Bento de Tamandua," 1869, APM SG 847, 254 (chapter 12).

63. "Compromisso da Irmandade de Nossa Senhora do Rosário dos Pretos do Arraial do Itabé, da Freguesia de N. Snr.ª do Pilar em ano de 1826," APM SP 959, chapter 3.

64. Ibid., chapter 4.

65. "Compromisso . . . Formiga," 1862, APM SP 959, chapter 1.

the same as that of king, was white or *pardo,* the main female judge should be black, or vice versa, in order to avoid discord in the brotherhood.[66] Toward the end of the nineteenth century, records show that whites participated in some festivals as festive kings and queens, although they were not called for in the compromissos. In these cases whites would have served as patrons of the festivals.[67]

Once again it is difficult to unpack what is meant by the ubiquitous use of this terminology based on color in the rosary brotherhoods *of the blacks.* The ongoing racial requirements for the administrative posts, even though in many cases they now included *pardos,* marks the official area in which the brotherhoods were interwoven with the power structure of the larger Brazilian society. It was in this arena that whites, and increasingly *pardos,* held the power. However, within the internal hierarchy of the brotherhoods, as expressed through the festival complex, the blacks held the positions of power and took care to organize the differences between the "blacks," and between blacks and whites when the latter were allowed to participate. This area of brotherhood activity also connected with the larger society, which deemed it to be festive, and later folkloric, but generally lacking in power— designations that assured the survival of the practices. And despite the negative associations connected with the term *black,* many nonslaves and even *pardos* and whites continued to actively participate in the black brotherhoods.

While some brotherhoods attempted to balance the power of their members, the brotherhood of the rosary in São Sebastião de Capituba tried to separate out some of the celebratory functions in another way, by restricting them to the slave population. Their first compromisso, dated 1849, included a special set of chapters for the slave population called "general clauses for the slave members" (*disposições gerais para os irmãos cativos*). These chapters indicated that slaves could not be elected to any administrative office; that they had to sing in the chapel one hour before the mass on Sundays and afterward pray three Our Fathers and a Hail Mary; and that the masters had to let their slaves attend the mass, making sure they were clean. These special clauses for slaves

<hr/>

66. Poel, *Rosário,* 199. In this compromisso, the main male and female judges had the role of the king and queen in the brotherhood (no king and queen are mentioned). Yet the present-day festival does have kings and queens; in the oral tradition the present-day participants recounted to Frei Chico the names of the kings and queens back to 1913. Ibid., 245–49.

67. See the accounts from Oliveira in V. J. Benfica, "A festa do Rosário, em Oliveira," originally published in the local newspaper the *Gazeta de Oliveira,* 9 October 1887, cited in its entirety in L. Gonzaga da Fonseca, *História de Oliveira* (Belo Horizonte, Brazil: Editora Bernardo Alvares, 1961), 329–32; and for São João del Rei, Copy of letter from Serianno Nunes Cardozo de Rezende to D. Silvério Gomes Pimenta, 13 August 1896, "Estatutos da Irmandade . . . de São João del Rei," 1841, MASSJ book 4.01.

also included the section on the king and queen, stating that on 1 October the slaves should nominate their king and queen and other people who were customary in the festival.[68]

Just eleven years later, however, the brotherhood in São Sebastião de Capituba submitted a new compromisso with "some alterations, which became necessary in the compromisso that has to rule these brotherhoods."[69] The new statutes did not include the special clauses for the slaves, and the king and queen were among those in the general listing of the members of the ruling board.[70] This unexplained change may have resulted from the disconnect between perceptions about the brotherhoods and realities lived within them. The original compromisso may have reflected the generally accepted perception that reinados were slave celebrations, as the municipal laws had decreed decades earlier. In fact, however, the positions of king and queen in other rosary brotherhoods had long been shared among slave and free members, and the change in this brotherhood's statutes probably reflects that reality. Thus, despite the association made by elites between black kings and queens and slavery (as expressed in law through the Postura), in practice those positions were held by blacks of high stature in the community of the brotherhood.

Compromissos of the nineteenth century began to regulate the role of women in the brotherhoods in ways never seen in the colonial period. Although women continued to participate on the ruling boards, as judges, and as queens, their power within the administrative structure eroded during the empire. Examples of these changes in gender roles abounded in the nineteenth-century compromissos. The revision of the statutes from São João del Rei, approved in 1841, specifically stated that only men could vote in the elections of the brotherhood.[71] Other compromissos gave specifically "domestic" and "feminine" tasks to the women officers. In the statutes from Oliveira, from 1860, eight brothers were to be elected to the ruling board and would have the responsibility of attending the meetings and the elections of the board. In addition, eight *zeladoras* (female caretakers) would be elected. They would be "in charge of washing and repairing the white clothes of the chapel and

---

68. "Compromisso, Irmandade de Nossa Senhora do Rosário e Almas de São Sebastião de Capituba," 1849, APM SP 959, "disposições geraes" chapters 1–6. The actual formation of this brotherhood, as in most cases, predates the *compromisso*. Already in 1837 the brotherhood had asked for a license to build its church, which was granted. Letter to the president of the province from Miguel de Noronha Pires, 22 September 1837, APM SP PP 1/9 caixa 09, doc. 18.

69. "Compromisso . . . de Capituba," 1860, AEAM 0253 Dom Antonio Ferreira Viçoso 1868, 03 02 014, intodution.

70. Ibid.

71. "Estatutos da Irmandade . . . de São João del Rei," 1841, MASSJ 4.01, chapter 2.

whatever else would be important for the cleanliness and splendor of the church."[72] In the statutes from Contagem, the duties of the sisters on the board and of the queen were described in a different chapter from that delineating the tasks of the men on the ruling board. The article stated that "the Sisters of the Board will help the Queen and the female judges in whatever will be necessary for the festival of the most holy Virgin of the Rosary," and an earlier article stated that the female judges would be responsible for the decoration of the church for the festival.[73] The responsibilities of women had clearly begun to be separate and distinct from those of the men, becoming the more domestic tasks of decorating, cleaning, and sewing for the festival. Clearly, members of the brotherhoods were not immune to the emerging rhetoric on female domesticity as it developed in the nineteenth century.

The requirements for the distribution of positions of power demonstrate that the members of the rosary brotherhoods were well aware of their differences—racial, ethnic, and gendered. Yet they knew it was necessary to regulate that diversity in order to maintain harmony in the brotherhood. In the colonial period, the creation of specific roles and hierarchies had been important to newly arrived Africans, who were anxious to re-create community using a mélange of elements drawn from different African groups and from European practices. One reason why internal balance was important was that the brotherhoods continued to engage in their ritual "work." As in the colonial period, an important element of that work was the care of the bodies and souls of the dead. In the nineteenth century, compromissos continued to address the question of the number of masses to be celebrated for the souls of different members, with kings, queens, and judges always receiving the highest number. The bells of the church would be rung to announce the funerals, and even this involved hierarchy. The board of the brotherhood in Ouro Preto complained of "irregularities in the ringing of the bell" at the death of members and ruled that the larger bell would be rung to announce the death of the people holding higher positions, and the smaller bell struck for the death of other members.[74]

Rituals of death, though they continued to be important, fell away from the documentary record in the nineteenth century. Few descriptions exist

72. "Compromisso da Irmandade de Nossa Senhora do Rozário da Freguezia da Villa da Oliveira," 1860, ACO, chapter 3.
73. "Compromisso da Irmandade . . . de Contagem,"ACBH, articles 42 and 39.
74. "Deliberação da Mesa Administiva," 1 November 1848, Irmandade de Nossa Senhora do Rosário, Alto da Cruz, 1846–1881, CC rol 085/0872-0965.

of the funerals of the rosary members beyond the outlines present in the compromissos and other official documents. Nevertheless, late twentieth-century congadeiros continue to practice rituals of death particular to rosary brotherhoods. I attended the funeral of a congado leader of the rosary brotherhood in the Community of the Arturos in Contagem in 1994, which incorporated drumming, singing, and special rituals for the person who had just died. The *vissungo*, or work song "from the time of slavery," that opened this chapter was traditionally sung by blacks in the communities in the highlands near Diamantina while they transported the dead in hammocks to the cemetery in the city, according to Ivo Silvério da Rocha, a congado leader in Milho Verde, who recorded the song in 1997 for folklorist Paulo Dias.[75] The first part of the song, as quoted in the epigraph, expresses the exhaustion of the bearers of the body as they transport it on foot the distance to Diamantina. The song continues:

> Padre Nosso com Ave Maria
> Securo camera qui tanazambê
> Tanazambê, ê, tanazambê, a
> Bamba jambê, a
>
> O caxinganguelê
> Vai-se embora com Deus
> Com Deus, com Deus
> Vai-se embora com Deus

The first line of the first stanza reads "Our Father with Hail Mary," referring to important prayers of the rosary devotion, and the last three lines repeat the phrase "go forth with God." The pallbearers sang this part of the *vissungo* when they were nearing the cemetery, in order to commend the soul of the dead (*encomendar a alma*) so it could more "easily enter the land of the ancestors."[76] African lyrics, identified as the language of "Banguela" by the singer, occur frequently in other songs of the congadeiros and evoke a memory of an African past. Without more documentary links to the nineteenth century, however, it is difficult to trace the dynamic unfolding of these traditions. By the late nineteenth century, the rituals of death had become an

75. Ivo Silvério da Rocha, a congado leader in Milho Verde, recorded by Paulo Dias. *Congado mineiro*, sound recording, Documentos Sonoros Brasileiros, Acervo Cachuera! Coleção Itaú Cultural, 2000. See liner notes by Paulo Dias.
76. Ibid. *Benguela* is the name *congadeiros* in Jatobá use to identify the African language they use in their songs.

internal, private matter of the brotherhood, practiced, if not in secret, certainly not on the public stage in the manner of the annual festivals.

The festivals and their coronations, by contrast, emerged in nineteenth-century Minas Gerais as exuberant expressions of the rosary brotherhoods as well as part of the popular folk culture of Minas Gerais. Nevertheless, the annual festival of the reinados and congados were considered to be for and of the blacks. Thus, the expression and affirmation of a common identity based on shared concepts of being "black" emerged most overtly in the feast day celebrations, which did the work of tying the diverse membership to a remembered African past, at the same time managing to create an important niche in the larger society.

Kings, Queens, and Festivals

In 1843, Count Francis de la Porte de Castelneau witnessed the election of a King of Congo from the balcony of the home of the baron of Sabará.[77] He commented:

> One thing worthy of note, the king had a black mask, as if he had a fear that staying in this country would fade his natural color. The court, whose costumes mixed all colors with extravagant decorations, was seated on either side of the king and queen; then came an infinity of other characters, the most considerable of which were without a doubt great captains, famous warriors or ambassadors of distant authorities, all dressed up in the style of the Brazilian Indians, with great headdresses of feathers, cavalry sabers at their sides, and shields on their arms. In this tumult, they mixed national dances, of dialogues between people, between these people and the king, or between the king and the queen, simulated battles and all types of somersaults worthy of very excited monkeys.[78]

Castelneau called this festival an "extravagant carnival" that seemed to combine practices brought from the coast of Africa with Brazilian traditions and religious ceremonies. The festival was celebrated on 27 December, which

---

77. Ilka Boaventura Leite, *Antropologia da viagem: Escravos e libertos em Minas Gerais no século XIX* (Belo Horizonte, Brazil: Editora UFMG, 1996), 142.
78. Conde Francis de la Porte de Castelneau, quoted in Cascudo, *Antologia*, 108.

coincided with the epoch of the rosary festivals in most cities, thus explaining the religious element to which Castelneau referred.

Like Martius several decades earlier, Castelneau called the king in the festival the King of Congo. References to a position called the King of Congo in the brotherhood books themselves still did not appear regularly in the nineteenth century, yet European travelers continued to call the black kings Kings of Congo. Although the Europeans' use of the term might be interpreted as their employment of a title common elsewhere in Brazil, such as in Rio de Janeiro and Recife, the title did have some local use. Limpo de Abreu, the local judge who so feared the slaves' interpretation of liberalism, commented that these slaves were led by a man "who is or who calls himself the King of the Congos."[79] It is unclear why the name did not emerge within the brotherhoods themselves until the oral tradition could trace it to the late nineteenth century. The few mentions of Kings of Congo in the documentary record, tied together with the oral tradition, strongly suggest that there was a figure known as the King of Congo in the brotherhoods and that the membership believed that it was important to keep that name out of the documentary record. The king, whether he took the title of King of Congo or not, helped to unite diverse groups of blacks in a single organization in order that the "work" of their ritual could be done.

It was not only outside observers who described the festivals. In the nineteenth century the books of the brotherhoods themselves began to contain clauses about their festivals. The inclusion in the Postura of the clause allowing reinados demonstrates that even in the beginning of the empire the authorities did not consider the traditions carried on inside the brotherhoods to be a threat to the status quo. After the promulgation of the Postura, when the coronations of kings and queens became legal once again, compromissos began to elaborate more about the position of the kings and queens and their meaning—or at least what the rosary membership wanted the authorities to believe they meant. One of the reasons brought forward was the similarity to the Feast Day of the Divine Holy Spirit (Festa do Divino). When members of the brotherhood in São Sebastião de Capituba, for example, eliminated the slave regulations in their compromissos in order to include the election of kings and queens from the general population, they explained that they would

79. Letter from Antonio Paulino Limpo de Abreu to the president and deputies of the provisional government, 14 February 1822, APM SP JGP 1/6, caixa 01, doc. 28.

80. "Compromisso . . . de Capituba," 1860, AEAM 0253 Dom Antonio Ferreira Viçoso 1868, 03 02 014, article 4.

elect the kings and queens "in the same way that is practiced in the nomination of the Emperor of the Divine Holy Spirit."[80] Likewise, the brotherhood in Milho Verde wrote that their coronation imitated the Festa do Divino, although their kings and queens would be black.[81] Even today, the festival of Our Lady of the Rosary in Minas Gerais is still contrasted with the Festa do Divino, the former being the "festival of the blacks" and the latter the "festival of the whites."[82]

Probably the most common explanation in the compromissos, however, for the coronations of blacks continued to come from the association of the black king with the three "kings" who were at the nativity of Jesus. The statutes from Formiga, for example, explained the reasons for having kings and queens thus: "[T]hey represent together the adoration shown by the three Kings to the newborn king, making offerings and celebrating with affectionate songs."[83] Likewise, the kings and queens in Contagem and their retinue were elected on 6 January, the Day of the Kings.[84] Despite this association, by the end of the empire many of the rosary festivals were being celebrated in early October, closer to the actual feast day of Our Lady of the Rosary and to the period during which festivals continue to be celebrated.[85]

The associations with Catholic holidays and imagery were, and continue to be, important to the participants in the festivals, but they only tell part of the story of the cultural mix that made up the rosary festivals. In fact, the nature of the particular Catholic festivals that were cited as templates for the rosary festival may have had special meaning for the Africans and their descendants who made up the membership in the brotherhoods. The Holy Spirit would certainly have been easily translated as an unseen spirit, and the Day of Kings celebration celebrated a black king. Clearly, even if "African" practices were hidden behind these Catholic associations, the possibility that these associations themselves were understood in a uniquely African way cannot be discounted. In fact, these discreet "cultural" elements are only

81. "Compromisso da Irmandade de N. Senhora do Rosário . . . da Freguezia de Milho Verde de Município da Cidade de Serro, Bispado de Diamantina, Província de Minas Gerais," 1863, APM SG 847, 95v–102v (chapter 9).

82. I found this to be true in Diamantina, Minas Gerais, on a visit to the *Festa do Divino* there in 1994. Carlos Rodrigues Brandão describes another case of this in Pirenópolis, Goiás, in his book *O Divino, o santo e a Senhora* (Rio de Janeiro: Campanha de Defesa do Folclore Brasileiro, 1978).

83. "Compromisso . . . Formiga," 1862, APM SP 959, chapter 1.

84. "Compromisso da Irmandade . . . de Contagem,"1867, ACBH, article 9 and article 38.

85. "Compromisso da Irmandade . . . de Milho Verde," 1863, APM SG 847, 95v–102v (chapter 12); "Compromisso da Irmandade de Nossa Senhora do Rosário de Cidade de Passos," 1873, APM SG 847, 286v-292 (chapter 7).

important in that they express a collective memory of "Africa," one that emerged out of associations that through their very organization, hierarchy, and flexibility expressed a uniquely "African" response, fostered by a remembered and shared African past.[86]

The coronation ceremonies were celebrated during the festival of the rosary, which continued to be listed in compromissos and the minutes of the meetings as festivals that included a sung mass, a sermon, and a procession.[87] As in the colonial period, the word *congados* never appeared in the statutes, but several of those documents in the second half of the nineteenth century mentioned that "we will admit to this festival all of the blacks from diverse nations, which accompany the retinue with their instruments as is customary."[88] These brief mentions in the compromissos recall Castalneau's account in which he describes the "ambassadors of distant authorities" who were the leaders of the different groups of congados. He specifically mentions the leaders being dressed in the "style of the Brazilian Indians, with great headdresses of feathers."[89] Castalneau's description recalls the groups of *mulatinhos* described in the *Aureo trono episcopal* from 1754, the dancers drawn by Carlos Julião in the late eighteenth century, and the present-day congado groups known as *caboclos, caboclinhos,* and *catopês* of the Serro do Frio region. Yet these groups with rich, feathered headdresses were only one of the "nations" that participated in the festivals.

As in the colonial period, records of the congados, the collective name for the dances of the different "nations," can most often be found in the accounting books of the brotherhoods. For example, the accounting books from Barbacena show that by the 1860s the brotherhood had various groups

86. Many of the cultural features of the festivals, as described in the nineteenth century, such as umbrellas, the specific colors used, and the hierarchies, would have embodied multiple meanings for the participants. It is important, however, in looking at these elements, to avoid the "plumber's shop" approach, going "in search of a widget like the one you have at home; enthusiasm may have to wait on patient labors of translation that recognize that each word, idea, or object is embedded in matrices of language, history, and ritual practice." Wyatt MacGaffey, "Twins, Simbi Spirits, and Lwas in Kongo and Haiti," in Heywood, *Central Africans,* 211.

87. See, for example, the minutes of the meetings from Mariana in "Termos de Meza, Mariana," 1747–1844, AEAM P27; from Ouro Preto (the Alto da Cruz brotherhood), "Deliberação da Mesa Administiva," cc rol 085/0872-0965; and from Barbacena, "Termos de Meza da Irmandade de Nossa Senhora do Rosário," 1825–1932, AEAM C21.

88. "Compromisso de Devotos . . . de Bambuhy," 13 julho 1862, APM SG 847, 42–42v (chapter 20); Lei no. 2156 de 15 november de 1875 approving and with a copy of the compromisso from the Irmandade da Nossa Senhora do Rosário da freguezia de Pimenta, in *Collecção das Leis da Assembléia Legislativa da Província de Minas Geraes* (Ouro Preto: Typographia de J. F. de Paulo Castro, 1876), 105; "Compromisso . . . Formiga," 1862, APM SP 959, chapter 21.

89. Castelneau in Cascudo, *Antologia,* 108.

going out and collecting alms for the festival. There are two extant accounting books for Barbacena, one from 1812 to 1830, and the other from 1866 to 1897.[90] When the second book began, the first years listed the alms of the reinado, which were the offerings of the king, the queen, and their retinue. That same year there were also alms collected by the Mozambiques, the same group that appeared in the 1820 compromisso from Pouso Alto fulfilling the same function as the other "African nations" listed in the accounting books from São João del Rei.[91] As the years went on, however, various other groups in Barbacena also appeared as groups collecting alms. In 1868 alms were collected from the "dances of the Indians" (dancadores de indios), in 1869 money was collected by the congado, and in 1871 the group called the mascarados (masked dancers) also appeared in the books. These names appeared for several years under different headings, then in 1882 were listed together for the first time as the "product of the Congado" (produto do Congado). Even in the last year of the book, 1897, already eight years into the republic, a payment was received from "the reinado and the dance of the Moors (do Reinado e Dança dos Mouros)."[92] During this entire period there was no mention of these activities in the minutes of the meetings, nor did these congados ever appear in the compromissos. The congados had become part of the custom—the folk tradition of the rosary festival in Minas Gerais.

The lack of mention of the congados in the police records supports the idea that the festivals had become a customary activity in the towns and villages of Minas Gerais. One exception to the documentary silence occurred in the town of Araxá, where, on the day after Christmas (the day the feast day celebrations usually occurred), the police found "a group of slaves near the chapel of Our Lady of the Rosary, about fifty slaves more or less and as soon as they saw the [policemen on their] rounds they began to awaken from their play, at which there were both men and women."[93] During the raid the police fined some of the participants and broke five drums, which were tied with ropes—described as being "painted and of ten palmas [hand widths] in size, with viscas [cords] of blue, green, red and white."[94] The subsequent police report of a group of slaves may have actually been about a group of

90. "Livro de Receitas e Despezas, Irmandade de Nossa Senhora do Rosário dos Pretos, Barbacena," 1812–1830 and 1867–1897, AEAM C32 and C22.

91. "Compromisso . . . de Pouso Alto," 1820, APM SP 959; "Livro de Receitas e Despezas da Irmandade de Nossa Senhora do Rosário," São João del Rei, 1805–1831, AINSR.

92. "Livro de Receitas e Despezas, Irmandade de Nossa Senhora do Rosário dos Pretos, Barbacena," 1867–1897, AEAM C22.

93. 26 December 1835, APM SPPP 1/12 caixa 1, doc. 16.

94. Ibid.

blacks, showing again the stereotyped association of blacks and the rosary festival with slavery. Nevertheless, if the brotherhood in Araxá was similar to almost all the other brotherhoods in the province, its membership would have been a mixture of slave and free.

The different "nations" clearly had several different roles in the rosary brotherhoods. Importantly, they collected alms for the festival through their dancing and songs. They seem to have dressed in costumes to do this, although we only have the description of one of these groups, the group dressed in feather headdresses. According to Castalneau, they were headed by captains, and thus, like the kings and queens, arranged themselves hierarchically. Only one of the designations appearing in the documents uses what we might call a "national" title, the Mozambiques, although the name for the collective activity, *congado*, certainly evokes the idea of Kongo. In addition, most of the names of the nations—*caboclo, caboclinho, mouros, índios*—evoke nonwhite groups. Clearly, the congados, like the reinados, were associated with blacks and served as one of the main celebratory components of the festival. A closer look at the rosary brotherhood in the small town of Oliveira helps to highlight some of the tendencies that were manifested in the rosary brotherhoods in the nineteenth century and will serve as a jumping-off point for the discussion of changes that would occur in the rosary brotherhoods in the twentieth century.

The Rosary Brotherhood of Oliveira

Oliveira began as a loose association of land grants that the Portuguese Crown ceded to settlers on the road between São João del Rei and the mines in Paracatu (northwest Minas Gerais) in the mid-eighteenth century. The hamlet soon became part of the parish of São José del Rei (present-day Tiradentes).[95] Like much of Minas Gerais, the parish of São José del Rei in the late eighteenth century had a large slave population. In 1795, the parish *rol* (census) identified a population that was 38.4 percent freeborn, 12.9 percent manumitted, and 48.7 percent slave.[96] Oliveira probably boasted a slave population of similar proportions to that of the rest of the parish. In the 1831 census of Minas Gerais, Oliveira had a population that was 40

95. Waldemar de Almeida Barbosa, *Dicionário histórico-geográfico de Minas Gerais* (Belo Horizonte, Brazil: Editora Saterb, 1971), 324–25.
96. Douglas Cole Libby and Clotilde Paiva, "Manumission Practices in Late Eighteenth-Century Brazilian Slave Parish: São José d'El Rey in 1795," *Slavery and Abolition* 21, no. 1 (April 2000): 102.

percent slave; 35 percent freeborn; and 25 percent of unknown "condition," probably many of these being *forros*.[97]

In Minas Gerais, slaves and freed blacks often gathered together in rosary brotherhoods within churches dedicated to Our Lady of the Rosary. The first record of such a church in Oliveira came from General Cunha Matos, who passed through the *arraial* in 1823 on his way to Goiás and he mentioned that the church of Our Lady of the Rosary was under construction. This comment indicated that an unofficial brotherhood of the rosary was already very likely in existence, because the cost of building such a church most often came from the brotherhood that sponsored it.[98] Two years later the peripatetic bishop Dom Frei José da Santíssima Trindade noted the presence of a nearly completed church of the rosary.[99]

Despite the early records of the rosary church and the large number of slaves and freed people in Oliveira, the rosary brotherhood in Oliveira did not officially come into existence until 1830, when its compromisso was approved by church and state authorities. The compromisso followed a standard format that laid out the organizational positions to be filled, the amount of annual dues each member was expected to pay, who could be a member, how often masses were to be celebrated, and how to care for the body and souls of the dead. It included the more orthodox elements of the feast day celebrations, such as provisions for a sung mass; a Te Deum; and, often, a sermon. Although the statutes did not include clear provisions for coronations and dances, accounting books of other brotherhoods as well as eyewitness accounts attest that these elements had been part of the feast day celebrations in rosary brotherhoods since the colonial period.[100]

The 1860 compromisso of the rosary brotherhood in Oliveira was unique in that it included a set of instructions for a *reinado*. According to the document, the brotherhood was to make the church ready, as was customary, for the annual festival called the Reinado do Rozário, "which could proceed under the authority of the police and the local representative of the bishop [*vigário da vara*]."[101] Further, the *reinado* was to occur on the same day as the Festa do Rozário. Because compromissos had to be approved by the

---

97. CEDEPLAR, 1831 census.

98. Barbosa, *Dicionário histórico-geográfico*, 325–26.

99. Ronald Polito de Oliveira, ed., *Visitas pastorais de Dom Frei José da Santíssima Trindade (1821–1825)* (Belo Horizonte, Brazil: Fundação João Pinheiro, 1998), 246.

100. Elizabeth W. Kiddy, "Brotherhoods of Our Lady of the Rosary of the Blacks: Community and Devotion in Minas Gerais, Brazil," Ph.D. diss., University of New Mexico, 1998," 173–84, 217–31.

101. "Compromisso da Irmandade . . . da Oliveira, 1860," ACO, chapter 6.

local as well as federal authorities, this admission of the reinado in the official statutes demonstrates that the local church and secular authorities did not oppose the celebration. Calling the reinado a *customary* activity, further shows that a continuity of tradition had already been established—demonstrating the likelihood that an unofficial rosary brotherhood had indeed existed well before the legal incorporation represented by the compromisso.

Further records of the Oliveira brotherhood drop out of sight until 1887, the year before the abolition of slavery in Brazil, when the local newspaper, the *Gazeta de Oliveira*, published a remarkable article about the annual reinado of the rosary.[102] Mestre Venâncio (V. J. Benfica), the author of the article, described the festival of Our Lady of the Rosary, noting that it was celebrated all over the empire, mostly in brotherhoods, and "especially those comprised of Africans and their descendants, as one exists in Oliveira, that predominate as if by enchantment and by a hereditary right they celebrate on those days."[103] The festival started with the raising of the masts, a novena, and the "strange figure of the bull [*boi*], that contains a person inside, and travels through the streets of the city accompanied by a multitude of people, mostly children."[104] At dawn the following day, one of the participants who had accompanied the *boi* traveled again through the streets beating a huge drum. As the day dawned, "there arrived from the farms around the city one after another, Mozambiques and *crioulos*, in great groups they call 'ternos.'"[105]

After the mass,

> saying good-bye to the coarse clothing of the farm, and dressing in clean shirts, little skirts and pants, pulling on colored tights and scarlet shoes, and putting on plumed headpieces, in the same manner others had hierarchical positions of captains, lieutenants, etc., dressed

102. The local newspaper probably expressed an interest in the celebration because it had become practice in many nineteenth-century brotherhoods to invite wealthy white patrons of the town to be "festive" kings and queens. Those kings and queens had the responsibility to help to sponsor the festival, while the "perpetual" kings and queens, and the kings and queens of the Congo, played more ritual roles in the festivals.

103. Benfica, "A festa do Rosário, em Oliveira," quote at 329. The local historian L. Gonzaga da Fonseca calls Benfica "mestre Venâncio" but does not give any additional information on his identity.

104. Ibid. The *boi do rosário* is not unlike the Bumba Meu Boi of the northeast of Brazil. Although not extremely common to the festivals to Our Lady of the Rosary in Minas Gerais, the *boi do rosário* also participates in the festival in Serro (during the raising of the masts), considered to be one of the longest-running festivals in Minas Gerais.

105. Ibid. *Ternos* are the name by which the groups of congadeiros are still known in Oliveira.

in rich and important military uniforms, united with the local population, followed by a banner on which you could see stamped the
image of the Virgin, divided into many "ternos," and led by their
chiefs, like warlike tribes distributed in hordes commanded by their
morubixabas, parade through the streets and plazas of the city,
singing, dancing, and playing various instruments, for example
adufes, drums, *canjares*, and others which names I do not know.[106]

These groups were the congados, whose purpose in going into the streets
was to

> fetch perpetual kings and queens (which are great in number, no
> doubt deriving from the name *reinado* which is given to the festival),
> princes and princesses, male and female judges, each one in their
> turn, and together one by one going to the house of the *festeira*, who
> is also called the queen, arriving at the house of the *festeiro*, who is
> called the king, both white, chosen in scrupulous secrecy and both
> elected by an absolute majority of votes by the greatest and most
> opulent people of that place, for which they are able to pay the
> expenses of the festival, which are not insignificant (that is, beyond
> everyone being obligated to give an alm of one hundred *mil reis* or
> more, on the occasion of the passing of the crowns).[107]

The groups led the kings and queens through the streets to the church of
the rosary; at their arrival they were "received there by the tolling of bells,
music and many fireworks, by the parish priest and a commission made up
of the treasurer, secretary, etc."[108] Interestingly, the writer clearly describes
the participation of whites in the roles of financial patrons of the festival
through their positions as annually elected kings and queens. The presence
of white kings and queens demonstrates once again the willingness of whites
to support, and participate in, the festivals of blacks, expressing a unique

---

106. Ibid., 330. *Adufe* is defined in the *Aurélio* as "Antigo pandeiro quadrado, de madeira,
com dois tampos de pergaminho, que encerram fieiras de soalhas." *Canjerê* is defined as
"Reunião de pessoas, geralmente negros, para a prática de feitiçarias." *Dicionário Aurélio Escolar
da Língua Portuguesa* 1 ed. (Rio de Janeiro: Editora Nova Fronteira, 1988). The *adufe*, now simply
called a *tamborim*, is the instrument still used to lead the group known as the Catupé in
Oliveira. It is a symbol of power and is itself considered to have power.
107. Fonseca, *História de Oliveira*, 330.
108. Ibid.

regional identity.[109] That identity, however, was profoundly conservative and clearly delineated the entrenchment of the patron-client relationship that obtained between whites and the black agricultural workers in Oliveira. Nevertheless, the black population devoted to Our Lady of the Rosary in Minas Gerais has been able to creatively use the social dynamics to maintain their festivals, which allowed them to build and maintain a strong and positive Afro-*mineiro* identity.

Mestre Venâncio was impressed with this apparent commingling of the races. He wrote that on the afternoon of the second day, whites and blacks again gathered together in the church "as if to show we are all brothers" and proceeded through the town, in such a way that "the observer, in seeing the huge number of people, would be astonished and amazed."[110] After the return of the procession the participants prayed a Te Deum and the festival ended. The author explained the participation of both blacks and whites by characterizing the festival as a town tradition, and he commented that even though it made a lot of noise, it was based on "traditional laws so well founded that, during the festivities and pastimes of those days, there is always the best order, [with participants] obeying one another hierarchically and blindly!"[111]

Conclusion

The Englishman Sir Richard Burton, who had spent significant stretches of his diplomatic career in Africa, recognized the fondness felt by Brazilian blacks for rosary beads, commenting that they seemed to "awaken [their] sense of home."[112] The rosary beads were an integral part of the devotion to Our Lady of the Rosary, which not only awakened a sense of home but also allowed the blacks to ritualize and actively remember their link to that homeland. Many elements of the description of the festival of Oliveira also point to an African past integrated into and blended with the Catholic festival. The central masts, the feathered headdresses, the kings and queens and hierarchical order of the events, the dancing and drumming, and the "good reunion," are only a few of the means by which the participants in the festivals actively remembered Africa. The description from Oliveira serves also as a

109. Bieber, "Postmodern Ethnographer," 59.
110. Fonseca, *História de Oliveira*, 331.
111. Ibid.
112. Richard F. Burton, *Explorations in the Highlands of the Brazil*, vol. 1 (New York: Greenwood Press, 1969), 83.

link between the festival there in 1887 to festivals that still occur today. There is still a *boi do rosário,* and there continue to be both annual kings and queens and "perpetual" kings and queens, demonstrating that both pairs participated in the festival, the former as patrons of the festival and the latter playing a ritual role. The important place of food and the sharing of it with the participants continues to be present. Even the description of the agricultural workers, shedding their soiled clothes and donning sumptuous outfits, could describe the participants in the current festivals. These links, however, should not be understood as rigid traditions that have not been modified in any way. In fact, their strength lies in the ability of the participants of the rosary brotherhoods to adapt to changes in the larger society. Until the end of the empire, many of those changes occurred slowly and did little to disrupt or even challenge patterns in the brotherhoods that had been established in the colonial period.

By 1887, however, the old patterns and relationships carried through the Imperial period were under serious attack. Throughout Brazil, the republican movement was gaining ground, slavery was on its last legs, and the monarchy was in its final two years. New ideas of order and progress, which elevated scientific principles to a religion while rejecting traditional religion as superstition, were on the rise. Concurrently with the rise of this movement in the secular arena, the Vatican kept up its pressure on the Brazilian church to turn more completely to Rome. Mestre Venâncio expressed the views of the Vatican when, despite his sympathy and admiration for the festival, he imagined a stranger passing through Oliveira on the day of the festival who might ask, "Wouldn't it, by chance, be better to leave out these solemnities, the dances of these people dressed like this, keeping only the religious cult, dedicated to the Virgin Mary, who is also venerated?"[113] Interestingly, he did not offer an answer to that question, but posed it in such a way that it seemed to come from a rhetorical stranger—a stranger representing the European-derived attitudes of the coast. Indeed, in the following decades, that voice from the "civilized" littoral would become increasingly strong in the small town of Oliveira and throughout Minas Gerais, as brotherhoods increasingly came under fire from the church, moving steadily toward romanization, and the government, which looked toward theories of order and progress as its guide.

113. Fonseca, *História de Oliveira,* 331–32.

PART THREE

6   CONGADOS AND REINADOS, 1888–1990

Eh, negro velho era cativo
a princesa libertou
negro velho era escravo
negro velho virou sinhô.

[Oh, the old black was a captive
The princess freed him
The old black was a slave
Then became the master.]

—*Lamento do negro* (Black's lament) from the
Missa Conga

The almost-four-hundred-year history of slavery in Brazil came to an end on 13 May 1888 with a decree signed by Princess Isabel, the emperor's daughter and regent. Just a little more than a year later, the sixty-seven-year empire in Brazil ended with a bloodless coup d'ètat on 15 November 1889. The new rulers sent Emperor Pedro II into exile in Europe and proclaimed the republic of Brazil under a new flag on which a slogan boasted of the positivist principles of order and progress. The young republic struggled to identify itself according to the new scientific principles implicit in that banner. It severed the church from the state, sending the church scrambling to reorganize itself. A clergy that increasingly turned to Rome viewed the traditional Brazilian brotherhoods with contempt, especially those that engaged in what the clergy understood to be profane dances. The new elite, weaned on "progressive" ideals of modernization and secularization, also scorned the old "folk" traditions. The twentieth-century tension between this nascent modernization and "folkloric" tradition finally severed the orthodox Catholic feast day celebrations from the heterodox expression of devotion—the dances and coronations of the reinado.

By the end of the twentieth century, Brazil had gone through several types of governments, and each change of government—despite the legal separation of church and state—would be accompanied by changes in the church. These changes sometimes complemented and supported the governments' projects and at other times served as a counterpoint to the changes they made. As they had in the centuries before, the participants in the celebrations, the congadeiros, found ways to redefine themselves throughout the century as they weathered the shifts in the religious and civil power structure. This strategy enabled the festivals and communities that sponsored them not only to survive but to grow in power and popularity in the second half of the twentieth century, in ways that had never been possible in the preceding centuries.

The First Republic

Many factors came together to hasten the end of the Brazilian monarchy. The emancipation of the slaves precipitated the collapse of that monarchy, but ideological shifts had already been laying the groundwork for the change for decades. Since the 1870s, new European ideas had been spreading through Brazil's emerging middle class, made up largely of military officers, intellectuals, and urban professionals. Many in this group, who wanted to see the end of the hegemony of the landed elite, embraced the philosophy developed by the French philosopher Auguste Comte, known as positivism. The Brazilian positivists understood their philosophy as a replacement of "Catholicism, Romanticism, and Eclecticism," the intellectual underpinnings of the landed elite.[1]

Several elements of positivism appealed to this group of Brazilian reformers. Positivism was understood to be a rational and scientific alternative to the current system. The philosophy also tended to be authoritarian and rationalized the continued concentration of power in the hands of a few, which appealed to both the intellectual elite and the military. The positivist vision of the family as the central social unit also appealed to the emergent Brazilian bourgeoisie, who saw the creed of the family as an acceptable alternative to the individualism that was stressed in other forms of nineteenth-century liberal thought.[2]

---

1. Thomas E. Skidmore, *Black into White: Race and Nationality in Brazilian Thought* (Durham: Duke University Press, 1993), 12.
2. Ibid., 12–13. See also João Cruz Costa, *A History of Ideas in Brazil: The Development of Philosophy in Brazil and the Evolution of National History,* trans. Suzette Macedo (Berkeley and Los Angeles: University of California Press, 1964), 182–202; and on positivism, see João

Many of the fledgling Brazilian republicans also embraced positivist philosophy. After the Paraguayan War, the republican movement began to expand—making the military/republican overthrow of the monarchy possible after the Republican Party began to court the military in 1887. Since the end of the Paraguayan War, the army had become increasingly discontented with the monarchy. The war had allowed the army to become a stronger and more united organization. Members of the military believed they were underpaid and underappreciated, and they resented the fact that military matters were often dictated by civilians who did not understand military concerns. Many military men believed that they had a duty, even a mission, to improve their country's political organization. When the republicans approached the armed forces, then, with the intention of staging a coup, they were warmly received. On 11 November 1889, several republicans, including Rui Barbosa and Benjamin Constant Botelho de Magalhães (a follower of Comte and an officer and professor in the military academy in Rio de Janeiro), met at Marshal Deodoro da Fonseca's house to convince him to lead a coup. Four days later, on 15 November 1889, the military and the republicans overthrew the empire.[3]

The coup and the republican governments that were established after the promulgation of the constitution in 1891, through the end of the First Republic in 1930, reflected the influence of the positivist thought of the times. Although the leaders claimed that Brazil was a republic, the governments were "oligarchical, authoritarian rule masquerading as republican democracy."[4] Elections were openly fraudulent, the political process was corrupt, and power was shared primarily by coffee barons from the states of São Paulo and Minas Gerais. Despite the importance of coffee, economically the First Republic experienced a shift toward industrialization and the inevitable urbanization that accompanied it, especially in the city of São Paulo and the planned city of Belo Horizonte, which became the capital of Minas Gerais in 1897.[5]

The move toward industrialization reflected the desire of the elites to bring Brazil into the "civilized" family of nations, represented most fully by Europe and increasingly by the United States. Socially these attitudes were reflected in racial policies of whitening. The elite optimistically believed that

---

Cruz Costa, *Panorama of the History of Philosophy in Brazil,* trans. Fred G. Sturm (Washington, D.C.: Pan American Union, 1962), 49–66; Wiarda, *Soul of Latin America,* 145–74.

3. E. V. d. Costa, *Brazilian Empire,* 228–33.

4. George Reid Andrews, *Blacks and Whites in São Paulo, Brazil, 1888–1988* (Madison: University of Wisconsin Press, 1991), 133.

whitening would eventually and inevitably rid Brazil of the dark-skinned races and their "degenerative" influence. This process would occur biologically, through immigration and miscegenation, and culturally, through either the repression or the co-optation of non-European practices.[6] As Kim Butler so cogently points out, "[T]o a people who associated Africans with barbarity and paganism, their descendants were antithetical to modernization, a social ill and a national problem to be remedied."[7]

Afro-Brazilians reacted to these attitudes in a variety of ways distinct to the particular regions in which they lived. The rapidly modernizing city of São Paulo experienced an upswing of social clubs, magazines, and eventually political activities initiated by Afro-Brazilians. In the more traditional northeast, Afro-Brazilians strengthened cultural practices that helped to build pride in their African past and strengthened their communities. The former strategy involved a co-optation of Euro-Brazilian organizations, in an attempt to integrate into Brazilian society; the latter strategy, of cultural assertion, entailed a conscious separation from those European-derived forms.[8] The Afro-*mineiro* population took a different route, and in some ways a middle route, by continuing with its rosary festivals, which had long been based on a Euro-Brazilian structure—the brotherhoods—with a content that was a distinct mix of African and European traditions. The festivals, which had already become part of local custom, became one of the main expressions of Afro-Brazilian culture in the state. Changes in the church, however, were beginning to lay the groundwork for significant alterations in the brotherhood structure, especially in regard to the associations' relationship with the church, that would become manifest after 1930.

The Brazilian Republic and the Separation of Church and State

For Brazilian elites, the nation's becoming a modern state and following positivist principles meant that the church could no longer play a role in

5. Ibid.; Kim D. Butler, *Freedoms Given, Freedoms Won: Afro-Brazilians in Post-abolition São Paulo and Salvador* (New Brunswick: Rutgers University Press, 1998), 24–26; Marshall C. Eakin, *Tropical Capitalism: The Industrialization of Belo Horizonte, Brazil* (New York: Palgrave, 2001), 33–38.
6. See Thomas E. Skidmore, "Racial Ideas and Social Policy in Brazil, 1870–1940" in *The Idea of Race in Latin America, 1870–1940*, ed. Richard Graham (Austin: University of Texas Press, 1990), 7–36; and Andrews, *Blacks and Whites*, 129–39.
7. K. D. Butler, *Freedoms Given*, 35.
8. Andrews, *Blacks and Whites*, 125–56; K. D. Butler, *Freedoms Given*, 59–66.

secular life. The provisional government that was set up after the coup immediately decreed the separation of church and state, which members of the constitutional assembly codified into law in 1891. The disestablishment of the church in the new constitution "went far beyond simple separation . . . and legislated the virtual isolation of the Church from the public realm."[9] The constitution was not proclaimed in the name of God; and it decreed freedom of religion, secularized all cemeteries, and banned religion from the schools. The government declared that it would support the Catholic clergy for one more year, after which the state could not subsidize any religion.[10]

Although the church had been clamoring for more freedom from state-generated bureaucratic constraints, it never supported the complete separation from the state, its base of institutional power. The church's dependence on the state had severely curtailed the development of its institutional framework, which had remained stagnant since colonial times. In 1889 there was only one archdiocese for all of Brazil, in Salvador, Bahia, and eleven dioceses served the vast country; only three of these had been founded during the empire. The abrupt separation of church and state pulled the rug out from under the church. In March 1890, the Brazilian bishops responded with a pastoral letter in which they thanked the founders of the new republic for ensuring the church liberties that it had not enjoyed during the empire, yet they maintained their stance that the church should remain linked with the state.[11] Although the bishops were not to get their wish during the First Republic, the pastoral letter symbolized a new beginning for the Brazilian church because it was the first time in all of Brazilian history that the bishops in Brazil had united to write a joint letter.[12]

Not surprisingly, the Brazilian church turned to Rome for support. The increasing influence of the ultramontane movement in Brazil, and the romanization of the Brazilian Catholic Church, was incipient at the end of the colonial period, spread during the nineteenth century, and came to fruition during the first years of the republic. The Roman church decided to assert its new influence on several different fronts. Pope Leo XIII encouraged the church to unite, urging the bishops to communicate among themselves and to hold regular meetings. The pope also stimulated institutional growth by creating

9. Thomas C. Bruneau, "Power and Influence: Analysis of the Church in Latin America and the Case of Brazil," LARR 8 (1973): 37.

10. Bruneau, *Political Transformation*, 30.

11. Ibid., 32–33.

12. C. F. G. de Groot, *Brazilian Catholicism and the Ultramontane Reform, 1850–1930* (Amsterdam: CEDLA, 1996), 79.

a second archdiocese in Rio de Janeiro and four new dioceses in 1893.[13] From then on, the growth in ecclesiastic divisions was exponential.[14] The successful spread of the institutional church in Brazil after the founding of the republic accompanied reform in the seminaries, which began teaching ultramontane doctrines to the seminarians. Finally, foreign priests were actively recruited so that the church could serve more Brazilians directly.[15]

An attempt to engage the Brazilian laity in a new outlook on Catholicism complemented the spread of the institutional church and the reform of the seminaries. This was to be done by substituting the popular and local devotions that were practiced in the traditional brotherhoods with universalistic devotions. The main devotion associated with the ultramontane reforms was to the Sacred Heart of Jesus, created by Pope Pius IX in the mid-nineteenth century. In addition, the ultramontane clergy hoped to replace the brotherhoods' old feast day celebrations with liturgical festivals that were associated with the new devotions.[16] The Jesuits took charge of spreading the devotion to the Sacred Heart by sponsoring a new lay association, called the Apostolado da Oração (Apostolate of Prayer). Pope Leo XIII also favored the devotion to the Sacred Heart, and, after disestablishment, the devotion, pious organization, and liturgical festivals associated with them spread quickly throughout Brazil.[17]

The ultramontane clergy hoped that the *apostolado* and other pious organizations would replace the traditional lay brotherhoods, which had come to be seen as perniciously independent and rife with questionable practices.[18]

---

13. Pope Leo XIII (pope from 1878 to 1903) became the Pope of the Rosary, because, in a circular of 7 September 1883, he officially named October the month of the rosary. Trindade, *Arquidiocese*, vol. 1, 258. Leo XIII is also widely known for his 1891 encyclical Rerum Novaram, which was directed against both socialism and economic liberalism. The encyclical became a strong source of impetus for the Catholic social movement.

14. Bruneau, *Political Transformation*, 33. Bruneau points out that the ecclesiastical divisions grew from 17 in 1900, to 30 in 1910, then to 58 in 1920. By 1964, the church had grown to 178 ecclesiastical divisions.

15. Groot, *Brazilian Catholicism*, 46–47.

16. Oliveira, "Catolicismo popular," 137–38.

17. Groot, *Brazilian Catholicism*, 104–5. The spread of the *apostolado* was so linked to the romanization of the church in the late nineteenth century and the twentieth that Ralph Della Cava suggested that it might be possible to draw a map of the expansion of the romanization in the church by mapping the founding dates of various branches of Apostolados da Oração in Brazil. Cited in Lisette van den Hoogen, "The Romanization of the Brazilian Church: Women's Participation in a Religious Association in Prados, Minas Gerais," *Sociological Analysis* 51 (summer 1990): 173 n. 6.

18. Leo XIII consecrated the whole human race to the Sacred Heart. The main associations and devotions to be spread by the ultramontane reforms were the Apostolado da Oração (devoted to the Sacred Heart of Jesus), the Pia Associação das Filhas de Maria, the Congregação Mariana (Immaculate Conception), the Liga de Jesus, Maria e José (Holy Family), and the Pia

The Religious Question of 1874 exposed many of the elite brotherhoods as hotbeds of Masonic activity that had the power to override the church's authority during the empire. The church also fought against what it understood to be profane activities and superstitions within the brotherhoods, especially during their feast day celebrations. Even during the empire, ultramontane priests had complained that the brotherhoods contained "all the obstreperous traits of Brazil's 'paganized Catholicism'" and that they even embezzled the contributions of their members.[19] One bishop advised a vicar, in 1909, to "let them [the brotherhoods] die little by little; at an opportune moment we just have to extirpate this alien body introduced by the devil into the organism of the church."[20]

Beyond the introduction of new devotions, the church clamored to play a larger role in the running of the long-established Brazilian brotherhoods. It wanted complete control over the administrative functions of the brotherhoods, which under the empire had been overseen by the state, and expressed its desire that the brotherhoods should submit willingly; needless to say, they were reluctant to comply. In 1892, the bishop of Rio de Janeiro attempted to take on the brotherhoods in his diocese. He wrote a pastoral letter in which he explained why the church should be able to take over the administration of the brotherhoods, claiming that they "did not stand in an autonomous position vis-à-vis the Church: they only administered a patrimony which was in fact God's, and *thus* should be controlled by the Church."[21] He gave the brotherhoods only four months to comply. The reaction was mixed. Some brotherhoods complied and others refused; the bishop had no means of forcing the latter. He appealed to Rome, and Rome wisely advised caution, seeing that this was a potentially explosive issue. Finally, the bishop turned away from his confrontational stance.[22]

The conflicts between the brotherhoods and the local priests were so great that the state stepped in to mediate the argument, despite the separation of church and state—resulting in a continuation of jurisdictional battles that had raged since the colonial period. In 1893 the parliament passed a new law that gave new legal status to the brotherhoods and made them accountable to the General Assembly of the parliament. Needless to say, the church

---

União de Orações e Culto Perpétuo a São José (Saint Joseph). Marjo de Theije, "'Brotherhoods Throw More Weight Around Than the Pope': Catholic Traditionalism and the Lay Brotherhoods of Brazil," *Sociological Analysis* 51 (Summer 1990): 194 n. 11.

19. Groot, *Brazilian Catholicism*, 90.
20. Dom Duarte, quoted in Groot, *Brazilian Catholicism*, 179 n. 26.
21. Groot, *Brazilian Catholicism*, 90.
22. Ibid., 90–91.

reacted negatively to this law, stating that the brotherhoods could never exert juridical authority without the express permission of the local bishop. In 1918, however, the Supreme Federal Tribunal ruled in favor of the arch-bishop of Rio de Janeiro when he stepped in and appointed a commission to study irregularities in the board of the Santíssimo Sacramento in the parish of São Christovão in Rio de Janeiro. This ruling recognized that the church was responsible for the activities of the brotherhoods, at least those activities done in the name of Catholicism.[23] After this ruling the church would maintain legal control over the brotherhoods. In the case of the rosary brotherhoods in Minas Gerais, however, this control would continue to be negotiated by the participants themselves.

Changes in Minas Gerais

Minas Gerais has been described by some scholars as the "most Catholic of Brazilian states,"[24] yet despite the increased presence of parish priests in the activities of the brotherhoods, the practice of religion remained largely in the hands of the laity, as it had since the colonial period. For example, the 1872 national census showed that on average in Brazil there was only one priest for every 4,202 inhabitants, but in Minas Gerais each priest had to serve 8,062 parishioners.[25] Clearly, the strength of the lay practice centered in the brotherhoods, which had maintained a strong and vital tradition since the colonial period. Lay involvement in brotherhoods and their devotions had not weakened religious fervor, however—on the contrary, it strengthened that fervor. For example, Minas Gerais resisted the national move toward secularization that had occurred after the founding of the republic. *Mineiro* lawmakers were not satisfied with the clause that stipulated taking religious education out of the schools, and in their own state constitution Catholic delegates managed to keep religious education in the state schools until 1906, when the positivist governor, João Pinheiro, abolished both religion in the schools and state subsidies to seminaries.[26]

The clergy in Minas Gerais had been involved in the spread of the ultramontane doctrine, albeit unevenly because of their small numbers,

---

23. Ibid., 91–93.
24. John D. Wirth, *Minas Gerais in the Brazilian Federation, 1889–1937* (Stanford: Stanford University Press, 1977), 91.
25. Groot, *Brazilian Catholicism*, 46–47.
26. Wirth, *Minas Gerais*, 90–91.

since the middle of the nineteenth century. Dom Viçoso, bishop of Mariana from 1844 to 1875, had done his best to follow the ultramontane principles. He had reformed the seminary, had attempted to reform the priests, and had spoken out openly against the emperor during the time of the Religious Question.[27] Dom Viçoso also trained the priest who would become his successor and the most influential bishop in Mariana during the First Republic, Dom Silvério Gomes Pimenta, a man who rose from extreme poverty and who himself probably had African descendants, to become the Bishop of Mariana in 1897, and then to become the first archbishop of Mariana when that locality was raised to an archdiocese in 1907.[28]

After disestablishment, the church in Minas Gerais expanded rapidly. Pope Leo XIII established three new ecclesiastical provinces (archdioceses) in Minas Gerais before 1930. He raised Mariana to an archdiocese in 1907, Diamantina in 1917, and Belo Horizonte in 1924 (shortly after it had become a diocese, in 1921).[29] In addition, the church established nine new dioceses during those same years.[30] Under the tutelage of Dom Pimenta, the church was "transformed from a weak dependency of the Empire to a self-confident, multilayered organization by World War I."[31] Dom Pimenta had risen quickly through the church hierarchy and had been to Rome four times. He represented the new type of ultramontane cleric—he participated in national and international conferences of bishops, he actively recruited Dutch and Belgian priests in Europe, and he promoted the new universalistic lay associations in Minas Gerais.

In 1910, Dom Pimenta codified his views on brotherhoods in his rules for the archdiocese. He conceded that lay brotherhoods had an important place in Catholicism because of their distribution of alms and their sustenance of hospitals and asylums. He added, however, that brotherhoods should have a specific purpose and that "unclassified and confused are the brotherhoods that express their purpose in vague and abstract formulas like these: to promote the glory of God, the splendor of Catholicism, etc."[32] Dom Pimenta recommended new brotherhoods be founded in accordance with the wishes of

27. Trindade, *Arquidiocese*, vol. 1, 217–43.
28. Ibid., 273–77, 290.
29. The state assembly of Minas Gerais, under the governorship of Afonso Pena, voted to move the capital from Ouro Preto to a "planned" city, which would be called Belo Horizonte. The city was built in the location that had previously been called Curral d'el Rey in the *comarca* of Sabará. The capital was officially moved in December of 1897. Barbosa, *História de Minas*, vol. 3, 652–55.
30. Trindade, *Arquidiocese*, vol. 2, 273.
31. Wirth, *Minas Gerais*, 91.

Rome, specifically mentioning the Brotherhood of the Sacred Family (Sagrada Família) which Pope Leo XIII had ordered to be established in all the parishes.[33] Finally, the new archbishop warned that the brotherhoods could partake in their festivals according to their statutes, but that they should not use their alms for profane ends, a restriction that had been continually reiterated since the colonial period.[34]

Brotherhoods of the rosary of the blacks symbolized the greatest fears of both the new secular state (wishing to modernize) and the church (seeking to unite and universalize practice and devotion). They were independent organizations that, on their feast days, played African drums and danced African dances, which, according to all the oral testimony, the church considered to be evidence of witchcraft and sorcery.[35] Nevertheless, Dom Pimenta, despite his introduction of new pious associations and his ultramontane leanings, did not engage in active repression of the brotherhoods of the rosary. Probably because of his leadership during the period of the First Republic, many rosary brotherhoods continued to celebrate their feast day celebration into the first half of the twentieth century.[36]

Brotherhoods of the Rosary After Abolition in Minas Gerais

The documentation of the rosary brotherhoods in the decades immediately following the abolition of slavery suggest that their members continued to engage in strategies through which they changed the necessary outward forms of the organizations while continuing the festivals that drew them together as a community and tied them to their history. The community in the rosary brotherhoods was built on an identity of being black, and being black continued to be defined by a common African past and the devotion to Our Lady of the Rosary. Although the ancestors of many of the participants in the rosary brotherhoods in 1888 would have been slaves, the identity in the community was not grounded in the commonality of the slave status. This conclusion is demonstrated by the lack on commentary in the books of

32. "Regimento da Diocese, 1910," AEAM Dom Silvério Gomes Pimenta 1910 04 1 027, chapter 28, no. 271.

33. Ibid., chapter 28, no. 276. C. F. G. de Groot also points out that one of Dom Silvério's greatest causes was to strengthen the family in Minas Gerais and to oppose civil marriage. Groot, *Brazilian Catholicism*, 118–19.

34. "Regimento da Diocese, 1910," AEAM Dom Silvério Gomes Pimenta 1910 04 1 027, chapter 28, no. 277.

the brotherhoods on the abolition of slavery or the founding of the Brazilian republic. The brotherhoods of the rosary, regarded by so many as "slave" organizations, would have seemed perfect locations for the abolitionist movement, yet no documentary evidence exists that verifies their participation in the abolition movement in Minas Gerais.

The trend in Minas Gerais in this matter once again diverges from patterns elsewhere in Brazil, where brotherhoods of the rosary participated in the struggle for the emancipation of the slaves. In São Paulo, for example, the famous mulatto abolitionist José do Patrocínio had ties to the Brotherhood of Our Lady of the Rosary.[37] The São Paulo abolitionist Antônio Manoel Bueno de Andrada wrote that the "brothers of the Rosary met almost daily with the other abolitionists," adding that "it was a revolutionary club."[38] In Rio de Janeiro, the rosary brotherhood, although not linked to the abolition movement, rewrote its statutes in the mid-nineteenth century to include several new provisions regarding the process of freeing its slave members, and in fact made it part of the overall mission of the brotherhood to engage in buying the freedom of its members.[39]

The documents in Minas Gerais do not offer evidence of the participation of the brotherhoods of the rosary in the abolition struggle. In fact, the extant minutes of the meetings are silent on that point and do not even comment on the final abolition of slavery in 1888.[40] Local legend in Sabará

35. Although, as C. F. G. de Groot points out, many other brotherhoods, not just those of the rosary, also engaged in what the clergy considered profane dances during their feast day celebrations. Groot quotes one Salesian missionary as stating that "the dances of S. Gonçalo abounded in Juniahy, but they were always smashed by us." The same missionary, however, made a bid for the retention of certain of the "semi-profane holidays" using the argument that the peasant was of a "pure spirit" and only lacked ecclesiastic instruction. Groot, *Brazilian Catholicism*, 84.

36. Theije, "'Brotherhoods,'" 194.

37. Michael Trochim, "The Brazilian Black Guard, Racial Conflict in Post-abolition Brazil," *The Americas* 44 (January 1988): 288. Kim D. Butler also points out that the brotherhoods of the rosary were the earliest African-Brazilian organizations, and that although they were politically active "during slavery and the abolition movement, [they] remained in the background of social activism between 1888 and 1938." Kim D. Butler, "Up From Slavery: Afro-Brazilian Activism in São Paulo, 1888–1938," *The Americas* 49 (1992): 185–86.

38. Antônio Manoel Bueno de Andrada, "A abolição em São Paulo," in Conrad, ed., *Children*, 469.

39. J. J. Costa, *Breve notícia*.

40. "Livro de Termos de Meza," Arraial de Bacalhau, AEAM Y12; "Termos de Meza," Barbacena, 1824–1932, AEAM C21 and C30; "Termos de Meza," Ouro Preto, 1791–1897, CC Freguesia de Nossa Senhora do Pilar, rol 82–83; "Termos Diversos," Irmandade de Nossa Senhora do Rosário dos Pretos, São João del Rei, 1864–1891, AINSR.

recounts that when the law was signed, members of the brotherhood of the rosary in that town halted construction on its large new church. The legend would seem to imply that the slaves were happy to be done with their obligations to Our Lady of the Rosary, because the purpose of the devotion was to address, and perhaps soften, the slave condition. Nevertheless, the hollow stone walls of that church still stand, and the devotion to Our Lady of the Rosary, kept alive by the blacks in Sabará, is still practiced within a humble chapel dedicated to Our Lady of the Rosary nestled against the back corner of the stone walls of the never finished church. The endurance of the devotion in Sabará, and throughout Minas Gerais, attests to the importance of Our Lady of the Rosary not only to slaves but to blacks of many conditions, as the colonial and imperial documentation also demonstrates. In fact, for present-day congadeiros, the signing of the Golden Law, which freed the slaves, by Princess Isabel entered their myth complex as a renewal of faith in the ability of Our Lady of the Rosary to answer their supplications; according to their legends, Our Lady of the Rosary guided Princess Isabel's hand.[41]

It may not have been the blacks who changed their attitudes after abolition; perhaps the elite, who had long participated in the rosary festivals, started to feel that the abolition of slavery meant that the "slave" celebrations no longer had a place. A letter at the end of the 1841 compromisso of São João del Rei sheds light on how the elite viewed the congado/reinado festival complex shortly after the abolition of slavery. Serianno Nunes Cardozo de Rezende, a white official, and a member of the São Joanense elite, served as the annual king, or the patron, of the brotherhood in 1896. He wrote a letter to the bishop of Mariana asking if the titles of *king* and *queen* in the brotherhood could be changed to *prior* and *prioress*. Rezende explained that the moniker of *king* "had traditionally been justified because of the tolerated existence of a special [celebration], sui generis, that was called the Congado, but which today has lost its meaning."[42] The bishop granted the request, with no commentary. Rezende's comment demonstrates that in the minds of some elites the end of slavery meant that a need no longer existed for the continuation of a "slave" celebration. That slave celebration, which in fact represented not the slaves alone but a large black community, however, turned out to have energy of its own. In 1909, the brotherhood wrote another letter

41. Dona Maria Geralda Ferreira, interview, 28 August 1996.
42. Copy of letter from Serianno Nunes Cardozo de Rezende to D. Silvério Gomes Pimenta, 13 August 1896, "Estatutos da Irmandade . . . de São João del Rei," 1841, MASSJ book 4.01. Serianno Nunes Cardozo de Rezende, at the time he wrote the letter, was also the president of the local Câmara and an important member of the Conservative Party. Aluizio José Viegas, conversation with the author, São João del Rei, 6 July 1997.

asking if the names of the heads of the brotherhoods could be changed back to *king* and *queen*, offering no explanation for change in attitude.[43] Dom Pimenta, the archbishop, granted this request, again without comment. The attitude of the bishop demonstrates that they were willing to have the concerns of the brotherhoods' festivals remain a local matter, while the request of the brotherhood members demonstrates that the coronations continued to have meaning for the black participants.

The books of other brotherhoods also attested to the continuation of the coronation of kings and queens and the celebration of the congados. The minutes of the meetings from Mariana between 1910 and 1926 listed, on the first page of the book, the seats of the *juizado* (the seating of brotherhood judges). The main male and female judges had the name of *Rêis* (Kings) in parentheses next to their titles.[44] A prince and princess of Our Lady of the Rosary were also present on the list, indicating that the brotherhood continued to elect the "court" of the reinado.[45] The accounting books from Barbacena listed money collected by the reinado and the "dance of the Moors" in 1897.[46] The minutes of the meetings were entitled the "Entry About the Festival of the Reinado" on two separate occasions in 1902. The entry recorded that "the reinado was received with the usual formalities at the door of the church" and that present in the procession were the king, queen, judges, and board members of the brotherhood.[47]

Despite the continuation of the festive practices in many of the brotherhoods, their official documentation reflects the changing attitudes of the church. These documents tended to stress the authority of the bishop and the archbishop while downplaying the annual festival celebration. The brotherhood in Barbacena, for example, not only continued into the twentieth century but wrote a new set of statutes in 1932. The statutes confirmed the authority of the archbishop through the inclusion of a clause stating that the brotherhood would show the accounts to the archbishop annually and that the brotherhood was subordinate to the "ecclesiastic authority in the archdiocese in which it is

43. Letter from the Irmandade de Nossa Senhora do Rosário dos Pretos to D. Silvério Gomes Pimenta, 6 February 1909, "Estatutos da Irmandade . . . de São João del Rei," 1841, MASSJ book 4.01.

44. This is interesting, considering that the brotherhood in Mariana did not have kings and queens listed in their elections between 1806 and 1855. "Termos de Meza," Mariana, 1747–1855, AEAM P27.

45. "Livro de Actas," Irmandade de Nossa Senhora do Rosário, Mariana, 1898–1926, AEAM Z30.

46. "Livro de Receitas e Despezas," Irmandade de Nossa Senhora do Rosário, Barbacena, 1866–1898, AEAM C22.

47. "Termos de Meza," Barbacena, 1825–1932, AEAM C21.

located."[48] It promised to promote the cult of the rosary in the appropriate month, October, as prescribed by Pope Leo XIII.[49] The brotherhood in Araçuaí also rewrote its compromisso in 1942 along ultramontane lines, promoting the festival according to the determinations of the bishop.[50] In fact, in contrast to the important part the feast day celebrations had played in the eighteenth and nineteenth century compromissos (although they had restricted themselves to the formal manifestations of the celebration), they were barely mentioned in the twentieth-century statutes of Barbacena and Araçuaí. These early twentieth-century compromissos also made no reference to a king or queen in the brotherhoods, yet the oral tradition in Araçuaí attests to the continuation of the election of kings and queens up to the present day.[51]

The documentary evidence, however, for the period up to 1950 is even more fragmented than that from the earlier period. The church in Brazil was experiencing a period of rapid change, and the very structure of the brotherhoods in which the rosary organizations had always existed was shifting, and in some cases breaking down. In fact, by about 1950, the very nature of the rosary brotherhoods would have changed, leaving on one hand the documents linked to rosary brotherhoods that remained associated with the Catholic Church, and on the other the festivals that splintered off and continued under the auspices of the participants themselves.

The Estado Novo and Catholic Action

The period of repression of the brotherhoods that started in the 1920s corresponded with the rise of the international group known as Catholic Action and with Getúlio Vargas's ascent to power. By the mid-1920s the power structure that underpinned the First Republic began to be challenged by groups that had been excluded from the national project: the poorer northeastern states, the southern states, the military, the middle class, workers, and the church, just to name a few.[52] Getúlio Vargas, a leader from the southern

---

48. "Novo Compromisso da Irmandade de N.S. do Rosário, Barbacena, MG," 1 September 1932, AEAM C21, chapter 2, article 3 and chapter VI, article 12.

49. Ibid., chapter 4, article 11.

50. "Estatutos para Irmandade de Nossa Senhora do Rosário," Araçuaí, MG, July 1942, printed in Poel, Rosário, 211–16.

51. Ibid., 245.

52. K. D. Butler, Freedoms Given, 31.

state of Rio Grande do Sul, rose to power in a military coup in 1930.[53] Vargas set up a corporate state in which different interest groups could have a voice in government, a move that opened the door to the formation of a black political party, the Brazilian Black Front, in São Paulo. The Black Front and all political parties were disbanded in 1937 when Vargas overthrew his own government and replaced it with an authoritarian government called the Estado Novo, or New State, which lasted until 1945.[54] After his ouster in 1945, Vargas returned again in 1950, democratically elected on a populist platform, and governed until 1954, when he committed suicide. Throughout his period in power many blacks supported Vargas, regarding him as the "father of the poor" because of rhetoric he used that placed him on the side of the people. Although historians have begun to question whether he actually achieved any substantial gains for the poor—mostly black—Brazilians, many remember him fondly as an advocate for their needs.[55]

For the black and poor members of the rosary brotherhoods in Minas Gerais, then, Vargas must have been a popular figure. He had no personal influence, however, on their local festivals. Changes in the church under the Vargas regime, however, did deeply affect the brotherhoods and their festivals. The church became one of the main interest groups able to assert their influence under Vargas, and it experienced a quick return to power during the two Vargas regimes. The central figure in the church's return to power in the state was Cardinal Sebastião Leme de Silveira Cintra, who did more than any other church official to reunite the church with the state in the second third of the twentieth century.[56] Through an alliance with Vargas, Cardinal Leme won important concessions, which were put into law in the constitution of 1934. That constitution, which began with the phrase "putting our confidence in God," gave the government the legal right to assist the church financially, banned divorce and gave full recognition to religious

53. Vargas had been a presidential candidate in the 1930 election but lost. Ibid., 33; Robert M. Levine, *Father of the Poor? Vargas and His Era* (New York: Cambridge University Press, 1998), 18–25.

54. See Michael L. Conniff, "Populism in Brazil, 1925–45," in *Latin American Populism in Comparative Perspective* ed. Michael L. Conniff (Albuquerque, University of New Mexico Press, 1982), 67–92.

55. See R. M. Levine, *Father of the Poor?* 100–111.

56. Cardinal Leme (1882–1942) had been archbishop in Olinda-Recife, coadjutor in Rio de Janeiro, and cardinal archbishop in Rio after 1930. His main concern was with gaining more influence for the church in Brazil. He wanted to win this influence by organizing, unifying, and finally pressuring the government to establish the church in its rightful place in public affairs. Bruneau, *Political Transformation*, 36–37; R. M. Levine, *Father of the Poor?* 35–37.

marriage, and gave permission for religious education to be conducted in public schools within school hours.[57] Although Vargas declared the 1934 constitution null when he established the Estado Novo in 1937, the concessions to the church remained in place. Cardinal Leme, however, beyond wanting increased state support, recognized the need to involve the laity as a means to increase influence. Deeply committed to doing so, Leme founded Catholic Action in Brazil in 1935.

Catholic Action had been started by the pope in 1922 in Europe as "an organization of laymen participating in the hierarchical Apostolate of the Church, outside of any party affiliation in order to establish the universal reign of Jesus Christ."[58] Cardinal Leme chose the Italian model for the Brazilian organization, which, like Vargas's government, was "centralized, corporate, and authoritarian."[59] However, it lost its power once it had achieved the goals of increased bureaucratic influence, and, according to historian Thomas Bruneau, Cardinal Leme died in 1942 distressed about the failure of the movement. Catholic Action did meet with some success in Minas Gerais, with its already strong history of lay movements among the elite and across the socioeconomic spectrum.[60]

The first archbishop of Belo Horizonte, Dom Antônio dos Santos Cabral, took an active role in turning the devotion of his region to a more romanized Catholicism and became a pioneer in promoting Catholic Action in Brazil. Popular accounts, both oral and printed, confirm that he engaged in an active campaign against the brotherhoods of the rosary and their festivals through the auspices of the organization.[61] Dom Cabral's attitudes toward the congados and reinados, and those of his colleagues in the archdiocese who had come into power in the previous half century, became clear in the constitution of the first synod of the archdiocese, held in 1944. The section of the constitution titled "On Religious Festivals" stated that the church must "eliminate the profane character that has been introduced into some of

57. The concession of teaching religion in the schools had already been won in the state constitution of Minas Gerais in 1929, because of a steady Catholic campaign to that effect. Wirth, *Minas Gerais*, 91.

58. Bruneau, *Political Transformation*, 45.

59. Ibid.

60. The question of the teaching of religion in the schools had galvanized the elite into strong Catholic lay movements and congresses throughout the first republic. Although Cardinal Leme's dynamism shifted the focus of Catholic activism to Rio de Janeiro, Minas Gerais remained a center of lay movements. Wirth, *Minas Gerais*, 198–99.

61. Pedrina de Lourdes Santos, interview, 7 September 1995; and Lima, *História de Nossa Senhora*, 61; Silveira, *Expansão da igreja*, 47.

[the festivals]."[62] More specifically, it stated that it would "[c]ombat the abuses, such as the dances of the reinados . . . and impede the use of alms collected in the name of religious festivals for profane ends."[63] As a result of the codification of this stance, many reinados throughout Minas Gerais were halted during the 1940s. According to the oral traditions, this represented a period of general repression of the festivals.

After 1950, congadeiros throughout Minas Gerais reemerged to begin their festivals again. Cardinal Leme's emphasis on the influence of the church and its reintegration into the state structure simply did not work after 1950. By then, many members of the church had begun to recognize the inability of the ultramontane and the political-influence model to engage the vast majority of the Brazilian laity. A rapid movement of industrialization and urbanization began in Brazil, and the church entered this now rapidly modernizing world "with a weak base of influence and an archaic influence model."[64] In response to changing attitudes, Catholic Action was reorganized on the basis of the French-and-Belgian model, which promoted penetration into different sectors of society, such as youths, women, and workers. The new groups that were founded, especially the youth groups, began to see firsthand the grave problems in Brazilian society, which, in turn, fostered in them a desire to work toward changing the system.[65] They participated in progressive movements that opened a space in which the rosary festivals, and their organizations, could emerge again onto the social stage of Minas Gerais.

Cabral's unified campaign, which was in many ways the culmination of the process of romanization, did succeed in forever changing the relationship between the official brotherhoods and the reinados/congados.[66] How the change was manifested depended on local factors within the individual communities, but there were three main tendencies. In the first, the "official" brotherhood and the reinado/congado split and both survived. An example of this is the case of São João del Rei, which had the earliest recorded rosary brotherhood in Minas Gerais, dating from 1708. After 1950, the brotherhood and the congados continued as vibrant, but separate institutions. The

62. *Constituições do primeiro sínodo da arquidiocese de Belo Horizonte,* 1944, 3a parte, 2, ACBH.

63. Ibid.

64. Bruneau, *Political Transformation,* 55–66, quote on 66.

65. The Juventude Universitária Católica (JUC) and the Juventude Estudantil Católica (JEC) were especially important in this new awareness of deep social inequalities. Ibid., 94–95.

66. On the relationship between the brotherhoods and romanization in the mid-twentieth century, see Oliveira, "Catolicismo popular," 137–40.

oral tradition in São João del Rei has it that the year 1950 marked the last time that the congados participated in a feast day celebration that was officially sanctioned by the brotherhood. The congados sang, danced, and played their drums at the door of the church, greeting the members of the brotherhood as the latter arrived back at the church after the procession.[67] After that year, however, the brotherhood continued in the church without the congado, and the congado continued, with their own kings and queens, in the neighborhood called Dom Bosco on the periphery of São João del Rei. There, the congadeiros practice their devotion in their own small chapel and have their own annual celebration to Our Lady of the Rosary. The official brotherhood, in recent years, has invited the Folia de Reis groups to play at the door of the church at Christmas, demonstrating some willingness to reincorporate what are called "folkloric" traditions back into their feast days.[68] The congados, however, have never been invited back, and some in the brotherhood do not think that the parish priest would allow them to be reunited.[69]

In the second tendency, the brotherhood continued—extremely weakened—without the congados.[70] This type of change occurred in such towns as Mariana and Ouro Preto. One of the rosary brotherhoods in Ouro Preto, on the Alto da Cruz in Antonio Dias, is located in the Church of Saint Iphigenia, which, according to legend, was built by the followers of Chico Rei. Nevertheless, sometime after the mid-twentieth century, the congado and reinado of that brotherhood ceased to exist. In recent years, the brotherhood of the rosary has been trying to resurrect the congado and celebrate their heritage as direct heirs to the "founder" of the congado in Minas Gerais, Chico Rei. They have sponsored several festivals but no longer have any groups of congadeiros, so they have had to bring those groups in from other towns.

In the third tendency, throughout Minas Gerais there were cases in which the brotherhood did not survive, but the congado endured as a vibrant

67. Aluizio José Viegas, conversation, 6 July 1997.

68. The Folia de Reis is associated with the *congadeiros* in many regions of Minas Gerais. For example, in Jatobá, Contagem, and Oliveira, the same people who participate in the congados also participate in the Folia de Reis at Christmas, making it another part of their annual ritual cycle.

69. Nelson Antunes de Carvalho, secretary of the Brotherhood of Our Lady of the Rosary in São João del Rei, interview with the author, 1 July 1997. The traditions of all the brotherhoods in São João del Rei have continued in a manner much stronger than in many other towns in Minas Gerais. For present-day brotherhoods in São João and their occasional conflicts with the diocesan church, see Theije, "Brotherhoods," 189–204.

70. I know of only one case in which the brotherhood and the *reinado/congado* complex remained together, in Serro, in the diamond-mining district. Their festival has continued through all the changes, and remains the high point of the ritual calendar for the entire town, not just the black population of the town. In fact, it is the only *congado/reinado* that has become a tourist attraction for people throughout Brazil.

form of devotion, the brotherhood in Oliveira serving as one example. Finally, there were congados and reinados that had never been associated with an "official" brotherhood, which survived on small farms away from the bustling towns of Minas Gerais. The history of these festivals is accessible only through oral testimony. For the twentieth century, it becomes possible to talk about particular case studies, pulling together not only the fragmented documentary record but also the testimony of participants who remember the stories their parents told them about the festivals in the early twentieth century. It is through these testimonies that some of the hidden transcripts of the festivals begin to surface. The case studies of Oliveira and Jatobá represent two different tendencies of communities of blacks devoted to the rosary. The festival in Oliveira emerged out of an official rosary brotherhood, while that in Jatobá was a rural manifestation of the rosary celebration, one that evolved on a landholding far from the eyes of the Catholic authorities yet still subject to the changes in church doctrine. These two case studies demonstrate how changes in the church, as well as the rhetoric of progress, was manifested on the local level in the first half of the twentieth century.

Changing Attitudes: The Festival in Oliveira

In the preceding chapter I discussed the origins of the rosary festival in the small town of Oliveira, Minas Gerais. Mestre Venâncio's report in 1887 in the *Gazeta de Oliveira* serves as one of the most detailed descriptions of a rosary festival from the nineteenth century, and it demonstrated that the celebration in Oliveira was respected enough in the community to be written about in its local newspaper.[71] Since that report, the *Gazeta de Oliveira*, which shortly thereafter was renamed the *Gazeta de Minas*, made a tradition of including stories on the festival of the rosary. An examination of those stories sheds light on the way the festivals began to be viewed by the elite in the interior of Minas Gerais. The reports demonstrated a gradual shift of local opinion regarding the feast day celebrations. Writers of the early articles continued to praise the festivals. For instance, the year after abolition (but some months before the proclamation of the republic), the *Gazeta de Oliveira* reported that the reinado was interrupted by a "torrential rain that would have put an end to the dances if it were not for the ardor of the dancers who rose above the severity of the

71. A search of several other local newspapers from the late nineteenth and early twentieth century yielded no positive results. The account from the local paper in Oliveira was the only one that I found, showing just how respected the festival was.

weather."[72] In both 1893 and 1894, brief announcements of the festivals revealed that people came from surrounding towns to take part in "the picturesque dances held to the strident sound of rustic instruments."[73] The next extant article is from 1913, and by then the tone has subtly changed.[74] The *Gazeta* reported that participation in the festival seemed lower, "but this did not take away the sparkle of the religious part and the enthusiasm for the profane part on the part of the 'blacks' that promote them."[75] Here, the author of the article made a clear distinction between the sacred and the profane, the latter being directly associated with the "black" community of Oliveira. The placement of the descriptor *black* in quotation marks may indicate that members of the "black" community may have been drawn together not only by skin color, which may have ranged widely in variation, but also as participants in the festival of the "blacks."

In 1918, according to another article, the tide of public opinion, at least as defined by the newspaper, had moved against the festival. The *Gazeta* reported: "In spite of the angry clamor against the African ceremony of the Congo through our streets, and the church prohibition that did not remain insensitive to the supplications of the blacks, the Congado still happened this year. For three days, Oliveira was overtaken by the multivocal, deafening rounds of the groups of blacks that wriggled in liturgical dances of barbarous and horrifying Hottentot or Mozambique rituals."[76] The article's writer articulated both secular and church objections to the festival and mentioned a diocesan prohibition, and this article diverged from previous ones in its hostile and racist tone. The rhetoric of interest and curiosity about the festivals had become a pejorative diatribe against "barbarous and horrifying" dances. Changing attitudes toward progress and modernization resulted in the characterization of the festival of the reinado as an African, pagan, and somewhat dangerous activity.

Despite the criticisms, however, the festival continued, demonstrating that people in Oliveira continued to enjoy the celebration. A rare photo from 1919 shows a group of Afro-*mineiro* participants dressed in military

72. *Gazeta de Oliveira* 57 ed. 30 setembro 1888, ACC, Pasta: Os Negros de Oliveira.

73. *Gazeta de Minas,* 367 ed., ACC Pasta: Os Negros de Oliveira.

74. The change in tone and attitude may have been, in part, due to the rise of the ultramontane lay organization in Minas Gerais called União Popular, which rose with great strength in Minas in response to the end of religious education in the schools under the leadership of Governor João Pinheiro in 1906. Wirth, *Minas Gerais,* 91.

75. *Gazeta de Minas,* 1341 ed., ACC Pasta: Os Negros de Oliveira.

76. *Gazeta de Minas,* 1607 ed., 20 de outubro de 1918, ACC Pasta: Os Negros de Oliveira. See Kim Butler's presentation of early twentieth-century objections to the "Africanization" of Carnival in Bahia. K. D. Butler, *Freedoms Given,* 183.

regalia on either side of a phenotypically white man crowned as the festive king. In front of the adults stands a group of children, dressed in their Sunday best, whose skin tone and features range from very "European" to very "African," belying the *Gazeta's* characterization of the festival.[77] In fact, in 1922 the *Gazeta* reported, "From October 18 to 22, the traditional festivals of Our Lady of Mercies and Our Lady of the Rosary occurred, bringing together an enormous gathering of the faithful and ending in a majestic procession."[78] Evidently, despite the pejorative discourse of some writers of the *Gazeta*, the rosary festival remained an important activity among much of the population in Oliveira.

For the members of the rosary brotherhoods, part of the importance of the festival lay in the power that the various captains and leaders in Oliveira had to manipulate unseen forces. This use of magic in the festivals was widespread, according to current participants, and the captains from the early part of the twentieth century are still talked about with a measure of awe. I discuss this aspect of the congados more thoroughly in the following chapter, but it is important to point out that the criticism of the authorities was based largely on the desire to become more modern—to wipe out "superstitious" practices and beliefs. Some white leaders might try to ban the festivals, while others might just make fun of what they interpreted as the ignorance of the blacks. Carolina Maria de Jesus recalls in her childhood memoirs, which are set in a small town in southern Minas Gerais, that a young man of the white elite of her town played on the blacks' superstitions during the congada. "To scare the blacks who danced the congada in the streets, he [Américo de Sousa] got up at three o'clock in the morning and made three crosses of ashes in the middle of the bridge that went to Rosário Plaza. When the blacks who were dancing the congada were going to cross the bridge and saw the crosses, they got afraid, thinking it was black magic. Ameriquinho, together with the other whites, laughed."[79]

In Oliveira after 1922, reports of the festival again disappeared from the *Gazeta*. In 1929, the town and ecclesiastical authorities had the old church of Our Lady of the Rosary torn down, with the promise to the black community that they would construct another church dedicated to her.[80] The statues of

77. Photo donated to the archive of the Casa da Cultura Carlos Chagas Oliveira by Sr. Firmino Moreira da Cruz, Ziziu, ACC Folder: Os Negros de Oliveira.

78. *Gazeta de Minas*, 1807 ed., 29 de outubro de 1922, ACC Pasta: Os Negros de Oliveira.

79. Robert M. Levine, ed., *Bitita's Diary, The Childhood Memoirs of Carolina Maria de Jesus*, trans. Emanuelle Oliveira and Beth Joan Vinkler (Armonk, N.Y.: M. E. Sharpe, 1998), 14.

80. Apparently, tearing down churches of the rosary was not unique to Minas Gerais. According to George Reid Andrews, the brotherhood of the rosary in São Paulo also had to

the saints in the old church were taken to the Church of the Stations of the Cross, where votaries of Our Lady of the Rosary no longer had control over them, and could no longer use them in their festivals without permission.[81] Oral testimony corroborates the difficulty that the festival encountered during those years. Local congadeiros tell of the festival being shut down in the early part of the century because two North American researchers, in their enthusiasm for the festival misrepresented it as a definitive expression of Brazilian Catholicism. According to these participants, the pope then personally banned the festival in Oliveira.[82] Frei Francisco Van Der Poel (Frei Chico) wrote of a similar incident in Araçuaí. The oral tradition from that town recounts how the festival closed between 1926 and 1935 and tells how even today participants believe that it was the pope who closed the festival during the same period—"Oh, my son, it was by order of the pope, I had to fulfill it. For me, the rosary festival always reigns, but the pope prohibited it, and so the festival closed down."[83] Nevertheless, according to the records of the monastery of Franciscan fathers in the diocese of Diamantina, the festival of the rosary had been banned "by the diocesan authority" between 1926 and 1935 "because of the frequent abuses that occurred during the festivals."[84] According to Frei Chico, then, it was the local clergy who blamed the closures on the pope in order to excuse themselves from the responsibility (and not lose face in front of) their parishioners. The case in Oliveira probably had similar local roots, also based on changes in the church in Minas Gerais.

The congado in Oliveira, however, despite this shutdown, and the following one that began in 1937, was able to continue, even though the original church and brotherhood that had housed it disappeared altogether.[85] The festival successfully reemerged in Oliveira in 1950, as its organizers recast it as folklore and downplayed its association with the church. According to the oral history,

---

fight to keep their church in the early twentieth century—they lost the battle, but were able to rebuild their church in a nearby area. Andrews, *Blacks and Whites*, 140.

81. The participants in the congado/reinado of Oliveira consider that their images no longer have a home. Every year before the festival they have to negotiate with the church to be able to use one or more of the images. In the three years in which I witnessed the festival, they were only allowed to use the image of Our Lady of the Rosary in their procession. The images of Our Lady of Mercies, Saint Benedict, and Saint Iphigenia were not allowed to leave the Igreja dos Passos where they are kept.

82. Heloisa Helena Maurício, secretary of the Association of Congadeiros in Oliveira, conversation with the author, Oliveira, MG, September 1994.

83. Seu Ermindo of Araçuaí quoted in Poel, *Rosário*, 250–51.

84. Quoted in Poel, *Rosário*, 250–51.

85. Dona Maria da Conceição Bispo Maurício, president of the Association of Congadeiros of Oliveira, interview with the author, 7 September 1995.

a respected white woman in town named Dona "Sinhâ" Saffi saw a miraculous apparition from the door of the church—an image of Our Lady of the Rosary bathed in light. Dona Saffi interpreted the vision as a command from Our Lady of the Rosary to help to reinstate the congado in Oliveira. She sought out the former King of the Congo, Geraldo Bispo dos Santos, and together they negotiated with the town authorities to allow the festival to begin again. The religious authorities, however, no longer wanted anything to do with the reinado or the brotherhood of the rosary. The bishop of Oliveira stated that whatever went on in the streets was not his responsibility but that of the police chief, thus effectively banishing the festival from the church.[86] In this way the festival was allowed to continue, recast, at least from the perspective of the officials, as a profane celebration. The festival has grown in both size and fame since that time, but it has done so under the auspices of a secular organization, the Associação dos Congadeiros de Oliveira (Association of Congadeiros of Oliveira).

After 1950, then, the split between sacred and profane, at least in the eyes of the secular and ecclesiastic authorities, became definitive. In 1959, the *Gazeta de Minas* published an editorial in which the author expressed that concept; "[T]he congado is the congado, a profane, interesting, and folkloric festival, a pastime that people of color like and that the simple folk of the town applaud."[87] The author asserted, however, that the congado could never be the feast day of the rosary, because "they are two distinct things. One is a pastime, the other devotion."[88] He concluded, "No one in good faith could claim for the congado the title of the Festival of the Rosary, because it has nothing to do with piety. It is only a fun public pastime."[89] The congadeiros themselves, however, never stop asserting the devotional nature of their festival.

The Festival in Jatobá

Ouro Preto, Mariana, Barbacena, and São João del Rei had all been locations of rosary brotherhoods that had survived since colonial times. Oliveira and Araçuaí both had had official rosary brotherhoods since the mid-nineteenth century. All these brotherhoods had been able to build their own churches

---

86. Ibid.
87. "Congado e Devoção a N. Senhora do Rosário," *Gazeta de Minas*, 1959, in ACC Pasta: Os Negros de Oliveira.
88. Ibid.
89. Ibid.

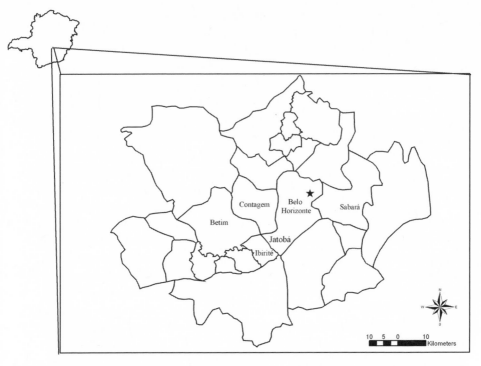

MAP 5.   Jatobá, Contagem, Betim and Ibirité, in the greater metropolitan region of Belo Horizonte.

and to gain recognition from the provincial and the ecclesiastic authorities, and they had been able to a certain extent to have the elite of the town participate in their organizations and their festivals. In other cases, however, organizations had developed with the purpose of promoting the devotion of Our Lady of the Rosary, which had never been formally incorporated by the church and state authorities. It is impossible to know how many undocumented organizations existed during the eighteenth and nineteenth centuries, but it is extremely unlikely that there were none.

The story of the brotherhood in Jatobá is one of a group of Afro-Brazilians who created a vibrant devotion based on Our Lady of the Rosary outside, or parallel to, the official church and state infrastructure. It is notable that the feast day celebration in Jatobá today closely resembles the other current feast day celebrations that started as part of "official" brotherhoods. This point is important for two reasons. First, Jatobá can serve as an example of rural devotions to Our Lady of the Rosary that have been lost from the historical record. Second, the rich oral tradition in Jatobá can serve as a hidden transcript to the types of devotions that went on even in the official brother-hoods but that did not appear in the official documentation.

The region known as Jatobá was identified in 1893 as the western border of Curral d'el Rei, in the district of Sabará, which in 1897 would become the new, planned state capital of Belo Horizonte.[90] Jatobá lies in the furthest southwest region of Belo Horizonte in a region known as the Vale do Jatobá, which today lies on the municipal frontier between Belo Horizonte, the industrial cities of Contagem and Betim, and the semirural municipality of Ibirité. According to the oral tradition, the Festa do Reinado de Nossa Senhora do Rosário started on a large farm (*fazenda*), Fazenda Pantana, owned by Alferes Antonio José de Freitas and his wife, Dona Pulquéria Pereira de Freitas, and located in the region of Ibirité. On the death of Antônio José de Freitas in 1833 the family assessed his estate. It included a total of fifty-seven slaves—nineteen Africans with ethnicities identified as Cabinda, Congo, Angola, Benguela, Monjolo, and Mozambique; thirty *crioulos*; one *mestiça*; one *parda*; and six listed without any information. In 1861 the estate was assessed again, with the widow Dona Pulquéria, herself a *parda* and the daughter of slaves according to oral tradition, as sole proprietor. The *fazenda* had forty-two slaves, more than half of whom were listed as *crioulo* and ten as African in origin.[91] Oral tradition has it that it was on this farm that the unofficial rosary brotherhood began.

At the end of the nineteenth century, discord within the brotherhood on the Fazenda Pantana in Ibirité led to the formation of a second brother-hood (also unofficial) in the neighboring region of Jatobá. Malaquinhas do Formigueiro, one of the leaders in the festival in Ibirité, precipitated the change. The earliest information about Malaquinhas was recalled by Seu Sebastião dos Santos in a 1993 interview with scholar and congadeira Leda Martins. Sebastião's identity card put his year of birth at 1895, but the oral testimony says that he was born in 1888. According to Sebastião, Malaquinhas was African, was short and skinny, had a face covered with scars, and was said to be very quarrelsome.[92] He founded the reinado in Jatobá because of

---

90. Later, Jatobá was incorporated as part of that city. The Fazenda Pantana became Vargem Pantana, incorporated into Contagem in 1919. In 1962 it became an independent municipality known by its popular name of Ibirité. L. M. Martins, *Afrografias*, 70–71, 81; see also "Processo de tombamento da Irmandade de Nossa Senhora do Rosário do Jatobá," no. 010869309568, Prefeitura de Belo Horizonte, Secretaria Municipal de Cultura, Belo Horizonte, 1995, 10–15.

91. L. M. Martins, *Afrografias*, 74–78, 83. The other categories of slaves in the 1861 assessment were *moleque* (young boy) and *pardo*. The only specific African ethnicities listed were two from Mina, one from Benguela, and one listed as *baçungis* (meaning unknown).

92. Ibid., 85. Seu Sebastião passed away in 1995.

an argument he had had within the brotherhood in Ibirité, where he was a captain of one of the congado groups, the Congo. Malaquinhas left in the middle of the festival with his Congo and subsequently chose a king and a queen and founded his own festival. Since then the festivals in Jatobá and Ibirité have remained separate, even though their members participate in the other's festival every year. Remembering the festival of his youth, Sebastião said that one year the queen of the festival would be from Jatobá and the king from Ibirité. The following year it would be the other way around. This recalls many of the nineteenth-century compromissos from official brother-hoods that would also regulate and try to balance the leadership positions.[93]

Where the oral testimonies diverge from the documentary record is in the way the participants recall the place of magic in the festivals. The stories told about the reinado of Jatobá by participants who remember those days are filled with magic, of the captains of the congado groups known as Mozambique and Congo and of the kings' and captains' abilities to manipulate forces of nature with a swing of their *bastões* (staffs) or with their swords or *tamborins* (small square frame drum used by some congado groups). Malaquinhas himself met his end through the magic of another captain. Dona Maria Geralda Ferreira, the matriarch of the festival in Jatobá, recalled that one of the captains from Mateus Leme, a town west of Contagem, put a spell on Malaquinhas to make him crazy. Malaquinhas wandered off into the woods playing his drum, and by the time he was found he was dead and completely naked, vultures having already eaten away his clothes.[94]

After the death of Malaquinhas the leadership of the festival passed to Seu José Basil de Freitas (grandfather of the current Queen of Congo), who became the leader of the festival as the King of Congo in 1910. José Basil was very black (*roxão*) and strong. He reigned over the festival for thirty-six years. After another argument within the Mozambique, José Basil passed the *bastão* of *capitão-mor* (captain general, leader of the festival) to Dona Maria's husband, Seu Virgulino Motta, in 1932. On the death of Virgulino in 1974, the leaders, on Virgulino's instructions, passed the *bastão* to Dona Maria's and Virgulino's son, João Lopes, who still presides over the festival. Both congadeiros and folklorists in Minas Gerais consider João Lopes to be one of the most traditional and powerful captains in Minas Gerais.

Mineiros involved with the rosary festival consider João Lopes to be traditional both because of his retention of and ability to use the occult knowledge passed on to him, and because of his use of the African dialect in

93. Ibid., 70 n. 1 and 84.
94. Dona Maria Geralda Ferreira, interview, 28 August 1996.

rituals in Jatobá. Just like the groups in Milho Verde in the diamond-mining district, the congadeiros in Jatobá call the language they use in their rituals Benguela. The long-reigning captain of the Mozambique in Jatobá, José dos Anjos Ferreira, Dona Maria's brother, talked about learning the African language in a 1983 interview:

> I learned the black language . . . because everyone in this region knew how to speak it. In Jatobá they spoke whichever was the African language of the blacks that came to work on the Fazenda do Pantana, of Sá Puchéria [sic.]. After abolition they stayed here. There were even those among us who know how to talk and sing in the language of the Indians. Other groups that came to the festivals spoke [the African languages] also, especially the very old people from Contagem (the Arturos). Nzambi, or Nzambiapungo is God who created everything. Kã-kã is also God. Kalunga also. Do you know the name of Our Lady of the Rosary? It is Manganá Mussambê, she is Mangana Indaruê. I learned the language on the farm. Our father spoke the languages, it was beautiful![95]

Oral traditions recount that José dos Anjos Ferreira, who was also a very well known *benzador* (healer), and the father of the King of Congo during the period in which I studied the festival, learned the African language from Malaquinhas and other ex-slaves who worked on the farms around the region. He taught it to his nephews, João Lopes and José Expedito da Luz Ferreira, first cousins who both became important leaders in the festival. Through this line of descent the language, at least in a ritual form, still exists within the festival complex in Jatobá.[96]

In Jatobá, despite the lack of legal incorporation, the festival came under the persecution of the church in the early 1940s. For seven years the festival took place secretly, in the house of the kings and queens.[97] For three of those

95. José dos Anjos Ferreira, interview with Eugênia Dias Gonçalves, 23 March 1983, excerpted in "Processo de Tombamento," 23.

96. João Lopes, interview, 5 October 1996; and José Expedito da Luz Ferreira, interview, 21 August 1995. Both these captains also know words and phrases outside the ritual complex. Leda Martins recounts the stories about the passing of the language in L. M. *Afrografias,* 94. Some scholars in Minas Gerais, most notably Eugênia Dias Gonçalves, have engaged in linguistic studies of the language used in the rosary festival in Jatobá, but these remain unpublished. See references to, and some citations from, her work in "Processo de Tombamento," 13–15.

97. Leda Martins writes that in the early part of the twentieth century the festival took place in private chapels built on private *fazendas,* such as the Chapel of Santo Antonio, built by Chico Novato on his farm in 1919. Although the date is not clear regarding when the church

years, 1947 through 1949, the festival had to shut down altogether. João Lopes claims that the reason that the festival stopped was because the church saw it as expressing witchcraft and sorcery; and Dona Leonôr, the present-day Queen of Congo, agrees that the church simply did not accept the festival.[98] Simultaneously with the tension between the church and the brotherhood, however, was the death in 1946 of the King of Congo, José Basil. In 1950, Virgulino and his brother-in-law José dos Anjos Ferreira mounted a campaign at the Folia de Reis to raise funds to build a new chapel. It was only through these efforts that the festival was able to begin again, in its own chapel built on Virgulino's and Dona Maria's land.[99] Since that time the festival in Jatobá has become one of the most important and well known in Minas Gerais.

The Congado After 1950

Historian of Minas Gerais Augusto de Lima Junior documented the changes occurring in brotherhoods such as those in Oliveira and Jatobá when he wrote in the 1950s that the reemergence of the *festa do rosário* "verified the exceptional fervor for these festivals, that is so dear to the hearts of *mineiros*, who reacted in this emergency, placing themselves on the side of the glorious patroness of Minas Gerais."[100] According to Lima, Our Lady of the Rosary, the traditional patron of the blacks, had become the patron of all of Minas Gerais. Despite the scorn of the church and some of the elite, this popular devotion had been able to shape general sentiment in Minas Gerais.

The changes after 1950, which for the most part caused the separation of the "religious" brotherhood from the festival complex, left the groups without an overarching structure to which the could ally themselves. In this vacuum, the congadeiros of Minas Gerais banded together in an extra-communitarian manner by forming a unified Association of Congadeiros (Associação dos Congadeiros de Minas Gerais) on 23 May 1954. The Associ-ation united many of the congados, at least in the central part of the state of Minas Gerais, around the capital of Belo Horizonte, into an organization that could act as the administrator of all the groups that carried on the festivals.

---

said that the congadeiros could not celebrate their festivals in a chapel, definitely by the 1940s this practice was forbidden. See L. M. Martins, *Afrografias*, 86.

98. João Lopes, interview, 5 October 1996; Dona Leonôr Pereira Galdino, Queen of Congo, interview with the author, Bairro Lindeia, BH, MG, 2 October 1996.

99. Dona Leonôr Pereira Galdino, interview, 2 October 1996; and João Lopes, interview, 5 October 1996.

100. Lima, *História de Nossa Senhora*, 61.

The association was a casual group of people who were concerned to see the traditions of the congados continued and who would gather together to discuss problems and traditions and ways to help communities of congadeiros. The association wrote statutes that were approved by both the state and the religious authorities. From then on, the various *guardas* (groups) and "brotherhoods" (they were still called brotherhoods even without the direct association to the Catholic Church) of congadeiros (defined as any group with more than one *guarda*) would turn in their statutes to the association rather than to the ecclesiastic and civil authorities.[101]

The opening that the congadeiros took advantage of occurred in the changing religious climate of the 1950s, when the Brazilian church, especially the liberal Conference of Brazilian Bishops (CNBB), moved toward a socially progressive and even revolutionary stance. Likewise, politically, the government opened significantly after the fall of the Estado Novo in 1945 and the creation of the Second Republic. Together, the church and the state in Brazil began to move in a more socially progressive direction.[102] In 1964 another military regime toppled the left-leaning government of João Goulart and put in place a military dictatorship that, like the positivists of the late nineteenth century, wanted Brazil to move forward as a "modern" nation. While less repressive than other dictatorships in the Southern Cone during the same period, the authoritarian regimes, especially in the first eight years, suspended civil liberties and quashed all dissent through fear tactics, such as torture and disappearances. The church, especially after the beginning of the most repressive phase of the regime in 1969, took a vocal stance against the policies of the government and in favor of human rights.[103] Until the end of the military regime, the church remained opposed to the actions of the government.

During the dictatorship, the congados continued to celebrate their festivals. Participants recall that the festivals did not change in any significant way in this period, only that they were required to submit the correct paperwork to the authorities. Once again, however, it was changes in the church that in some regions created friction with brotherhoods. The Second Vatican Council (1962–65) defined a new model for church influence by emphasizing the

101. Célia Lourdes Ferreira, interview, 25 December 1996; *Associação dos Congados de Nossa Senhora do Rosário de Minas Gerais—Estatutos* (Belo Horizonte, Brazil: Gráfica e Eidtora Cultura, sd).

102. Bruneau, "Power and Influence," 40; Kevin Neuhouser, "The Radicalization of the Brazilian Catholic Church in Comparative Perspective," *American Sociological Review* 54 (April 1989): 237–38.

103. Maria Helena Moreira Alves, *State and Opposition in Military Brazil* (Austin: University of Texas, 1985), 153–59.

importance of the laity and attempting to bring the church into the modern world by enacting such changes as celebrating mass in the vernacular. These changes might seem to be in harmony with the already existing brotherhood emphasis on lay involvement, but in fact brotherhood members, and not just members of the rosary brotherhoods, were opposed to many of the changes and wanted to continue their "traditions" as they had for centuries. The clergy, although progressive, often saw "popular" religious expression as superficial and at odds with the new stance of the church. Sociologist Marjo de Theije studied these conflicts between the post–Vatican II church and the brotherhoods in São João del Rei, and concluded:

> For the brotherhoods, the traditions are the very essence of being a Catholic and form part of their identity and history. For the clergy, including the bishop, the traditional ceremonies are mere externals that stand in the way of the implementation of liturgical innovations and do not contribute to real faith. They consider the traditions a purpose in itself, separated from religion, whereas the laymen deem the ceremonies to be an important part of their perception of faith.[104]

The revolutionary movement known as liberation theology emerged from the opening of Vatican II and, because of its emphasis on empowering the poor, might also seem to have appealed to the members of the rosary brotherhoods in particular. Nonetheless, I heard criticisms of a local priest who was a proponent of liberation theology, blamed for his opinions because some brotherhood members believed that priests should not be involved in politics. The reaction to Vatican II and to liberation theology highlights the fundamentally conservative nature of the brotherhoods in Minas Gerais—conservative in the literal sense, in that their main goal is to preserve traditions that have served to identify them for centuries.

Progressive priests did not always enter into conflict with the brotherhoods; in fact, many priests were tolerant of popular religious expressions and saw them as a way to bring the participants closer to the church.[105] These attitudes allowed the congadeiros to develop the Missa Conga, or the "Congo Mass" which has become a central part of the rosary "traditions" today. An anthropologist and president of the Association of Congadeiros at that time,

---

104. Theije, "Brotherhoods," 201. On the views of the church on popular religion in Brazil, see Waldo Cesar, "O que é 'popular' no catolicismo popular," *Revista eclesiástica brasileira* 36, no. 141 (1976): 5–18.
105. Theije, "Brotherhoods," 198.

Romeu Sabará, wrote the mass together with Padre Nereu Teixeira in 1973. They took the mass to the archdiocese, which approved it as a mass for the congado.[106] The Missa Conga reflects the increasing concern of the Brazilian clergy in the 1970s and 1980s regarding issues of race and discrimination.[107] In fact, the Lament at the Door of the Church, an excerpt of which opened this chapter, is a key dramatic moment in the mass. It dramatizes the blacks' being locked out of the church, followed by the priest flinging open the doors and ushering the blacks in to worship. This scene clearly acts out the church's new acceptance of the devotion of the blacks.[108]

In 1976, the association became a federation, which elevated the organization to a level at which they would be recognized by municipal and state laws.[109] The objective of the federation has been to maintain the "traditions" and the roots of the congados and to help groups and brotherhoods of congadeiros to continue. In all, about 150 groups are associated with the federation. Fifty of these are groups in Belo Horizonte, and the other one hundred are located in small towns and cities throughout the state of Minas Gerais. The federation is divided into an administrative board and a *conselho deliberativo* (deliberative council) and has a King and Queen of Congo who represent the state of Minas Gerais. The King of Congo claims direct descent from Chico Rei. During the period of my research in Brazil in the late 1990s, the federation held informal meetings once a week in central Belo Horizonte in a condemned building fondly called *balança mais não cai* (it rocks, but it doesn't fall). Once a month the members meet in an outlying neighborhood in their organization headquarters. The federation recently received approval to get funding from the city to renovate its center and build a dormitory to house visiting congadeiros. Clearly, the federation as a unit has been able to influence the authorities in ways that individual groups never could.[110]

---

106. Célia Lourdes Ferreira, interview, 25 December 1996; and "Dom Serafim pede perdão por todos opressores da raça negra," *Estado de Minas,* 14 May 1988. There already had been a mass in which the congadeiros participated during the festivals before 1973, but it did not include the singing, playing, and dancing of the congadeiros.

107. Andrews, *Blacks and Whites,* 203–4.

108. Although the blacks had their own churches, of the rosary and of other devotions, there is no evidence that the groups of congadeiros were ever allowed to play their drums inside the churches until after 1950 (in their own chapels) and after Vatican II in parish churches.

109. Statutes of the Federação dos Congados de Nossa Senhora do Rosário do Estado de Minas Gerais (Ex-Associação), Pública pela Lei Estadual 5.586 de 30-10-70 e Municipal no. 2.648 de 10-9-76.

110. Célia Lourdes Ferreira, interview, 25 December 1996. Célia pointed out that many of the groups in Minas Gerais are not affiliated with the federation, but its goal is to include everyone.

In 1988, at the one-hundred-year anniversary of the abolition of slavery, events were planned throughout Brazil to either celebrate the date or criticize the lack of progress that had been made in creating equal opportunities for blacks in Brazil.[111] The church and state in Minas Gerais decided that one way to commemorate the date would be to hold a Missa Conga in the sports stadium called the Mineirinho. Seven thousand people attended the mass, celebrated by the archbishop of Belo Horizonte, Dom Serafim, who was assisted by thirty-four priests.[112] In order to celebrate the abolition of slavery, the *mineiro* Church honored its own local Afro-Brazilian tradition, demonstrating the importance of the Congado to the Afro-*mineiro* population, and to *mineiro* identity in general.

In Minas Gerais since the 1970s there has been a huge surge of interest in the congados, much of this generated by a dedicated group of folklorists who recognize the festivals as being an important part of the cultural heritage of the state. These folklorists, most of whom are associated with the Comissão Mineiro de Folclore (*Mineiro* Commission on Folklore), have studied and documented many festivals throughout the state. Other interest has been sparked by members of the clergy who seek to embrace these practices, rather than push them away, especially in the current competition of the religious marketplace of Brazil. The congadeiros are aware of this new interest, which has enabled them to emerge confidently onto the landscape of popular devotion in Minas Gerais. In fact, on any given weekend during the cycle of the rosary—August 15 to October 31—in any small town or neighborhood of Belo Horizonte a visitor might hear the drums of the congadeiros or see costumed groups playing their music and singing through the streets on their way to "fetch" the kings and queens of their festivals.

In the twentieth century, local changes in the festivals have occurred in response to any number of conditions in particular locations. In Oliveira, for example, certain congado groups have stopped temporarily and others have begun, the locations of different aspects of the festival have changed, people have died, and positions of power have been passed on. Likewise, in Jatobá, changes in personnel within the groups and even in leadership positions are not infrequent. Since the colonial period the books of the brotherhoods have attested to these types of local and relatively minor alterations. The constant change is part of the brotherhoods' ongoing negotiation both with the church and state powers and within their own populations. It is not that the

111. Andrews, *Blacks and Whites,* 211–33.
112. "Dom Serafim pede perdão por todos opressores da raça negra," *Estado de Minas,* 14 May 1988.

traditions are "invented" in the sense that Hobsbawm and Ranger propose, but rather that they are constantly unfolding in response to changing circumstances.[113] Nevertheless the underlying work of the festivals, and of the organizations of the rosary brotherhoods, has remained relatively stable. They continue to function to bring the community of blacks together, a community joined by the devotion to Our Lady of the Rosary and by a common heritage and memory of Africa.

Conclusion

The Congados and Reinados of Our Lady of the Rosary have managed to survive in Minas Gerais throughout three centuries, but the most challenging period they have experienced has been the past century, when the Roman church and modernization of Brazil combined to challenge the festivals and their underlying devotions. Yet the congadeiros resisted the changes and created ways to continue their celebrations, including the formation of the statewide organization that could bring their concerns into the political arena.

Recognition, however, along with the chronological distance from the African roots of the festival, has brought with it new problems. First, the festivals' marginalization by the official church throughout much of the twentieth century has caused them to be cast as "folklore" in the sense of "secular." The congadeiros themselves, however, understand their festival as devotional. In addition, scholars who have examined the festivals have named certain ones to be more or less "traditional" (often relying on the testimony of one or another brotherhood leader), setting up new power struggles within and between the brotherhoods. Finally, at the dawn of the twenty-first century, fewer young people are willing to continue traditions that seem anachronistic. These are all challenges that the congadeiros must face. Yet the congadeiros have been successful in overcoming obstacles in the past. They have created a historical continuum by which the cosmologies brought from Africa and rearticulated in Minas Gerais in the form of a heterodox Catholicism could resist the alienation of slavery, the attacks of the church, and, so far, the entropic effect of modernization.

The communities dedicated to Our Lady of the Rosary have been successful because of their most tenacious "tradition"—their ability to adapt and reshape themselves externally in order to keep the rituals that identify

113. Eric Hobsbawm and Terence Ranger, *The Invention of Tradition* (Cambridge: Cambridge University Press, 1983).

them as a community of blacks and as descendents of Africans. This community expresses a particular culture, but a culture that has been constantly unfolding—social memory, in the parlance of Thomas Abercrombie.[114] By the twentieth century, that adaptation involved the communities presenting themselves to the world as a group of secular organizations. Nevertheless, all the congadeiros today, without exception, agree that their festival is devotional and not a form of folklore (secular) and frequently made this assertion to me—clearly, in order that I could better understand the depth of meaning that the festival held for them. The field of folklore no longer recognizes an opposition between folklore and religion, and folklorists in Minas Gerais today agree that the celebration is devotional. Nevertheless, the congadeiros themselves developed their own understanding of the intellectual currents in the history of Afro-Brazilian folklore, and they continue to define the rubric of *folklore* as being oppositional to *religion*, as it was also defined through much of the twentieth century by prominent anthropologists and folklorists.[115] By allowing the festival to be recast as folklore, however, the participants have been able to ensure its continuation. In fact, the Congados not only have survived, but have, in many cases, been accepted back into the church as important popular, and religious, expressions.

114. Abercrombie, *Pathways*, 21.
115. For example, Arthur Ramos identified the Afro-Brazilian trance cults as religious. He did a disservice to the Central African culture, however, when he categorized the festivals that he identified as the Congos to be *folklore* of African derivation, manifestations of Afro-Brazilian culture that either never had or had lost their religious significance. He identified the brotherhoods of the rosary, and their practice of crowning kings and queens, as being a transport of the system of African secular "secret societies." See Arthur Ramos, *The Negro In Brazil*, trans. Richard Pattee (Philadelphia: Porcupine Press, 1980), 95; and Arthur Ramos, *As culturas negras no novo mundo* (Rio de Janeiro: Civilização Brasileira, 1937), 369.

7 VOICES OF THE CONGADEIROS

Cem anos de abolição
não pude comemorar
cadê a libertação
que a lei Aurea ficou de me dar?

[One hundred years of abolition
I can't celebrate
Where is the liberty
That the Golden Law promised?]

—Pedrina de Lourdes Santos, captain of the
Mozambique of Our Lady of Mercies, Oliveira, MG

As the brotherhoods of the rosary came under attack in the first half of the twentieth century, the participants found ways to develop that ensured the survival of their devotion. In many cases, the festivals were separated from the official church and remained independent or became aligned with the Federation of Congadeiros. Thus, rather than the institution of the brotherhood simply sponsoring the festival, as was historically the case, the festival became the sponsor of the institution. Therefore, to study the devotion to Our Lady of the Rosary in the present, the focus must turn away from the brotherhoods to the people who participate in the annual festivals. A look at how the participants view their own history and devotion sheds light on the tenacity of the devotion through centuries, as well as the centralizing symbols of blackness and devotion to Our Lady of the Rosary.

The power dynamic between the congadeiros and the larger world in which they live is the most enduring facet of the continuum that stretches from the colonial period to the present in the rosary organizations. Dirks, Eley, and Ortner point out that although anthropologists in recent years have severely questioned the idea of the durability of culture, the concept of culture itself has expanded with "Foucaldian notions of discourse, and Gramscian notions of hegemony," both of which "emphasize the degree to which culture is grounded in unequal relations."[1] Thus, the notion of the durability of unequal power relations that shape cultures has supplanted the concept of the durability of a given culture itself. It is within this theoretical realm that the history of the brotherhoods can link with the present-day *Congado/Reinado*; in fact, it is in the discussion of power relations in society that anthropology and history have been able to find common ground.[2]

The communities of congadeiros, however, were not passive recipients within the unequal power relations that surrounded them. They actively shaped their world, within the constraints of their society, through the maintenance of rituals and the promulgation of narratives that served as a foundation for the identity of their communities. They creatively used the society to shape a tradition that would appear nonthreatening to the whites and, at the same time, maintain links to a remembered past. The present-day congadeiros continue these strategies. The ritual action of the congados and reinados happens within communities of congadeiros who have their own interpretations of the factors that have kept them together. The interpretations emerge in the myths, legends, and narratives that form the bedrock of the congadeiros' social memory. Four main themes constantly emerge through their words: race and class, shared faith, common concepts of power, and the importance of passing on their shared history.

Being "Black" in the Festivals of the Rosary

An important function of the brotherhoods of the rosary, and of the present-day feast day celebration to Our Lady of the Rosary, has been to negotiate the ongoing racial and economic inequalities that are pervasive in Brazilian society. Scholars have long acknowledged that the scale from black to white in Brazil represents a continuum that can be mediated by an increase in wealth. This outlet has created ambiguous race relations, the very ones that cause many elite Brazilians to claim that Brazil suffers from class, not race, discrimination. In the 1950s, Marvin Harris attempted to define the fluid categories in his study of race relations in a rural town in Minas Gerais. He found that a "negro" in Brazil was any of the following: a poverty-stricken white, mulatto, or black; a poor mulatto or black; or a black of moderate

---

1. Nicholas B. Dirks, Geoff Eley, and Sherry B. Ortner, eds., *Culture/Power/History: A Reader in Contemporary Social Theory* (Princeton: Princeton University Press, 1994), 3.
    2. Ibid., 6.

wealth. By contrast, a "white" would be a wealthy white, mulatto, or black; a white or mulatto of moderate wealth; or a white who is poor.[3] Harris pointed out, however, that what mediated the scale, in fact, was race. He also found that all the studies confirmed that "[t]he Negro consistently tends to minimize and narrow down the negatively infectious scope of being Negro, and the white tends to exaggerate and broaden it. The white tends to strip the Negro of worth and dignity because he is a Negro, and the Negro tries to cling to his dignity and attain worth despite it. *But everyone believes it is better to be white.*"[4] Much has changed in Brazil in the fifty years since Harris's study, yet discrimination and lack of opportunities for blacks have remained fairly constant. The authors of all the studies conducted in the years since Harris's, right up to the most recent, agree that race has remained the most dominant category of discrimination in Brazil.[5]

Despite the ongoing discrimination, the rosary festivals of the blacks provide a counterpoint to the prevailing discourse on race. They serve to acknowledge the discrimination in Brazilian society but also to express pride in a cultural *and* physical African heritage. In fact, the Festa do Rosário is known as the feast day of the blacks even in cases in which black participants are no longer in the majority.[6] The legend of Our Lady of the Rosary serves as a foundation myth for the blacks' devotion to Our Lady of the Rosary and for the pride that has emerged within the devotion. The version below is one that Dona Maria told on three separate occasions during interviews, and the one that I summarized in Chapter 2. According to Dona Maria, the following story takes place in Africa.

> Long ago some slaves were down at the shore, and they saw Our Lady out in the waves with the infant Jesus on her lap. The sea was rough, and the water rocked her from one side to the other. The slaves went to their master and told him that they had seen Our

3. Marvin Harris, "Race Relations in Minas Velhas: A Community in the Mountain Region of Central Brazil," in *Race and Class in Rural Brazil: A UNESCO Study*, ed. Charles Wagley, 2d ed. (New York: Columbia University Press, 1963), 62–81.

4. Harris, "Race Relations," 59.

5. See the recent monograph by France Winddance Twine, *Racism in a Racial Democracy: The Maintenance of White Supremacy in Brazil* (New Brunswick: Rutgers University Press, 1998); the many excellent essays in Rebecca Reichmann, ed., *Race in Contemporary Brazil: From Indifference to Inequality* (University Park: Penn State Press, 1999); and the insights of John D. French, "The Missteps of Anti-imperialist Reason: Pierre Bourdieu, Loïc Wacquant, and Michael Hanchard's *Orpheus and Power*," Duke University Working Paper no. 27, n.d.

6. See Brandão, *Divino*, 94–97; and Carlos Rodrigues Brandão, *A festa do santo de preto* (Goiânia: Universidade Federal de Goiás, 1985), 48–49.

Lady in the middle of the sea sitting on the water. And the master said to them, "Who is it that saw Our Lady in the waves? Would Our Lady appear to the blacks? If she was going to appear, she would appear for us, the whites, who are able to make a little chapel for her, because I'm sure she doesn't have a place to live." And the slave said, "No, *sinhô*, this morning, at six o'clock you go, go there and I'll show you there in the middle of the sea." So early the next morning the master went there with the black and saw Our Lady seated there with the child in her lap, rocking in the waves. And he looked, and looked, and looked, and finally said, "this isn't for you, no! I'll call for a priest and we'll have a procession and the priest will get her out of the waves." And he called his friends, and the priest, and they had a beautiful procession and the priest prayed, and called to her—they made a big bouquet of flowers and offered it to her, but she did not move. On the next day they called the bishop, they took him to the edge of the sea to get her out. And the bishop brought that big brotherhood with their big procession and the bishop prayed and called up to heaven but Our Lady just rocked there on top of the waves. So, the bishop left and told the master that he should just leave her for the blacks. If the bishop couldn't get her out of the water, no one could—except maybe the blacks because they found her.

So, the blacks returned to the slave quarters at midnight and formed a *terno* [group]; it was a *terno* of Congo. And during the days they went to the woods to cut wood, hollow it out, and make some drums. . . . Then those of the Congo went there, played every salutation to Our Lady, but she just rocked, she did not leave her place. When the Congo went to leave, this is what it said in the newspaper, that the water came, rose up and covered half of her body. All of the waters began to open and she returned to bob in the waves. So they said good-bye and left and told the others that they couldn't get her out, they had called and praised her and asked for her blessing but she did not leave.

And so the *terno* of Mozambique formed. They had already prepared [all the drums]. They made all of them in the forest, you know, they made all the instruments and they went there to the edge of the sea. They arrived there at the sea, the seven old blacks, and they sang for her in the African dialect. They sang for her for a long time at the edge of the sea, calling her, and she rocked, it looked like she would come and she didn't come, it looked like she would come and she didn't come. Fine, she didn't leave her place.

After them the slaves arranged the three Candombe, the three oldest blacks that existed in the time of slavery. It was those three, with the three drums . . . and they went to the edge of the sea around midnight and began to play their drums. The water of the sea trembled, so they were filled with courage and they continued to play and to call her. So they stayed from midnight until six in the morning, and Our Lady moved forward to a certain point in the waves and turned and stayed there in the water with the infant Jesus in her lap.

And the next night at midnight the three returned, the three blacks arrived at the edge of the sea and sang for her, and cried for her . . . and she went and came, she went and came walking, and they were playing the *tambu* [large drum], and she came walking, came walking. Before she arrived the Mozambique came and made a circle around the three drums. Then she stopped and then the Congo arrived, everyone playing those notes, and everyone played in their own way, each one sang according to his ability, and she came and went, she came walking. The Mozambique opened up a space and the black went with the big drum and put it at the very edge of the sea, and Our Lady came and sat on top of the drum.[7]

Not only did Our Lady of the Rosary appear to the blacks, to the slaves; in fact, she preferred their devotion over that of the whites. The legend then describes how, even after she was called from the sea, the whites tried to take her and put her in their chapel and lock the door against the slaves, but Our Lady escaped and went back out to the sea. Finally, after three times, the blacks went and made their own chapel to her in the woods, and there she stayed.[8]

7. Dona Maria Geraldo Ferreira, interview, 17 August 1995. All the stories of the saints have been subject to change, and here, too, there are several variations, some of which have been published. For some of the other versions told in Jatobá, see L. M. Martins, *Afrografias*, 49–55.

8. Dona Maria told me that she had read this legend in a newspaper from the small town of Oliveira when she was in her twenties. As Clare Sammells pointed out in the *American Folklore Society News*, "People who cannot read sometimes assume that literate writings must be true, or more valid, by virtue of being written rather than spoken. The assumption continues today, in our literate society, that things that are written down have more weight than those

Just as there are different versions of the festivals themselves, there are several variations of this legend told throughout Minas Gerais. One element with many permutations is the specific group that calls Our Lady of the Rosary from her location; this depends on which groups of congados participate in the festivals in that particular region. Other versions of the origin stories might deviate where Our Lady was found; in some she has to be coaxed out from a cave, in others from a tree, and in others from a river.[9] All the versions, however, contain the main theme of Our Lady of the Rosary stubbornly ignoring the attempts of the whites and the church authorities to call her out of her place. Instead, she accepts the dancing and singing of the blacks. The style of the story clearly comes from the European medieval apparition tradition, in which images refuse to move from the site where they have been discovered or revealed.[10] Nevertheless, the story is designed to actively evoke the memory of the origin, and reason for being, of particular congado communities. No single group had success in calling Our Lady to the shore; it took the united effort of all of them to accomplish the task. Here, many different "nations" joined together on the basis of their status as "blacks" and united under the protection of Our Lady of the Rosary. This, in miniature, tells the story of the movement from African to Afro-Brazilian, yet with the maintenance of a ritual memory of the differences that had existed in the days of slavery. The practice of the devotion to Our Lady of the Rosary in the feast day celebrations make space for the continuation of ethnic identities in the rituals, while simultaneously asserting the unity of the participants as blacks. The legend opens the space for a collective memory that links the heirs of the rosary tradition with an African homeland.

José Expedito da Luz Ferreira, the main captain of the Mozambique in Jatobá, built on this story to tell of the origin of the type of rosary used by the blacks, a rosary made from the seeds of the plant called the *lágrimas de Nossa Senhora* (tears of Our Lady).

> According to what the old black said, when Our Lady sat on top of the *tambu* the master of the black thought that the black was a witch doctor and began to beat him, mistreating him. So, Our Lady cried and a drop of the tears from her eyes fell in the sand and there grew a plant. That plant grew there that moment, with the little fruit that is called *conta-de-lágrima* [bead of a tear]. The

---

that were merely heard." Clare Sammells, "The Internet and Folklore," *American Folklore Society News* 26 (December 1997): 17.

   9. Pedrina de Lourdes Santos, interview, 24 August 1995.

   10. Christian, *Apparitions*, 17–19.

blacks collected those fruits and made a rosary. And that is what is still called the rosary of the tears of Our Lady. And that is the rosary that we pray today.[11]

Although this story is told much less frequently than the myth of Our Lady of the Rosary, the congadeiros all use the rosary made from seeds known as the *contas-de- lágrima*. According to a captain of a Mozambique of Our Lady of Mercies in Oliveira, Antonio Eustáquio dos Santos, the rosary of tears is the only true rosary; the others are not authentic.[12] Today, both the long, complete rosaries (fifteen decades) that are worn during the festivals and the crowns of many kings and queens, another potent symbol within the festival, are made out of the "tears" of Our Lady of the Rosary. The coronation of the kings and queens re-enacts, according to the participants, the final, glorious rosary meditation—the coronation of Our Lady in heaven. In addition, congadeiros always wear a rosary of five decades (*terço*) around their necks. These rosaries and *terços* are said to be the weapons (*armas*) that protect the congadeiros from possible harm, as seen in the folk saying that opened the first chapter of this book.[13] Thus, the rosary is not only passive protection but also a weapon with which to fight the hardships and injustices of life.

The story of Chico Rei, also recounted earlier in this book, is the origin myth of the congado in Minas Gerais. It provides another basis for a positive racial consciousness among the congadeiros. Like the legend of Our Lady of the Rosary, the story is told often, sometimes in private, formal interviews, at other times as part of the festivals themselves. Chico Rei remains an important mythical figure for the congadeiros of Minas Gerais. Unlike Zumbi, the hero of the Quilombo dos Palmares in the northeast of Brazil, who was king of a community that separated itself physically from the whites, Chico Rei, according to the legends, succeeded in society by maintaining his sense of inner worth, despite his position as a slave. Pedrina de Lourdes Santos, captain of the Mozambique of Our Lady of Mercies in Oliveira (Fig. 5), explains the importance of Chico Rei to the community of congadeiros:

> Chico Rei was just as important as Zumbi, only his way of fighting, his tactics let's say, were different. For me, Chico Rei was one of the first abolitionists here, because, in a different way, instead of fighting,

11. José Expedito da Luz Ferreira, interview, 21 August 1995
12. Antonio Eustáquio dos Santos, captain of the Mozambique of Our Lady of Mercies, Oliveira, interview with the author, 25 September 1995.
13. Célia Lourdes Ferreira, interview, 25 December 1996.

or fleeing his situation, he tried to live in that extremely difficult, conflictual situation, trying to show the people his value in that way inside of that situation. And the whole time he showed through how he lived, through his behavior, that there are many ways to do that, it did not only have to be through flight.

. . . Chico Rei was a person, an emperor who was made a slave, and, and, and, still continued with his human dignity . . . they said to him, "you are a slave, and you will work like a slave," but inside himself he never felt like a slave. This is what people need to learn, that despite forces outside of ourselves that compromise us, like what we are living right now, these forces only have power if we permit them to. . . . Chico Rei created his own way to live in very, very difficult situations, and he was able to pass through them with great majesty . . . because the majesty of Chico Rei, for me, was not only the crown of Congo that he wore, but from the moment he was able to live this, his majesty transcended the physical crown, and he really gained a heavenly crown. And it is that crown that the festival passes, you see?

. . . He never felt like a slave and it was that that set him apart, and because he never felt like a slave he never had to flee to a *quilombo* because inside himself he always remained free.[14]

The crowns of Our Lady of the Rosary and Chico Rei, then, are two transcendent crowns that together with the *coroa*, or crown, of the rosary, give the congadeiros the sense of self-worth, dignity, and majesty that has allowed the community of congadeiros to flourish.

According to Captain Pedrina, the festival serves as a place where "the blacks," who are people in the lower classes, can "be somebody." In her analysis, the process of social inversion, especially in the festival in Oliveira, allows the people of the lower classes to come out and "own" the streets for the time of the festival. More important to her, just as it was to Mestre Venâncio a century earlier, however, is the role that the festival plays in bringing people of different social classes and backgrounds together: "Blacks, whites, rich, poor, gays, prostitutes, all are respected in the grand moment of the festival, all are praised, applauded and treated courteously without discrimination. This is one of the great forces I see in this festival, it is the

14. Pedrina de Lourdes Santos, interview, 29 June 1997.

FIG. 5.   Captain Pedrina de Lourdes Santos and Captain Antonio Eustáquio dos Santos, a sister and brother who together lead the Mozambique of Our Lady of Mercies in Oliveira. Between them is a young congadeira, one of more than two dozen who participate in this group.

moment when the differences in the world disappear, at least for those who are there participating."[15]

However, Captain Pedrina remains critical of the social and economic situation of the lower classes of Oliveira and of the situation of blacks in general in Brazil. She is one of the few who have truly been able to rise up out of poverty, in her case, by putting herself through an accounting program and securing a relatively high paying job in a bank in Belo Horizonte. She did this while raising three children with her husband, Francisco, also from Oliveira. While she fights racial discrimination at a personal level on a daily basis, she channels her political energy, to fight against discrimination, into the festival of Our Lady of the Rosary, which she considers to be an expression of her African roots. She writes much of the new music that her Mozambique performs and uses the music to criticize the reigning social order. For the celebration of the one-hundred-year anniversary of the abolition of slavery, she wrote this song, which she performed at the microphone on the main festival stage in Oliveira:

In the time of slavery	No tempo de cativeiro
the life of the black was just	
to work	vida de negro era só trabucar
he worked all day	trabucaba o dia inteiro
and still only earned the whip	e ainda ganhava o chiquirá
Look, long live liberty	Ora viva a liberdade
slavery has already ended	cativeiro já acabou
but we still don't have equality	mas ainda nos falta igualdade
between the black and the master	de negro para senhor
One hundred years of abolition	Cem anos de abolição
I can't celebrate	não pude comemorar
where is the liberty	cadê a libertação
that the Golden Law promised?	que a lei Aurea ficou de me dar?[16]

Dona Maria, of Jatobá, also talks about the inequality that she sees around her. Although she does not like to talk about slavery, because it was such a sad time, she admits that life had actually become much easier in her lifetime. In earlier years, she and her husband had enjoyed some material wealth; at one time they owned twenty-three acres of farmland in the Jatobá

---

15. Pedrina de Lourdes Santos, interview, 24 August 1995.
16. Ibid.; and *Os negros do rosário* (Belo Horizonte, Brazil: Trem da História, 1987), sound recording. *Trabucar* is the vernacular that many congadeiros use for *trabalhar* (to work).

valley. They hired men to help them farm. She laughs and shakes her head, saying that girls today complain, as she compares their lives to hers when she was a young mother; "I raised fourteen children, no, fifteen—twelve of mine and three others. I gave birth to them, raised them, put them in school, and all of them learned, everyone in my family knows how to read and write, not deep study, but everyone knows how to read and knows how to write. . . . I cooked, I washed, I ironed, I had children, I sent the children to school, I carried firewood on my head so I could cook for my husband, for everyone."[17] As Belo Horizonte spread out and enveloped Jatobá, and after the death of her husband, Virgulino, in 1974, Dona Maria began to sell off their land. She donated the small piece of land she lives on now to the brotherhood. According to Dona Maria, she has been poor, then rich, and now is poor again, but she has remained steady in her devotion to Our Lady of the Rosary.[18]

Although she remains philosophical rather than bitter about the trajectory her life has taken and feels that, in general, life has improved for blacks in Brazil, she criticizes the exploitation she sees around her. Like Pedrina, Dona Maria uses the metaphor of slavery to explain continued economic discrimination:

> Slavery ended, but it didn't end, because today, the people today are slaves all the same, think about it, slaves. People work, everyone works for these companies, and people have rights, but they are all mistreated, abused! Those that want to work to earn their daily bread are mistreated, almost like slaves, only that they aren't tied to a whipping post. But everything else still exists. And there are a lot of poor souls in this world, in this Brazil, who are slaves. The poor who have no place to sleep, no place to stay—persecuted. And the police, who grab some poor guy and beat him until he falls on the ground, or drag him to a place far away, kill him and throw him in the water. This is all from the time of slavery. And what about slavery? Did it end? Slavery didn't end! As long as the world was the world there has been slavery. As long as the world is the world slavery will never end.[19]

The festival of the rosary, however, has allowed the congadeiros to negotiate the inequality, both class and color based. The moment of the festival is

17. Dona Maria Geralda Ferreira, interview, 28 August 1996.
18. Ibid.
19. Ibid.

a celebration of their African roots and a triumph of negritude. João Lopes
(Fig. 6), the head of the festival in Jatobá, sums up this attitude when he says:

> The crowning of Our Lady, everywhere you go to see it, you can be
> sure that the crowning of Our Lady is only done by the blacks
> [negros], it's not a dance, not a festival of the whites . . . so many
> whites say they won't go to the festival of Our Lady of the Rosary
> because it's a celebration of the blacks. I'll tell you a story. There
> was a white that went to the festival of the blacks, and he said,
> "Wow, what a smell! This is the smell of blacks!" He said it close to
> a black, who replied, "I'm the son of Zambi [God], and what's more,
> of Our Lady, and if you, sir, are sensing some smell, leave, because
> today I'm a black, yes, sir!"[20]

A Community of Faith

One of the most important means through which the congadeiros have
combated both race and class prejudice, not to mention overcome physical
odds, has been their faith. The faith of the congadeiros, like the African traditions and the sixteenth-century Catholicism from which it developed, does
not separate the profane from the sacred elements. As Captain Pedrina
explains, "[The black] never separated religion from private life, religion and
life are all one thing."[21] Part of the nature of the belief systems that inter-
twine life and religion so intimately is the reliance on action rather than
liturgy to express the devotion. Pedrina explains that "to pray, for the black,
does not mean just genuflection, it is not concentration nor silence. On the
contrary, to pray is to dance and sing and to let the *ngoma* [music] fly."[22]

The active elements of the congadeiros' faith have to do with taking
care of practical matters, especially the two basic needs of keeping food on
the table and maintaining health.[23] These are both necessities that are
addressed only inadequately by the Brazilian government now, and were

---

20. João Lopes, interview, 17 August 1995. It is important to note that João Lopes and
Pedrina de Lourdes Santos use the term *negro* instead of *preto* in these accounts. Kim Butler
discusses the negative connotation associated with the term *negro*, as opposed to the term
preto. Its use in these narratives emphasizes the speakers' awareness of that negative, and
specifically racial, connotation and their desire to demonstrate how the congados confront, and
even invert, those connotations. See Kim Butler's discussion in *Freedoms Given*, 57–58.

21. Pedrina de Lourdes Santos, interview, 24 August 1995.

22. Ibid. In Jatobá I was told that *ngoma* meant "guarda," one of the generic names for a
congado group, but to Pedrina, from Oliveira, it signified the music of the drums.

FIG. 6.   João Lopes, *capitão-mor* of the rosary festival in Jatobá. He is wearing a hat that he made out of *contas-de-lágrima*, or beads formed from the tears of Our Lady of the Rosary

not at all at the turn of the twentieth century. Dona Maria remembers the abject poverty of her childhood, when she always felt hungry and cold. At the time, her father did not believe in the congado.

> I was a child when I remember the groups of congadeiros passing by our door on their way to the houses of the participants there below, there on the edge of the train tracks. We would go through the backyards down there, in the middle of the trees, so we could see the congado pass. Papa didn't like it at all. He thought that the congado was witchcraft, sorcery, only of bad things, that there was

nothing good about it. Later, he asked for an explanation of what the congado was, and what the story of Our Lady of the Rosary was when the blacks took her from the middle of the sea. He witnessed her, opened his heart to faith and love in Our Lady of the Rosary; and because of this his life turned around and we never went hungry again.[24]

According to the legends, Our Lady of the Rosary showed her preference for the blacks' form of devotion, and congadeiro stories of positive reversals of fortune and return to health continue to be attributed to the strength of their devotion to her. Other specialist saints, who were part of the brotherhood tradition from the beginning, are also known for their abilities to help in the day-to-day lives of the congadeiros. Of all the other saints celebrated by the congadeiros, none is more important than Saint Benedict. In the early years of contact, Our Lady of the Rosary, with her white color, may have been understood as a spirit and as more removed from the lives of her devotees; in contrast, Saint Benedict has always shared many personal associations with the participants. He was black, was the child of slaves, and worked in the kitchen, a job traditionally associated with domestic workers, who in Brazil are overwhelmingly black. He is the patron saint of the kitchen, and many miracles are attributed to him, most having to do with keeping enough food on the table.

According to official Catholic history, Saint Benedict the Black (1526–89) was born in Sicily and gained a reputation in his day for sanctity and miracles. He joined an order at a young age, and although he eventually was made the superior of his house, he preferred to work in the kitchen.[25] The congadeiros keep the basic outlines of this story, but go on to elaborate about specific miracles that he performed. These stories range from exact duplicates of other saint's stories to decidedly "African" variations. Frei Chico, who worked extensively in the north of Minas Gerais, where he engaged in exhaustive research about the Afro-Brazilian population, narrated to me many versions of the story of Saint Benedict that he collected among congadeiros in Araçuaí. In one, Saint Benedict, a cook in a monastery, sneaked food out to give to poor people in the nearby town. The monks suspected that Benedict was stealing and hid on the road to catch him. When they saw him, they jumped out and demanded to see what he had hidden in his robe. The food,

23. The two others that complement those are finding housing and jobs.
24. Dona Maria Geralda Ferreira, interview, 17 August 1995.
25. Butler, *Butler's Lives*, vol. 2, 30.

however, had miraculously turned into flowers, which fell out onto the road. The monks were satisfied and continued on their way, as did Benedict. The flowers then turned back into food which he used to help feed the people.[26] The congadeiros in Belo Horizonte and Oliveira told snippets of this tale. The moral of the story for the congadeiros is clear: Saint Benedict wanted to share his food with the poor of the village; the authorities did not want him to do so and tried to trap him, but God sent a miracle that enabled him to fulfill God's will, which was to help the poor and hungry.

Some of the Saint Benedict stories relate more closely to the plight of the Brazilian slaves and present-day blacks and recall their strategies to resist and undermine the authority of the masters. Dona Conceição Bispo in Oliveira recounts another Benedict story:

> Saint Benedict is the protector of the kitchen. If a person is short of cash, or lacks something they need, it is enough to ask him and he gives to the people. Saint Benedict was in the convent, he worked in the convent with the Franciscan monks. Once he had a desire to see a mass, and he had already been an altar boy, and then he worked there, but they would not let him go [to mass], in the old days the black had no rights, you know? And so one day he went to the convent and said, knowing that there was a very beautiful mass in the convent, and he said that he was going to see the mass. And they said that he couldn't, that he couldn't, and he said, "but I'm going."
>
> [He went, and] one of the monks said to him, "You have to make lunch to serve, at eleven o'clock it has to be ready. You can't stay to see the mass." But Benedict just stayed there leaning against the wall, and waiting to see the mass. After some time the monk said to him, "Benedict, you go to the kitchen to make lunch because at eleven o'clock the lunch has to be ready to serve to everyone who will be there—the guests and everyone." And Benedict said OK, and waited there at the door of the church, with the monk who also stayed at the door, and [Benedict] stayed there watching the mass with the monk looking over at him all the time.

---

26. Frei Francisco Van Der Poel, conversation with the author, 26 September 1994. This is identical to a story published about Queen Isabel of fourteenth-century Portugal, which serves as an origin myth for the Feast Day Celebration of the Divine Holy Spirit. Mari Lyn Salvador, "Ritual Exchange in Azorean Festivals," in *Time out of Time: Essays on the Festival,* ed. Alessandro Falassi (Albuquerque: University of New Mexico Press, 1987).

When the mass ended, he left running to go inside where they had the kitchen, and when he was running he sensed the smell of food, and when he arrived there the fire, the pans were on the wood stove as full as could be with food. And he stayed walking back and forth, until the monk came in and asked, "Benedict, who made all this food?" And Benedict replied, "It was me." The monk said, "No, it wasn't you." And he thought that the food would not be good, but Benedict said that he could try it, and everyone thought it was marvelous. It was the multiplication of food![27]

The story reflects many practical dilemmas that must have been common to slaves and their descendants—the present-day low-income blacks in Brazil. Benedict wants to go to mass but he is told that he cannot. Three times Benedict outright disobeys the orders of the monk, all three times showing an impressive passive resistance. In the first case Benedict simply decides to attend the mass even though he has been told that he cannot. The second time, he simply ignores the monk. Finally, Benedict responds verbally, in apparent agreement with the monk, but nonetheless continues to hold his ground by the church door.

These types of resistance echo some of the ways in which the early *mineiro* brotherhoods responded to the authorities. For the congadeiros, Benedict obeys God's orders above those of humans, and when he returns to the kitchen God has rewarded him for his loyalty by filling his pots with food. When the monk asks who made lunch, however, Benedict does not give the credit to God, preventing a misunderstanding about possible witchcraft. Instead, he states that he made the food, thus preventing any unnecessary discussion about the miracle that had occurred. This part of the story may describe metaphors for earlier methods of hiding from the authorities practices that were considered to be magical events.

Although many of the congadeiros today do not earn much money, in interviews they never expressed lack of food as their biggest preoccupation. Instead, the question of health is their greatest concern.[28] When asked about their devotion to Our Lady of the Rosary, most of the congadeiros responded with stories regarding their health, and it is because of health problems that

---

27. Dona Maria da Conceição Bispo Maurício, interview, 7 September 1995.

28. This emphasis on addressing health problems through devotion is not unique to the congadeiros; in fact, R. Andrew Chesnut posits that the move toward Pentecostalism is a direct outgrowth of the desire for solutions to poverty-generated health problems. R. Andrew Chesnut, *Born Again in Brazil: The Pentecostal Boom and the Pathogens of Poverty* (New Brunswick: Rutgers University Press, 1997), 5.

FIG. 7. The directorate of the festival in Oliveira. Left to right: Capitão-mor Geraldo Bispo dos Santos Neto, Secretary Heloísa Helena Maurício, Secretary Maria Rita de Castro Santos, and president of the Association of Congadeiros of Oliveira Dona Maria da Conceição Bispo Maurício. Respectively, they are the son, daughter, daughter-in-law, and wife of Geraldo Bispo, the former King of Congo who was instrumental in getting the festival started again in the 1950s.

they most often make promises to Our Lady of the Rosary and the other saints of the festivals. Many congadeiros recount the success of those supplications by telling stories of healing miracles at great length and in extensive detail. Dona Conceição of Oliveira (Fig. 7) told a story about the miracle that saved her oldest daughter, who had been dying of croup.

> The first blessing that I received from [Our Lady of the Rosary], that was very important was for Aparecida, the name of my oldest daughter. She had the croup, the sickness, you know? A very dangerous sickness. It was a time here in Oliveira when many children had already died, and there was no more medicine to be found—it's the only thing that stops it, the medicine, if you give it right away. We had a doctor, he was my mother's doctor, and I took my daughter to

him. We arrived there, and for a long time I could feel the heat of the
fever. And so, I arrived there and when he examined her he said,
"She won't make it to three o'clock this afternoon." This was in the
morning that I took her. And so I started to cry, and he said, "You can
take her, I'm not going to prescribe medicine because she only needs
a will, you know, an obituary, so you can bury her, but she's not
going to make it to three o'clock in the afternoon." I said, "But sir,
you have to do something." And he said, "I can't do anything." I left
thinking, "Our Lady of the Rosary will not let my daughter die."

As the story continues, Dona Conceição searched for medicine at the house
of a rich farmer, because he used it for his horses, but he did not have any.
Finally, she returned to town and although there had not been any of the
medication in the pharmacy earlier, a shipment had just arrived. She rushed
there and they gave her daughter a dose. She told them that she would
return to buy more.

Then we arrived in the house and put her into the bed, with that
horrible fever. And my mother told me, "Go take a bath, and take
off those clothes, you are as hot as the child." And we left the child
in the bed, we had made the bed totally white, and put a red cloth
that people say is good to lower the fever. And I went to take a bath
and my godmother stayed there in the bedroom with her. When
some time had passed, my mother was crying in the kitchen at
lunchtime, I arrived at the door of the kitchen and there was the
[photo of the] Church of the Rosary, and I asked Our Lady of the
Rosary to not let my daughter die. If she would cure her—that year
I hadn't been able to do the festival, I hadn't been able to do anything, because I had also been sick and I didn't have any money—
but the next year I would dress her as a princess and make a very
beautiful festival. And it seems as if Our Lady said, "Amen," you
know? Because when I heard my godmother call me, "Goddaughter,
come here, run here"—when she said, "Run here," I thought that my
daughter had died, because I couldn't believe anything else. And so
I started to cry and my mother was crying too, and my godmother
was insisting, "Come here, Maria, come here, goddaughter, come
quickly so you can see something." And I didn't have the courage,
and then she came to the door of the dining room and said, "Maria,
come here, come here goddaughter so you can see something." But
when I looked over at her, she was laughing, but it wasn't possible

that my daughter would be dead and she would be laughing, and I perked up. When I arrived in the bedroom my godmother said, "Look there on the floor," and there was phlegm so big that I don't know how it got through her throat . . . the fever was gone and the phlegm left—it was a miracle, the phlegm came out all bloody, that is to say, it was a type, it was an operation done by Our Lady.[29]

In the end, the doctor came by at three o'clock and told Dona Conceição that she could "paint a miracle," because the child should have died.[30] This story demonstrates how, according to the interpretation of the congadeiros, Our Lady has a power to cure illness that goes beyond the medical profession's ability. The doctor did not even bother to prescribe medicine; he simply, and coldly, told Dona Conceição that her child was going to die. Not accepting that, however, she asked Our Lady to intercede to save the life of the child. And in exchange, Dona Conceição promised to continue with the festival and to enter her daughter as a princess.

Dona Conceição's story describes a common theme of the healing stories—the inefficacy and coldness of the medical profession and the triumph and mercy of the saints. In order to gain that mercy, however, sometimes the promises have to be very large, such as making a lifetime of commitment to the festival. The captain of the Mozambique in Jatobá, José Expedito da Luz Ferreira, made his commitment to the festival in this manner. When he was young he did not like to dance in the festival and was embarrassed to participate in the congado. Then, "I took a fall from a tree, and landed on my back and had three fractures in my spinal column. Then the doctor told me that I would only leave the wheelchair to go to the cemetery, that I would never again be a man in any way. From the waist down had died. So I made a promise to Our Lady of the Rosary, that if I would have the force in my legs at least to be able to walk I would return to dance in the reinado, because I really didn't like to dance the reinado."[31] He was thirty at the time; when he was interviewed, he was fifty-nine and still dancing in the congado. After this miracle, he fulfilled his promise by making a lifetime commitment to the festival, to become one of the strongest leaders in the festival of Jatobá.

The saints, then, serve to link the people intimately with the divine, listening and responding to the congadeiros' troubles when the secular,

29. Dona Maria da Conceição Bispo Maurício, interview, 9 September 1995.
30. The saying "to paint a miracle" comes from the tradition of painting ex-votos depicting a miracle that occurred.
31. José Expedito da Luz Ferreira, interview, 21 August 1995.

social world does not. These stories, however, do not differ much from other manifestations of what is often called "folk" or "popular" Catholicism in Brazil and throughout the world. Where the devotion of the congadeiros diverges from those other practices is in how they manifest their relationship to power, demonstrated in the stories of Saint Benedict and Our Lady of the Rosary. Yet the congadeiros maintain a relationship with a different kind of power—one that can be manipulated—to which they connect to protect themselves against the negative forces that surround them.

Discourse on Power

The congadeiros have always existed in an unequal power relationship with both the secular and religious authorities. Read one way, the trajectory of the history of the congadeiros and the festival of the rosary is one solely of the negotiation of this power dynamic. The very endurance of the festivals, even when their underpinning organizations were undermined by the church, shows the success of one method by which the congadeiros resisted the authorities. They engaged in an active struggle to keep their devotion alive, a struggle that has involved not only social strategies within the Western framework but also something that might be called an African response to the ongoing inequalities and injustices. This strategy involves the manipulation of natural forces, forces that cannot be seen, but that, according to John S. Mbiti, pervade all the other elements of African traditional religions.[32] Beyond material "survivals" within the congados and the cross-cultural significance of many of the symbols and actions within the festivals, the occult use of these natural forces marks the congados as a tradition with significant ties to the African past of the ancestors of the present-day participants. The congadeiros' relationship to the forces has created dynamic tensions between the congadeiros and the church and secular authorities, but also, and more predominantly, between different groups of congadeiros.

Because the manipulation of the forces represents a link to practices that have traditionally been frowned on by the church as sorcery and magic, its presence within the Congado has been the area of greatest concern to the Catholic Church, of which the participants are well aware. In interviews and informal conversations, all the participants agree that the church traditionally thought of the festival as *macumberia* (witchcraft), or *coisa do feiticeiro* (a thing of the witch doctor). Many of the participants agree with the church's

32. Mbiti, *African Religions*, 3; see also Sweet, *Recreating Africa*, 104–5.

analysis of their past, commenting that in the old days the festival was *porcaria* (filthy) and *bobagem* (foolishness) because of the common use of "magic" within the ritual complex. These opinions are based on the stories told of the old, powerful captains of the festival of Our Lady of the Rosary, who had the ability to play tricks or challenge rivals through manipulating natural forces. These abilities evoke, and are heirs to, worldviews brought from Africa. In their study of African American Protestantism in the southern United States and the British Caribbean, Betty Wood and Sylvia R. Frey generalized that in Africa,

> [e]very town and village had one or more ritual experts who, by virtue of their special sensitivity to the supernatural or of long years of training, had access to these mystical forces and through the power of ritual and the use of talismans and amulets were able to manipulate them for the benefit of individuals or communities. . . . No clear distinction existed between the respected religious office of priest and of magician, nor were the functions of priest and sorcerer always differentiated.[33]

James H. Sweet demonstrates that many of these ritual positions and practices came over whole cloth to Brazil.[34] It is not surprising, however, that little evidence exists through which to trace the evolution of these specialists within the brotherhoods of the rosary, and certainly these types of abilities would have been subject to adaptations as the brotherhoods themselves were through the centuries. The legends of the congadeiros, however, attest to the continuation of ritual specialists who, as the authors quoted above assert, had access to mystical forces and the ability to manipulate them. For the congadeiros, those specialists have been the captains of the congados and Kings of Congo, and the congadeiros recall these figures with a mixture of awe and pride.

The congadeiros in Jatobá talk about several powerful captains from their own and neighboring festivals, who walked great distances to participate in one another's festivals. They speak fondly of Pedro Alcântara of Betim, Júlio Juliano from Ibirité, and João Crioulinho from Itaúna. Some of the captains were considered extremely dangerous. Juscelino Cascalho would invite groups from other Congados to his festivals, other captains who were "less educated,

33. Frey and Wood, *Come Shouting*, 16; see also Mechal Sobel, *Trabelin' On: The Slave Journey to an Afro-Baptist Faith* (Princeton: Princeton University Press, 1988), 5–10.
34. For his main arguments on this, see Sweet, *Recreating Africa*, 227–30.

who didn't have a good understanding of things," simply to play tricks on them. Some of the tricks might be one captain's causing another to be paralyzed in his tracks. In another case a captain crossed a bridge and kept another captain from finding the bridge, even though it was right in front of him. According to Dona Maria of Jatobá, in this particular case the King of Congo had to be called to break the spell.[35]

Dona Maria, who lived her entire life in Jatobá, commented that the captains from Oliveira were considered to be exceedingly powerful.[36] One of the most famous captains in Jatobá, Edson Tomas dos Santos, came originally from Oliveira. He "spoke and sang in African and was famous for hypnotizing his enemies with a look and enchanting women, who were attracted to his broad smile and distinguished eyes."[37] According to one story, a young girl laughed at him as he walked by during a festival. He laughed back and asked her why she was laughing. She commented that she had no reason to laugh, then suddenly fell into a fit of laughing and just as suddenly fell sound asleep. No one could wake her for the entire festival. When he finally woke her up at the end of the day he admonished her "not to laugh at things you do not understand."[38]

Zé Aristides from Contagem is remembered as an especially powerful personality. He taught Dona Maria's husband, Virgulino, much about the Congado. The Queen of Congo in Jatobá, Dona Leonor Galdino, describes Zé Aristides as having been "very, very wise, just like Chico Rei, and he always used a yellow umbrella."[39] Zé Aristides would throw his staff (bastão), which had been made during the time of slavery, on the floor, and it would turn into a snake. But Zé Aristides was not the only captain with this skill. Congadeiros from many different regions tell similar stories about the transformation of a ritual cane or a stick into a snake. Dona Maria of Jatobá describes an incident when "there was this black. He looked like this [demonstrating] to one side, and he made some wood turn into a snake, he made a vine turn into a snake."[40] Other objects could also be transformed into snakes. Captain Antonio Eustáquio dos Santos recalls that in Oliveira,

---

35. Dona Maria Geralda Ferreira, interview, 28 August 1996.
36. Oliveira was the only town in the interior that was mentioned as having powerful captains; the rest who were fondly remembered in Jatobá were from regions that, for the most part, border directly with Jatobá.
37. L. M. Martins, *Afrografias*, 95.
38. Ibid., 95–96.
39. Dona Leonor Pereira Galdino, interview, 2 October 1996.
40. Dona Maria Geralda Ferreira, interview, 17 August 1995.

[t]here was another captain, too, named Gandu. In fact until today his daughter is the Perpetual Queen of the Crowning of [Our Lady of] Mercies. . . . This captain danced in a *terno* of Congo, so he wore a scarf around his neck and a straw hat. He took off the hat and the scarf, and he threw the scarf—OK, this is the story my father told me—he threw the scarf onto the ground and it transformed into a snake. So he kept singing and he took off his hat and threw the hat near [the snake] and the hat transformed into a hawk, and the hawk grabbed the snake and ended up circling in the sky. Now, for me this is a story.[41]

Many stories all relate the ability of certain captains to manipulate natural forces, such as one of the most frequently told stories in Oliveira—that of the magic banana tree. Captain Antonio Eustáquio heard these stories from his father, the former captain of the Mozambique. The story occurred in the garden of the patio where the *terno* gathered together to prepare to go to the Reinado.

My father had an uncle called Belisário who was a medium. He had a great ability, and in reality he really worked a lot with this. So it happened, they all sang, and he sang many things, and threw his *bastão*, he tapped it there several times and there appeared a banana tree. The tree grew fast, and there grew a bunch of bananas that ripened immediately, and Belisário picked the bunch, took off the bananas, and threw them to the dancers that were there. I heard this story, but I didn't see it with my own eyes, I didn't have that opportunity.[42]

The late Raimundo Lopes do Santos (Seu Dário), a former King of Congo in Oliveira, was present when the banana tree grew. When he recounted the story, he added that Belisário "told each of the soldiers [dancers in the congado groups] to take one [banana], don't take two, only one. Then, he said, 'OK people, only one, don't take more,' and all that was left over he took and ate, and then he disappeared, no one saw him!"[43] Another common form of the manipulation of nature was a captain's ability to send a swarm of wasps to

41. Antonio Eustáquio dos Santos, interview, 25 September 1995.
42. Ibid.
43. Raimundo Lopes dos Santos, Guarda Fiscal, interview with the author, Oliveira, MG, 10 September 1996. João Lopes of Jatobá also sings a song about the ability of the old masters to make a banana tree grow overnight: "Minha mãe mandô me chamá/lá no pé de mulungu/oi de

annoy and injure other groups of congadeiros. Seu Dário recalls that he was in the middle of a *terno* when a swarm of wasps came and started biting everyone in the group, who then scattered in every direction. The captain of the group ordered the wasps away, and the whole swarm just disappeared.[44]

In all these stories, it is striking that the magic was directed against equals and not against the masters or bosses. When I asked Dona Maria if the magic helped the blacks to fight against cruel masters; she quickly answered yes. She told a story about the magic that helped a slave escape a cruel master. "There was a black and the master was searching for him to punish him, so this black hid himself on the road, he turned into a termite. The master passed by, but escaping, the black stayed there, saw the master in the distance, and got up and went away. And so it was that many blacks won before the time of slavery."[45]

The power of these captains to manipulate the forces was usually manifested through the use of ritual objects. The *bastões* of the leaders of the festivals and the captains of the Mozambiques remain some of the most important ritual objects of the festival. The captains often tell long stories about the history of their *bastão* and of who passed it on to them, because the receipt of this ritual object conferred the legitimacy to the power position they held in the ritual complex. Dona Maria tells the story of how João Lopes received his *bastão* while he was still in her womb:

> The *bastão* of [João Lopes] was picked up in the street . . . from the captain of the Mozambique from here, I don't know what happened, because at that time I didn't understand anything, I just followed along, just followed along, but I paid attention to everything that happened. We arrived at a crossroads, and I don't know what happened—a revolt in the middle of the Mozambique. The Mozambique stopped like this [gesturing], as if ants had been thrown onto the fire, and everything scattered. The leader threw the *bastão* there on the ground and stepped over it and left too. And he said whoever wants to pick it up, do it.

> So, the royalty stopped, and I was there a little in front of the King of Congo—with one child in my arms, the other following along, and

---

dia plantá bananera/oi de noite tocá Caxambu/chora ingoma." Cited in the liner notes of the sound recording *Congado mineiro.*

44. Raimundo Lopes dos Santos, interview, 10 September 1996.
45. Ibid.

my stomach awaiting this one [João Lopes]. So, when the royalty stopped I walked like this [demonstrating], and stood on one side of the *bastão*, looking at it there on the ground. So, Seu Zé Basil turned his head and said, "Oh, Maria, if you have the courage pick up the *bastão* for me, I'm still afraid to pick it up." Even then I had an altar to Our Lady here in the old house that was here. I put it there on the altar, and it may have been eight days later when they had a rehearsal. Seu Zé Basil gave the *bastão* to Virgulino. Virgulino was incredible in the Congo, he played guitar, and he left that position and took charge of the *bastão*, took charge of the Mozambique. He had a new meeting and put all new dancers and took charge, until he died.[46]

Once a captain receives the *bastão* it is his or her responsibility to treat it with care. For instance, the *bastão* is always kept on an altar, and it can never be turned upside down.[47] José dos Anjos Ferreira Filho, the King of Congo in Jatobá during the time I did my fieldwork, recalls that his father, who was the powerful captain of the Mozambique for many years, and Dona Maria's brother, never let anyone touch his, not even his wife. He would also never let anyone see his ritual preparation of the *bastão*.[48] Although the use of these kinds of ritual objects recalls an African past, the participants can also turn to biblical sources to explain antecedents to their practice. For some, the *bastões* represent the staff that Moses "used as he crossed the Red Sea"; in order to show God's power, Moses threw down and it turned to a snake.[49] Moses' long journey, of course, led his people out of slavery, just as the captains of the congados during the time of slavery may have used their abilities to supercede the slave condition, in large part by helping to form communities of faith and power.

José Expedito admitted that a *bastão* "had a little power in agreement with the force and the faith that a person has in Jesus and in Our Lady."[50] João Lopes agreed when he commented that a ritual object such as the *bastão* cannot have any power if the person using it is not pure in his or her thoughts. According to João Lopes, the two most dangerous threats to his power are

46. Dona Maria Geralda Ferreira, interview, 17 August 1995.
47. Seu Sebastião Pinto de Souza, captain of the Mozambique of Our Lady of the Rosary, interview with the author, Oliveira, 18 September 1995.
48. José dos Anjos Ferreira, King of Congo of Jatobá, interview with the author, Tirol, BH, MG, 28 August 1996.
49. José Expedito da Luz Ferreira, interview, 21 August 1995. Exodus 4:1–7 in *The New Oxford Annotated Bible with Apocrypha, New Revised Standard Edition* (New York: Oxford University Press, 1994).
50. José Expedito da Luz Ferreira, interview, 21 August 1995.

women and drink. These could cause him to "lose my dignity, I would lose my dignity, and I would lose all of the supernatural forces that I have. In the first place, you, women. In the second place, *cachaça* (Brazilian rum). Women and drink are the saddest things, the saddest things for the masculine in the congado."[51] This belief is probably the cause of the Federation of Congadeiros' ban on drinking and its requirement of celibacy during the festivals, to prevent dilution of the power that is possible in the festivals.

Another way to manipulate natural forces in the past was through the use of *pontos* (literally "points") during the festivals, both drawn (*riscados*) and sung (*cantados*). *Pontos*, which are widely found in Umbanda and other Afro-Brazilian trance religions, are songs or drawings that function as concentrated points of communication with the other world. Often, in those religions, these items will refer to, and call down, a specific god or goddess, or a *preto velho* or *caboclo* spirit. Captains in the congados are careful to stress that *pontos* were used in the past but no longer are. They emphasize that the two religions (the trance religion and Catholicism, as expressed in the congado) must remain separate.

Many captains in Oliveira, however, recalled that the congadeiros used *pontos riscados* in Oliveira at the crossroads, already dangerous and liminal places. Captain Pedro Aponísio of the Catupé of Our Lady of the Rosary in Oliveira commented that his group does a ritual movement known as a *meia-lua* (half moon) at crossroads. The *meia-lua* is a movement in which the two lines of dancers, or in some festivals just the captains, do a figure eight around each other, which they do because, according to Captain Pedro Aponísio, back in the time of the old congadeiros they said that the evil spirits lived at the corners, so if they did a *meia-lua* the good spirits would accompany them."[52] Sometimes captains who really wanted to bring down some magical power would draw the circle of the *ponto* and put inside it the five-pointed star (*cinco Solomão*) made out of the tears of Our Lady taken from a broken rosary. If another captain reached this symbol, which was thought to be an especially powerful one, he would not let his dancers pass because of the danger. According to Seu Dário, "It's dangerous, you know, if a person jumped over one they would fall, or get sick, it's dangerous, very dangerous!"[53]

The captains of the congados also consider the *pontos cantados* to be extremely dangerous. Many of the older captains say they no longer use the

51. João Lopes, interview, 5 October 1998.
52. Seu Pedro Aponízio, captain of the Catupé of Our Lady of the Rosary, interview with the author, Oliveira, MG, 11 September 1996.
53. Raimundo Lopes dos Santos, interview, 10 September 1996.

pontos cantados during the festival to Our Lady of the Rosary. They complain that young captains, who have not received a good education in the ways of the congados, sing *pontos* without even being aware of what they are doing. The *pontos cantados* function very much like the *pontos riscados*, giving the captain the ability to call down certain forces. Nevertheless, according to the captains, the *pontos* are some of the oldest songs of the congados. Eustáquio Cristiano, captain of the Catupé of Our Lady of the Rosary in Oliveira, sang a couple of the *pontos* for me during an interview.

If you go, go turn there	Se vai, vai torna aí
The wood that doesn't sway	O pau que não balança
is about to fall.	'ta na hora de cair.
The hatchet that cuts	O machado que cortar
I don't know if it's a termite hill	eu não sei se esse é cupira
Or a jacaranda tree.	ou se é jacarandá.

This captain added that it is all right for people who know how to deal with them to sing these.

The captains have, in addition to the traditional access to powers, the responsibility to protect their groups from the malevolent forces that other captains may call down. The rituals that the captains perform before the groups leave the places where they gather in Oliveira, or before they leave the *terreiro* (yard) in front of Dona Maria's house in Jatobá, are carried out to protect the group from those unseen dangers. Captain Eustáquio Cristiano explained that the captains always have to ask the protection of the *pretos velhos* before going out to the festival: "All of the captains have the responsibility to ask for help, you know, from the guides, because they don't only have to prepare themselves with the saints of the festival, because they help a lot, but we also have the obligation to prepare with our guides . . . the *pretos velhos* who are the protectors."[54] According to Seu Eustáquio, asking protection of the *pretos velhos* does not contradict tenets of the Catholic faith. He comments that it doesn't interfere because "it is all the word of God."[55]

João Lopes explained that the raising of a flag eight days before the festival is to begin serves to both warn the spirits and ask for the protection of the *pretos velhos* during the time of the festival.

---

54. Eustáquio Cristiano, captain of the Catupé of Our Lady of the Rosary, interview with the author, Oliveira, MG, 10 September 1996.

55. Ibid.

[The flag] is there on top of that mast. We are under the guard of all of them up in heaven: Our Lady of the Rosary, Saint Benedict, Saint Iphigenia, Our Lady of Mercies, the warning flag. The warning flag symbolizes *one,* a warning that we are about, through the noise we make here on earth speaking, singing, with our instruments, warning all the spirits that follow the Reinado de Nossa Senhora do Rosário—that was first done in heaven and second on earth—warning them that we are about to do the second Reinado of Our Lady. And, we are also, during that event, saying that we require their protection . . . we are asking their protection. In the festival of the Reinado they all come, if they don't come . . . the Reinado only serves to destroy everything, because who did the Reinados were the old spirits, the Africans who came from Africa.[56]

The *pretos velhos* are well known in the trance religion of Umbanda, but the congadeiros fervently maintain that they keep their traditions separate from such religions, although many of the congadeiros also participate in one or the other of those trance religions.[57] Célia Lourdes Ferreira, a *mãe-de-santo* (mother of the saint/leader of a Candomblé or Umbanda center) who also participates in the festival in Jatobá, commented that all the *pretos velhos* in Candomblé "invoke, sing to, and talk a lot about Our Lady of the Rosary."[58] The *mãe-de-santo* adds that when the *pretos velhos* are about to do some work, or bless someone, they call on Our Lady of the Rosary to protect and to help them. Nevertheless, Our Lady of the Rosary, according to Célia, does not represent one of the *orixás* (gods) of the pantheon; she only functions in a capacity as the patroness of the *pretos velhos.*[59]

The way that the communication between the two worlds occurs in both the trance religions and in the congado, as João Lopes pointed out, is through the "noise" that the congadeiros make on earth. The congadeiros consider the drums of the congados to be of fundamental ritual significance. All the captains, often with the help of the dancers, make their own drums in a traditional way, buying the hides for the heads, curing and drying them

---

56. João Lopes, interview, 17 August 1995. The first reinado that João Lopes refers to here is the crowning of Our Lady of the Rosary in heaven, which is the last of the fifteen mysteries of the rosary.

57. Roger Bastide also found this to be true in the northeast of Brazil. Bastide, *African Religions,* 54.

58. Célia Lourdes Ferreira, interview, 25 December 1995.

59. Ibid.

themselves, and tying them on to the drums with heavy ropes. The drums themselves are thought to have their own lives, and they are baptized and given names. The congadeiros consider groups that do not make their own drums to be less traditional and more "folkloric."

In both Oliveira and Jatobá, some especially powerful drums are infused with their own life and play by themselves. In Oliveira, Seu Dário explained that one famous old captain of the Catupé, Arlindo, had a drum that played by itself. "Arlindo had a drum in that house there, now it's there at Dona Conceição's house. She [the drum] played alone, without anyone putting a hand on her, she played by herself . . . she played rrrummmm, rrrummmm, rrrummmm . . . and Arlindo would say, 'Leave her there, she's happy, she's content, leave her there to play alone.'"[60] João Lopes in Jatobá often hears the drums of the Candombe playing in his small room at night. "So, if I told you these drums played by themselves you would think it was a lie, right? Sometimes when I'm sleeping here I lie down and turn off the lights, I lie down and turn off the lights and the drums begin to play, brummmmm, brummmmm, brummmmm, principally on the eve of our festival these instruments play constantly by themselves here. There are even people who are afraid to pass by!"[61]

For João Lopes, the tradition of "magic"—the manipulation of forces usually not controlled by human beings—has continued in the festival. As his predecessors were in their time, he is considered one of the most "powerful" captains today. Much of the native exegesis proclaims that in the present-day festival the witchcraft (macumberia) has stopped. Other participants maintain that the forces still exist and that they are even more dangerous today because they are more hidden. How the captains manipulate the forces derives from the occult knowledge that only they keep.

The manipulation of the natural forces through the care and manipulation of ritual objects, the use of highly charged sacred drawings and songs, the playing of drums to call down the sacred, and the link to the ancestors through the pretos velhos—all form the foundation of how congadeiros understand their world. Captains and kings, ritual experts who are taught orally, learn to manipulate the physical world. The captains can link their knowledge to their predecessors, who came from Africa or had been taught by Africans. This element of the congadeiros' past does not emerge in the documentary record; it remained safe, buried within the hidden transcript.

60. Raimundo Lopes dos Santos, interview, 10 September 1996.
61. João Lopes, interview, Itaipu, BH, MG, 5 October 1996.

Teaching the Traditions of a Shared Past

One of the major problems facing the captains of the congados today is what they perceive as the lack of heirs to their tradition. While not all the congadeiros agree on the exact form of the tradition, there is a general consensus that some traditions within the festivals are in danger of dying out. The congadeiros fear that the youth of today are not serious enough to accept the responsibilities and ritual obligations that being a full participant in the festival entail. Because the traditions of Our Lady of the Rosary need to be passed from generation to generation orally in order for them to continue, teaching becomes extremely important. Captains of groups consciously pick someone to follow them, as do the Kings and Queens of Congo. Then, the captain has the responsibility to pass on that tradition, and for all the captains with whom I spoke, this responsibility is a heavy weight.

One of the most popular stories of the leaders of the congadeiros relates how the tradition was passed on to them. João Lopes earned his *bastão* when he was in his mother's womb. Perhaps, he says, it was this circumstance that gave him the will to learn the traditions of the congados and to acquire Benguela, the ritual language of the congados of Jatobá. He talks about all the curiosity, the vocation, and the enthusiasm he has had for the congado since his youth and recounts how his uncle taught him the African language, as well as the *pontos*, the prayers and the fundaments of the congado.[62] Despite his good education, João Lopes did not become *capitão-mor* until 1974, upon the death of his father, Virgulino, who on his deathbed told João Lopes, "Don't let the reinado stop!"[63] João Lopes started as *capitão-mor* the very next year, and he invited twice as many people just to see if he could fill his father's shoes. The day after the festival, João Lopes went down to the chapel and it was in flames, everything was destroyed—"crowns, flags, everything! Charcoal!"[64] According to João Lopes, it was a test that Our Lady of the Rosary had given him. He had to make everything new, by hand; since then, he has been the undisputed leader of the festival in Jatobá.

A captain can have the *bastão* passed on even when he or she is not ready to receive it, as in the case of Captain Antonio Eustáquio, of the Mozambique of Our Lady of Mercies in Oliveira. When he was passed the responsibility he was just a drummer, and he felt he was not ready to take on the leadership

---

62. Ibid. For a more elaborate rendition of this story, see L. M. Martins, *Afrografias*, 105–7.

63. João Lopes, interview, 5 October 1996.

64. Ibid.

position of captain. He was even embarrassed to wear the skirt, the uniform of the captains of the Mozambiques. When his father suddenly grew ill, he called Antonio to his bedside and began to pass on the traditions. Antonio asserts that his father died before he could pass on everything, yet Antonio took the *bastão* and has gone on to become one of the most well respected captains in Oliveira.

Kings and Queens of Congo also need to be taught their responsibilities in the festival. They are also often passed the crown from a parent or an aunt or uncle. Amásia do Rosário, the Queen of Saint Benedict in Oliveira, received the crown from her aunt, who lived to be ninety-seven years old. The aunt's crown had originally been passed from Amásia's great-grand-mother, "from the time of slavery," according to Amásia. Just as the men pass the traditions down through the male line, the women, who in the past did not participate in the congado, passed the crowns of the reinado down through the female line. The passing, however, did not go from mother to daughter, but often from an aunt to a niece, through extended kinship ties. The crowns, like the *bastões,* have important ritual obligations attached to them, especially in bringing with them the responsibility of participation in the festivals. Echoing the experiences of João Lopes and Captain Antonio, Amásia received the crown at her aunt's deathbed and has never missed a festival since receiving it.[65]

At times the "traditions" taught in one region can be misunderstood in another region. Several years ago, the Mozambique in Jatobá decided to make their uniforms out of homespun cotton, so they would wear the same clothes that the slaves would have worn. They did this in a conscious homage to their ancestors. When they went to participate in a festival in another town, one of the Queens of Congo commented that she was "dying of shame" because of the simplicity of the costumes. According to the participants from Jatobá, this was a case in which the queen had not been properly instructed in the meaning of the festival—she was more concerned with luxury than with tradition.[66]

The question of how the tradition is passed, and concern that it be passed correctly, have also become important issues in the Federation of Congadeiros of Minas Gerais, which created a deliberative council in order to make sure that the traditions are being secured by the various festivals. João Lopes, considered one of the most traditional captains, was the president of the council when I

65. Amásia Maria do Rosário, Queen of Our Lady of Mercies, interview with the author, Oliveira, MG, 14 September 1995.
66. Célia Lourdes Ferreira, conversation, 30 September 1995.

was doing my fieldwork. The federation sends representatives to all the festivals to ensure that they do not diverge from what the federation defines as the tradition of the congado, to prevent it from becoming mere "folklore." Some of the things it wants to prevent, for instance, would be a king dancing during the festival, a dancer who goes into a bar, or dancers participating out of their uniforms. When the federation determines that a festival has broken one of the traditions, its participants are called to meet with the members of the federation to see how the problem can be solved.[67]

The federation requires that all the congadeiros be Catholics; this is one of their obligations, despite the seemingly contradictory presence of many African traditional practices and beliefs. Célia Lourdes Ferreira explains it like this: "Look, they have to be Catholic, but in truth the Congado is African in origin. So, in fact, many congadeiros are congadeiros and are spiritists also, either Umbandistas or Candomblé practitioners, without it interfering with the religion, it works together. When he is a congadeiro, he is a congadeiro and is doing his things in the congados without mixing things up. But everything comes from the same origin."[68]

While the congadeiros see no conflict between "African" and Catholic traditions, some priests still believe the Congado to be far from the Catholic doctrine and refuse to participate. Some of the congadeiros feel that the priests do not accept the festival because of the priests' "ignorance." To solve that, the congadeiros see it as their responsibility to teach their priests about the festivals, to educate them on why it is part of the Catholic tradition. For example, after much coaxing, a priest in a neighborhood near Jatobá allowed the Missa Conga to be held in the parish church. As a cautionary measure, however, he sprinkled *agua benta* (holy water) on the congadeiros as they entered the church. The congadeiros were quite upset by what they perceived to be a lack of respect, and later, after the completion to the festival, they went to the priest and discussed the meaning of the festival with him at great length. The priest accepted the congadeiros' explanation, and they have celebrated the Missa Conga there ever since without any need for the holy water.[69]

Since Vatican II, many priests in the church, especially those familiar with the culture of Minas Gerais, have become increasingly tolerant of the Congado, although the degree of this tolerance varies greatly from region to region. Certain priests, such as Frei Chico, have enthusiastically embraced

67. Ibid.
68. Ibid.
69. Célia Lourdes Ferreira, interview, 21 August 1995.

the congado and Afro-Brazilian culture. Frei Chico worked for more than twenty years in the rural village of Araçuaí and wrote a book about the festival of the rosary there. For the past several years he has lived near Belo Horizonte, celebrating the Missa Conga in Jatobá every year. Other priests have expressed the need to work with people using their faith as a jumping-off point, rather than scorning the practices that the people already had.

Despite the conscious work to secure their traditions, some captains feel that the festival no longer is the powerful ritual event that they knew in the past. For instance, in Oliveira many of the congadeiros commented that the costumes in the festival used to be very simple, and that the participants were never very neat. One old captain in Oliveira, Geraldo da Glória, would always dance barefoot, like the slaves did before him. The captain of the Mozambique of Our Lady of the Rosary exclaimed that the festival had become more than it needed to be, that it had become too political. He went on to say that "now it's a tourist thing, our tourism."[70] He continues to lead his group, however, for Our Lady of the Rosary, but added that he would probably not pass on the tradition, that he would be the last one, because he just did not see anyone with the necessary qualities to take on the responsibility.[71]

João Lopes, the head of the festival in Jatobá, expressed similar concerns, stating that if he could not find anyone both willing and able, the traditions will die with him. Yet many of the congadeiros argue that the old captains said the same thing when João Lopes was a boy. For a festival that has lasted so long and withstood so much, it seems almost impossible that the late twentieth century would see its destruction. Perhaps Dona Maria said it best when she commented: "This congado comes from the beginning of the world. No one knows the beginning of it, and no one knows the end."[72]

Conclusion

The four themes that run through the narratives of the congadeiros demonstrate some of the ways in which they construct their own world—separate from but intimately tied to the larger society in which they are embedded. They remember and celebrate the heroes of their past, such as Chico Rei, who—mythic or real—serve to make sense of their responses to the larger

---

70. Sebastião Pinto de Souza, captain of the Mozambique of Our Lady of the Rosary, Oliveira, interview with the author, Oliveira, MG, 18 September 1994.

71. Ibid.

72. Dona Maria Geralda Ferreira, interview, 17 August 1995.

power structure. They place that history within the larger context of Brazilian history and present-day identity politics when they make comparisons between Chico Rei and the much celebrated Zumbi of Palmares. Their annual rearticulation of ties to the *pretos velhos* connect them to an even more distant past, inhabited by ancestors who continue to protect them from unseen dangers. Within that protected arena, the congadeiros articulate their own concepts of power, based very much on the foundation of their tradition of faith and the community. They engage in rituals and tell stories that allow them to actively remember their own heritage not only as Afro-Brazilians but as congadeiros. As congadeiros, they are heirs to the long tradition of the lay religious brotherhoods dedicated to Our Lady of the Rosary, which developed over centuries at the particular crossroads of multiple European and African influences that came together in Minas Gerais.

CONCLUSION

Se a morte não me matar, tamborim
se a terra não me comer, tamborim
ai, ai, ai, tamborim
eu tenho de chorar com'ocê tamborim.

If death does not kill me *tamborim*
if the land does not eat me *tamborim*
ai, ai, ai, tamborim,
I must sing [cry] with you, *tamborim.*

—Song of the Catupé in Oliveira to close the festival

The history of the brotherhoods of the rosary demonstrates that the congadeiros constantly negotiated an ongoing interplay of economic, political, racial, and gendered factors expressed through the specific power dynamic of the Atlantic World, Brazil, and Minas Gerais; in other words, the brotherhoods have had to balance the forces of change and continuity in order to survive. For the congadeiros, the word *tradition* identifies what is perceived to have continued in the festivals. When they call an action "traditional," they imply that for them, as descendants of Africans, of slaves, and as blacks, it comes from their shared past. It is part of the shared set of symbols that identify them as a persistent people.[1] Despite the congadeiros' outlook on the stability of their traditions, the historical record, including their oral accounts, often demonstrate that elements of the rituals that the congadeiros consider to be traditional constitute some of the most dynamic elements within the festivals. However, the most continuous element has been the ability of the brotherhoods to maintain community through a constant interplay

---

1. George Pierre Castile and Gilbert Kushner, eds., *Persistent Peoples: Cultural Enclaves in Perspective* (Tucson: University of Arizona Press, 1981), xv–xxii.

between their community, the outside world, and the unseen world. In fact, the flexibility of the concept of tradition, embodied in the idea of negotiation, has facilitated the endurance of the communities' devotion and practice. In this conclusion, I examine the ideas of continuity and change through the lens of tradition, community, and spirit. The members of the brotherhoods were not a changing community held together by inert traditions. On the contrary, flexible traditions that rearticulate links to a shared past have insured the continuation, and persistence, of a people.

Tradition

As discussed in the previous chapter, culture, for much of the first century of anthropological studies, was considered to be enduring, in that it changed slowly if at all. Within that model, the traditions of those cultures were the backbone of that stability, passed intact from one generation to the next.[2] Scholars' former emphasis on the durability of tradition included a sidebar in the case of Afro-Brazilian traditions. The relative purity of traditions in Afro-Brazilian religions became a major concern of scholars and participants in those religions after the turn of the twentieth century.[3] Traditions, both among participants and scholars, have been defined by outward forms, such as rituals, festivals, foods, and language. Traditions that show more purity and less syncretism have been favored by scholars and, in being favored, have gained prestige in their own communities.[4] Recent research suggests that much of the responsibility for the identification of some groups as "more pure" than others comes from certain participants—informants for the scholars—themselves.[5] These influences only exacerbate the autoidentification of certain groups as traditional and the competition between the groups for the increased prestige that scholarly recognition brings.

The scholarly focus on the purity of traditions has also affected the congadeiros, even though academics have only recently begun to take an interest

2. Dirks, Eley, and Ortner, *Culture/Power/History*, 3. See also Hobsbawm and Ranger, *Invention of Tradition*.

3. This began with the doctor-anthropologist Raimundo Nina Rodrigues at the turn of the twentieth century in Salvador, Bahia. See Skidmore, *Black into White*, 53–64.

4. See the excellent examination of this problem in Beatriz Góis Dantas, *Vovó Nagô e papai branco: Usos e abusos da Africa no Brasil* (São Paulo: Editora Graal, 1988).

5. J. Lorand Matory, "The English Professors of Brazil: On the Diasporic Roots of the Yoruba Nation," *Comparative Studies in Society and History* 41, no. 1 (1999): 72–103.

in them. Scholars are choosing certain groups to study, thus giving those groups prestige and a certain influence within the larger community of congadeiros. Many of the main informants who are sought out consider themselves to be the most traditional. Yet many practices that are identified as traditions in the brotherhoods have been constantly evolving. The danger in overvaluing the end product of certain developments over others sets up another power dynamic within the communities of congadeiros that has always been present but could become even more exaggerated.

Historical documentation demonstrates that the brotherhoods, and certain practices within them, continued from the colonial period through the Brazilian Empire, the First Republic, and the vast changes in the twentieth century to today. Yet what can be gleaned from the documents relative to traditions in the brotherhoods shows that many practices called traditions in today's festivals were constantly in flux. How many kings and queens were crowned in a given year, how many saints were venerated during the festivals, how many masses were said or sung for a given festival, or even whether the festival could occur (whether it was threatened by financial problems in the brotherhood) all changed constantly through the history of the brotherhoods. Even which groups of congados participated in the festival changed. The documents reveal these changes but, unfortunately, rarely record the attitudes of the participants about the changes.

The congadeiros today judge their own and one another's relative change and continuity against what they understand to be tradition, but the concept of tradition changes from person to person and from group to group. Tradition for the congadeiros, as for adherents of the Afro-Brazilian religions of the northeast, has been linked to the relative abundance or purity of African "traits," such as the retention of African languages. Among the congadeiros the concept of tradition also includes the retention of slave traditions—as in the preference for certain foods, dirt yards, dancing in bare feet, and the way the drums are made—or traditions from the older brotherhoods, such as collecting alms or picking up the kings and queens at their homes. Traditions also include the manner of clothing used; for example, a skirt worn over pants is considered traditional for many of the congado groups.

Traditions vary from region to region. Historically, the brotherhoods of the rosary developed regionally, and variations emerged in relative isolation from one another, as evidenced today in the regional characteristics of different groups of festivals. Although the Federation of Congadeiros seeks to unite those groups, competition remains heated between them. For instance, groups occasionally travel to different regions to participate in festivals but often complain afterward that they were not treated well, or that the host festival "traditions" were not correct, or worse, that the host group had lost its traditions.

The leaders' attacks on the traditions of other groups can be understood as an extension of the "traditional" rivalries between groups and between powerful captains. They also reflect, however, the self-identification of groups as more or less traditional in comparison with those of other regions. Even so, within brotherhoods, the idea of tradition remains a fluid category, as some of the practices considered traditional are actually relatively recent additions. For example, the Candombe is considered by most congadeiros today to be the most traditional group, in fact the ancient source, of the Congado. However, the festival in Jatobá did not start a Candombe until after João Lopes took charge of the festival in 1974. The next most traditional group of congados in Jatobá is considered to be the Mozambique, yet everyone freely admits that, in fact, the Congo was the original, and for a while the only, congado in the festival in Jatobá.[6] Other rituals have also been mutable in Jatobá, often changing together with the shifting demography of the area. For instance, João Lopes admitted that certain late-night processions through the street were no longer done, because many of the new residents to the area did not know what the congado was and so might endanger the congadeiros.[7]

Similarly, the traditions in Oliveira have been dynamic because of the constant negotiation with the town and church authorities. For instance, the festival in Oliveira includes the figure of Princess Isabel, representing that monarch's role in freeing the slaves, although she never traditionally played a part in the festivals. Her inclusion was a compromise on the part of the congadeiros to make the festival more acceptable to those authorities, yet it is criticized by participants who would like to see the festival become more traditional. To others, the presence of Princess Isabel has in itself become an important part of the tradition. The internal dynamic of the Oliveira festival has also changed. Although the Mozambiques are considered the most traditional group, the Catupé was the first group to exist in Oliveira, and in this way is the most historical. For example, the fact that the groups no longer go through the town collecting alms has also changed the dynamic of the festival, yet that occurred because the festival expanded to eight days and many participants cannot take off work or school in order to engage in those practices.

The elements that participants call traditional, then, have been dynamic through the years and centuries. Some groups, such as the Candombe, that

---

6. Leonôr Pereira Galdino, interview, 2 October, 1996.
7. João Lopes, interview, 5 October 1996.

seem to be more overtly "African" in form and ritual turn out to be more recent, while features that might be called more syncretic, including the crowning of kings and queens and the participation of those groups called Caboclos and Caboclinhos have persisted for centuries. This shift corresponds to an increased self-identification and awareness of the communities as "African" as they have had to more self-consciously negotiate the larger society since the romanization of the Brazilian church and, more recently, since the onset of the media attention given to certain parts of Afro-Brazilian history (although not the *mineiro* Congado traditions) around the one hundredth anniversary of the abolition of slavery, in 1988.[8]

The bundle of traditions that make up the Congados, however, is not invented in the sense that Hobsbawn and Ranger imply simply because they are recent. Instead, they show the dynamism of tradition in response to the outside world. For instance, groups called Mozambiques have existed in Minas Gerais since the beginning of the nineteenth century, just not at the festivals of Jatobá and Oliveira. The presence of the Mozambique in these festivals may demonstrate a cross-fertilization that occurred as communications improved throughout the twentieth century.

Community and Spirit

Many of the traditions of the Congado have been dynamic and flexible, but at their core exist many general practices that have remained stable, for instance, the brotherhoods' constant devotion to Our Lady of the Rosary and their use of drumming to open a ritual space in which to express that devotion. The practices have endured because of the consistency of the underlying structure—the cosmology. This structure reflects concepts drawn from African traditional thought, such as the concepts of healing and celebration, the pragmatic approach to change, and the interaction of the seen and the unseen worlds, all of which have endured in the congados. Likewise, the structures of power, including an articulated hierarchy and an understanding and nurturing of patron-client relationships, have endured.[9] More fundamentally, however, what has endured in the brotherhoods and among the congadeiros is the lack of separation between sacred and profane, a feature that, in the past, was shared by African traditional worldviews and sixteenth- and seventeenth-century Christianity.

8. Andrews, *Blacks and Whites*, 218–24.
9. See Miller, "Central Africa," 42.

Over time, the link between the sacred and the profane created a circular dynamic within the brotherhoods through which the formation of community and the endurance of religious beliefs and practices constantly reinforced each other. The center of this dynamic, of course, was the symbol of Our Lady of the Rosary, which served to bridge the many cultures that gave birth to the brotherhoods and to connect the past and present of the devotion. Not surprisingly, her cross-cultural presence has been the most obviously enduring factor in the brotherhoods. Our Lady of the Rosary and other symbols within the festival act and react in a world that radiates out in concentric circles from the individual, to the family, to the community, to modern Brazil, and finally to the spirit and to God. The keyword here, however, is *community*. The interchange between community strength and devotional life created and continues to create a social Möbius strip that constantly reinforces both.

The individual within this complex makes a link with the spirit by offering private prayers and requests that are answered by Our Lady of the Rosary.[10] Joseph M. Murphy points out that the diaspora traditions he studied seek "to develop an intimate relationship between individuals and the spirit."[11] In their worldview, congadeiros have received graces from Our Lady of the Rosary and other saints whom they praise in the festivals and have the possibility of gaining certain supernatural abilities through a strong link with the spirit, granted according to a congadeiro's strength of devotion to Our Lady and his or her observance of specific rituals that reinforce the link.

The individual, however, by no means stands alone. Only through the unity of the community can the individual's association with the unseen world be efficacious—only then can the special powers have meaning. The spirit is brought into public ceremonies to help the community.[12] Among the congadeiros, the family and neighborhood define the boundaries of the community, and their importance cannot be overstated. The directorates of the organizations, the congados, and the royalty are complexes that are all based

---

10. The participants often express the belief that Our Lady of the Rosary does not actually grant the wishes, that she intercedes with God/Jesus on their behalf, thus enabling their requests to be granted. The thanks, however, usually go to her.

11. Joseph M Murphy, *Working the Spirit: Ceremonies of the African Diaspora* (Boston: Beacon Press, 1994), 190.

12. Again, Murphy points this out for the diaspora ceremonies he observed. All those ceremonies involved the inducement of trances. According to Célia Lourdes Ferreira, the lack of trances in the congado is the thing that makes the festival of the rosary different from Umbanda and Candomblé. In fact, although stories are told of some participants, or whole groups, falling into trance, everything is done to bring them out of it quickly. The lack of trance, however, does not make the congados any less of a diaspora tradition. Célia Lourdes Ferreira, interview, 25 December 1996.

in the family, the neighborhood, or both. The festival has served to sustain those affective ties in a society in which poverty threatens to pull them apart. In a social world that sought to break up families during the colonial period and given the precarious state of families in lower-income neighborhoods in industrial Brazil today, this emphasis on family and other affective bonds in the congados have served to make the entire community stronger.

The community of congadeiros has extended beyond the localized festivals to include a larger community, united in a statewide association, the Federation of Congadeiros. This organization consists of people of the same social backgrounds who, despite their frequent differences, share common experiences and histories. In this way, the festivals have expanded out of their own communities and are serving to unite a population that has traditionally been kept apart by both physical (lack of access to information) and ideological (the myth of racial democracy) means. Whether the congadeiros will be able to improve the situation of the participants in a political way has yet to be seen, but congadeiros are already sponsoring communal workshops and cottage industries in individual communities and are being sought out to endorse candidates in both local and state elections (Fig. 8).

The festival of the crowning of Our Lady must be understood in its relationship to the larger Brazilian society. The festival does, on one level, serve as a system of social redress.[13] In the case of the congadeiros, however, the festival has historically served to resolve conflicts not only within the community but also between the community and the social system in which it is embedded. The festival, then, negotiates with the social structure and serves, if not to resolve, at least to mediate, the inherent conflict present in an ongoing asymmetrical social system.

Finally, this relationship of the participants with the reality beyond the social structure—with the spirit—must be taken into consideration if one wishes to understand how the festival "works" and how it has endured. Murphy asserts that "the dynamism of diasporan ceremony is not only a cathartic release of tension—though of course it is that—but it is also a profound view of the relationship between human and spirit."[14] The festival of the rosary reinforces the link with the spirit in several ways. First, on the surface, it serves to thank Our Lady and the other saints represented in the festivals. Second, it calls on the *pretos velhos* that link the congado with an African past. And third, it links the participants with their ancestors, their traditions, and their own pasts.

---

13. Victor Turner, *The Anthropology of Performance* (New York: PAJ, 1986), 34–35.
14. Murphy, *Working the Spirit,* 180.

FIG. 8.   Congadeiros have recently become more active in politics. This car, which in 1996 sat outside the main meeting place of the rosary festival in Novo Progresso, a neighborhood in Belo Horizonte, exhorts the public to "vote congadeiro."

African traditional worldviews considered the saints, the *pretos velhos*, and the ancestors to be part of an extensive spirit world. Whether an outside observer wants to believe in the miracles and magic powers negotiated through the saints who are venerated in the festivals does not matter. The participants have a profound belief in these things, and this belief affects all aspects of their lives. Anthropologist Wyatt MacGaffey quotes J. Pouillon, who observed that "it is only the nonbeliever who believes that the believer believes in God: to the believer his belief is knowledge, that is, perceived and experienced fact."[15] For the congadeiros, their direct link with the spirit world, made possible by the continuation of the festival, is perceived and experienced fact.

The brotherhoods provided a space for the establishment of a community by the slaves and free blacks of Minas Gerais. Those communities centered around the powerful image of Our Lady of the Rosary. Leaders were chosen who could help to negotiate the relationship between the brotherhood mem-

15. MacGaffey, *Religion and Society*, 1.

bership and the larger society, and others were chosen who could do the same with the unseen world. The communities created the conditions in which a coherent cosmology could be formed; the community and its cosmology, mutually reinforcing, created conditions in which were forged an enduring, persistent people who embraced common symbols of a shared past and a shared cosmology. Further, the community and its cosmology gave that population a way to interact and negotiate with the larger social structures.

The community has resisted an unjust social system not through armed struggle or political debate, but, like Chico Rei, through strengthening their link with the unseen world, which in turn strengthens the very foundation of their communities. They gain ritual efficacy and community solidarity through traditional symbols of power: the rosary that protects them, the drum that opens up the ritual space, the staff that manipulates that space, and the transcendent crown symbolizing the congadeiros' link with the spirit that defines their lives in the social realm.

Final Thoughts

The examination of the history of the Brotherhoods of Our Lady of the Blacks in Minas Gerais provides insight into the complicated and messy dynamic of transnational culture that resulted from the forced migration of millions of Africans to the Americas. Although much has been written on this subject and on various regions, the study of the brotherhoods offers a new perspective on several aspects of this dynamic.

First, the exploration of the earliest brotherhoods as reformulation of an African cosmology based in a heterodox mix of African worldviews and folk Christianity recasts the brotherhood members as active players in their own lives, supplanting their image as passive receptors of the hegemonic moral discourse. In many ways, the brotherhoods were simultaneously places of assimilation and of resistance. Their members learned to survive through the tactics of negotiation, subterfuge, and endurance, demonstrating that there were a wide range of responses to slavery, responses that push out against the confines of the simple bipolar opposition of resistance and accommodation.

Second, the endurance of the brotherhoods over a period of centuries offers a look at how Africans became Afro-Brazilians. The *mineiro* brotherhoods of the rosary were heterogeneous: the populations always included Africans from several regions, Brazilian-born blacks and mulattos, men and women, slaves and free. Despite, or perhaps because of, this mixture, the brotherhoods remained coherent organizations, changing with the requirements of the time but enduring all the same. In addition, despite the heterogeneity, a form of devotion endured that retained non-European worldviews and practices. The nineteenth-century accounts attest to the use of drumming and dancing during the feast day celebrations, the crowning of kings and queens, and the playing of groups with names such as Congo and Mozambique. The population in the brotherhoods actively chose to retain these aspects of their cultures even as they became (or perhaps enabling them to become) Afro-Brazilians.

Third, the active form of devotion within the brotherhoods turned out to be more resistant than the organization of the brotherhoods themselves. When the Brazilian church turned to Rome in the beginning of the twentieth century, all the heterodox brotherhoods came under scrutiny. But, even with an active campaign against them, the festivals of the brotherhoods of the rosary endured, retaining their heterodox basis in African traditional practices and worldviews and popular Catholicism. Through these festivals, the congadeiros express an overt sense of pride in their blackness in a country in which the elite deny the existence of racial strife.

Finally, the story that the congadeiros tell is not one of exploitation but of victory in the face of slavery and the economic domination and exploitation of the capitalist system.[16] The congadeiros do not speak of victory over the economic inequalities extant in contemporary Brazil; instead, they celebrate quotidian victories gained by Our Lady of the Rosary on their behalf. Borrowing James Scott's metaphor of "weapons of the weak," these victories have long constituted part of the arsenal of the congadeiros to combat the asymmetric social and economic system in which they have lived for centuries. As proclaimed in the popular saying that opened Chapter 1 of this book, "The beads of my rosary are artillery bullets."[17] These metaphorical weapons have enabled the congadeiros to "resist" in the sense of *resistência*, the Portuguese word meaning both "to resist" and "to endure." The devotion to Our Lady of the Rosary has allowed the congadeiros a ritual efficacy that has enabled them to maintain strong family and community structures built on their shared and remembered past, as well as a positive ethnic/racial consciousness, despite centuries of cultural, social, and economic oppression.

---

16. I use the word *victory* here because this is the term that the congadeiros themselves use when one of their promises is fulfilled by Our Lady. They say she has been "victorious."

17. See Chapter 1, n. 2.

Table 1   Membership of the brotherhoods of Our Lady of the Rosary

Place of Origin	Atlantic Islands	Central Africa	East Africa	West Africa	Brazil	Unknown
"Nation"/Other Discrete Group	Cabo Verde	Angola	Mozambique	Coura	Cabra	Cachante
	São Tome	Bamba		Courano	Crioulo	Canboda
		Bambambila		Fon	Exposto	Canguica
		Bambamboira		Fula	Ladino	Carabari
		Bango		Gome	Mulata	Catanga
		Benguela		Lada	Pardo	Caxanche
		Cabinda		Mina		Chibante
		Cabunda		Nago		Coboes
		Caconde		Sabaru		Cobu
		Cambunda				Coutam
		Camunda				de Nação
		Camundonga				Embala
		Cassange				Goymeno
		Comundongo				Grangui
		Congo				Granju
		Ganguella				Ladano
		Macangana				Mafumba(i)
		Monjolo				Monbica
		Mucumbe				Mopoco
		Quicamba				Mosangano
		Rebollo				Mosumbe
		Songo				Mucoso
						Mugumbe
						Muhambe
						Pemeno
						Soro

Table 1 Membership of the brotherhoods of Our Lady of the Rosary (continued)

Place of Origin	Atlantic Islands	Central Africa	East Africa	West Africa	Brazil	Unknown
						Timbu
						Toco
						Xambu

SOURCES (nations and other groups): "Assentos de Irmãos," Irmandade de Nossa Senhora do Rosário, 1750–1886, Mariana, AEAM P28; "Entradas de Irmãos," Irmandade de Nossa Senhora do Rosário dos Pretos, São João del Rei, 1747–1806, AINSR; "Livro de Termos de Meza," Irmandade de Nossa Senhora do Rosário, Arraial de Bacalhau, Freguesia de Nossa Senhora da Conceição de Guarapiranga, 1758–1893, AEAM Y12.

SOURCES (regions): J. D. Fage, An Atlas of African History, 2d ed. (London: Edward Arnold, 1978); Mary C. Karasch, Slave Life in Rio de Janeiro, 1808–1850 (Princeton: Princeton University Press, 1987); John K. Thornton, Africa and Africans in the Making of the Atlantic World, 1400–1680 (Cambridge: Cambridge University Press, 1992); Pierre Verger, Fluxo e refluxo do tráfico de escravos entre o golfo do Benin e a Bahia de Todos os Santos dos séculos XVII a XIX, 2d ed., trans. Tasso Gadzanis (São Paulo: Editora Corrupio, 1987).

NOTE: The groups identified are from the membership of the brotherhoods of Mariana, São João del Rei, and Arraial de Bacalhau for the period 1750–1860.

Table 2   Membership of the rosary brotherhood in São João del Rei

Decade	Atlantic Islands		White		Brazil		Central Africa		East Africa		West Africa		Null[a]		Unknown[b]		Grand Total
	number	%	number	%	number	%	number	%	number	%	number	%	number	%	number	%	
1750s	0	0.00	0	0.00	1	04.00	6	22.22	0	0.00	2	7.41	18	66.67	0	0.00	27
1760s	0	0.00	0	0.00	9	25.71	9	25.71	0	0.00	2	5.71	15	42.86	0	0.00	35
1770s	0	0.00	2	1.16	37	21.38	30	17.34	0	0.00	8	4.62	96	55.49	0	0.00	173
1780s	0	0.00	2	0.85	35	14.96	49	20.94	0	0.00	21	8.97	124	52.99	3	1.28	234
1790s	0	0.00	10	1.63	118	19.25	163	26.59	1	0.16	32	5.22	288	46.98	1	0.16	613
1800s	2	0.48	3	0.72	72	17.22	73	17.46	0	0.00	20	4.78	247	59.09	1	0.24	418
Total	2	0.13	17	1.13	270	18.00	330	21.98	1	0.07	85	5.64	788	52.59	5	0.33	1500

Source: Entradas de Irmãos, Irmandade de Nossa Senhora do Rosário dos Pretos, São João del Rei, 1747–1806, AINSR.

[a] Null indicates that no information was given about the origin of the member.
[b] "Unknown" indicates African nations that could not be identified.

Table 3   Leadership positions in the rosary brotherhood of Arraial de Bacalhau, Guarapiranga

Decade	Atlantic Islands		Brazil		Central Africa		East Africa		Unknown[a]		West Africa		Total
	number	%	number	%	number	%	Number	%	number	%	number	%	
1760s	5	1.81	57	20.65	162	58.70	0	0.00	7	2.54	45	16.30	276
1770s	7	2.48	59	20.92	170	60.28	2	0.71	17	6.03	27	9.57	282
1780s[b]	1	2.00	28	56.00	16	32.00	0	0.00	2	4.00	3	6.00	50
1790s	4	0.73	284	51.92	211	38.57	0	0.00	10	1.83	38	6.95	547
1800s	5	0.94	262	49.34	231	43.50	1	0.19	9	1.69	23	4.33	531
1810s	0	0.00	313	67.02	137	29.34	1	0.21	5	1.07	11	2.36	467
1820s	0	0.00	154	59.46	92	35.52	1	0.39	1	0.39	11	4.25	259
1830s[c]	0	0.00	18	64.29	8	28.57	1	3.57	1	3.57	0	0.00	28
Total	22	0.90	1175	48.16	1027	42.09	6	0.25	52	2.13	158	6.48	2,440

SOURCE: "Livro de Termos de Meza," Irmandade de Nossa Senhora do Rosário, Arraial de Bacalhau, Freguesia de Nossa Senhora da Conceição de Guarapiranga, 1758–1893. AEAM Y12.

NOTE: Only 2,440 had their geographic origin/ethnicity identified.

[a] "Unknown" indicates unidentified location of African nation.
[b] The numbers for this decade are low because no elections were listed from 1778 to 1789.
[c] 1830 was the last year of the election lists, so this represents only that year, not the decade.

Table 4   New members of the rosary brotherhood in Cachoeira do Campo

Decade	Members				
	Female		Male		
	number	%	number	%	Total
1720s	69	47.59	76	52.41	145
1730s	5	45.45	6	54.54	11
1740s	49	44.95	60	55.05	109
1750s	36	55.38	29	44.61	65
1760s	60	46.51	69	53.49	129[a]
1770s	63	38.89	99	61.11	162[b]
1780s	48	52.18	44	47.82	92[b]
Total	330	46.28	383	53.72	713

SOURCE: "Entradas de Irmãos," Irmandade de Nossa Senhora do Rosário, Cachoeira do Campo, AEAM AA25 and AA26.

[a]In this decade there were two entries in which it was impossible to ascertain the gender of the incoming member.
[b]In each of these decades there was one entry in which it was impossible to ascertain the gender of the incoming member.

Table 5   New members of the rosary brotherhood in Ouro Preto, Paróquia de Pilar

Decade	Members				
	Female		Male		
	number	%	number	%	Total
1720s	88	45.59	105	54.40	193
1730s	160	35.48	291	64.52	451
1740s	138	33.33	276	66.67	414
1750s	29	31.18	64	68.82	93
1760s	1	33.33	2	66.67	3
Total	416	36.04	738	63.95	1154

SOURCE: "Entradas de Irmãos," Irmandade de Nossa Senhora do Rosário, Ouro Preto 1724–1760, CC Paróquia de Pilar, rol 81.

Table 6   New members of the rosary brotherhood in Cachoeira do Campo

Decade	Members						
	Forro		Free		Slave		
	number	%	number	%	number	%	Total
1720s	15	10.34	50	34.48	80	55.17	145
1730s	7	63.64	1	9.09	3	27.27	11
1740s	15	13.76	51	46.79	43	39.45	109
1750s	13	20.00	29	44.62	23	35.38	65
1760s	8	6.11	75	57.25	48	36.64	131
1770s	13	7.98	78	47.85	72	44.17	163
1780s	4	4.30	49	52.69	40	43.01	93
Total	75	10.46	333	46.44	309	43.10	717

SOURCE: "Entradas de Irmãos," Irmandade de Nossa Senhora do Rosário, Cachoeira do Campo, AEAM AA25 and AA26.

Table 7   Membership of rosary brotherhood of Ouro Preto, Paróquia de Pilar

Decade	Members						
	Forro		Free		Slave		
	number	%	number	%	number	%	Total
1720s	21	10.88	17	8.29	156	79.79	193
1730s	26	5.76	41	9.09	384	85.14	451
1740s	27	6.52	46	11.11	341	82.37	414
1750s	6	6.45	12	12.90	75	80.65	93
1760s	0	0.00	0	0.00	3	100.00	3
Total	80	6.93	115	9.96	959	83.10	1154

SOURCE: "Entradas de Irmãos," Irmandade de Nossa Senhora do Rosário, Ouro Preto 1724–1760, CC Paróquia de Pilar Rol 81.

Table 8   New members of the rosary brotherhood in Mariana

| Decade | Members | | | | | | |
| | Forro | | Free | | Slave | | |
	number	%	number	%	number	%	Total
1750s	149	37.63	11	2.78	234	59.6	396
1760s	49	23.11	20	9.43	143	67.45	212
1770s	1	4.76	8	38.09	12	57.14	21
1780s	16	9.82	24	14.72	123	75.46	163
1790s	7	18.92	3	8.11	27	72.97	37
1800s	3	12.00	8	32.00	14	56.00	25
1810s	2	6.45	10	32.26	19	61.29	31
1820s	1	1.35	22	29.73	51	68.92	74
1830s	7	7.61	38	41.30	47	51.09	92
1840s	5	2.91	94	54.65	73	42.44	172
1850s	0	0.00	184	69.43	81	30.57	265
1860s	0	0.00	171	70.66	71	29.34	242
1870s	1	0.86	102	87.93	13	11.21	116
1880s	0	0.00	48	94.12	3	5.88	51
Total	241	12.70	743	39.17	911	48.13	1897

SOURCE: "Assentos de Irmãos," Irmandade de Nossa Senhora do Rosário, 1750–1886, Mariana, AEAM P28.

Table 9   New members of the rosary brotherhood in Barbacena

| Decade | Members | | | | | | |
| | Forro | | Free | | Slave | | |
	number	%	number	%	number	%	Total
1810s	54	20.38	102	38.49	109	41.13	265
1820s	4	5.06	53	67.09	22	27.85	79
1830s	3	23.08	4	30.77	6	46.15	13
1840s	1	5.26	11	57.89	7	36.84	19
1850s	2	4.00	25	50.00	23	46.00	50
1860s	0	0.00	45	51.72	42	48.28	87
Total	64	12.48	240	46.78	209	40.74	513

SOURCE: "Entradas de Irmãos," Irmandade de Nossa Senhora do Rosário, Barbacena, 1812–1840 and 1841–1863, AEAM C31 and C26.

GLOSSARY

arraial	a hamlet or small village
bastão	the staff used by the captains of certain congado groups as their sign of power.
Caboclo/Caboclinho	the term *caboclo* refers literally to a person with mixed Indian and Portuguese heritage. It can also mean a country bumpkin. In Minas Gerais the name refers to one of the congado groups that are found mostly in northern Minas Gerais. The dancers and musicians wear headdresses of brightly colored feathers and snap their bows and arrows in syncopated rhythms as they dance.
Candombe	one of the current congado groups in Minas Gerais, considered in the legends of the congadeiros to be the ancient ancestor to the congado. The Candombe is also one of the most secretive of the congado groups, and usually its rituals are not open to the public. The Candombe uses three drums of varying sizes that are baptized and given names in a fire ceremony. The musicians in the Candombe also use a friction drum called a *puita* and various rattles as well as call-and-response singing and a special kind of dance.
capitão-mor	literally the captain major of the festival. It is one of the highest positions in the present-day brotherhoods, sometimes even more important than the King of Congo.
compromisso	the incorporating statutes of a lay religious brother-hood.
congadeiro/a	a person who participates in the Congado and who is part of a community that sponsors a festival.
Congada	Afro-Brazilian celebrations in the state of São Paulo and further south that are often associated with Our Lady of the Rosary and Saint Benedict. Although

some nineteenth-century travelers referred to the celebrations they saw in Minas Gerais as congadas, the documents from that region and the participants themselves always use the masculine *os* ending.

congados   refers to the different ritual groups (*guardas* and *ternos*) that participate in the festival of the rosary. Folklorists in Minas Gerais refer to these groups as the "seven brothers," which are named the Candombe, Mozambique, Congo, Caboclo/Caboclinho, Catupé/Catopê, Marujo, and Vilão. Different regions will have different types of groups; for example, festivals in the region around Oliveira will tend to have Mozambique, Catupé, and Vilão; whereas around Belo Horizonte, the Candombe, Mozambique, and Congo predominate. In the far north there are other groups, such as the Tamborzeiros of Araçuaí. Historically the groups were referred to as the "ambassadors" to the King of Congo, and today they play an important role in escorting the royalty of the festival to different locations. They also played, and in some cases continue to play, a role in collecting alms for the festival.

Congado   in Minas Gerais this term is the vernacular for the Feast Day of the Crowning of Our Lady of the Rosary, which includes the dancing and singing of the congados as well as the coronation of the kings and queens of the festival.

crioulo/a   during the time of slavery referred to a Brazilian-born black.

dízimo   a tithe.

forro/a   a freed slave.

guarda   like a *terno*, a *guarda* is a group, specifically a congado group.

irmandade   a lay religious organization or confraternity, usually organized around a specific saint or devotion of the Catholic Church. These organizations, known as *cofradías* in Spain and Spanish America, were and continue to be widespread throughout the Iberian world. Although the term translates literally as "brotherhood," some *irmandades,* specifically those dedicated to Our Lady of the Rosary, welcomed women into their membership.

matriz   the main parish church of any town.

mineiro   of or from the state of Minas Gerais.

padroado real   the royal patronage of the Portuguese and then Brazilian Crown over the Catholic Church in its territories, granted to the Portuguese royalty through a series of papal bulls in the fifteenth century and lasting until the end of the empire in 1889. It granted the Grand Master of the Order of Christ (first Prince Henry the Navigator and then successive kings of Portugal and emperors of Brazil) the right to oversee practically all aspects of the church, including collecting the tithe, naming bishops, and censoring letters from Rome.

pardo/a   a person of or with the appearance of mixed African and European ancestry.

por devoção   refers to the act of taking on a position in the brotherhood voluntarily because of the strength of the person's devotion.

pretos velhos   the spirits of old blacks, often the spirits of black African slaves who died in Brazil.

provedor   the local official, or supervisor, who oversaw the running of the brotherhoods for the Crown. The position was often held by the crown judge or the local justice of the peace.

quilombos   runaway slave communities.

reinado   the coronation of kings and queens of the rosary festivals. It can also refer to the entire component of the festival that involves the royalty, including their retinues and guards.

Reinado   the name that the congadeiros themselves often prefer to use, rather than Congado, for the annual feast day celebration of the crowning of Our Lady of the Rosary.

sinhô/sinhâ   the vernacular term used in the time of slavery for the master/mistress of the slaves.

terno   like a *guarda,* a *terno* is a group, specifically a congado group.

BIBLIOGRAPHY

ARCHIVES AND MANUSCRIPT COLLECTIONS

Arquivo da Casa da Cultura Carlos Chagas, Oliveira, MG
Arquivo da Catedral de Oliveira, Oliveira, MG
Arquivo da Cúria Metropolitana, BH, MG
Arquivo Eclesiástico da Arquidiocese de Mariana, MG
Arquivo da Irmandade de Nossa Senhora do Rosário, São João del Rei, MG
Arquivo Nacional do Brasil, Rio de Janeiro, RJ
Arquivo Público Mineiro, Belo Horizonte, MG
Casa Borba Gato, Sabará, MG
Casa dos Contos, Ouro Preto, MG
Fundação Biblioteca Nacional, Rio de Janeiro, RJ
Museu de Arte Sacra, São João del Rei, MG

PUBLISHED PRIMARY MATERIAL

Almeida, Cándido Mendes de, ed. *Código philippino ou ordenações do reino de Portugal*. 14th ed. Rio de Janeiro: Typographia do Instituto Philomático, 1870.

Antonil, Andre João (pseud.). *Cultura e opulência do Brasil por suas drogas e minas*. São Paulo: Melhoramentos, 1976.

Associação dos Congados de Nossa Senhora do Rosário de Minas Gerais—Estatutos. Belo Horizonte, Brazil: Gráfica e Eidtora Cultura, n.d.

Avila, Affonso. *Resíduos seiscentistas em Minas: Textos do século do ouro e as projeções do mundo barroco*. Vol. 1, *Triunfo eucarístico*. Belo Horizonte, Brazil: Centro de Estudos Mineiros, 1967.

Barbot, James. *Barbot on Guinea: The Writings of Jean Barbot on West Africa, 1678–1712*. Vols. 1–2. Edited by P. E. H. Hair, Adam Jones, and Robin Law. London: Hakluyt Society, 1992.

Barlaeus, Gaspar. *História dos feitos recentemente praticados durante Oito Anos no Brasil*. Translated by Cláudio Brandão. Rio de Janeiro: Ministério de Educação, 1940.

Barros, João de. *The Asia of João de Barros*. Extracted in *The Voyages of Cadamosto, and Other Documents on Western Africa in the Second Half of the Fifteenth Century*. Edited and translated by G. R. Crone. London: Hakluyt Society, 1937.

———. *Décadas da India*. In *The Voyages of Cadamosto and Other Documents on Western Africa in the Second Half of the Fifteenth Century*, edited and translated by C. R. Crone. London: Hakluyt Society, 1937.

Benfica, V. J. "A festa do Rosário, em Oliveira." Originally published in the *Gazeta de Oliveira*, 9 October 1887. Cited in its entirety in L. Gonzaga da Fonseca, *História de Oliveira* (Belo Horizonte, Brazil: Editora Bernardo Alvares, 1961), 329–32.

Bishop, Elizabeth. *The Diary of Helena Morley*. Translated by Elizabeth Bishop. New York: Ferrar, Straus and Cudahy, 1957.

Bosman, William. *A New and Accurate Description of the Coast of Guinea*. Originally published 1705. London: Frank Cass, 1967.

Brásio, Padre António, ed. *Monumenta missionaria africana: Africa Ocidental (1685–1699)*. Vols. 1–15. Lisbon: Academia Portuguesa da História, 1985.

Burton, Richard F. *Explorations in the Highlands of the Brazil*. Vols. 1–2. New York: Greenwood Press, 1969.

Cadamosto. *The Voyages of Cadamosto, and Other Documents on Western Africa in the Second Half of the Fifteenth Century*. Edited and translated by G. R. Crone. London: Hakluyt Society, 1937.

Cadornega, António de Oliveira de. *História geral das guerras angolanas, 1680*. Vols. 1–4. Edited by José Matias Delgado. Lisboa: Agência-geral do Ultramar, 1972.

Cavazzi de Montecúccolo, Pe. João António. *Descrição histórica dos três reinos do Congo, Matamba e Angola*. Translated by Pe. Graciano Maria de Leguzzano. Lisbon: Junta de Investigações do Ultramar, 1965.

Ciruelo, Pedro. *Pedro Ciruelo's A Treatise Reproving All Superstitions and Forms of Witchcraft, Very Necessary and Useful for All Good Christians Zealous for Their Salvation*. Translated by Eugene A. Maio and D'Orsay W. Pearson. Cranbury, N.J.: Associated University Presses, 1977.

Códice Costa Matoso, Coleção das notícias dos primeiros descobrimentos das minas na América que fez o doutor Caetano da Costa Matoso sendo ouvidor-geral das do Ouro Preto, de que tomou posse em fevereiro de 1749, & vários papéis. Belo Horizonte, Brazil: Fundação João Pinheiro, 1999.

Collecção das leis da Assembléia Legislativa da Província de Minas Geraes. Ouro Preto, Brazil: Typographia de J. F. de Paulo Castro, 1876.

Colleção das leis do Império do Brasil, 1860. Vol. 23, pt. 2. Rio de Janeiro: Typografia Nacional, 1860.

Compromisso da Irmandade de Nossa Senhora do Rozário na freguezia da Conceyção da Villa do Príncipe do Sêrro do Frio no Anno de 1728. Serro, Minas Gerais, Brazil: Irmandade de Nossa Senhora do Rosario, 1979.

Congado mineiro. Sound recording. Documentos Sonoros Brasileiros, Acervo Cachuera! Coleção Itaú Cultural, 2000.

Constituições do primeiro sínodo da arquidiocese de Belo Horizonte. Belo Horizonte, Brazil: n.p., 1944.

Constituições primeiras do Arcebispado da Bahia, feitas, e ordenadas . . . 12 de junho de 1707. São Paulo: Antônio Louzada Antunes, 1853.

Costa, Joaquim José. *Breve notícia da irmandade de Nossa Senhora do Rosário e São Benedito dos homens pretos do Rio*. Rio de Janeiro: Tipografia Politécnica, 1886.

CEDEPLAR . 1831 Census in Minas Gerais. Database. Compiled and organized by CEDEPLAR, Faculdade de Ciências Econômicas, UFMG, Belo Horizonte, Brazil.

Debret, Jean Baptiste. *Viagem pitoresca e histórica ao Brasil*. Vol. 2. Translated and edited by Sérgio Milliet. São Paulo: Livraria Martins Editora, 1954.

Dias, Fr. Nicolau. *Livro do Rosário de Nossa Senhora (Edição fac-similada da edição de 1573)*. Lisbon, Biblioteca Nacional, 1982.

Estado de Minas (Belo Horizonte, Brazil), 14 May 1988.

Ewbank, Thomas. *Life in Brazil*. New York: Harper and Brothers, 1856.

Julião, Carlos. *Riscos illuminados de figurinhos de Brancos e Negros dos usos do Rio de Janeiro e Serro do Frio*. Introduction by Lygia da Fonseca Fernandes da Cunha. Rio de Janeiro: n.p., 1960.

Koster, Henry. *Travels in Brazil*. London: Longman, Hurst, Rees, Orme, and Brown, 1816.

Letter from the Conde de Assumar to Dom João V, 20 April 1719. *RAPM* 3 (1898): 265.

Mathias, Herculano Gomes. *Um recenseamento na capitania de Minas Gerais, Vila Rica—1804*. Rio de Janeiro: Arquivo Nacional, 1969.

"Memoria Histórica da Capitania de Minas-Geraes." *RAPM* 2 (1897): 425–518.

"Nomeação de Antônio de Albuquerque." *RAPM* 11 (1906): 685.

Oliveira, Ronald Polito de, ed., *Visitas pastorais de Dom Frei José da Santíssima Trindade (1821–1825)*. Belo Horizonte, Brazil: Fundação João Pinheiro, 1998.

Os negros do rosário. Sound recording. Belo Horizonte, Brazil: Trem da História, 1987.

"Processo de Tombamento da Irmandade de Nossa Senhora do Rosário do Jatobá." No. 010869309568. Prefeitura de Belo Horizonte, Secretaria Municipal de Cultura, Belo Horizonte, Brazil, 1995.

"Religioens, clerigos e mater.ᵃˢ Eclesiasticas." *RAPM* 16 (1911): 393–403.

Rugendas, João Maurício. *Viagem pitoresca através do Brasil*. Translated by Sérgio Milliet. São Paulo: Livraria Martins, 1954.

Santos, Pedrina de Lourdes. "O Reinado em Oliveira." *Boletim da Comissão Mineira do Folclore* 15 (1992): 37–41.

Thomaz, Manoel Fernandes. *Indice alphabetico das leis extravagantes do Reino de Portugal*. Coimbra, Portugal: Imprensa da Universidade, 1843.

PUBLISHED AND UNPUBLISHED SECONDARY SOURCES

Abercrombie, Thomas A. *Pathways of Memory and Power: Ethnography and History Among an Andean People*. Madison: University of Wisconsin Press, 1999.

Abreu, Martha. *O império do divino: Festas religiosas e cultura popular no Rio de Janeiro, 1830–1900*. Rio de Janeiro: Nova Fronteira, 1999.

Aguiar, Marcos Magalhães de. "Vila Rica dos confrades: A sociabilidade confrarial entre negros e mulatos no século XVIII." Master's thesis, Universidade de São Paulo, 1993.

Alves, Maria Helena Moreira. *State and Opposition in Military Brazil*. Austin: University of Texas, 1985.

Andrade, Mario de. *Danças dramáticas do Brasil*. São Paulo: Livraria Martins Editora, 1962.

Andrews, George Reid. *Blacks and Whites in São Paulo Brazil, 1888–1988*. Madison: University of Wisconsin Press, 1991.

Araújo, Alceu Maynard. *Cultura popular brasileira*. São Paulo: Instituto Nacional do Livro, 1973.

———. *Folclore nacional: Festas, bailados, mitos e lendas.* Vol. 1. São Paulo: Edições Melhoramentos, 1964.

Arens, William W., and Ivan Karp, eds. *Creativity of Power: Cosmology and Action in African Societies.* Washington, D.C.: Smithsonian Institution Press, 1989.

Ariès, Philippe. *The Hour of Our Death.* Translated by Helen Weaver. New York: Oxford University Press: 1991.

———. *Western Attitudes Toward Death: From the Middle Ages to the Present.* Translated by Patricia M. Ranum. Baltimore: Johns Hopkins University Press, 1974.

Ashe, Geoffrey. *The Virgin.* London: Routledge and Kegan Paul, 1976.

Azevedo, Paulo Cesar de, and Maurício Lissovsky, eds. *Escravos brasileiros do século XIX na fotografia de Christiano Jr.* São Paulo: Editora Ex Libris, 1988.

Banker, James R. *Death in the Community: Memorialization and Confraternities in an Italian Commune in the Late Middle Ages.* Athens: University of Georgia Press, 1988.

Barbosa, Waldemar de Almeida. *Dicionário histórico-geográfico de Minas Gerais.* Belo Horizonte, Brazil: Editora Saterb, 1971.

———. *História de Minas.* 3 vols. Belo Horizonte, Brazil: Editora Comunicação, 1979.

———. *Negros e quilombos em Minas Gerais.* Belo Horizonte, Brazil: n.p., 1972.

Barman, Roderick J. *Brazil: The Forging of a Nation, 1798–1852.* Stanford: Stanford University Press, 1988.

Bastide, Roger. *African Civilisations in the New World.* Translated by Peter Green. New York: Harper and Row, 1978.

———. *The African Religions of Brazil: Toward a Sociology of the Interpenetration of Civilizations.* Translated by Helen Sebba. Baltimore: Johns Hopkins University Press, 1978.

Bastide, Roger, and Florestan Fernandes. *Brancos e negros em São Paulo: Ensaio sociológico sôbre aspectos da formação, manifestações atuais e efeitos do preconceito de côr na sociedade paulistana.* São Paulo: Companhia Editora Nacional, 1959.

Bennett, Herman L. "A Research Note: Race, Slavery, and the Ambiguity of Corporate Consciousness." *Colonial Latin American Historical Review* (Spring 1994): 207–13.

Bergad, Laird W. "After the Mining Boom: Demographic and Economic Aspects of Slavery in Mariana, Minas Gerais, 1750–1808." *LARR* 31, no. 1 (1996): 67–97.

———. *Slavery and the Demographic and Economic History of Minas Gerais, Brazil, 1720–1888.* New York: Cambridge University Press, 1999.

Bethell, Leslie, ed. *Colonial Brazil.* Cambridge: Cambridge University Press, 1991.

Bieber, Judy A. "Postmodern Ethnographer in the Backlands: An Imperial Bureaucrat's Perceptions of Post-independence Brazil," *LARR* 33, no. 2 (1998): 37–72.

———. *Power, Patronage, and Political Violence: State Building on a Brazilian Frontier, 1822–1889.* Lincoln: University of Nebraska Press, 1999.

Birmingham, David. "The African Response to Early Portuguese Activities in Angola." In *Protest and Resistance in Angola and Brazil,* edited by Ronald H. Chilcote, 11–28. Berkeley and Los Angeles: University of California Press, 1972.

———. *A Concise History of Portugal.* Cambridge: Cambridge University Press, 1993.

Birmingham, David, and Phyllis M. Martin, eds. *History of Central Africa*. 2 vols. London: Longman, 1983.

Black, Christopher F. *Italian Confraternities in the Sixteenth Century*. Cambridge: Cambridge University Press, 1989.

Bockie, Simon. *Death and the Invisible Powers: The World of Kongo Belief*. Bloomington: Indiana University Press, 1993.

Booth, Newell S., ed. *African Religions: A Symposium*. New York: NOK, 1977.

Borges, Célia. "Devoção branca de homens negros." *Cadernos de ciências sociais* 2 (October 1992): 29–35.

———. "Irmandades do rosário: Participação e dinâmica social em Minas no séc. XVIII." *Anais Universitários: Ciências Sociais e Humanas* 6 (1995): 239–53.

Boschi, Caio César. *Os leigos e o poder: Irmandades leigos e política colonizadora em Minas Gerais*. São Paulo: Editora Ática, 1986.

Bowser, Frederick P. *The African Slave in Colonial Peru, 1524–1650*. Stanford: Stanford University Press, 1974.

Boxer, Charles R. *The Church Militant and Iberian Expansion, 1440–1770*. Baltimore: Johns Hopkins University Press, 1978.

———. *The Golden Age of Brazil, 1695–1750: Growing Pains of a Colonial Society*. Berkeley and Los Angeles: University of California Press, 1962.

———. *The Portuguese Seaborne Empire, 1415–1825*. New York: Alfred A. Knopf, 1969.

———. *Race Relations in the Portuguese Colonial Empire, 1415–1825*. Oxford: Clarendon Press, 1963.

Brandão, Carlos Rodrigues. *O Divino, o santo e a Senhora*. Rio de Janeiro: Campanha de Defesa do Folclore Brasileiro, 1978.

———. *A Festa do santo de preto*. Goiânia, Brazil: Universidade Federal de Goiás, 1985.

———. *Peões, pretos e congos: Trabalho e identidade étnica em Goiás*. Brasília: Editora Universidade de Brasília, 1977.

———. *Sacerdotes de viola: Rituais religiosos do catolicismo popular em São Paulo e Minas Gerais*. Petrópolis, Brazil: Editora Vozes, 1981.

Brandes, Stanley. "The *Posadas* in Tzintzuntzan: Structure and Sentiment in a Mexican Christmas Festival." *Journal of the American Folklore Society* 96 (July/September 1983): 259–80.

———. *Power and Persuasion: Fiestas and Social Control in Rural Mexico*. Philadelphia: University of Pennsylvania Press, 1988.

Brandon, George. *Santeria from Africa to the New World: The Dead Sell Memories*. Bloomington: Indiana University Press, 1997.

Brásio, Padre António. *Os pretos em Portugal*. Lisboa: Pelo Império, 1944.

Brown, Diana DeG. *Umbanda: Religion and Politics in Urban Brazil*. Ann Arbor: UMI Research Press, 1987.

Bruneau, Thomas C. *The Church in Brazil: The Politics of Religion*. Austin: University of Texas Press, 1982.

———. *The Political Transformation of the Brazilian Catholic Church*. London: Cambridge University Press, 1974.

———. "Power and Influence: Analysis of the Church in Latin America and the Case of Brazil." *LARR* 8 (1973): 25–51.

Burns, E. Bradford. *A Documentary History of Brazil*. New York: Knopf, 1966.

———. *The Poverty of Progress: Latin America in the Nineteenth Century.* Berkeley and Los Angeles: University of California Press, 1980.

Butler, Alban. *Butler's Lives of the Saints.* 4 vols. Edited and revised by Herbert Thurston and Donald Attwater. New York: P. J. Kenedy and Sons, 1956.

Butler, Kim D. *Freedoms Given, Freedoms Won: Afro-Brazilians in Post-abolition São Paulo and Salvador.* New Brunswick: Rutgers University Press, 1998.

———. "Up from Slavery: Afro-Brazilian Activism in São Paulo, 1888–1938." *The Americas* 49 (October 1992): 179–206.

Camargo, Monsenhor Paulo Florêncio da Silveira. *História eclesiástica do Brasil.* Petrópolis, Brazil: Editora Vozes Limitada, 1955.

Campolina, Alda Maria Palhares, C. Melo, and M. Andrade. *Escravidão em Minas Gerais: Cadernos do arquivo 1.* Belo Horizonte, Brazil: Secretaria de Estado da Cultura, 1988.

Cardozo, Manoel S. "The Lay Brotherhoods of Colonial Bahia." *Catholic Historical Review* 33 (1947): 12–30.

Carneiro, Edison. *Negros bantus: Notas de etnografia religiosa e de folclore.* Rio de Janiero: Civilizição Brasileira, 1937.

Carrato, José Ferreira. *As Minas Gerais e o primórdios do Caraça.* São Paulo: Companhia Editora Nacional, 1963.

Carvalho, José Murilo de. "Elites and State Building: Brazil." *Comparative Studies in Society and History* 24 (July 1982): 378–99.

Cascudo, Luís da Câmara. *Antologia do folclore brasileiro.* São Paulo: Livraria Martins Editora, 1965.

———. *Dicionário do folclore brasileiro, segundo edição.* 2 vols. Rio de Janeiro: Instituto Nacional do Livro, 1962.

Castile, George Pierre, and Gilbert Kushner, eds. *Persistent Peoples: Cultural Enclaves in Perspective.* Tucson: University of Arizona Press, 1981.

Cesar, Waldo. "O que é 'popular' no catholicismo popular." *Revista eclesiástica brasileira* 36, no. 141 (1976): 5–18.

Chesnut, R. Andrew. *Born Again in Brazil: The Pentecostal Boom and the Pathogens of Poverty.* New Brunswick: Rutgers University Press, 1997.

Chirimini, Tomás Olivera. "Candombe, African Nations, and the Africanity of Uruguay." In *African Roots/American Cultures: Africa in the Creation of the Americas,* edited by Sheila S. Walker, 256–74. Lanham, Md.: Rowman and Littlefield, 2001.

Christian, William A., Jr. *Apparitions in Late Medieval and Renaissance Spain.* Princeton: Princeton University Press, 1981.

———. *Local Religion in Sixteenth-Century Spain.* Princeton: Princeton University Press, 1981.

Clarence-Smith, William Gervase. "Review Article: The Dynamics of the African Slave Trade." *Africa* 64 (1994): 275–86.

Connerton, Paul. *How Societies Remember.* New York: Cambridge University Press, 1989.

Conniff, Michael L., ed. *Latin American Populism in Comparative Perspective.* Albuquerque: University of New Mexico Press, 1982.

Conrad, Robert Edgar. *Children of God's Fire: A Documentary History of Black Slavery in Brazil.* 2d ed. University Park: Pennsylvania State University Press, 1994.

————. *The Destruction of Brazilian Slavery, 1850–1888.* 2d ed. Malabar, Fla.: Krieger, 1993.

————. *World of Sorrow: The African Slave Trade to Brazil.* Baton Rouge: Louisiana State University Press, 1986.

Cooper, Frederick. "The Problem of Slavery in African Studies." *Journal of African Studies* 20 (1979): 103–25.

Coppos, Odette. *Congadas (folclore).* Rio de Janeiro: Editora Pongetti, 1971.

Corrêa, Iracema França Lopes. *A congada de Ilhabela na festa de São Benedito.* São Paulo: Editorial Livramento, 1981.

Costa, Emília Viotti da. *The Brazilian Empire: Myths and Histories.* Chicago: University of Chicago Press, 1985.

Costa, Iraci del Nero da. *Populacões mineiras: Sobre a estrutura populacional de alguns núcleos mineiros no alvorecer do século XIX.* São Paulo: Instituto de Pesquisas Econômicas, 1981.

Costa, João Cruz. *A History of Ideas in Brazil: The Development of Philosophy in Brazil and the Evolution of National History.* Translated by Suzette Macedo. Berkeley and Los Angeles: University of California Press, 1964.

————. *Panorama of the History of Philosophy in Brazil.* Translated by Fred G. Sturm. Washington, D.C.: Pan American Union, 1962.

Craemer, Willy De, Jan Vansina, Renée C. Fox. "Religious Movements in Central Africa: A Theoretical Study." *Comparative Studies in Society and History* 18 (October 1976): 458–75.

Curtin, Philip. *The Atlantic Slave Trade: A Census.* Madison: University of Wisconsin Press, 1969.

Curtin, Philip, Steven Feierman, Leonard Thompson, and Jan Vansina. *African History from Earliest Times to Independence.* 2d ed. London: Longman, 1995.

Curto, José C., and Paul E. Lovejoy, eds. *Enslaving Connections: Changing Cultures of Africa and Brazil During the Era of Slavery.* Amherst, N.Y.: Humanity Books, 2004.

DaMatta, Roberto. *Carnivals, Rogues, and Heroes: An Interpretation of the Brazilian Dilemma.* Translated by John Drury. Notre Dame: University of Notre Dame Press, 1991.

Dantas, Beatriz Góis. *Vovó Nagô e papai branco: Usos e abusos da Africa no Brasil.* São Paulo: Editora Graal, 1988.

Degler, Carl. *Neither Black nor White: Slavery and Race Relations in Brazil and the United States.* Madison: University of Wisconsin Press, 1971.

Diniz, Domingos. "Congado ou reinado de Nossa Senhora do Rosário." *Boletim da Comissão Mineira de Folclore* 11 (1987): 39–43.

Dirks, Nicholas B., Geoff Eley, and Sherry B. Ortner, eds. *Culture/Power/History: A Reader in Contemporary Social Theory.* Princeton: Princeton University Press, 1994.

Duffy, James *Portugal in Africa.* Baltimore: Penguin Books, 1962.

Eakin, Marshall C. *Tropical Capitalism: The Industrialization of Belo Horizonte, Brazil.* New York: Palgrave, 2001.

Fernandes, Florestan. *The Negro in Brazilian Society.* Edited by Phyllis B. Eveleth. Translated by Jacqueline D. Skiles, A. Brunel, and Arthur Rothwell. New York: Columbia University Press, 1969.

————. "The Negro in Brazilian Society: Twenty-five Years Later." In *Brazil, Anthropological Perspectives*, edited by Maxine L. Margolis and William E. Carter, 96–113. New York: Columbia University Press, 1979.

Ferretti, Sérgio Figueiredo. *Repensando o sincretismo*. São Paulo: Editora da Universidade de São Paulo, 1995.

Flynn, Maureen. *Sacred Charity: Confraternities and Social Welfare in Spain, 1400–1700*. Ithaca: Cornell University Press, 1989.

Fonseca, L. Gonzaga da. *História de Oliveira*. Belo Horizonte, Brazil: Editora Bernardo Alvares, 1961.

Fraginals, Manoel Moreno, ed. *Africa in Latin America*. New York: Holmes and Meier, 1984.

Freitas, Judy Bieber. "Marginal Elites: Politics, Power, and Patronage in the Backlands of Northern Minas Gerais, Brazil, 1830–1889." Ph.D. diss., Johns Hopkins University, 1994.

————. "Slavery and Social Life: Attempts to Reduce Free People to Slavery in the Sertão Mineiro, Brazil, 1850–1871." *Journal of Latin American Studies* 26 (1994): 597–619.

French, John D. "The Missteps of Anti-imperialist Reason: Pierre Bourdieu, Loïc Wacquant, and Michael Hanchard's *Orpheus and Power*." Duke University Working Paper no. 27, n.d.

Frey, Sylvia R., and Betty Wood. *Come Shouting to Zion: African American Protestantism in the American South and British Caribbean to 1830*. Chapel Hill: University of North Carolina Press, 1998.

Freyre, Gilberto. *The Masters and the Slaves: A Study in the Development of Brazilian Civilization*. 2d ed. Translated by Samuel Putnam. New York: Alfred A. Knopf, 1956.

————. *Sobrados e mucambos: Decadência do patriarcado rural e desenvolvimento do urbano*. 2 vols. 5th ed. Rio de Janeiro: Livraria José Olympio Editora, 1977.

Galeano, Eduardo. *Open Veins of Latin America*. Translated by Celdric Belfrage. New York: Monthly Review Press, 1997.

Geertz, Clifford. "Blurred Genres." *American Scholar* 49 (Spring 1980): 165–79.

————. *The Interpretation of Cultures*. New York: Basic Books, 1973.

Gomes, Núbia Pereira de Magalhães, and Edimilson de Almeida Pereira. *Do presépio à balança: Representações sociais da vida religiosa*. Belo Horizonte, Brazil: Mazza Edições, 1994.

————. *Negras raízes mineiras: Os Arturos*. Juiz de Fora, Brazil: Editora da Universidade Federal de Juiz de Fora, 1988.

Gomez, Michael A. *Exchanging Our Country Marks: The Transformation of African Identities in the Colonial and Antebellum South*. Chapel Hill: University of North Carolina Press, 1998.

Gorender, Jacob. *O escravismo colonial*. São Paulo: Editora Ática, 1978.

Goulart, Maurício. *A escravidão africana no Brasil: Das origens à extinção do tráfico*. São Paulo: Editora Alfa-Ômega, 1975.

Graham, Richard, ed. *The Idea of Race in Latin America, 1870–1940*. Austin: University of Texas Press, 1990.

Gray, Richard. "'Como vero Prencipe Catolico': The Capuchins and the Rulers of Soyo in the Late Seventeenth Century." *Africa* 53 (1983): 39–54.

Groot, C. F. G. de. *Brazilian Catholicism and the Ultramontane Reform, 1850–1930*. Amsterdam: CEDLA, 1996.

Guimarães, Carlos Magno. *A negação da ordem escravista: Quilombos em Minas Gerais no século XVIII*. São Paulo: Icone Editora, 1988.

Halbwachs, Maurice. *The Collective Memory*. Translated by Francis. J. Ditter Jr. and Vida Yazdi Ditter. New York: Harper and Row, 1980.

Harris, Marvin. "Race Relations in Minas Velhas: A Community in the Mountain Region of Central Brazil." In *Race and Class in Rural Brazil: A UNESCO Study*, edited by Charles Wagley, 47–81. 2d ed. New York: Columbia University Press, 1963.

Hemming, John. *Red Gold: The Conquest of the Brazilian Indians*. Cambridge: Harvard University Press, 1978.

Herskovits, Melville J. *The Myth of the Negro Past*. New York: Harper and Brothers, 1941.

Heywood, Linda M. "The Angolan-Afro-Brazilian Cultural Connections," *Slavery and Abolition* 20, no. 1 (1999): 9–23.

———. "Portuguese into African: The Eighteenth-Century Central African Background to Atlantic Creole Cultures." In *Central Africans and Cultural Transformations in the Atlantic Diaspora*, edited by Linda M. Heywood, 91–113. New York: Cambridge University Press, 2001.

———, ed. *Central Africans and Cultural Transformations in the Atlantic Diaspora*. New York: Cambridge University Press, 2001.

Higgins, Kathleen J. *"Licentious Liberty" in a Brazilian Gold-Mining Region: Slavery, Gender, and Social Control in Eighteenth-Century Sabará, Minas Gerais*. University Park: Pennsylvania State University Press, 1999.

Hilton, Anne. *The Kingdom of Kongo*. Oxford: Clarendon Press, 1985.

Hobsbawm, Eric, and Terence Ranger. *The Invention of Tradition*. Cambridge: Cambridge University Press, 1983.

Hoogen, Lisette van den. "The Romanization of the Brazilian Church: Women's Participation in a Religious Association in Prados, Minas Gerais." *Sociological Analysis* 51 (Summer 1990): 171–88.

Hoornaert, Eduardo. *Formação do catolicismo brasileiro, 1550–1800*. Petrópolis, Brazil: Editora Vozes, 1974.

———. *História da igreja no Brasil*. Petrópolis, Brazil: Editora Vozes, 1977.

Karasch, Mary C. "Central African Religious Tradition in Rio de Janeiro." *Journal of Latin American Lore* 5 (1979): 233–53.

———. "Minha Nação: Identidades escravas no fim do Brasil colonial." Translated by Angela Domingues. In *Brasil: Colonização e escravidão*, edited by Maria Beatriz Nizza da Silva, 127–41. Rio de Janeiro: Editora Nova Fronteira, 2000.

———. *Slave Life in Rio de Janeiro, 1808–1850*. Princeton: Princeton University Press, 1987.

Kiddy, Elizabeth W. "Brotherhoods of Our Lady of the Rosary of the Blacks: Community and Devotion in Minas Gerais, Brazil." Ph.D. diss., University of New Mexico, 1998.

———. "*Congados, Calunga, Candombe:* Our Lady of the Rosary in Minas Gerais, Brazil," *Luso-Brazilian Review* 37, no. 1 (2000): 47–61.

———. "Ethnic and Racial Identity in the Brotherhoods of the Rosary of Minas Gerais, 1700–1830." *The Americas* 56, no. 2 (October 1999): 221–52.

————. "Who Is the King of Congo? A New Look at African and Afro-Brazilian Kings in Brazil." In *Central Africans and Cultural Transformations in the Atlantic Diaspora*, edited by Linda M. Heywood, 151–82. New York: Cambridge University Press, 2001.

Klein, Kerwin Lee. "On the Emergence of Memory in Historical Discourse," *Representations* 69 (Winter 2000): 127–50.

Kopytoff, Igor. "Ancestors as Elders in Africa," *Africa* 41, no. 2 (April 1971).

————. "Slavery." *Annual Review of Anthropology* 11 (1982): 207–30.

————, ed. *The African Frontier: The Reproduction of Traditional African Societies.* Bloomington: Indiana University Press, 1987.

Kubik, Gerhard. *Angolan Traits in Black Music, Games, and Dances of Brazil: A Study of African Cultural Extensions Overseas.* Lisbon: Centro de Estudos de Antropologia Cultural, 1979.

Lamas, Dulce Martins, and Suely Brígido. " A festa do rosário de alguns aspectos musicais." In *A música na história de Minas colonial*, edited by Maria da Conceição Rezende Fonseca, 567–70. Belo Horizonte, Brazil: Editora Itatiaia, 1989.

Landes, Ruth. *The City of Women.* Albuquerque: University of New Mexico Press, 1994.

Lara, Silvia Hunold. "Significados Cruzados: As embaixadas de Congos no Brasil colonial." Paper delivered at the Twentieth Conference of the Latin American Studies Association, Guadalajara, Mexico, April 1997.

Law, Robin. *The Slave Coast of West Africa, 1550–1750: The Impact of the Atlantic Slave Trade on an African Society.* Oxford: Clarendon Press, 1991.

Leacock, Seth, and Ruth Leacock. *Spirits of the Deep: A Study of an Afro-Brazilian Cult.* New York: Anchor Books, 1975.

Leite, Ilka Boaventura. *Antropologia da viagem: Escravos e libertos em Minas Gerais no século XIX.* Belo Horizonte, Brazil: Editora UFMG, 1996.

Leite, Serafim. *História da companhia de Jesus no Brasil.* 10 vols. Rio de Janeiro: Civilização Brasileira, 1938–50.

Levine, Daniel H., ed. *Constructing Culture and Power in Latin America.* Ann Arbor: University of Michigan Press, 1993.

Levine, Robert M. *Father of the Poor? Vargas and His Era.* New York: Cambridge University Press, 1998.

————, ed. *Bitita's Diary: The Childhood Memoirs of Carolina Maria de Jesus.* Translated by Emanuelle Oliveira and Beth Joan Vinkler. Armonk, N.Y.: M. E. Sharpe, 1998.

Libby, Douglas Cole. "Proto-industrialisation in a Slave Society: The Case of Minas Gerais." *Journal of Latin American Studies* 23 (1991): 1–35.

————. *Transformação e trabalho em uma economia escravista: Minas Gerais no século XIX.* São Paulo: Editora Brasiliense, 1988.

Libby, Douglas Cole, and Clotilde Paiva, "Manumission Practices in Late Eighteenth-Century Brazilian Slave Parish: São José d'El Rey in 1795." *Slavery and Abolition* 21, no. 1 (2000): 96–127.

Lima, Augusto de, Júnior. *História de Nossa Senhora em Minas Gerais.* Belo Horizonte, Brazil: Imprensa Oficial, 1956.

Lloyd, P. C. "Sacred Kingship and Government Among the Yoruba." *Africa* 30 (July 1960): 221–37.

Lovejoy, Paul E. *Transformations in Slavery: A History of Slavery in Africa*. Cambridge: Cambridge University Press, 1983.

————. "The Volume of the Atlantic Slave Trade: A Synthesis." *Journal of African History* 23 (1982): 473–501.

Lucas, Glaura. "Os sons do rosário: Um estudo etnomusicológico do congado mineiro—Arturos e Jatobá," 2 vols. Master's thesis, University of São Paulo, 1999.

Lupi, João. *Moçambique, Moçambiques: Itinerário de um povo afro-brasileiro*. Santa Maria, Rio Grande do Sul, Brazil: Santa Maria Edições Universidade Federal de Santa Maria, 1988.

MacGaffey, Wyatt. "African Religions: Types and Generalizations." In *Explorations in African Systems of Thought*, edited by Ivan Karp and Charles S. Bird, 301–28. Bloomington: Indiana University Press, 1980.

————. "Comparative Analysis of Central African Religions." *Africa* 42 (1972): 21–31.

————. "Dialogues of the Deaf: Europeans on the Atlantic Coast of Africa." In *Implicit Understandings: Observing, Reporting, and Reflecting on the Encounters Between Europeans and Other Peoples in the Early Modern Era*, edited by Stuart B. Schwartz, 249–67. Cambridge: Cambridge University Press, 1994.

————. *Kongo Political Culture: The Conceptual Challenge of the Particular*. Bloomington: University of Indiana Press, 2000.

————. *Religion and Society in Central Africa: The BaKongo of Lower Zaire*. Chicago: University of Chicago Press, 1986.

Machado Filho, Aires da Mata. *O negro e o garimpo em Minas Gerais*. Rio de Janeiro: Livraria José Olympio, 1943.

Mallon, Florencia. "The Promise and Dilemma of Subaltern Studies: Perspectives from Latin American History." *AHR* (December 1994): 1491–515.

Martins Filho, Amilcar, and Roberto B. Martins. "Slavery in a Nonexport Economy: Nineteenth-Century Minas Gerais Revisited." *HAHR* 63 (1983): 537–68.

Martins, Leda Maria. *Afrografias da memória: O reinado do rosário no Jatobá*. São Paulo: Editora Perspectiva, 1997.

Martins, Maria do Carmo Salazar. "Revisitando a província: Comarcas, termos, distritos e população de Minas Gerais em 1833–35." In *Quinto seminário sobre a economia mineira*, 13–29. Belo Horizonte, Brazil: UFMG/CEDEPLAR, 1990.

Martins, Saúl. *Congados: Família de sete irmãos*. Belo Horizonte, Brazil: Serviço Social do Comércio (SESC/ARMG), 1988.

Marzal, Manuel M. "Transplanted Spanish Catholicism." In *South and Meso-American Native Spirituality*, edited by Gary H. Gossen, 140–69. New York: Crossroads, 1997.

Matory, J. Lorand. "The English Professors of Brazil: On the Diasporic Roots of the Yoruba Nation." *Comparative Studies in Society and History* 41, no. 1 (1999): 72–103.

Maxwell, Kenneth R. *Conflicts and Conspiracies: Brazil and Portugal, 1750–1808*. New York: Cambridge University Press, 1973.

————. *O Marquês de Pombal*. Translated by Saul Barata. Lisbon: Editora Presença, 2001.

————. "Pombal and the Nationalization of the Luso-Brazilian Economy." *HAHR* 48 (November 1968): 608–31.

Mbiti, John S. *African Religions and Philosophy.* New York: Anchor Books, 1970.

Meecham, J. Lloyd. *Church and State in Latin America: A History of Politico- ecclesiastical Relations.* Chapel Hill: University of North Carolina Press, 1934.

Meyer, Marlise. *Caminhos do imaginário no Brasil.* São Paulo: Editora de Universidade de São Paulo, 1993.

Meyers, Albert, and Diane Hopkins, eds. *Manipulating the Saints: Religious Brotherhoods and Social Integration in Postconquest Latin America.* Hamburg, Germany: Wayasbah, 1988.

Miers, Suzanne, and Igor Kopytoff eds. *Slavery in Africa: Historical and Anthropological Perspectives.* Madison: University of Wisconsin Press, 1977.

Miller, Joseph C. "Central Africa During the Era of the Slave Trade, c. 1490s–1850s." In *Central Africans and Cultural Transformations in the American Diaspora,* edited by Linda M. Heywood, 21–69. New York: Cambridge University Press, 2001.

———. "The Paradoxes of Impoverishment in the Atlantic Zone." In *History of Central Africa,* vol. 1, edited by David Birmingham and Phyllis M. Martin, 118–59. London: Longman, 1983.

———. "Retention, Reinvention, and Remembering: Restoring Identities Through Enslavement in Africa and Under Slavery in Brazil." In *Enslaving Connections: Changing Cultures of Africa and Brazil During the Era of Slavery,* edited by José C. Curto and Paul E. Lovejoy, 81–121. Amherst, N.Y.: Humanity Books, 2004.

———. *Way of Death: Merchant Capitalism and the Angolan Slave Trade, 1730–1830.* Madison: University of Wisconsin Press, 1988.

———, ed. *The African Past Speaks: Essays on Oral Tradition and History.* Kent, England: Wm. Dawson and Sons, 1980.

Mintz, Sidney W. *Caribbean Transformations.* Chicago: Aldine, 1974.

Mott, Luiz. *Rosa Egipcíaca: Uma santa africana no Brasil.* Rio de Janeiro: Editora Bertrand Brasil, 1993.

Motz, Marilyn. "The Practice of Belief." *Journal of American Folklore* 111 (1998): 339–55.

Mukuna, Kazadi wa. *Contribuição bantu na música popular brasileira.* São Paulo: Editora Parma, n.d.

Mulvey, Patricia. "Black Brothers and Sisters: Membership in the Black Lay Brotherhoods of Colonial Brazil." *Luso-Brazilian Review* 17, no. 2 (1980): 253–79.

———. "The Black Lay Brotherhoods of Colonial Brazil: A History." Ph.D. diss., City College of New York, 1976.

Murphy, Joseph M. *Working the Spirit: Ceremonies of the African Diaspora.* Boston: Beacon Press, 1994.

Neuhouser, Kevin. "The Radicalization of the Brazilian Catholic Church in Comparative Perspective." *American Sociological Review* 54 (April 1989): 233–44.

New Catholic Encyclopedia. 18 vols. New York: McGraw Hill, 1967.

Nora, Pierre. "Between Memory and History: Les Lieux de Mémoire." Translated by Marc Roudebush. *Representations* 69 (Winter 2000): 7–25.

Oderigo, Néstor Ortiz. *Calunga: Croquis del Candombe.* Buenos Aires: Editorial Universitaria de Buenos Aires, 1969.

Oliveira, Pedro A. Ribeiro de. "Catolicismo popular e a romanização do catolicismo brasileiro." *Revista eclesiástica brasileira* 36, no. 141 (1976): 131–41.

Pagden, Anthony. *European Encounters with the New World*. New Haven: Yale University Press, 1993.

Patterson, Orlando. *Slavery and Social Death: A Comparative Study*. Cambridge: Harvard University Press, 1982.

Parreira, Adriano. *Economia e sociedade em Angola na época da Rainha Jinga, século XVII*. Lisbon: Imprensa Universitária, 1990.

Peel, J. D. Y. "The Pastor and the *Babalawo:* The Interaction of Religions in Nineteenth-Century Yorubaland." *Africa* 60 (1990): 338–69.

Pike, Ruth. "Sevillian Society in the Sixteenth Century: Slaves and Freedmen." *HAHR* 47 (August 1967): 344–59.

Poel, Frei Francisco Van Der. *Os homens da dança: Religiosidade popular e catequese*. São Paulo: Edições Paulinas, 1986.

———. *O rosário dos homens pretos*. Belo Horizonte, Brazil: Imprensa Oficial, 1981.

Poole, Stafford. *Our Lady of Guadalupe: The Origins and Sources of a Mexican National Symbol, 1531–1797*. Tucson: University of Arizona Press, 1995.

Price, Richard. *Maroon Societies: Rebel Slave Communities in the Americas*. Garden City, N.Y.: Anchor Press, 1973.

Ramos, Arthur. *As culturas negras no novo mundo*. Rio de Janeiro: Civilização Brasileira, 1937.

———. *The Negro in Brazil*. Translated by Richard Pattee. Philadelphia: Porcupine Press, 1980.

Ramos, Donald. "A influência africana e a cultura popular em Minas Gerais: Um comentário sobre a interpretação da escravidão." In *Brasil: Colonização e escravidão*, edited by Maria Beatriz Nizza da Silva, 142–62. Rio de Janeiro: Editora Nova Fronteira, 2000.

———. "Community, Control, and Acculturation: A Case Study of Slavery in Eighteenth Century Brazil." *The Americas* 42 (April 1986): 419–52.

———. "A Social History of Ouro Preto: Stresses of Dynamic Urbanization in Colonial Brazil, 1695–1726." Ph.D. diss., University of Florida, 1972.

———. "Vila Rica: Profile of a Colonial Brazilian Urban Center." *The Americas* 35 (April 1979): 495–526.

Reichmann, Rebecca ed. *Race in Contemporary Brazil: From Indifference to Inequality*. University Park: Pennsylvania State University Press, 1999.

Reis, João José. *A morte é uma festa, ritos fúnebres e revolta popular no Brasil do século XIX*. São Paulo: Companhia das Letras, 1991.

———. "Identidade e diversidade étnicas nas irmandades negras no tempo da escravidão." *Tempo* 2, no. 3 (1997): 7–33.

———. *Slave Rebellion in Brazil: The Muslim Uprising of 1835 in Bahia*. Translated by Arthur Brakel. Baltimore: Johns Hopkins University Press, 1993.

Reis, João José, and Flávio dos Santos Gomes, eds. *Liberdade por um fio: História dos quilombos no Brasil*. São Paulo: Companhia das Letras, 1996.

Reis, João José, and Eduardo Silva. *Negociação e conflito: A resistência negra no Brasil escravista*. São Paulo: Companhia das Letras, 1988.

Rocha, Leopoldo da. *As confrarias de goa (séculos XVI–XX), conspecto histórico-jurídico.* Lisbon: Centro de Estudos Históricos Ultramarinos, 1973.

Rodrigues, Raymundo Nina. *O animismo fetichista dos negros bahianos*. Rio de Janeiro: Civilização Brasileira, 1935.

Russell-Wood, A. J. R. "Ambivalent Authorities: The African and Afro-Brazilian Contribution to Local Governance in Colonial Brazil." *The Americas* 57 (July 2000): 13–36.

———. *The Black Man in Slavery and Freedom in Colonial Brazil*. New York: St. Martin's Press, 1982.

———. "Black and Mulatto Brotherhoods in Colonial Brazil: A Study in Collective Behavior. *HAHR* 54 (1974): 567–602.

———. *Fidalgos and Philanthropists: The Santa Casa da Misericórdia of Bahia, 1550–1755*. Berkeley and Los Angeles: University of California Press, 1968.

———. "Prestige, Power, and Piety in Colonial Brazil: The Third Orders of Salvador." *HAHR* 69, no. 1 (1989): 61–89.

———, ed. *From Colony to Nation: Essays on the Independence of Brazil*. Baltimore: Johns Hopkins University Press, 1975.

Ryder, A. F. C. "Missionary Activity in the Kingdom of Warri to the Early Nineteenth Century." *Journal of the Historical Society of Nigeria* 2 (1960): 1–26.

Sagrista, Rafael Ortega. "La Cofradía de los Negros en el Jaén del Siglo XVII." *Boletin del Instituto de Estudios Giennenses* 12 (1900), 1–10.

Salles, Fritz Teixeira de. *Associações religiosas no ciclo do ouro*. Belo Horizonte, Brazil: Universidade Federal de Minas Gerais, 1963.

Salvador, Mari Lyn. "Ritual Exchange in Azorean Festivals." In *Time out of Time: Essays on the Festival*, edited by Alessandro Falassi, 244–60. Albuquerque: University of New Mexico Press, 1987.

Sammells, Clare. "The Internet and Folklore." *American Folklore Society News* 26 (December 1997): 17.

Saunders, A. C. de C. M. *A Social History of Black Slaves and Freedmen in Portugal, 1441–1555*. Cambridge: Cambridge University Press, 1982.

Scarano, Julita. "Black Brotherhoods: Integration or Contradiction?" *Luso-Brazilian Review* 16 (Summer 1979): 1–17.

———. *Devoção e escravidão: A irmandade de Nossa Senhora do Rosário dos Pretos no distrito diamantino no século XVIII*. São Paulo: Nacional, 1976.

Scheper-Hughs, Nancy. *Death Without Weeping: The Violence of Everyday Life in Brazil*. Berkeley and Los Angeles: University of California Press, 1992.

Schuler, Monica. "*Alas, Alas, Kongo": A Social History of Indentured African Immigration into Jamaica, 1841–1865*. Baltimore: Johns Hopkins University Press, 1980.

Schwartz, Stuart B. "Patterns of Slaveholding in the Americas: New Evidence from Brazil." *AHR* 87 (February 1982): 55–86.

———. "Resistance and Accommodation in Eighteenth-Century Brazil: The Slaves' View of Slavery." *HAHR* 57 (1977): 69–81.

———. *Sugar Plantations in the Formation of Brazilian Society, Bahia, 1550–1835*. Cambridge: Cambridge University Press, 1985.

———, ed. *Implicit Understandings: Observing, Reporting, and Reflecting on the Encounters Between Europeans and Other Peoples in the Early Modern Era*. New York: Cambridge University Press, 1994.

Scott, James C. *Domination and the Arts of Resistance: Hidden Transcripts*. New Haven: Yale University Press, 1990.

———. *Weapons of the Weak: Everyday Forms of Peasant Resistance*. New Haven: Yale University Press, 1985.

Silva, Eduardo. *Prince of the People: The Life and Times of a Brazilian Free Man of Colour.* London: Verso, 1993.

Silva, Maria Beatriz Nizza da, ed. *Brasil: Colonização e escravidão.* Rio de Janeiro: Editora Nova Fronteira, 2000.

Silva, Rosa Cruz e. "The Saga of Kakonda and Kilengues: Relations Between Benguela and Its Interior, 1791–1796." In *Enslaving Connections: Changing Cultures of Africa and Brazil During the Era of Slavery,* edited by José C. Curto and Paul E. Lovejoy, 245–59. Amherst, N.Y.: Humanity Books, 2004.

Silveira, Vicente. *Expansão da igreja católica em Minas Gerais.* Belo Horizonte, Brazil: Imprensa Oficial, 1983.

Skidmore, Thomas E. *Black into White: Race and Nationality in Brazilian Thought.* Durham: Duke University Press, 1993.

Slenes, Robert W. "Comments on 'Slavery in a Nonexport Economy.'" *HAHR* 63 (1983): 569–90.

Smith, E. Valerie. "The Sisterhood of Nossa Senhora da Boa Morte and the Brotherhood of Nossa Senhora do Rosário: African Brazilian Cultural Adaptations to Antebellum Restrictions." *Afro-Hispanic Review* 11 (1992): 58–69.

Soares, Mariza de Carvalho. *Devotos da cor: Identidade étnica, religiosidade e escravidão no Rio de Janeiro, século XVIII.* Rio de Janeiro: Civilização Brasileira, 2000.

Sobel, Mechal. *Trabelin' On: The Slave Journey to an Afro-Baptist Faith.* Princeton: Princeton University Press, 1988.

Souza, Laura de Mello e. *Desclassificados do ouro: A pobreza mineira no século XVIII.* Rio de Janeiro: Editora Graal, 1986.

———. *O diabo e a terra de Santa Cruz.* São Paulo: Companhia das Letras, 1989.

Souza, Marina de Mello e. *Reis negros no Brasil escravista, história da festa de coroação de Rei Congo.* Belo Horizonte, Brazil: Editora UFMG, 2002.

Stein, Stanley J. *Vassouras: A Brazilian Coffee Country, 1850–1900.* Princeton: Princeton University Press, 1985.

Strickland, D. A. "Kingship and Slavery in African Thought: A Conceptual Analysis." *Comparative Studies in Society and History* 18 (July 1976): 371–94.

Sweet, James H. *Recreating Africa: Culture, Kinship, and Religion in the African-Portuguese World, 1441–1770.* Chapel Hill: University of North Carolina Press, 2003.

Tannenbaum, Frank. *Slave and Citizen: The Negro in the Americas.* New York: Alfred A. Knopf, 1947.

Theije, Marjo de. "'Brotherhoods Throw More Weight Around Than the Pope': Catholic Traditionalism and the Lay Brotherhoods of Brazil." *Sociological Analysis* 51 (Summer 1990): 189–204.

Thomas, Hugh. *The Slave Trade: The Story of the Atlantic Slave Trade, 1440–1870.* New York: Simon and Schuster, 1997.

Thompson, Robert Farris. *Face of the Gods: Art and Altars of Africa and the African Americas.* New York: Museum for African Art, 1993.

———. *Flash of the Spirit: African and Afro-American Art and Philosophy.* New York: Vintage Books, 1984.

Thornton, John K. *Africa and Africans in the Making of the Atlantic World, 1400–1680.* Cambridge: Cambridge University Press, 1992.

————. "Early Kongo-Portuguese Relations: A New Interpretation." *History in Africa* 8 (1981): 183–204.

————. *The Kingdom of Kongo: Civil War and Transition, 1641–1718*. Madison: University of Wisconsin Press, 1983.

————. *The Kongolese Saint Anthony: Dona Beatriz Kimpa Vita and the Antonian Movement, 1684–1706*. Cambridge: Cambridge University Press, 1998.

————. "Legitimacy and Political Power: Queen Njinga, 1624–1663," *Journal of African History* 32, no. 1 (1991): 25–40.

————. "On the Trail of Voodoo: African Christianity in Africa and the Americas." *The Americas* 44 (January 1988): 261–78.

————. "Religious and Ceremonial Life in the Kongo and Mbundo Areas 1500–1700." In *Central Africans and Cultural Transformations in the American Diaspora*, ed. Linda M. Heywood, 71–90. New York: Cambridge University Press, 2001.

————. "The Role of Africans in the Atlantic Economy, 1450–1650: Modern Africanist Historiography and the World-Systems Paradigm." *Colonial Latin American Historical Review* (Spring 1994): 125–40.

————. "Traditions, Documents, and the Ife-Benin Relationship." *History in Africa* 15 (1988): 351–62.

Thurston, Herbert, and Donald Atwater. *Butler's Lives of the Saints*. New York: Kennedy and Sons, 1956.

Tinorhão, José Ramos. *As festas no Brasil colonial*. São Paulo: Editora 34, 2000.

————. *Os negros em Portugal: Uma presença silenciosa*. Lisbon: Editorial Caminho, 1988.

Toplin, Robert Brent. *The Abolition of Slavery in Brazil*. New York: Atheneum, 1972.

Trindade, Cônego Raymundo. *Arquidiocese de Mariana, subsídios para a sua história*. 2 vols. 2d ed. Belo Horizonte, Brazil: Imprensa Oficial, 1953.

Trochim, Michael R. "The Brazilian Black Guard: Racial Conflict in Post-abolition Brazil." *The Americas* 44 (January 1988): 385–401.

Turner, Victor. *The Anthropology of Performance*. New York: PAJ, 1986.

————. *Dramas, Fields, and Metaphors: Symbolic Action in Human Society*. Ithaca: Cornell University Press, 1974.

————. *The Ritual Process: Structure and Anti-structure*. Ithaca: Cornell Paperbacks, 1991.

Twine, France Winddance. *Racism in a Racial Democracy: The Maintenance of White Supremacy in Brazil*. New Brunswick: Rutgers University Press, 1998.

Vansina, Jan. *Kingdoms of the Savanna*. Madison: University of Wisconsin Press, 1966.

————. *Oral Tradition: A Study in Historical Methodology*. Translated by H. M. Wright. Chicago: Aldine, 1965.

Vasconcelos, Diego. *História antiga da Minas Gerais*. 2 vols. Rio de Janeiro: Imprensa Nacional, 1948.

Verger, Pierre. *Fluxo e refluxo do tráfico de escravos entre o golfo do Benin e a Bahia de todos os santos dos séculos XVII a XIX*. 2d ed. Translated by Tasso Gadzanis. São Paulo: Editora Corrupio, 1987.

————. *Trade Relations Between the Bight of Benin and Bahia from the Seventeenth to the Nineteenth Century*. Translated by Evelyn Crawford. Ibadan: Ibadan University Press, 1976.

Vieira, Padre Antônio. "'Children of God's Fire': A Seventeenth Century Jesuit Finds Benefits in Slavery but Chastises Masters for their Brutality in a Sermon to the Black Brotherhood of Our Lady of the Rosary." In *Children of God's Fire: A Documentary History of Black Slavery in Brazil*, 2d ed., edited by Robert Edgar Conrad. University Park: Pennsylvania State University Press, 1994.

Wallace, Anthony. *Religion: An Anthropological View*. New York: Random House, 1966.

Warner, Marina. *Alone of All Her Sex: The Myth and the Cult of the Virgin Mary*. New York: Vintage Books, 1976.

Weber, Max. "Ethnic Groups." In *New Tribalisms: The Resurgence of Race and Ethnicity*, edited by Michael W. Hughey, 17–30. New York: New York University Press, 1998.

Wheeler, Douglas L., and René Pélissier. *Angola*. Westport, Conn.: Greenwood Press, 1978.

Wiarda, Howard J. *The Soul of Latin America: The Cultural and Political Tradition*. New Haven: Yale University Press, 2001.

Wilkins, Eithne. *The Rose-Garden Game: A Tradition of Beads and Flowers*. New York: Herder and Herder, 1969.

Winston, Anne. "Tracing the Origins of the Rosary: German Vernacular Texts." *Speculum: A Journal of Medieval Studies* 68 (July 1993): 619–36.

Winston-Allen, Anne. *Stories of the Rose: The Making of the Rosary in the Middle Ages*. University Park: Pennsylvania State University Press, 1997.

Wirth, John D. *Minas Gerais in the Brazilian Federation, 1889–1937*. Stanford: Stanford University Press, 1977.

Zamith, Rosa Maria Barbosa. "Aspectos internos do fazer musical num congado de Minas Gerais." *Revista Música* (São Paulo), 6 (May/November 1995): 203–27.

INDEX